Contents

Part 3: Strategies and Techniques

Part 4: Reporting 305

Preface

This volume of readings has been compiled by the course team which produced *E364 Curriculum Evaluation and Assessment in Educational Institutions*. This is an Open University course for educational professionals with a particular interest in the topical issue of evaluation, and the problems of responding to the often conflicting demands of accountability.

This Reader forms only one component of the course, which also includes written texts, radio and TV programmes and face-to-face tuition.

Although these readings, some of which were specially commissioned for this volume, were initially selected to support students studying the course, they also stand in their own right, thus presenting for the first time in one place important articles linking together evaluation and accountability.

Introduction

The 1960s and the early 1970s were periods of growth in education and a forward-looking view of curriculum development. The Schools Council, following on the tradition of the Nuffield Foundation, was particularly instrumental in developing large-scale curriculum projects, such as the *Humanities Curriculum Project (14-16)*. Such projects produced materials and techniques which were intended to reform various aspects of education in schools. There emerged however, a pessimism about the impact of centralized curriculum development initiatives. The economic restrictions of the late 1970s and early 1980s, coupled with this pessimism, provided a sombre background for evaluation.

The curriculum projects of the 'happier' period had formed a nucleus for the development of a cadre of curriculum evaluators, and from this the British literature on evaluation grew. It did so as a result of the discourse among the professional evaluators, and was dominated by methodological concerns such as quantitative *v.* qualitative methods and illuminative *v.* 'experimental' evaluation models. This was accompanied by an increase in stature for 'evaluation' as an object of study, promoted by such institutions as the Centre for Applied Research in Education at the University of East Anglia.

Some of these evaluators were also pessimistic about centralized curriculum development and the interest in evaluation moved away from the learning materials produced by the projects to a concern for effects in the classroom. So too an interest in the teacher as researcher increased. This assumed that change stems from the involvement of the teacher in investigations of what occurs in his or her classroom. The growth of school-based INSET combines with this to provide a focus at the institutional level, through such activities as curriculum review.

This increasing professional awareness of what goes on in schools and colleges coincides with an increasing public concern for accountability: demands for information about what occurs in schools and a need for assurance that 'quality' is being maintained or even improved. Such concern can, under some models of accountability, conflict with increased teacher involvement and control over the curriculum and its development, an argument taken up in the first part of the Reader. So the debate about evaluation moves away from purely methodological issues to one of purposes: why is the evaluation being done? Is it to satisfy public demands or for the teacher's or the school's own development? Evaluation now takes on a different role: not only serving projects and being within the control of professional evaluators. Instead evaluations are being increasingly performed as a response to public demands. The nature of the evaluation, who performs it and who controls it are now the central issues debated in the literature.

Tertiary education has a different and largely uncharted history of curriculum development and evaluation. Central initiatives by the Council for National Academic Awards and the Technician and Business Education Councils have dominated the scene and account for a good deal of the energy expended in curriculum development. There is evidence emerging of a lack of such development at the 'learning interface', despite the pervasive control exercised by these central agencies. Their resolve however, has not been shaken, unlike their less powerful school counterpart, the Schools Council. Like the initial efforts in the school sector, curriculum development within colleges has been preoccupied with planning, and evaluation has not been a central concern. The tertiary sector has remained surprisingly unaffected by the kinds of accountability demands for evaluation made on schools, and the concerns of schools have therefore dominated the literature.

The Reader has elements of all these movements in evaluation and accountability in the last two decades. The first part considers various conceptions of accountability, upon which the various responses of evaluation will be based. Sockett argues for accountability based upon a recognition of teacher professionalism, whereas Sallis argues for a partnership between 'client and professional'. In an area of much polemical argument the emerging results of the research projects on accountability, spawned largely by SSRC, have added a welcome empirical base to the debate. We have included contributions from three of these. Becher *et al.*, in investigating policy options, produced an analysis of a range of types of accountability. At the opposite end of the spectrum of approaches to that advocated by Sockett, Wood and Gipps investigated local authority testing programmes, feared by some as a crude and therefore misleading mechanism which may be used to judge schools.

The second part of the Reader considers various ways in which institutions might respond to pressures for increased accountability. These range from self-evaluation on an assumption of total teacher professionalism and autonomy, to an alternative assumption requiring inspection by other (superior) professionals. Becher *et al.* in their consideration of school-based accounting accept teacher autonomy and present a framework and basis for this kind of response. This is taken up in a later article by Simons, *Process Evaluation in Schools*; she however sees the justification of self-evaluation as a continuing part of professional practice, not as a short-term response to political pressure.

Sizer presents a management perspective on how to define quality of education through the definition of indicators. Although this approach may be unacceptable to many, the definition of what counts as quality is essential to any judgement of education. The empirical difficulties are well illustrated in the debate on the Rutter study summarized by Doe. Inspections of schools, particularly when conducted by HMI, are often controversial affairs and so a response to accountability which attempts to combine the 'impartiality' of the outsider (the inspector) with the knowledge of the insider (the teacher) looks attractive. The use of outsiders to 'audit' an evaluation done by insiders is uncommon in Britain, particularly at school level; Vaughan and Manning in their description of the North Central Association of Schools and Colleges describe such an approach in the North American context of accreditation.

Although the debate about evaluation has shifted, methodology still has an important place. The choice of approaches and techniques will determine the usefulness of the information and the credibility of the evaluation. The importance rests not so much on which of the competitive methodologies is intrinsically better but which is *appropriate* for the circumstances of the evaluation. Part 3 covers this topic, comprising three sections: an historical review of strategies; techniques for in-school evaluation; and examples and blueprints. Lawton presents six models which show the historical development of the thinking in this area, ranging from the evaluation of an educational programme against pre-specified goals, to an evaluation concerned with the portrayal of the processes involved. Such descriptive accounts enable a range of audiences – teachers, parents and governors – to learn what is going on, and it is claimed this can be done without prescribing the judgements they are expected to make. Illuminative evaluation is in this tradition, and Parlett and Parsons both address this approach. Techniques cannot be entirely divorced from strategy: Steadman provides a comprehensive review of strategies and techniques and is concerned, not with defending a particular stance, but with presenting a repertoire for the would-be evaluator. Simons examines techniques of unstructured interviews for use in schools. Delamont and Hamilton, in considering classroom research, argue for qualitative portrayals of classrooms by unstructured observational methods rather than the approach of interaction analysis, employing pre-specified observation schedules.

An important focus for those who seek to portray the full picture of an educational process and its products is the study of a particular instance or case. This is particularly true for those involved with evaluation in their own institution. Becker and Stenhouse discuss respectively: the problems of inference and proof in ethnographic study and the conduct, analysis and reporting of case study research. The concern with methodology is not only to provide information of a kind which the 'users' (teachers, parents, governors and local authority politicians) can understand and have confidence in, but to fit approaches and techniques to the purpose of the evaluation. This is brought out in the articles by Parlett, on departmental evaluation in higher education, and by Simons in her argument for democratic principles in school-based evaluation. Finally, the checklist by Elliott and Harlen includes such considerations in both the planning and reviewing of an evaluation.

The final aspect of any evaluation (before in fact changes are implemented), that of reporting, is the subject of Part 4. A result of the pressure for accountability is a greater concern for communication, in the case of schools, with parents. Thus the problem of reporting evaluation has to be seen as part of the question of the general issue of communication with such outsiders. Becher *et al.* formulate a typology of various kinds of communication with parents, and Gibson and Clift and others develop the specific areas of written communications and pupil reports respectively.

In the case of secondary schools and colleges, examination results represent a form of reporting of evaluation. But because they selectively represent the institution and mask a good deal of complexity, their publication is controversial. Shipman considers how they can be presented – an issue which in the early eighties is likely to be of growing interest as part of the public's 'right to know' the achievements or otherwise of educational institutions.

Robert McCormick

PART 1: ACCOUNTABILITY

Editor: Robert McCormick

1.1 Accountability: Purpose and Meaning
H. Sockett

The purpose of an accountability system is in part contained in the meaning of the word, which, at a simple level, is to hold someone to account. Yet the main point on which all its advocates would agree is that it is an attempt to *improve* the quality of education, and, it is sometimes added, to *prove* that this is being done. It is tempting to argue that accountability in a system must have *one* purpose. Yet, if there are a variety of parties on either side of an accountability relation they may interpret that purpose differently and have additional purposes of their own. A parent may see it as ensuring that his child gets fair treatment; the adviser may see it as a major way of deciding which teachers to put up for promotion. Once we go beneath the generality of purpose expressed in the phrase 'improvement' we are bound to get to particular and divergent purposes. Purposes may be more or less specific, and are of immense heterogeneity. It is therefore inappropriate to say accountability has one purpose or, at this point, to discuss such varied purposes further. We may turn to the problem of *meaning*.

To say that an agent is accountable for his actions to another is not merely to say that he is *able* to deliver an ACCOUNT, but to assert that he is *obliged* to do so. Such an obligation may be held to exist, in the central case, by virtue of a legal contract, a detailed undertaking of a promissory character, or an unwritten agreement without force in law. The agent has the right to use resources, which are not his own, for purposes which are negotiated between him and the provider to whom he is accountable. In the central case too, I believe the provider is the beneficiary of the agent's stewardship of these resources.

The central case is located most easily in industrial enterprises, in the accountability relation between a board of directors and the company shareholders. Frequently, however, the nominal providers and beneficiaries establish bodies to whom account is given and who act on the provider's behalf. Thus a Minister is accountable to Parliament for

Sockett, H. (1980), 'Accountability: the contemporary issues', in H. Sockett (ed.), *Accountability in the English Educational System*, Hodder & Stoughton, pp. 10-12.

the activities of his department, Parliament acting on behalf of the citizen tax-payer providers.

The provider of the resources may contract with an agent for the use of his skills: for the use of these skills the agent is accountable. Thus a company employs a man as managing director. The skills he offers are the skills of administration and management. A pharmaceutical company will employ research chemists, whose skills are used not merely in the gradual perfection of drugs already under manufacture, but for the development of new drugs to combat particular diseases or afflictions. The company's resources are at the disposal of both manager and chemist; both are accountable for the way they use those skills.

There are some exceptions which deserve notice. First, although a barrister contracts his services to the client through a solicitor, neither solicitor nor client can hold the barrister accountable. The reason given for this practice is that the barrister has no control over the outcome of the case – that is a matter for the jury and the judge. But the barrister is expected to do his best when he presents the case, to work out the best arguments, to use his skills in cross-examination and to present the case with all the verve and tenacity at his command. If he fails to come up to these standards, then it is not the solicitor or the client to whom the barrister is accountable, but to professional peers represented by the Bar Council. Second and likewise, a doctor, while in certain respects accountable to the National Health Service as his employer, is also accountable to the BMA as the governing body of his profession. The details of particular cases which are dealt with by the respective professional bodies are to hand, but the question they debate is not whether certain results have been achieved, but whether professional standards of integrity and practice have been adhered to. In these cases the accountability is, as it were, negative rather than positive. It is invoked as a procedure in cases of breaches of professional standards, not in terms of inadequate outcomes. Barristers don't report their successful cases to the Bar Council, nor do doctors return to the BMA lists of people cured of rubella.

If then we examine various forms of accountability we may discern one distinction of significance. In the central case the agent is accountable for *outcomes and results*, while in the exceptional cases mentioned the agents are accountable to *codes of practice*, that is, codes of professional principles. We might say that the managing director is *accountable* to the company employing him as a steward of resources, and think of the barristers as *answerable* to their professional peers, though nothing hangs on the terminology. They are simply different forms of accountability.

Now whether a man is seen as accountable in *either* of these senses, he must accept moral responsibility for his activities. An individual manager may of course be more concerned with moral obligations to his employees than with contractual obligations to the providers. Manufacturers of dangerous drugs may *feel* more responsible to their customers than to their shareholders. A notorious insurance financier was held up to moral approbrium for his apparent refusal to countenance the *moral* claims of his clients. Furthermore, there may be hierarchies of accountability, e.g. within a company, but no such hierarchy can exist within either accountability as answerability or straightforward moral responsibility. For the answerable professional or the moral agent, the buck always stops here.

There is therefore little to be gained from examining the meaning of accountability as if we expected such an examination to give us a *direct* clue to what *form* of accountability is appropriate. Rather we have a rough-hewn meaning, i.e. the obligation to deliver an account of what is done. Then we have noted two different ways in which this might be done, ways which point to different forms of accountability, i.e. accountability for results, and accountability in terms of professional codes of practice.

1.2 Beyond the Market Place: A Parent's View
J. Sallis

Almost inescapably, in any discussion of the accountability of school to parent, one gets drawn into the language of commerce, and consumerism. One has to consider all the ways in which education resembles, or differs from, other goods and services, in an attempt to establish relevant relationships between giver and receiver. I think this is necessary if one is to illuminate the dark places and expose some of the undemocratic habits still found in the education service. Yet it is also depressing and inadequate, and even though I must follow these winding paths to their end, I hope before concluding the chapter to reach a point from which there is a view beyond the market place.

If you were to ask a sample of parents at the school gates 'Is this a good school?' you would conclude from the answers either that there wasn't a lot wrong with the education system or that loyalty was an encouragingly common human quality. In some senses both conclusions would be justified. Were you to ask instead 'Could this school be improved?' you would realize that popular satisfaction with the service was qualified in some degree. If you went on to ask 'Does the school seek *your* opinions on ways in which it could be improved?' you would be bound to conclude that many parents did not expect to be consulted in these terms. Finally, if you asked 'Does the school make sure you understand and consent to what it proposes to do for your child?' the great majority would look totally bewildered, never having been asked to consent to anything more than a German measles injection or the payment of 50p towards a school trip, never expected to understand more than the reason why soft shoes should be worn in the hall or at most why the timetable couldn't provide physics *and* housecraft for some poor fourteen-year-old trying to hedge her bets.

You would find, if you asked the last question of a big enough sample, a sophisticated few who would tell you in no uncertain terms that most schools don't accept any obligation to earn our trust in this overt way, in fact that schools are not accountable enough to those

Sallis, J. (1979), 'Beyond the Market Place: a Parent's View', in J. Lello (ed.), *Accountability in Education*, Ward Lock Educational, pp. 110-16.

whose lives they directly affect. Many thinking parents are dissatisfied with the remote accountability provided by an elected government which lays down broad policies and an elected LEA administering the local service. Even those who don't formulate such things feel increasingly a sense of vague unease and helplessness in the face of the school's pretty substantial independence of both central and local control and their own limited grasp of what they should expect from it.

It is remarkable that parents' expectations of schools should be so confused, and that schools' recognition of parents' needs should have grown so slowly, when for fifteen years there has been a steady development of consumerism in all other spheres of our lives. I think, indeed, that education is at an earlier stage than industry and commerce in the development from simple, even austere, well understood and fiercely monitored objectives (with which we emerged from the Second World War and continued into the early 1950s) to bewilderingly rich and varied offerings, expensive and luxurious, cheap and cheerful, cheap and nasty, eye-catching and empty or plain and good. This immense freedom and variety in the supply of consumer foods, combined with the development of many new techniques: drip-dry, non-stick, self-clean, etc. after the austerity of war, first excited then frightened. In the fright, value for money, fitness for purpose, fair shares for all, suddenly didn't seem such dull virtues after all.

I speak of these times in the world of commerce with feeling, for in the mid-1950s I was a very young person working in what is now called the Department of Trade and Industry and concerned with the consumer goods industries. Being young I was allowed the occasional luxury of flying kites and making outrageous suggestions, most of them arising from concern about the very low status of the consumer in our economy. I was indeed a new consumer myself, concerned when out of about £15 a week the handle came off the only saucepan and a toe went through the new sheet. The newspapers were full of even worse things like flock-printing where the pattern dissolved in water or disintegrated in sunlight.

It was the wrong moment to suggest that the consumer needed more protection, for most of my elders had been through too many years of rationing and regulations, strong but unglamorous textiles, practical if unstylish furniture. The embers still glowed from the bonfire of controls they had helped to fuel, and the doctrine of *caveat emptor* reigned supreme. The shops were full of varied and attractive goods, the first flood of cheap imports from the East nearly washed the counters away. The idea that one might again specify the warp and weft strength of sheets or even lay down how double was a double sheet seemed remote, even mean and miserable. If you wanted to buy a very expensive Egyptian cotton sheet, which wasn't *the* most durable but oh-so-soft, or a cheap bright towel which lasted just till you hated the colour, wasn't this what we all dreamed of in those dull days of austerity and fair shares?

I even remember saying in the canteen that the manufacture of nightdresses in children's sizes should be made illegal. True, mothers could still make them, but if they were made unfashionable they would soon stop. What an interference with freedom! I was, I hasten to say, concerned with the freedom of thousands of girls to grow up without bursting into flames, and the problem was partially solved by the development of a flame-resistant finish which was fairly cheap and comfortable, but still hasn't stopped the home dressmaker. The sophisticated educationist won't look far for the relevance of this story either, as he sees everywhere how freedom for the individual has its high price.

Yet, in five years, consumerism was becoming a fashionable concept and in ten was well established. By this time I was more concerned as a consumer with the tensile strength of nappies, the safety of pram harnesses and the order in which ingredients were named on baby dinners in jars. I took a wry pleasure in the growth of kite marks and seals of approval, of consumer groups and consumer magazines, safety and durability pursued often on an international scale, and stronger legislation to protect the consumer against false claims, price-fixing and restrictive practices. The buyer might still need to beware, but it was tacitly accepted that he deserved impartial advice and some protection.

I don't think the analogy is at all fanciful. When we were young, education too had a certain simple austerity in its objectives and methods, and we felt we understood them. Visionaries might already have been dreaming dreams in the late forties and fifties, but most people in education were busy with roofs over heads and teachers to fill those heads with knowledge of a kind still broadly the subject of consensus. For the majority we were still a long way from primary education stemming from the child and his world — and one of the most urgent reasons for communicating better is to stop people frightening us into throwing all this away. We were also a long way from educating *all* young people well beyond childhood, never mind trying to do so in the same institutions, never mind trying to do so for a changing world and on shifting social sands.

But just as the shops filled with bewildering speed with new, varied, eye-catching goods, so education exploded with new ideas, objectives and techniques, some durable, some less so, some good value for money, some not. Freedom to experiment was as precious to many then as freedom in the market place to my senior colleagues. Gradually the intervention in and assessment of what was taught and how, by central and local government, decreased. There was, relatively speaking, plenty of money to spend, and elected members both locally and nationally concentrated on providing the facilities for all this to happen.

Somewhere along this road, public understanding got left behind, and without understanding, confidence is soon in jeopardy. The bewildering variety, newness and eye-appeal of what was on offer at first excited, then, more slowly than in the world of goods and services, frightened. From that fright we have to recover, perhaps painfully, for the child's sake.

For the child is the consumer. But the parent is his representative. And the parent is, unlike any other consumer, a compulsory participant. Not only is he obliged by law to see that his child is suitably educated, he is also told in one learned study after another that his informed support is the most important single factor in his child's success. Many schools, perhaps even most schools, make admirable arrangements to inform and involve parents, though rarely to treat them as partners in the process. The growth of good practice is very encouraging, and the only depressing thing to me is that the LEAs, who are responsible for the efficiency of the local service, and therefore the sum of the effective relationships of child, parent and school, are so slow to see that if well-informed parent support is vital to effectiveness, it is *their* legal responsibility to secure it. I believe this will soon have to be spelt out. It is not enough that the necessary communication should develop in a haphazard way — it must be organized.

At this point teachers quite rightly say that trust is the basis of all our social relationships, and the more complex the activity, the blinder the trust has to be. Why don't you trust us, they say, as you do others who have had an expert training to perform services for you? One sympathizes, for no experts, except perhaps the paperhanger, are such victims of the enthusiastic amateur. In fact, however, we must in the nature of things trust educators more blindly than other professionals, and with something more precious than we entrust to anyone but the doctor. Grandmother's lace shawl sent to the Rapid Dry Cleaners may be priceless, but it's only lace and memories, and even the past can't compete with the future. The dry cleaner tells us if he thinks it risky (the poor teacher isn't so free!) and if the damage will only respond to some further dangerously drastic treatment, he comes back for our consent. Consent exists in some form in all our relationships with other professionals, and it has three components rarely present in education. One is consensus about objectives, which as I have said we perhaps came nearer a generation ago before education tried to attempt so much, for so many, against such an unsettled social background. The solicitor must know whether he is conveying a house, bequeathing our property, or dissolving a marriage. The decision is not his, although the clever words in which he translates our intentions are his. We even tell him the price of the house, the beneficiaries of the will and the grounds of the divorce, subject always to his advice on the practicalities. Which brings us to the second component in consent, the exchange of information about methods, their limitations and implications. The doctor, seeing our blood-count is too low for an anaesthetic, has to explain why he must treat the anaemia before the gallstones. The garden designer makes sure we know the bed must be limed if we want azaleas in our particular soil, and he shares with us the secret life of apple trees before we choose mates for ours. Finally, and with education, like medicine, it can be pretty final, there must be some dialogue to judge the success of what has been done. The three elements together can be described as consent, but to me they are also components of accountability, and the most important is information. Without it we cannot judge whether the objectives are realistic, even if we support them, cannot approve the programme, cannot assess the outcome. Nor, which is the most important part of all, can we play our vital part unless we understand what is to be done, how it is to be done, and what can be expected at the end. Here we come to the respect in which education really *is* different from all other professional activities, which, with all their safeguards for the customer, leave him still very much a passive element. I shall return to this, for it constitutes my view beyond the market place, and is crucial in the definition of a properly accountable relationship between teacher and parent. For the parent is a partner.

Teachers must forgive us if we sometimes seem a bit shrill. It is only because we know that mistakes cannot afterwards be rectified. In this respect, as in others I shall come to, the consumer analogy is a cruelly false one. We may, with all the protection now given to us, walk out of a shop with a new pair of shoes in return for a pair that split. At worst we can resolve never to buy there again. But a child has only one chance. We do not *want* to make the school accountable for failure. We want to be sure that avoidable failure doesn't happen.

Educators sometimes argue that they are in a special position because of the complex nature of their accountabilities. Teachers are answerable, they say, to their head, the LEA as their employer, and to their parents, as well as being constrained by many external factors such as national and local guidelines, examination requirements and the needs of employers. Yet even a humble power station worker is answerable to his line manager, his employer, and in a sense to the consumer of electricity, and many employees in industry work within constraints of safety and quality specifications and the needs of preceding or following processes. The real difference is that in the school there may be a conflict between accountability in a collective sense, through parent bodies and governors, and accountability to the individual parent as partner in the education of his own child. Until all parents have a recognized status in the process, and the confidence to maintain it, there is a danger that such collective mechanisms as exist for schools to explain, justify and monitor what they are doing will be dominated by minorities of parents whose confidence is greater than their fellows, but whose interests are not necessarily those of the majority.

Teachers often use this as an argument against improving collective accountabilities at all. But surely we need partnership at both levels, collective involvement in policy to give strength and direction to parent aspirations, and individual rights to make sure there is no barrier in the last resort between the individual and the school? The latter is the best guarantee that the base of parent activity will broaden in time.

This was at least the feeling of seven members of the Taylor Committee who signed a note of extension to the Committee's Report. That note urged the establishment of individual rights to the means to perform the statutory individual duty, rights to those good habits of communication which the Committee went so far as to list as desirable practice.

The Taylor Committee Report, in fact, sees its new-style governing body as a means of ensuring the accountability of schools to their communities, and gives parents an *equal* status with other parties in the process. It is difficult to see how such a body can work if it is excluded, as many teachers' organizations would advocate, from a share in curriculum decisions, for all the reasons given earlier in the discussion of consent as a vital element. 'Oversight' of the curriculum in some Articles of Government was a bad word, suggesting as it does something Olympian, remote – even careless! It is insight we need, not oversight.

We are already moving away from consumerism as a goal in education, the key being in the word 'partnership'. No discussion of consumer aspirations is complete, however, without a mention of the concept of choice, which is an essential component in the market place ideology. Information, guarantees, standards, are needed by the buyer so that he may *choose* well. There the road ends. In education the concept of choice, so superficially appealing, has many pitfalls. In no other activity does the exercise of positive and well-based choice change the nature of that which is *not* chosen, and which those less able to choose have to accept. We are not *part* of that non-fading, strong absorbent new towel, however smugly we wrap ourselves into it. We are not part of the trouble-free new television set, even if metaphorically glued to it. The less satisfactory towels and TV sets bought by others are made no worse by our action. But we and our children are part of our schools, and we change them. Choice is only demanded because some schools are thought to be better than others and its very exercise widens the gap. It is more urgently demanded because parents are not satisfied that without it they have any influence at all. It is this that we must change, for otherwise the operation of market forces will impose cruel sacrifices on the majority whenever there is slack in the system.

The answer, I submit, is already sketched out in the law, but so far not translated into universal practice. We do not consume the education provided by schools. We share responsibility with the school for the education of our children. The school must satisfy us about what it is doing, but without us it cannot be satisfactory, and we must be given the means to play a responsible part. This is surely the key to that gate from which we can see beyond the market place. School and parents must be accountable to each other for their contributions to a shared task. Any suggestion that some parents are better than others at supporting their children at school arouses acute sensitivities, but no greater than those involved in the conspiracy of silence and embarrassment which surrounds the question of variable teacher quality. From these sensitivities only the child suffers, since there is little hope of improving either the school or home input until we have outgrown them. Outgrowing them does of course require a revolutionary move forward in relationships and attitudes, an advance towards open schools in a sense perhaps not yet attainable.

Beyond the market place, then, we leave behind the vocabulary of consumerism, with its talk of the cost of this and the price of that. We talk instead of the value of things and of needs and remedies. For in the end there is something deeply inappropriate about the idea of the satisfied customer in education, however well informed, protected and indulged. We cannot in any case isolate our personal satisfaction from the health of the system as a whole, since the quality of what is done in schools profoundly affects everybody. We have paid dearly in the past for failure to educate the majority, and shall surely pay more dearly if we fail in future. The only hope is to establish and work for the ideal of the parent as committed partner. 'The Partnership' as one of my fellow Taylor Committee members said, 'must be real, and must be built' (Flower, 1978).

Reference
Flower, F. (1978), *Where*, June.

1.3 Towards a 'Professional' Model of Teacher Accountability
H. Sockett

Here Sockett continues his argument put forward in the first reading of this section by exploring accountability based on codes of practice, a position which Sallis, in the last reading, is unlikely to see as part of the Taylor 'Partnership'.

What might be an alternative to this results-based model as so far described? If we notice the difference outlined above, namely the difference between a system based on results and a system based on principles, the characterizing differences of an alternative can be seen as follows:

(a) accountability would be *for* adherence to principles of practice rather than *for* results embodied in pupil performances,

(b) accountability would be rendered *to* diverse constituencies rather than *to* the agglomerate constituency of the public alone,

(c) the teacher would have to be regarded as an autonomous professional, not as a social technician, within the bureaucratic framework of a school and the educational system.

(d) the evaluation through measurement of pupil performances (the 'how' of accountability) would be replaced by a conception of evaluation as providing information for constituents allied to a system of proper redress through a professional body.

The development of such a system of accountability can be supported through the following considerations. First, while a teacher certainly has influence over children and must take a measure of responsibility for their achievements and failures, the mere testing of results assumes that a teacher has greater control than is possible. Second, by shifting the focus of accountability on to results only, we fail to consider the quality of the conditions and opportunities for learning – the schooling process, if you like – within which much more sophisticated judgements may be made about a teacher's effectiveness. Third, if the object of the

Sockett, H. (1980), 'Accountability: the Contemporary Issues', in H. Sockett (ed.), *Accountability in the English Educational System*, Hodder & Stoughton, pp. 19-22.

accountability exercise is to improve the quality of teaching (because through that better results, *inter alia*, will come) then it is on that quality that attention should be focused. If therefore the profession was able to articulate what it regarded as the positive standards of good teaching it would itself be providing a measure of accountability.

But does the notion of accountability to principles of practice or codes of conduct provide tight enough criteria of accountability? Clearly much work needs to be done on this, but if we look at the way in which the Council for National Academic Awards has radically altered the style of course planning in many institutions of higher education we can easily see how, in the field of curriculum design and planning alone, a group of professional peers making judgements about their colleagues' work can and does contribute to improvements of standards. Those standards are, almost entirely, at a level of principles of practice; that is, they demand care, thoroughness of preparation, extensive consultation with teaching staff within an institution, detailed understanding of objectives and so on. The Council does not dictate syllabuses, but if an institution wants to promote a syllabus, it has to produce it *properly*, i.e. in accordance with certain standards.

There is no reason why this kind of procedure should not be extended, that is, why groups of professionals should not be able to establish detailed codes of conduct in each branch of professional activity, be it syllabus construction, assessment, styles of teaching or whatever. Our present professional code tends simply to rule certain codes of behaviour out, e.g. professionals must avoid sexual entanglements with pupils, or, teachers should not be sarcastic; but no positive code has emerged. Underpinning an emerging code of this kind would be the educational principles to which Peters has consistently drawn attention, the concern for truth and objectivity, for rationality, and open-mindedness, for relevance and so on. A familiar danger, for example, in a classroom is for a teacher to put children in the situation of having to guess what the teacher wants, rather than answer the question as such. The detailed study of classrooms, though still in its infancy, can begin to produce codes of classroom conduct at this highly specific level from the basis of high-flown principles.

The diversity of a teacher's constituents mentioned above, suggests that a mere results-based system will obliterate many crucial differences between the parties. A professional model of accountability would take account of these differences in two particular respects: the drawing-up of the 'contract' or 'covenant', i.e. the discussion with parties on what the schools ought to be doing and what individual teachers ought to be doing, and the delivery of the account, that is, producing the kinds of justifications and explanations which are relevant to the concerns of these very different parties. Schools and teachers are well experienced in this. Their reports to inspectors and advisers are very different from the kinds of explanations that are offered to School Parliaments or Councils. What the headmaster says at an open day is different from what he will say when addressing the Rotary Club. The reports are not in conflict, of course: they simply are addressed to different groups or 'constituents'. [. . .]

It is clearly the case that, within this conception of accountability to principles of practice, the assumption is being made that the teacher aspires to the status of an autonomous professional; he will make defensible rational judgements within a corpus of understanding shared with his fellow professionals. He will not be seen as, simply, a rather clever child-minder or a social technician carrying out the directives of a bureaucracy. Accepting that this view of the profession and its members might be hotly contested, it is nevertheless critical that it be asserted, though not here argued, because it draws attention to the need for an advocate of any accountability system to expound the conception of the teacher lying beneath the skin of his proposals.

Finally, there is a growing body of work on the evaluation of schooling (MacDonald, 1977) which provides the kind of detailed development necessary if the evaluation undertaken within the professional model is to provide relevant information to the varied constituents. These developments suggest that a style can be found in which judgements can be systematically made about a teacher's adherence in his practice to a professional code of conduct. They further imply that the reports that issue can be made public, thereby accepting the legitimacy of a person's right to know; a Freedom of Information Act which applied to schools would have more than mere results to attend to. However, such evaluation studies do not simply bring information to the constituents; they are a vital component in the development of our understanding of the processes and the products of schooling, and that provides the basis for increasingly informed conversations between teachers and their constituents.

How might practical progress in this direction be promoted? First, the profession should seek self-government, not to protect its members, but because only in that way can it produce a system of accountability consonant with educational purposes. Second, the profession will have to attend to the problems of what it is legitimate for a teacher to say and to do, i.e. to give an account of what academic freedom means in the context of compulsory schooling. Third, the profession must devise positive codes of conduct, not warnings, particularly in the following areas:

(i) classroom conduct and relationships with pupils,
(ii) professional conduct in staffrooms and within the hierarchical structure of schools,
(iii) relationships with parents,
(iv) the implications of self-government for schooling administration.

Fourth, these codes would be made public and would be accessible to the layman; they would not be sets of ponderous jargon-packed legislation. They would incorporate disciplinary procedures, opportunities for sanctions and redress of grievances. Fifth, since it is in the teaching-learning transactions that the task of education and schooling goes on, the profession must tackle the way in which the good professional is rewarded by being promoted out of the classroom. Sixth, the profession as a body must be in much closer relationship with the researchers and theorists attempting to develop appropriate modes of evaluation.

In a previous essay (Sockett, 1976) I have attempted to fill out the background to these arguments. It is necessary to point out that they entail a fresh start from a base both of attention to principles and codes of practice *and* the recognition of teaching as a self-governing profession. Whether the teachers' unions, as currently constructed, provide a satisfactory base for that is not a matter that can be dealt with here.

References

MacDonald, Barry (1977), *Accountability, Standards and the Progress of Schooling*, mimeo, CARE, University of East Anglia.

Sockett, H. (1976), 'Teacher Accountability', in *Proceedings of the Philosophy of the Educational Society of Great Britain*, Vol. 10.

1.4   A New Partnership for Our Schools

This extract from the Taylor Report considers the role of the governing body in the evaluation of a school — the way of improving schools' accountability in the collective sense as Sallis put it in the second reading of this section.

Keeping under Review the Life and Activities of the School

6.34 As a first step in keeping under review the degree to which the school is achieving its goals and making progress towards its aims, the governing body will want to decide what information and advice it will need in respect of those activities of the school which it considers of particular importance as indicators of the school's progress.

6.35 The primary source for this information and advice will be the headteacher and especially his staff, and the success of the operation will depend upon their contribution. Like all other organizations, schools produce in the course of their everyday business a great deal of information about many aspects of their work. Often this serves a single, specific purpose and is then discarded. Even when preserved it is not always in a form which facilitates its further use. We think that this represents a lost opportunity. The information flowing into and within the school, on those matters which can indicate progress in important respects, should be assembled and processed in such a way that it can be readily used by the governing body. Whilst the information required by the governors will vary from school to school it might be helpful to mention a few obvious items which we would expect to be collected. In all schools information about applications for places at the school, records of attendance and suspensions would be helpful, together with records of out of school activities including details of school societies and educational visits. In the case of primary schools information about relevant secondary provision and, in the case of secondary schools, information about examination results and employment opportunities in the area, might be added. In addition to basic information of this kind, the governors would no doubt also wish to have periodic reports of

Department of Education and Science (1977), *A New Partnership for Our Schools* (The Taylor Report), HMSO, pp. 55-9.

a more qualitative nature on the major departments of the school and its pastoral system as well as the headteacher's assessment of the school's general progress.

6.36 The governing body would also be concerned to obtain information on how the school is seen by the community which it serves. It would be for the governing body to decide upon the type of information required and the means of obtaining it but again, for purely illustrative purposes, we note some possibilities: the views of the school's parents, pupils and supporting staff: the pre-school provision available locally; the views of the governing bodies of other schools, to which pupils, in the case of primary or middle schools, normally transfer; the views of local people (based on observation and experience) and, in the case of secondary schools, the views of employers and institutions of higher and further education.

6.37 We believe that it will help individual governors to gain insight into the nature of the educational opportunities being provided and into the complexities of the teacher's task if they visit classes in progress. We therefore *RECOMMEND that where the governing body considers it appropriate and desirable and has worked out with the teachers procedures for the purpose, individual governors should have the opportunity of seeing classes at work*. It should be emphasized that governors should not see themselves in the role of inspectors. Where the attention of a governor is drawn to difficulties affecting a particular class or teacher, he should inform the chairman in order that the matter can if necessary be taken up in the first place with the headteacher and perhaps with the local education authority adviser concerned.

6.38 The total number in the local education authority advisory/inspection service has grown substantially in recent years to the present level of about 1,800 advisers in England and Wales. The purpose of the advisory service is to promote high standards of performance by teachers and of attainment by pupils both in basic skills and studies and in education in its wider sense. This purpose is principally achieved through the provision of advice, based on wide experience and knowledge, to head and other teachers and by reference to example to show where and how high standards are achieved and maintained. Whilst the relationship of advisers with teaching staff will normally be one of mutual support, the advisory team exercises a leadership role in the area of curriculum innovation, in-service training and staff development programmes. In those circumstances where the efficiency of a particular school or teacher is giving cause for concern, the advisory team may assume an inspectorial role and report as required to the governing body and to the local education authority.

6.39 Viewed overall, the local education authority advisory service has developed in a haphazard way. In the past a local interest in, or current concern about, a particular area of the curriculum, for instance mathematics, modern languages, English, physical education or religious education, often resulted in the appointment of a specialist adviser to work in this field. This has led to the local education authority advisory service having at present in some areas a certain imbalance. Although the opportunity presented by local government reorganization was taken to achieve a better balance and improved structure, there nevertheless remains a preponderance of advisers who are primarily subject specialists rather than general advisers who, in addition to having a specialist role, are able to take an overview, to assess and to give advice upon the school as a whole, its organization, overall development, and progress, following the tradition and practice of HM Inspectorate. The Inspectorate has become smaller (there are now only about 300 HM Inspectors available for work in approximately 28,000 schools in England and Wales) and there are heavy demands upon it to assist in preparing policy advice on national issues for the Secretaries of State, as well as for HM Inspectors to concern themselves with the work and standards of individual schools. We therefore regard it as a matter of urgency that more general advisers should be made available through the local education authority advisory service. This will be essential if the role we have envisaged for the new governing bodies is to be filled. [. . .]

6.41 We recognize that any increase in the number of general advisers will also mean a substantial extension of the in-service training programme for advisers at present in post. At the same time, it is clear to us that if any general adviser is to work effectively, this adviser must be able to call on support from, and work within, a well-balanced advisory team.

6.42 We therefore *RECOMMEND* that:

(a) *Every local education authority should take steps to ensure that the services of a general adviser are regularly available to each of its schools and that the general adviser will be available for consultation with, and report to, the governing body on request.*

(b) *All local education authorities should review the adequacy of their advisory/inspection service in the light of the requirements which we propose for the new governing bodies and should take early steps to strengthen these services as necessary, aiming at a minimum of one adviser to every 20,000 of its total population at the earliest possible date.*

(c) *Local education authorities, grouped on an area basis and in collaboration with HM Inspectorate, should establish panels consisting of local education authority advisers, HM Inspectors, and other appropriate agencies to arrange in-service training to assist local education authority advisers to identify and to develop the necessary skills to work more effectively as general advisers.*

6.43 We recognize that in some areas these proposals will involve substantial additional expenditure but we regard them as of the highest priority. We also recognize that the establishment of a local education authority network of general advisers throughout the country may take some time to achieve and that until this position is reached, some governing bodies may find themselves exceptionally in urgent need of the assistance of a general adviser before one has been assigned to their school. In these circumstances, we hope that chief education officers and education committees will deal sympathetically with requests for assistance from governing bodies.

6.44 In paragraphs 6.35 to 6.43 we have indicated the major sources from which the governing body will derive its information and advice on the life and activities of the school. *We RECOMMEND that this material should be brought together in each school with the purpose of creating an effective but unobtrusive information system for the governing body.* Individual governing bodies will have their own views on what is best in their local situation and we do not suggest that there should be any standard pattern. *We RECOMMEND that the head-teacher be made responsible for developing the governing body's information system, working with general guidance provided by the governing body about the aspects of the school's activities on which information is required and the form in which it is required.*

6.45 The governing body would be able to put the information collected to short- medium- and long-term use. We would not wish to lay down any firm guidelines on how governing bodies should use their information systems in the short and medium terms. By quickly reflecting any substantial changes over a wide range of the school's activities it would be an important aid in keeping the school under continuous review. When any particular question arose, the governing body could look to the school's information system to provide up-to-date material with a helpful bearing upon the matter. In the course of each school year we think the governing body should ask the headteacher to arrange for the relevant information to be brought together in reports on particular sectors of the school (e.g. the school's pastoral system or a teaching department). Finally, the system would be the basis on which at longer intervals the governing body would ask for the production of a complete and coherent picture of the school so as to appraise the school's progress as a whole and consider the extent to which its development matched their intentions. This would also be an appropriate occasion for a periodic general reconsideration of the school's aims and objectives.

6.46 In considering how often governing bodies should appraise the progress of their schools in this way, we must distinguish between the first and subsequent occasions. In general we think it unlikely that the information for a first complete appraisal would be available for several years after the introduction of this approach. Some governing bodies will find it relatively easy to conduct such an appraisal sooner than this, but we would not wish others to feel obliged to do likewise. We think that each governing body should be encouraged to work at a pace which it finds appropriate to its particular situation. Nonetheless we think it important to set a limit to the time spent by any governing body in producing its first appraisal of its school's progress. We therefore *RECOMMEND that every governing body produce a first general appraisal, however incomplete, within four years of its formation.* We are reluctant to specify a term for subsequent appraisals as the experience of the first few years will provide the only basis for a well-informed decision. We hope that governing bodies would be able to appraise their school's progress in total every two or three years, and certainly not less often than every four years. *We RECOMMEND that the exact term should be decided by the local education authority after consultation with the governing bodies of the schools in its area.*

6.47 The procedures outlined in paragraphs 6.34 to 6.46 have two advantages to which we wish to draw particular attention. First, neither the continuous reviewing nor the periodic appraisals of the school's progress should interrupt the normal running of the school. Second, the direct involvement of the teachers and others working in the school would, we believe, not only improve the quality of the review and appraisal processes but also facilitate the staff's acceptance of proposals for any action needed in consequence.

1.5   Accountability in the Middle Years of Schooling

This extract is the conclusion to the report of the research project which investigated, by interviewing parents, teachers, local authority officers, governors and politicians, various views on accountability.

Conclusions

ASPECTS OF ACCOUNTABILITY

In Parts 3 and 4 of our Report, we have been concerned with reviewing the armoury of techniques and procedures which schools and LEAs respectively can deploy in the context of accountability. We now turn, in the concluding stages of our analysis, to a consideration of the different purposes which these techniques and procedures may be called upon to serve.

Three points deserve to be borne in mind by the reader in working through the arguments we shall now rehearse. The first is that accountability can have a positive as well as a negative aspect. It need not be seen simply as a burdensome necessity in meeting external obligations. If properly designed and implemented, an accountability policy can also provide a defence against outside attempts to limit autonomy and the enjoyment of legitimate rights and powers. Such attempts might take the form of political encroachments on freedom, or the unjustified erosion of financial entitlements, as well as campaigns to undermine reputation through the media or to destroy it through libellous gossip.

Second, accountability – as we have come clearly to recognize in the course of our study – is a two-way process. Any LEA, in satisfying its external obligations to maintain proper educational standards, must also see itself as answerable to its teachers and its schools, and must strive actively to sustain its supportive relationships with them.

The third point leads on from these. It is possible to approach accountability as a process of mutual negotiation, in which something is conceded – say, some professional prerogative which contemporary

East Sussex Accountability Project (1979), *Accountability in the Middle Years of Schooling: An Analysis of Policy Options,* University of Sussex, mimeo, pp.96-107.

values call into question – and something gained – perhaps a firm declaration of public trust, a renewed guarantee of essential autonomies, or an insurance against future encroachment. Such an approach must call for a gradualist and long-term strategy, based on careful consultation between the authority and its schools. It could be expensive in time and effort, and could risk exasperating public patience. But the alternative, of imposing an apparently cheap, quick and easy solution, against the wishes of the schools, might in the end prove a hollow victory. It would at best achieve conformity without conviction; at worst it could lead to the general debilitation which now characterizes many school systems in North America.

SIX MODES OF ACCOUNTABILITY

In the attempt we now make to knit together the diverse strands of our analysis and to give them a coherent shape, we have inevitably had to oversimplify or sharpen a number of familiar distinctions as well as to introduce some new ones of our own. We wish to acknowledge the crudity and occasional artificiality of the barriers which we have found it necessary to erect in marking out the terrain for further exploration. We recognize and welcome the fact that they will be transcended by the subtleties of future political debate.

As we noted in the Introduction to this Report, it is possible to distinguish three facets within the broad meaning of the term accountability: (1) *answerability* to one's clients ("moral accountability"); (2) *responsibility* to oneself and one's colleagues ("professional accountability"); (3) and *accountability* in the strict sense to one's employers or political masters ("contractual accountability").

These distinctions are exemplified in different ways by schools on the one hand and Education Committees on the other. Schools are primarily answerable to parents, but legally accountable to the LEA (in some circumstances directly, in others via their managers). Education Committees are answerable to their schools, but constitutionally accountable to the electorate (either directly, or via their governing Council). Both have also to acknowledge certain responsibilities to their own professional consciences and to their peers.

We have earlier remarked that accountability must meet two basic interconnected demands: (1) the preservation and, where possible, enhancement of overall levels of performance through *maintenance* procedures; (2) the detection and amelioration of individual points of weakness through appropriate *problem-solving* mechanisms.

Taking these two sets of considerations together, we can distinguish six different modes of accounting, as follows:

1. Answerability for maintenance;
2. Answerability for problem-solving;

3. Responsibility for maintenance;
4. Responsibility for problem-solving;
5. Strict accountability for maintenance;
6. Strict accountability for problem-solving.

Between them, these six modes serve to draw attention to the demands which might – in principle if not always in practice – be made on schools and LEAs. We shall accordingly use them as the basis for our subsequent discussion. First, we shall look at the pattern of possible expectation as it relates to schools, taking this to be a matter of legitimate interest also to the Education Committee and its officers. After that, we shall sketch out the set of requirements for accountability which might be levied on the Authority itself.

THE ELEMENTS OF SCHOOL-BASED ACCOUNTING

As we noted in Part 3 of this Report, there is a variety of possible ways in which the schools might elect to meet their answerability to parents for the maintenance of standards – the first mode in our list. The parents' awareness of what their children's schools are doing may be promoted through regular communication on individual pupils' progress, or by allowing ready parental access to classrooms and teachers, or by encouraging a general atmosphere of open enquiry. Other forms of provision would include explanations of curricular aims and teaching methods, accounts of overall policy, and reports on general standards of performance.

The second mode concerns the school's potential problem-solving strategies, and especially its means of responding to matters of parental concern. These may include early disclosure of problems – whether affecting individual children or relating to wider issues – where this seems appropriate in averting later crisis; and the prompt acknowledgement and investigation of – and subsequent response to – expressions of parental grievance. All parents have a right to know what the appropriate procedures are within the school if they wish to raise a complaint.

The professional responsibilities which might be exercised by schools in the course of their own internal maintenance – the third mode in our list – could be expected to include the development of good relationships with parents on the one hand and the authority on the other, alongside various forms of domestic monitoring of standards and the regular review of staffing, curricula and teaching arrangements. Schools may also – insofar as their reputations are interdependent – be called upon to exercise professional responsibility towards one another. Junior and middle schools must, moreover, share responsibility with the infant and secondary schools to which they are linked, for the long-term interests of their pupils.

Table 1: Elements of Schools' Accountability

	Answerability (to parents)	Responsibility (to self and peers)	Strict Accountability (to LEA direct or via managers)
Maintenance	1: – Regular communication on individual children's progress (via written reports etc.); – Accounts of overall policy (via prospectus etc.). Explanation of curricular aims and methods; – Reports on general standards of performance, academic and other (via open days, speech days etc.); – Encouragement of better parental awareness of school's activities and endeavours (via ready access to classrooms and staff, atmosphere of open enquiries and discussion).	3: – Domestic monitoring of standards; – Regular review of staffing, curricula and teaching arrangements; – Promotion of good relationships with parents (via school social occasions etc.); – Promotion of good relationships with feeder and receiving (secondary) schools; – Promotion of good relationships with managers, advisers, and LEA as a whole.	5: – Observation of mandatory and constitutional procedures; – Meeting of centrally agreed specifications; – Openness to authorized visitation; – Readiness to justify curricular goals and methods and overall policies; – Readiness to account for pupil performance standards.
Problem-solving	2: – Notification to all parents of complaints procedures; – Prompt acknowledgement and investigation of parental complaints, confirmation of action taken; – Early disclosure to parents, where appropriate, of problems (i) relating to individual children (ii) involving wider issues.	4: – Screening of individual children at risk (via internal reporting, pupil records, tests, etc.); – Provision of remedial help to children in need; – Awareness of incipient points of weakness; – Anticipation of potential crises.	6: – Reporting of unresolved external complaints and grievances; – Reporting of unresolved internal difficulties; – Development of effective means to deal with problems arising.

NB: The entries above are not intended to be comprehensive. They are meant only to indicate possible expectations or demands in each category. They should *not* be taken as indicating policies which are necessarily feasible, desirable or deserving of priority at the school level.

The fourth mode, relating to internal problem-solving, would include – on the institutional front – being aware of and taking steps to rectify incipient points of weakness, and the vigilant anticipation of potential crisis; and – in relation to individual children – the sensible use of screening procedures (such as pupil records and diagnostic tests) to identify and give remedial help to those at risk.

The fifth mode – strict accountability for maintenance – is concerned with the accountability of each school to its LEA for overall quality of provision. Here, one might note its explicit obligation to observe mandatory and constitutional accounting procedures and to meet centrally-agreed specifications. Implicit expectations would include the school's openness to informal visitation by authorized representatives of the authority, its readiness to justify (if reasonably called upon to do so) its curricular goals and methods and its overall policies, and its similar readiness to account for below-average levels of pupil performance.

The sixth and last mode focuses on the ways in which the schools do or should account to the LEA with respect to problem-solving. In this context, they have a clear duty to report on all such grievances or complaints deriving from external sources, and all such internal difficulties, as they are not themselves able to resolve satisfactorily within a reasonable period of time. They would also properly be expected to develop, on their own initiative, appropriate means of anticipating and dealing with such problems as may in fact arise.

These various elements of school-based accounting are summarized in Table 1. We have not attempted to mark out the distinctions between those items which are universally applicable, those which are common practice, and those at present observed by few schools or none. We have not made any of the subsidiary differentiations between informal and formal, mandatory and constitutional procedures. Nor have we attempted to single out those particular policy options which remain presently available to schools. All such categories are dependent on context: the demarcation lines between them will vary from one time and one place to another. Any reader who wishes to define them for his own purposes will, we hope, have no difficulty in doing so.

THE ELEMENTS OF AUTHORITY BASED ACCOUNTING

It is possible to categorize the different components – both actual and potential – of an authority's programme of accountability in much the same way as we have just done in relation to a school's. The same list of six modes will serve for this, and we shall examine them in the same order as before.

The first mode, in this setting, concerns an authority's answerability to its schools for the quality of its maintenance activities. Among the possible items under this head, we may note the obligation of an authority to provide each school with the resources appropriate to carry out its essential tasks and to meet the reasonable expectations made of it. The LEA will also have a general responsibility for the quality, morale and well-being of its professional teaching staff (one particular expression of this might be the institution of systematic forms of personnel development). Authorities may also be expected to support their schools as institutions, both by accrediting (and, where appropriate, publicizing) good practice, and by coming actively to their defence – in general or in particular – when their overall standards are subjected to demonstrably unjust or unreasonable criticism. Schools, it may be argued, have a natural right to seek an explanation of their authority's policies on accountability.

LEAs are, as our second mode suggests, also answerable to schools in regard to problem-solving. That is to say, they have a moral duty to help schools both to identify potential difficulties and to tackle practical issues for which external support is likely to be necessary or desirable. The former obligation is commonly met through testing programmes designed to pick out areas of weakness or through types of diagnostic visitation procedure. [. . .] Issues serious enough to call for outside help may involve individual children, particular teachers, or the institution as a whole. The forms of response will vary accordingly: they may include intervention by the Area Office, the temporary presence in the school of advisers, the decision to make extra resources available, or – in the last resort – the transfer or dismissal of staff or even the closure of the school. Furthermore, when a particular complaint registered by a parent or other outside agent (including the press) can be shown to be without basis, the school or teacher concerned may have a right to expect the authority's full backing in contesting it.

An authority's professional responsibility to keep its affairs in good order constitutes the third mode in our list. It is discharged in part by fostering good relationships with its schools and teachers (not to mention its own advisory and administrative staff), and in part by cultivating and enhancing its relationships with the public. Good housekeeping will imply an effective set of procedures for evaluating and reviewing current policy: it can also crucially depend on the ability of officers and members to work together, and the forcefulness of the arguments they are able to muster in their annual bids to Council for resources. The demands of mutual responsibility between different authorities, and between local and national administration, could also be included in this general category.

Turning next to internal problem-solving by the LEA – the fourth mode – we reiterate a point made by one of the officers we interviewed during the course of our study. Committee members and their staff, besides responding to problems which have already arisen, or acting on issues which they can identify as likely to arise, are called upon to

Table 2: Elements of LEAs' Accountability

	Answerability (to schools)	Responsibility (to self and peers)	Strict Accountability (to electorate, direct or via Council)
Maintenance	1: – Provision of adequate resources to enable schools to meet LEA's expectations; – Promotion of quality and morale of teaching staff (e.g. via personnel development schemes); – Support of schools (in general or particular) by (i) accreditation and dissemination of good practice; (ii) defence against unfounded general criticisms by members of public or press; – Justification of authority's own policies on accountability.	3: – Development of effective member/officer teamwork; – Preparation of convincing proposals for resources; – Systematic evaluation and review of current policies; – Promotion of good relationships with schools; – Promotion of good relationships with public (via encouragement of better general awareness of schools' activities and endeavours).	5: – Certification of overall standards (via monitoring tests and visitations); – Specification of agreed general goals and specific curricular policies (via manifestos, guidelines etc.); – Disclosure of nature and extent of LEA's maintenance procedures.
Problem-solving	2: – Assistance in identifying potential difficulties (via screening tests, diagnostic visits etc.); – Assistance, when appropriate, in tackling problems relating to (i) individual children; (ii) particular teachers; (iii) school as a whole; – Defence against unfounded specific complaints by parents, public or press.	4: – Continuing improvement of strategies for identifying and responding to problems; – Awareness of incipient points of weakness in system; – Enhancement of abilities to accommodate and respond to unforeseen political pressures.	6: – Effective handling of externally-generated problems (serious/unresolved complaints, unforeseeable crises); – Effective handling and rectification of problems generated within system; – Disclosure of LEA's available measures for problem-solving; – Wide notification of grievance procedures; – Prompt acknowledgement and investigation of public complaints; confirmation of action taken.

NB: The entries above are not intended to be comprehensive. They are meant only to indicate possible expectations or demands in each category. They should certainly *not* be taken as indicating policies which are necessarily feasible, desirable, or deserving of priority at the LEA level.

accommodate rapidly to unforeseen political pressures from outside the educational arena and to devise swift and effective ways of meeting them.

Our fifth mode concerns the accountability of elected members to their constituents for the maintenance of overall standards within the education service. [. . .] Particular forms of certification include authority-wide testing designed for general monitoring purposes, routine visitation programmes with the same ends in view, and the specification of general aims and curricular policies. An important – but generally neglected – aspect of this form of accountability is the public disclosure of the nature and extent of the maintenance procedures adopted by the authority in respect of its schools.

The final mode – the sixth in our list – draws attention to the authority's obligations to account to the public for the effectiveness of its problem-solving. In this context, its general abilities to predict, handle and rectify problems come under critical scrutiny. Such problems (whether relating to children, teachers or schools) fall into two groups: those which arise externally, in relation to a particular grievance, or to some unforeseeable quirk of circumstance; and those which are generated internally, as a result of malfunctioning or maladministration within the system. If either type of issue is inadequately handled, the LEA must ultimately take the blame. Hence the potential importance of making widely known what measures are in fact available to deal with both eventualities. A closely related obligation is to notify the public of the most appropriate forms in which to register possible complaints. Over and above this, the authority will be expected to ensure that any actual complaints are properly acknowledged; that they are carefully investigated, and (where necessary) dealt with; and that the fact that this has been done is duly notified to the original complainant.

In concluding this summary review of the elements of authority-based accountability, we must rehearse the caveats expressed in the previous section on accountability at the level of the individual school. The considerations set out in Table 2 take no account of time and place, the state of existing practice, or the key policy areas awaiting further consideration. Our concern has been with identifying possible forms of demand for accountability – which we take to be a proper function of policy analysis – rather than with evaluating the significance of those demands in practice – which constitutes a first stage in the formulation of policy proposals as such.

ACCOUNTABILITY IN THE WIDER POLICY CONTEXT

We shall conclude our Report with a brief consideration of the place of accountability in the overall scheme of things – in the whole policy framework of a school and an authority. One way to approach the question is to reflect on what we, as members of the research team, have learned in the course of our two years' work on the Project.

Although we tried not to let our preconceptions influence the course of our enquiries, we certainly had some sketchy notions at the outset of where the investigation might lead us. One of these was that the schools probably held the key to some of the more crucial policy choices, and that school-based accountability procedures were likely to be the focal point of our attention. Another was that accountability would transpire to be closely concerned with the development of good public relations, and that we might need to give particular attention to this aspect. A third was that accountability might begin to emerge as a new heading in the LEA's budget, and that any policy proposals would have to justify their costs alongside competing claims on resources. As our work developed, we found ourselves forced to recognize that we had got each picture out of focus. It was not that we were plainly mistaken in our vision, but rather that we had caught a blurred and slightly distorted image of what was there to be seen. In each case, the reasons – when we hit on them – were instructive.

Schools are undeniably important components in educational accountability, but our hope of building up a policy framework on the Every School for Itself principle was foredoomed. What we at first failed to realize was that, in terms of accountability, the ruling principle must be that No School is an Island. Public reputation presupposes interdependence, not independence – the one school with a bad name contaminates the ninety-nine with a good. So while each must do the best it can in its own cause, the collective interest must in the end be protected by the authority (which is there to guard it) rather than by the schools (who are there to serve it). That is why our Report has turned out to be as much about the authority's options as it is about the schools' – though we did not start out with that expectation.

As our many interviews and discussions over the past two years have shown, it is also clearly the case that the successful discharge of accountability must involve the education service in more open dialogue, more vigorous publicity, a more conscious promotion of public relations, than has been its practice in the past. But to equate accountability with communication skills – as we were at first inclined to do – would be to overlook a host of other activities which we now recognize as relevant to our theme. They are those which concern the internal well-being of the system: the identification and amelioration of problems, the proper exercise of professional responsibilities, the efforts at self-appraisal, the enhancement of existing skills, and many others we have touched on in the course of our Report. In the long term, these may turn out to be more important than mere improvements in the techniques of presentation, persuasion and pacification, for they can have a catalytic effect in the regeneration of morale and self-respect, and hence in winning the respect of others. The best way of all of earning public confidence is the most direct: namely to be clearly seen as doing a good job. Again, therefore, while we have no wish to repudiate our initial concern with improved communications with parents and others, our explorations have taken us a long way beyond that point.

At one stage in our thinking, we toyed with the idea of presenting some kind of cost-benefit exercise which could match accountability against other areas of policy. We felt that our analysis would be incomplete if we were not able to present some rationale, however sketchy, to enable the authority to decide whether it wished to commit new resources in this area, and if so what scale of commitment it might sensibly make. We soon came to realize that the task was self-defeating. The elements of accountability are so diverse, multifarious and pervasive that there is simply no way of separating them out and displaying them as a separate entry in an inventory of tasks or commitments, whether at the level of the authority or at that of the school. Accountability, far from being — as our initial preconception had it — an element among others in the system, is an important aspect of the way the system itself works.

Very few of the activities with which this Report has been concerned — take school prospectuses, pupil records, county-wide testing schemes, or formal inspection — were the product of William Tyndale or Mr Callaghan's Ruskin speech. They were there — albeit undisclosed, unnoticed and unnamed — long before accountability became the political fashion; and they will doubtless long survive it. What that fashion has done is to call for a more explicit framework of expectations — summarized in Tables 1 and 2 — a framework which may clarify priorities and show the interconnections between activities hitherto separately conceived.

The time may come when accountability becomes a major influence on policy decisions. If so, it may perhaps serve not only to encourage the critical review of existing policies but also to identify the new initiatives which may be needed in response to changes in external circumstance. Such speculation, however, lies at the margins of our present understanding. All we can now say with confidence is that our initial presupposition was mistaken. Accountability — to revive a once much-quoted catchphrase — is not so much a programme, more a way of life.

1.6 How do Parents Choose and Judge Secondary Schools?

J. Elliott

We have included here an extract from a chapter 'How do Parents Choose and Judge Secondary Schools?' from the Cambridge Accountability Projects' case study of a school (Uplands), which has to respond to the danger of falling rolls in a situation of free parental choice. One response was an information brochure. The extract picks up the research in the year following the worries about falling rolls.

Success in the Market Place

In his report to the governors on 11 June 1980 Philip King wrote:

> Recently staff have been pleased, and some even a little relieved, to learn that in the annual inter-schools competition to recruit new pupils we have attracted 10 per cent more than might be regarded as a mathematical 'fair share'.

The intake for September 1980 had risen to over 135 pupils compared with the 1979 figure of 121. How had this come about? Which factors — 'the new brochure', 'the open-evening', 'the grapevine' — constituted important influences on parental choice? Also why had so many parents chosen Uplands? Interviews with a small group of existing parents had suggested that within the middle-class section of the local community there might be a substantial number of parents who shared Uplands' liberal — progressive ideals, believing that their child's 'personal happiness at school' and 'opportunities for personal and social development' were as, or even more, important than academic achievement and exam success.

The summer term 1980 'Evening for New Parents' provided me with an opportunity to explore these questions further. I drafted a questionnaire which King and his staff allowed parents (one per family) to complete during the coffee period. Thirty-two parents representing

Elliott, J. (1981), 'How do Parents Choose and Judge Secondary Schools?', in *A School in the Market Place*, Cambridge Accountability Projects, University of Cambridge Institute of Education.

sixty-four families did so.

The three major sections of the questionnaire were concerned with:

(a) What sources of information most influenced choice? (Section 5)

A number of statements, derived from interviews with existing parents [. . .] were listed and the respondents asked to assess the extent to which they were *Very Influential, Influential,* or *Not Influential* choice factors. Space was made for respondents to add additional sources of influence.

(b) Who made the choice in the family (Section 3), e.g. 'my child', 'mother and father jointly', 'mother, father and child'?

The items in this section may have elicited distorted responses because:

 (i) I neglected to include a 'mother and child jointly' category. Three parents however inserted it.

(ii) I suspect some parents responded in terms of the choice pattern they felt ought to, rather than did, obtain.

(c) Reasons for choice? (Section 4) In this section a large number of statements, again derived from previous interviews with existing parents, were listed. Respondents were first asked to place a tick beside those which expressed their own reasons for choice, and then to rate them in order of importance. Foolishly I neglected one very obvious reason; namely 'we have older children at the school already'. However, respondents had an opportunity to include it in the additional spaces provided. [. . .]

DISCUSSION (1) WHO CHOOSES?

Fifty-six per cent of respondents claimed that choice of school was jointly made by mother, father and child. A further 31 per cent claimed it was jointly made by mother and father, and only 6 per cent that it was made by either mother alone or mother and child jointly. No respondents claimed that the choice was entirely the child's. However, from the frequency with which 'our child wanted to go there' was cited as a 'top 3' consideration, it is clear that many children had a major if not final say in choice of school.

DISCUSSION (2) INFLUENTIAL SOURCES OF INFORMATION

The results of Section 5 on the information sources which influence choice are illustrated in Fig. 1. It is clear:

(a) That the open day for new parents was *very influential* in determining choice for almost half the respondents and *influential* for another quarter.

This suggests that 'the critics' I spoke to at the end of the day were a minority amongst the evening audience, who had indeed

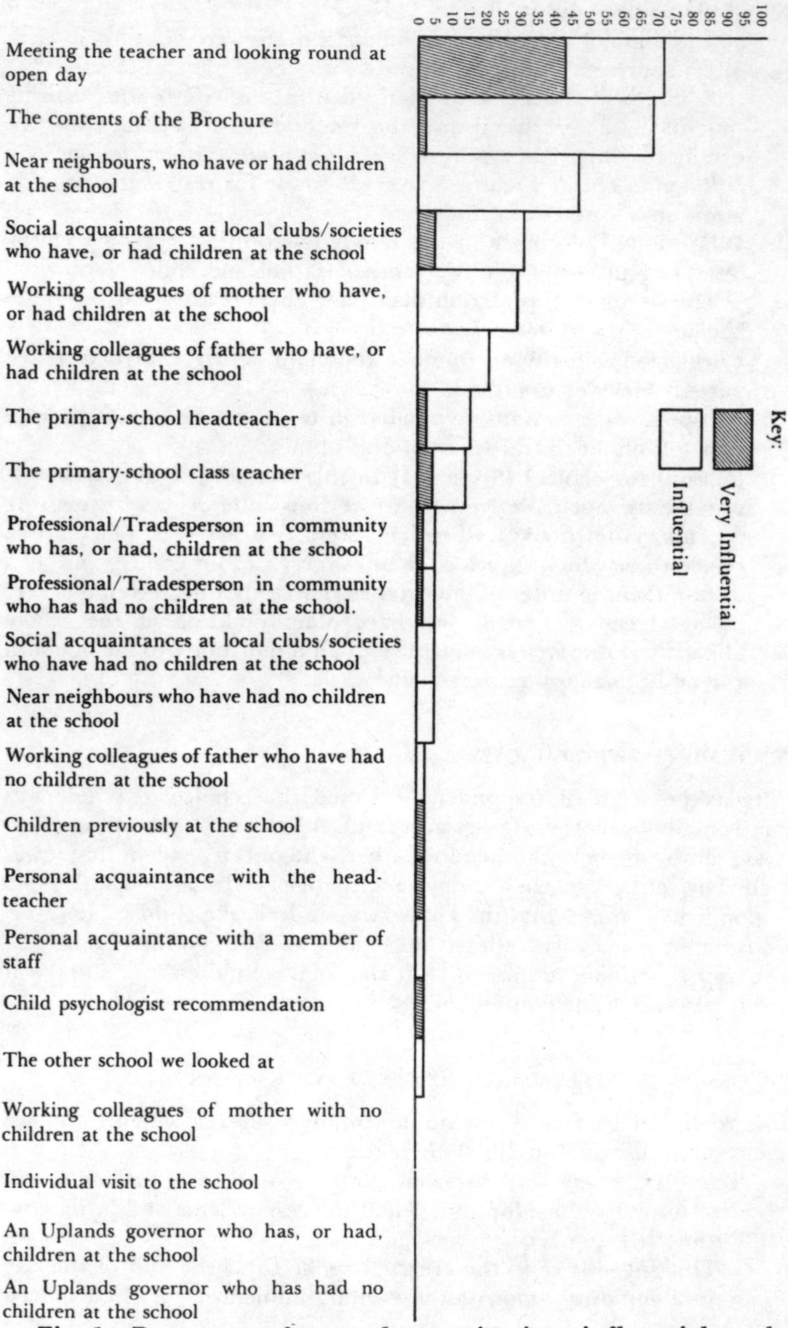

Meeting the teacher and looking round at open day

The contents of the Brochure

Near neighbours, who have or had children at the school

Social acquaintances at local clubs/societies who have, or had children at the school

Working colleagues of mother who have, or had children at the school

Working colleagues of father who have, or had children at the school

The primary-school headteacher

The primary-school class teacher

Professional/Tradesperson in community who has, or had, children at the school

Professional/Tradesperson in community who has had no children at the school.

Social acquaintances at local clubs/societies who have had no children at the school

Near neighbours who have had no children at the school

Working colleagues of father who have had no children at the school

Children previously at the school

Personal acquaintance with the head-teacher

Personal acquaintance with a member of staff

Child psychologist recommendation

The other school we looked at

Working colleagues of mother with no children at the school

Individual visit to the school

An Uplands governor who has, or had, children at the school

An Uplands governor who has had no children at the school

Key:

Very Influential

Influential

Scale: 0 5 10 15 20 25 30 35 40 45 50 55 60 65 70 75 80 85 90 95 100

Fig. 1   Percentage of respondents rating item influential on choice

already made up their minds. However, it contradicts the view of one member of staff that parents have already made up their minds prior to the open day.

This result also indicates the danger of interpreting criticisms expressed at 'question time' as expressions of a majority view. School staff can develop a quite false impression of parental attitudes at formal meetings (and so can researchers).

(b) That the brochure elicited a positive response from the majority of respondents but was not an over-riding influence. As the only source of information to prospective parents it is unlikely to persuade.

(c) That existing or past parents of the school play a major role on 'the grapevine' in influencing choice. Neighbours, work colleagues, and social contacts who have not had children at the school are far less influential. The results also confirm the impression gained through interviews that parents' choices are not determined by grapevine information from a single source, and that although the grapevine is influential it is the 'going to see for ourselves' which is more likely to be the major determinant.

(d) That primary-school heads and staff influenced the choices of only a minority of respondents. This again confirms the impression gained in interviews with primary-school heads [. . .] that they tend to adopt a neutral line, and suggests that some staff at Uplands have tended to overestimate the amount of influence they exert.

DISCUSSION (3) REASONS FOR CHOICE

My interviews with a small group of existing parents about their reasons for choosing Uplands [. . .] suggested that at least for some parents:

(a) The proximity of the school to home was an important reason for choice.

(b) Their child was given a major say in choice of school.

(c) Their child's 'personal happiness' and 'opportunities for personal and social development' were as, and perhaps more, important than their 'opportunities for academic success' at school.

(d) Mothers more than fathers tended to ascribe greater importance to 'happiness at school' and 'opportunities for personal/social development' than fathers.

(e) The extent to which the school was well-organized was an important reason for choice.

Fig. 2 outlines the results of section 4 of the questionnaire in a form which will hopefully allow us to explore the extent to which these hypotheses apply.

The diagram shows that a large minority (28.5 per cent) cited 'the nearest school' as an important consideration, but only 12.5 per cent

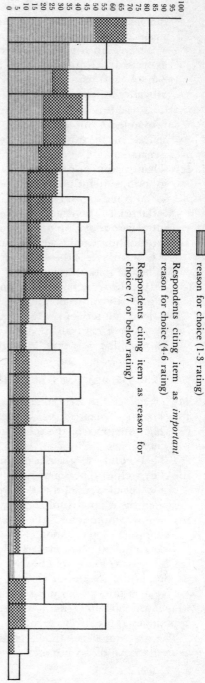

Provides a balanced, all-round education

Our child wanted to go to the school

Curriculum caters for child's personal/ social as well as academic level

Children generally are happy at the school

Parents can easily approach the head/staff about their child's progress

New children enter a personal rather than impersonal atmosphere

It is the nearest school

The teachers care for children as individuals

The policy of teaching to mixed-ability groups will benefit our child

The school is well managed and efficient

The headmaster has 'put his roots down' and will remain for some time

The school will give our child the examination opportunities he/she needs

The children get on well with the teachers

Discipline is good

The school is good at keeping parents informed about problems and progress of children

The teachers make sure children acquire basic skills they need for the future

The integration of subjects in the lower school makes sense

Children are stretched in the classroom

The school has good exam results

Child's friends at the school

Children enjoy lessons

We have older children at the school

Parents can freely air their worries about the school's policies and practices

The school's uniform policy is sensible

Children are made to work in lessons

Teachers know their subjects and how to put them across

Respondents citing item as *very important* reason for choice (1-3 rating)

Respondents citing item as *important* reason for choice (4-6 rating)

Respondents citing item as reason for choice (7 or below rating)

Fig. 2   Percentage of respondents citing item

cited it amongst their 'top three' reasons for choice. This will surprise those who assume that most parents opt for 'convenience' rather than other considerations. However, one must remember that this question-naire was completed at a formal evening for new parents, circumstances likely to attract more middle-class than working-class parents. Earlier I suggested that working-class parents tended to accept the advice of primary heads and send their children to the nearest school, and that positive choice would mainly be exercised by middle-class parents. This would explain why only a small minority of respondents placed 'nearest school' amongst their top three reasons for choice.

'Our child wanted to go to the school' is revealed to be a *very important* reason for a large minority of parents (37.5 per cent). In fact it emerges as second in popularity within the 'top three' category. This result confirms an impression gained when interviewing existing middle-class parents; that there is a substantial number of child-centred middle-class parents in the Central area community.

The diagram also reveals the extent to which opportunities for personal and social as well as academic development (rated 1-3 by 28 per cent and 4-6 by 9 per cent) loom higher in respondents' scale of priorities in choosing a school than opportunities for exam success (rated 1-6 by 12 per cent) or the school's exam record (rated 1-6 by 9 per cent). The former consideration can be closely linked with 'provides a balanced, all-round education'; the most popular consideration (rated 1-3 by 50 per cent and 4-6 by 19 per cent), and with 'the teachers care for children as individuals' (rated 1-3 by 12.5 per cent and 4-6 by 12.5 per cent) and 'the policy of teaching to mixed-ability groups will benefit our child' (rated 1-3 by 12.5 per cent and 4-6 by 6 per cent).

'Children generally are happy at the school' (rated 1-3 by 22 per cent and 4-6 by 19 per cent) also emerged as a major reason for choice by a substantial number of respondents. A linked reason also frequently cited, was 'new children enter a personal rather than impersonal atmosphere' (rated 1-3 by 19 per cent and 4-6 by 12.5 per cent).

A closer analysis of mothers' (15) and fathers' (17) reasons for choice revealed that one-third of the mothers tended to rate 'children generally are happy here' amongst their 'top three' reasons compared with about one-eighth of the fathers. However, almost as many fathers as mothers cited this item as *a reason*. The questionnaire provided no evidence that this reason applied more to daughters than sons.

No difference in priorities between mothers and fathers was apparent with respect to 'opportunities for personal/social as well as academic development'. Interestingly more father respondees did not, as I had anticipated, place 'good examination results' or 'opportunities to take exams' amongst the 'top three'. In fact, although no differences in this respect were apparent, rather more mothers than fathers cited these reasons as *a reason*.

If any conclusion can be inferred from the questionnaire responses it is that there is, within the local community, a substantial number of middle-class parents who place 'the development of the whole child, through an all-round education' and 'their child's personal happiness at school' above all other considerations when exercising choice. The liberal−progressive image of Uplands appears to match the educational values of a significant section of the local community. Such 'external support' could mean that the school does not have to change its ethos in order to survive in the market place.

If the original advocates of 'parental choice' intended it as a mechanism for bringing schools into line with a common set of community values, perhaps those which emphasize academic achievement, my interviews and the questionnaire responses suggest they may have seriously underestimated the extent to which value-pluralism exists in communities. However, it may well be that parents' value-priorities change as their children move up the secondary school age-range. From the standpoint of new parents, 'examinations' and 'employment prospects' are half a decade into the future. The 'New Education Act' in insisting that schools publish their examination results may have incorrectly assessed the kind of information many parents feel they need at the time of choice.

If more mothers than fathers placed items linked with 'personal happiness' in the 'top three' category, were there any reasons which fathers tended to rate more highly than mothers? My interviews with existing parents suggested that some ascribed great importance to the quality of school management. 'The school is well managed and efficient' was cited as a reason by 37.5 per cent of respondents; 12.5 per cent rating it 1-3 and 6 per cent 4-6. Although analysis revealed little difference between the numbers of mothers and fathers citing this as *a reason* almost one-third of the fathers rated it amongst their 'top three' while none of the mothers did. This supports an impression I gained in interviews with existing parent-fathers, many of whom occupy managerial roles in local industry. They tend to be very sensitive to management issues, and apply models of managerial competence derived from their own experience to schools. Philip King appears to meet their criteria for 'a good manager', and it is interesting that although 'the headmaster has put his roots down' is only rated 1-3 by 9 per cent of respondents, a further 22 per cent rated it 1-6 and in all 44 per cent cited it at least as *a reason* for choice.

Interestingly the 'discipline is good', and 'uniform policy makes sense' items were not frequently cited amongst the 'top six' reasons, although 28 per cent cited the former and 56 per cent cited the latter as a reason. Perhaps both were felt to be covered by, and subordinate to, 'the management' item. However, the fact that 56 per cent of respondents felt Uplands' flexible 'colour-code' dress policy was sensible, reflects again a match between a substantial proportion of parents and the liberal image of the school.

Finally Fig. 2 suggests that a school's capacity to communicate with parents about their children is an important consideration for a significant number of parents. 'Parents can easily approach the head/staff about their child's progress' achieves fourth place amongst the most frequently cited 'top three' reasons, with 22 per cent of the respondents rating it so. A further 12.5 per cent rated it in the 4-6 category. 41 per cent of respondents cited 'the school is good at keeping parents informed about children's progress and problems' as *a reason*, and 12 per cent cited it amongst their 'top six' reasons for choice.

1.7 An Enquiry into the Use of Test Results for Accountability Purposes
R. Wood and C. Gipps

This project aimed to evaluate the impact of testing programmes in classrooms on school practices, and on educational policies at local and national levels. This article is an interim report of the Evaluation of Testing in Schools Project, based on a survey of local authorities and interviews with senior officers of LEAs. It reveals much less anxiety about testing in a climate of accountability than is commonly thought.

1 Origin and Scope of the Project

The origin of the project lies in a seminar held in Cambridge in September 1977 which resulted in the book, *Accountability in Education*, edited by Tony Becher and Stuart Maclure (1978), still the best treatment of accountability in the British context, despite the overdone anti-testing polemic. A direct consequence of this seminar was a decision by the Social Science Research Council, through its Educational Research Board, to set up a panel to spend £200,000 on research relevant to accountability. The Institute of Education was awarded a little less than half that sum to carry out a three-year project (January 1980 – January 1983).

The point about this project is that it offers, for the first time we believe, the opportunity to investigate the world of testing, a world which includes:

– the purposes of testing, stated and hidden, at local authority *and* school levels, where we think of four purposes: monitoring (the subject of this paper), screening, assisting inter-school transfer (which includes selection) and individual diagnosis.

– the political dimension of testing, evident in dealings between local authority administrators, education committees, teachers and teacher associations and in the ways disclosure of results to outside parties, notably parents, is handled.

– technical matters such as choosing tests, making sense of manuals, the fitness of score distributions for the purpose intended, reporting

First publication.

of results to lay people and, in general, all those aspects of testing which we might agree are in need of demystification.

– the rejection of standardized or off-the-shelf tests in favour of tailored (LEASIB)[1] or home-stitched products and the growth of forms of assessment other than tests, such as checklists and guidelines with accompanying tasks.

– the interpenetration of testing and teaching as manifested in day-to-day classroom activity.[2]

– the work of the Assessment of Performance Unit (APU), especially as it affects local authority attitudes and actions although, in fact, we are engaged in a full-scale evaluation of the APU.

II Sources of Information

We have two primary sources of information on which to draw. The first comprises the answers to a questionnaire sent by us to all local authorities (bar the Scilly Isles) in April 1980. This questionnaire asked LEAs if they were testing and, if so, who they were testing and with what tests, why they were testing (purpose), what they did with the results (follow-up), whether they had plans to change in the future, plus a few questions covering the disclosure of results, the APU and accountability-motivated initiatives other than testing, notably self-evaluation. The questionnaire was necessary because the information we wanted did not exist. Certainly the DES claimed not to have it, because Rhodes Boyson said so in Parliament.[3]

The response to the questionnaire exceeded expectation. Replies were received from 94 out of 104 LEAs, a rate which may be compared with the 93 replies out of 146 (unreorganized LEAs) the Bullock Committee (Bullock, 1975) received in 1973 when it asked LEAs whether they had carried out any reading surveys in the past three years. It seems reasonable to attribute the higher response rate to greater interest and activity in the testing field these days, due in part to the Bullock Report.

The second source of information is the set of transcripts of semi-structured interviews with senior officers from 30 selected LEAs. These LEAs were chosen from the questionnaire returns so as to put us in touch (hopefully) with as many varieties of testing (and the absence of it) as possible. The interviews, which usually lasted about two hours, were conducted variously with one (rarely), two, three, four, five and on one memorable occasion nine persons (the best part of an education committee) and obviously the mixtures of interviewees varied in function and rank, unavoidably we think. The ideal grouping was reckoned to be the chief or principal educational psychologist, the senior adviser for primary education (where testing is most intensive) and where appropriate the administrator responsible for carrying out the testing programme (where there was one).

III Findings

In what follows results from the questionnaire bearing on this paper are spliced with relevant gleanings from the interviews and couched in the form of statements, whose meaning and implications will be discussed later.

TEST CONTENT

Reading is by far the most common attainment tested. Of the 90 LEAs which completed the questionnaire or gave information by letter, 71 reported regular authority-wide surveys of reading covering at least one age group (plus a further four which tested 'English'). A comparison with Bullock (1975, p.257) shows that 50 of the 93 responding LEAs reported that they did some sort of objective testing but only a handful carried out regular reading surveys.[4]

Mathematics, in one form or another, that is arithmetic, is tested in 36 of the authorities we know about. Only one authority tests mathematics (for monitoring purposes) and nothing else. The more recently a testing programme has been introduced the more likely it is to have a mathematics test in it.

Verbal or non-verbal reasoning tests are used by just under half (39) of the reporting authorities, *three more than test mathematics*. Some of this usage is in connection with surviving 11-plus schemes. We estimate that 15 LEAs are still selecting at or around age 11, sometimes only in geographical pockets. There may be more for we now know that two 11-plus schemes were not reported in the questionnaire.

AGES TESTED

The most common age for testing reading is 7-plus, that is, early in the primary school, indeed as Bullock recommended (8-plus used to be more common) (Bullock, 1975, p.247). Most testing occurs in primary schools, as has always been the case. At the secondary level there is a little more testing at all ages than Bullock reported, but a significant change comes at age 13. 11 LEAs are now testing reading at this stage, which in 1973 was untested. This change is probably connected with the growth of middle schools, since testing of reading before and/or after transfer is common practice. Where testing occurs towards the end of compulsory schooling, the subject tested is rather more likely to be mathematics than reading. A decision to test mathematics at 15-plus as often as not springs from interchanges with industry.

PURPOSE OF TESTING

Of the purposes to which tests are put, *screening* refers to that process whereby test scores are used, either exclusively or in combination with other indicators, to single out children thought to be in need of closer scrutiny and perhaps, ultimately, special treatment. *Monitoring*, by contrast, is the business of examining *group* scores, where the groups may be classes, school age cohorts or authority-wide age cohorts, with a view to making comparisons.

Screening, almost by definition, implies that all children are tested, although it is possible to imagine an authority or school deciding that it was pointless testing certain children because they would certainly fall outside the screen. Monitoring does not necessarily imply any particular testing plan although it is not necessary to test all children; comparisons can be made using samples, indeed most people, with the APU in mind, probably think of monitoring strictly in terms of sampling, or *light sampling* as it is called. In practice, however, most LEAs which claim to be monitoring engage in blanket testing, partly or perhaps mostly because they wish to screen at the same time, or have thought that they are screening and also because light sampling of the order of 10 per cent is not thought to provide enough information on which to base inter-school comparisons.

To come now to the purposes of testing mentioned by LEAs, and focusing on reading, the most often cited reason given for testing was screening. Of the 71 LEAs with reading surveys only five did not give screening as one of their reasons although two of these, it should be said, took the position that screening involves far more than a mere inspection of test scores. Statements that testing is meant to satisfy a multiplicity of purposes were common: a typical reply, 'The tests are administered to monitor performance across the Authority, to indicate resource requirements and to enable decisions to be made on appropriate curriculum (sic)'. Some officers admit to disquiet about using tests for so many different purposes; there are, in fact, technical limitations on how far you can use the same test to screen *and* monitor effectively.

Where mathematics testing is concerned, LEAs are readier to allow that they are monitoring and nothing else. Indeed some differentiate quite clearly between the screening of reading and the monitoring of mathematics. This, in itself, says a lot. The idea of treating innumeracy or mathematical disability is regarded in some quarters as quite novel, if not the subject for a joke.

WHY DO LEAs MONITOR?

Monitoring is of two kinds. There is monitoring of authority-wide results, which involves comparison with ostensibly national norms and there is monitoring of school results, which involves comparing schools. An authority may do both from the outset or end up doing both, having started with the first kind.

As to cause, there is no doubt that the agonizings about 'standards' which were a feature of the middle 1970s persuaded some authorities, but by no means all, that they ought to be monitoring. The response took various forms:

— setting up testing programmes with the object of monitoring alone;
— setting up testing programmes with the stated object of screening but with the intention of monitoring also;
— using existing screening programmes for monitoring purposes;
— augmenting existing schemes on the ground that, having proved to be workable and acceptable, the machinery is there to extend testing, a 'knock-on' effect, if you like.

Here are examples of the first and last forms:

In 1974 the Chief Education Officer of a certain authority sees the way the wind is blowing and asks his officers to draw up plans for a monitoring programme. Even before Callaghan makes the Ruskin speech (the opening of the so-called 'Great Debate') he has persuaded the education committee that it would be prudent to introduce his programme.

Members of an education committee perceive that there is national concern about mathematics achievement, are aware that there is already a reading screening programme in the authority and want to know what the 'standard' of arithmetic is in their schools, so they extend the screening to include maths.

But not all monitoring initiatives stemmed from 'standards' rhetoric, as these two examples show.

Following reorganization in 1974 (often a critical factor in the development of testing) a new authority wishes to get its bearings, in particular it wishes to understand what levels of achievement it can expect and so wants to compare itself with the 'national picture'. It starts collecting 'O' level and CSE results. Then someone on the education committee says, 'These are fine as far as they go but what about some information on younger children, some test scores, maybe? Can we see how our 9-year-olds compare on reading with 9-year-olds nationwide?'

In 1975 there is a fight for resources among different departments within an authority. Education officers decide they need to know where the local children stand in comparison with the 'national average'; if their performance is below par they will feel able to ask for more resources.

The point – which will surprise no one – is that no single causal explanation will fit all authorities which claim to be monitoring. The corollary is that there is almost certainly great variation in what is meant by monitoring. It could be anything from a casual inspection of results one afternoon to a full-scale intervention exercise based on the results.

LIGHT SAMPLING

Sampling is practised in twelve authorities only. Blanket testing is, therefore, the norm. Sampling is usually of children, except in two authorities where schools are sampled. Where participation in testing schemes is voluntary, as it is in a few LEAs, the percentage of children tested will fall below 100 per cent but rarely below 70 per cent. Of those authorities that sample, a 10 per cent fraction is considered too low in the smaller authorities, where 25 per cent is more common.

FOLLOW-UP

This is the subject about which we know least, largely because we have not observed follow-up in practice. Answers to the questionnaire are not too helpful containing, as they do, a certain amount of what we suspect to be pious hand-waving in the direction of that all-purpose phrase 'allocation of resources'. What we can say is that in accountability terms we have seen no sign that any LEA is following up in textbook fashion, i.e. beating teachers over the head with test results. On the contrary, the tone employed by officers is invariably benign, with phrases like 'positive discrimination' liable to crop up. It is possible that the 'big stick' is kept up the sleeve and produced on occasion – one officer did talk about giving schools 'a kick up the pants' – but, not surprisingly, there was reticence on this subject.

IV Discussion

That the testing of reading should continue to be given so much more attention than the testing of mathematics or indeed any other skill – only one LEA reported testing perceptual skills and that at age 4 – is something which we shall be writing about elsewhere. We also need to ponder on the fact that verbal and/or non-verbal reasoning are tested more often than mathematics. Then there is the question of why reading is thought susceptible to remediation whereas mathematics is not, at least not yet, although an educational psychologist we know is working on it.

Sticking strictly to the terms of the paper it is necessary to consider what emerged as our major findings:

Monitoring is much less common than screening, in fact testing is used at least as much in connection with school transition as for monitoring schools' performance;

Light sampling is used only by a small number of authorities;

Monitoring procedures come about in many different ways and there is no single explanation;

While there is some mystery surrounding the use to which monitoring results are put it looks as if they are not used to make schools or teachers accountable in anything like the classic manner. To our knowledge there is no authority which publishes 'league tables', i.e. named school results.

To take the last one first, we are not sure what a full-blown 'accountability through testing' model should look like but we assume it would have the following features, at least.

1. Monitoring initiated by officers or at the instigation of the education committee.
2. Results collated centrally and analysed on a school-by-school basis.
3. School results made available to the education committee in 'league table' form, perhaps also to the media.
4. Schools said to be performing below par asked to explain themselves.

(We stop short of adding American-style actions such as dismissing teachers or keeping students at school.)

The chief reason why this scenario does not occur is that teachers, individually, in groups and through their associations, have made it abundantly clear to officers that 'league tables' are not on. If anything is an iron law, it is that. Officers in their turn have done everything in their power to dissuade education committee members from requesting league tables and, as far as we can tell, have always succeeded. The most members might get, in a large authority, are summarized results at a divisional level.

Maurice Peston, in a stimulating paper (1981), argues that the accountability debate is to a considerable extent to do with a jockeying for position between teachers, officials and politicians and the relationship of all of them to parents, pupils and society in general. In this analysis, monitoring procedures can be seen as a *contract* between officials and teachers aimed at excluding politicians, not to mention the other groups (who barely get a look in at all), from access to named school data, and so prevent unwelcome enquiries. There are trade-offs, of course. Teachers have to accept the tests while officials deny themselves the opportunity, if they ever wanted it, of getting public leverage from test results. Any leverage they do exert has to be private and that, in fact, is the form the contract takes. Typically schools are assured that results will be used confidentially and *professionally* which means, for example, an adviser talking over below par results with the head of the school. It is the significance of such meetings – they may be symbolic – and the consequences, which remain to be explicated.

Anyone reading some of the contributions to the Becher–Maclure volume might come away with a strong impression of 'administrators eagerly embracing testing and test data as satisfying their need for administrative neatness and the appearance of objectivity' (Peston, 1981, p.226). It would be idle to deny that LEAs contain people with this cast of mind, although the consequences might be fairly harmless, or to dispute the fact that test results, providing they turn out right, offer a highly convenient way of keeping critics at bay. All the same, as a general description of administrators the quotation will not do. If it did, there would not be LEAs about which it could be said that they could do far more with test results than they do. Several have data on all children but choose to look only at small samples. There are LEAs which do not collect data centrally. We know of one LEA which never got round to making use of test scores gathered three years ago and has had to admit that the data are now worthless. And there is an LEA which tests 60,000 children with not inexpensive tests and gives as its sole reason 'To give teachers some idea of the general ability of the children they teach'.

There are officers who use testing for opportunistic reasons, there are officers who subscribe to testing for sincere reasons, believing that schools should be more accountable and that test data, limited though they may be, are part of the evidence. And there are officers who have intellectual reservations about testing, or just plain distaste for it, in both cases perhaps harking back to 11-plus. Some of these people have resisted testing in debate, others have resorted to delaying tactics ('wait for the APU and LEASIB'). Others have bowed to *realpolitik* but are working away at converting education committees and colleagues, sometimes, to what they regard as a more enlightened outlook – 'guidelines is what we should be aiming for'. Finally, there are those officers who have no strong feelings one way or the other about testing as a source of information but who realize that testing can be messy, can cause problems (computers), can store up trouble for the future (with heads and unions), can get out of control (if results fall into the wrong hands) and so on. Testing can spoil administrative neatness as well as enhance it.

Then there are the teachers. If the theorem is that administrators eagerly embrace testing then a rider would seem to be that teachers wholeheartedly reject testing, both on ideological and education grounds. From the enquiries we have made, that is a caricature of the way things are. It would appear, in the main, that teachers, and particularly headteachers, are every bit as keen on testing as administrators. The best empirical confirmation of that statement is what happens when, in a sampling context, heads are offered the opportunity of testing the children who are not part of the light sample. In one LEA operating a 10 per cent sampling policy, where that offer was made, 92 per cent of schools tested 100 per cent of children in an age group. In another LEA which had to proceed carefully over light sampling because it was feared it might be the thin end of the wedge, the teachers through their associations trust the authority sufficiently now to be asking for blanket testing. As a third illustration consider the

LEA which, on reorganization and the abandonment of 11-plus, offered primary heads, unwisely it believes in retrospect, the chance of continuing testing or giving it up. Opinion was almost unanimous in wanting to retain testing and has been so ever since, despite mounting attempts by the officers to cut back on the volume of testing, which is considerable.

Three observations come to mind. There is an *inertia* about testing – once introduced, rarely withdrawn. Heads come to rely on it, new reasons are found for continuing with it.

Memories of 11-plus have faded; the newer testing schemes are regarded differently.

The interesting question now may well be 'What use do heads make of test results?' That we intend to find out.

V Current Developments

This paper was written in January 1981 when education cuts were biting hard. The effects will still be felt in a year's time so we want to say something about a recent development we have noticed, and suspect we will see more of, that is, the use of testing expressly for the allocation of resources.

Accountability is only an issue in a crisis, says Peston (1981). Well, this certainly is a crisis but one that seems to be diverting attention in the LEAs away from concern over standards. Is testing an issue only when there is nothing more urgent? More than one authority told us that education committee members are no longer concerned about standards and have almost forgotten about the testing programme. Now they are more concerned with cuts and the new Education Bill. That seems to be logical. Why worry about standards when you are told daily that they must fall and the only question is 'By how much?'?

Against this background two LEAs to our knowledge have introduced testing programmes for the avowed purpose of allocating resources. One of these, which hitherto has shown no interest in installing a centralized testing programme, is testing to provide data which it believes will assist in carrying out what it calls a 'staffing policy'. Teachers and their associations have accepted the package on the grounds that somehow teaching jobs will be conserved.

The arguments the authority uses for testing are familiar. With every head shrieking for help, who do you help most? If you're not careful you end up helping those who shout loudest. Therefore we need objective data to enable us to cut the cake fairly and, more importantly, for it to be seen to be cut fairly, should we ever have to defend our decisions publicly. At the same time this authority – and others – maintains that information gained from testing is only one factor taken into consideration when decisions are made. There is, however, as House remarks (in Becher and Maclure, 1978, p.211), a strong tendency for quantitative data to overwhelm other sources of information, whatever the protestations to the contrary.

The relative weights given to 'hard' and 'soft' data is one matter: the principle by which resources should be allocated, or perhaps more correctly, reallocated, is another. There seem to be two extreme possibilities: give resources to the schools with the poorest results which, if it works, will tend to equalize achievements across schools *or* give resources to those schools with the best results where payoff is most likely, and let the schools with the poorest results go to the wall. The first course of action is conventional wisdom while to mention the second in public is more or less taboo, although it might turn out to have some bearing on schools closure policies.

Supposing schools learn the rules of the game, say, poor results mean more resources, and behave accordingly. What happens then? Don't we move towards a payment by results situation, but in reverse? Or to situations which have occurred in America, specifically in Michigan and Florida, where as Becher and Maclure (1978, p.220) maintain, 'the use of tests to improve standards tends to be ineffectual when failure in schools carries no penalties and success brings no rewards'. In Michigan, particularly, plans to discourage schools from 'implicitly or explicitly' taking steps to depress test scores in order go get continued funding caused tremendous controversy among teachers and were never implemented because they were perceived not as an incentive, but as a penalty, singling out teachers with pupil failures (see Madaus, 1979, for useful background and interesting thoughts on the test-based funding theme).

Of course we have nothing like the same system here but likely problems can be foreseen. Take an LEA where it is *believed* that resource allocation hinges on test results, whatever actually happens. Heads know their test scores, they know their resource allocation, all they need to do is compare notes with their neighbours and before long there's unrest, both from those who feel they deserve more and those who feel they need more.

To return to accountability, the question is, 'Are we closer than ever before to the introduction of accountability procedures, overt and covert, and hinging on test results?' Peston's prediction would suggest we are; if scarce resources are channelled according to test scores, will the recipients be required to demonstrate that they have produced improvements from the input? What about other schools receiving fewer resources? Will they be required to show that their performance standards have not fallen off? Or fallen off as much as might have been expected? But how do you calculate how much that should be? Might there not be a sort of 'Three-day week' phenomenon at work with more productivity coming from fewer resources? None of these questions featured in the project proposal: it is a measure of how events are moving that they should now seem so important.

Notes
1. Local Education Authorities and Schools Item Banks (LEASIB), an NFER project designed to provide LEAs and schools with tests in mathematics and language tailored to their curricular practices.
2. This work will be largely in the hands of Barry Stierer, an SSRC PhD linked award student attached to the project who will be studying the teaching and testing of reading in the primary school.
3. Reply to Mrs Renée Short (reported in *Education*, 4 April 1980, p.367).
4. By the time this paper appears another, provisionally entitled 'The Testing of Reading in LEAs: Bullock Seven Years On', will be available or perhaps will have been published.

References
Becher, T. and Maclure, S. (eds.) (1978), *Accountability in Education*, NFER Publishing Co.
Bullock, A. (ed.) (1975), *A Language for Life* (The Bullock Report), HMSO.
Madaus, G. F. (1979), 'Testing and Funding: Measurement and Policy Issues', *New Directions for Testing and Measurement*, No. 1, Jossey-Bass.
Peston, M. (1981), 'Accountability in Education: Some Economic Aspects', *Educational Policy Bulletin*, Spring.

PART 2: RESPONSES
Editors: Philip Clift and Mary James

2.1 Policy Options at the School Level
A. Becher, M. Eraut and J. Knight

These extracts, based on a report of the East Sussex Accountability Project, review the range of approaches to school-based accounting: from routine strategies for problem-solving to more formal procedures. A brief discussion of self-assessment checklists, monitoring by indicators, school-based evaluation and audited self-assessment, serves as a useful introduction to subsequent articles which describe particular approaches in more detail.

Approaches to School-based Accounting

Many of the proponents of school-based accounting have focused rather more on the principle than the practice; and where particular approaches have been suggested, they have been illustrative rather than definitive. The review that follows is necessarily brief but does at least indicate some of the issues that remain to be explored. In particular it distinguishes between four different forms of accountability, [. . .] developing at school level the distinction [. . .] between problem-solving and maintenance.

Problem-solving is very much part of the natural system of accountability[. . .]. It includes both the habitual practices by which all teachers keep their eyes and ears open, look out for problems and assure themselves that, at least at a superficial level, all is well; and the informal and multifarious procedures by which heads watch over their schools. It does not attempt to focus on any particular issue or to seek evidence that is not fairly readily available.

Maintenance procedures can be usefully subdivided between those that are primarily concerned with pupil progress and those that involve some form of school self-evaluation. Unlike the more informal problem-solving procedures, the systematic monitoring and review of pupils' progress and well-being takes place within a formal framework of records and reports, tests and examinations[. . .].

Evaluation procedures at school level have provided the focus for

Becher, A., Eraut, M., Knight, J. (1981), 'Policy Options at the School Level', abridged from Chapter 5 of *Policies for Educational Accountability*, Heinemann Educational Books.

recent discussions of the merits and feasibility of school-based accounting, but it has not always been clear what kind of review was intended. Some suggestions, for example, seem to concentrate on self-reporting or the provision of information for external audiences. Others have suggested school self-assessment or internal evaluation, in which there is a deliberate attempt to search for strengths and weaknesses in a school's practice and to consider alternative approaches. There remains the question whether the outcomes of such evaluations should be reported, and if so to whom. Advisers, governors and parents are among the more obvious candidates. One new departure would be audited self-assessment which involves an external auditor or panel of auditors in viviting the school and certifying or commenting on its reports[. . .].

Problem-solving

The detection of individual points of weakness can be pursued by two quite distinct strategies, which we have chosen to call spotting and scanning. Spotting rests on the assumption that any signs of trouble will be readily detected by the watchful observer, who therefore needs to make no special arrangements to gather additional evidence. Its effectiveness depends both on the frequency of observation and on the perceptiveness of the observer. It is, for example, reasonable to expect that an alert and sensitive teacher can effectively trouble-spot in his own classroom, but less reasonable to suggest that he could do this on a brief visit to someone else's classroom. Scanning, on the other hand, implies a more systematic attempt to gather evidence about potential problems. It is deliberate, contrived and sometimes time-consuming: so it tends to be seen as only supplementary to incidental observations. In the nature of things, both heads and teachers encounter enough problems without seeking them out: so they have a natural reluctance to go out of their way to look for more.

The teacher's regular trouble-spotting activities include routine marking and observing pupil behaviour in class; his scanning activities include giving diagnostic tests, analysing a batch of exercise books and making systematic entries in the record book. A head can trouble-spot by walking round the school, visiting classrooms and talking to teachers and pupils; but he is equally likely to have problems drawn to his attention by other people – teachers, ancillary staff, parents, and members of the local community. Primary heads also carry out a variety of scanning activities – reviewing teachers' record books, looking over pupils' work, reading reports and record cards, looking at test or examination results and personal testing of pupils. Year tutors' responsibilities, in contrast, are usually confined to spotting. Neither they nor primary teachers with special responsibility for particular subjects would consider it appropriate or politically feasible to review the work of pupils other than their own. Greater delegation takes place in secondary schools, but the procedures for monitoring other teachers' classrooms are correspondingly limited. The head of school does not have the time and the head of department does not have the authority. However, [. . .] all teachers receive information relevant to trouble-spotting in the natural course of events. Chance meetings with parents or pupils, access to the grapevine and comments from other schools can all indicate problems which may need further investigation.

Problem-solving is thus a normal part of professional life. All teachers engage in spotting, perhaps with varying degrees of success; but there is much greater variation in the enthusiasm and commitment with which scanning activities are pursued. Good spotters probably need to give less time to scanning, but few people are likely to admit that they are not good spotters. Ultimately it is the head who is responsible for the effectiveness of problem-solving activities, but most schools would benefit from some internal discussions about how they do it, how well it works, and what they find to be the principal difficulties. [. . .]

Reviewing Policy, Performance and Procedures

The review of policy, performance and procedures is central to the notion of school-based accounting. It can take a number of forms: internal self-assessment, external reported self-assessment and audited self-assessment. But in practice, the two most immediate concerns – will teachers be prepared to do it?, and will it ever amount to more than whitewash? – have tended to obscure discussion of difficulties and deeper implications.

[. . . While] detailed reports on the curriculum would be valued by parents and help to create an atmosphere of trust [a] consideration of school self-accounting raises three major issues:

(i) The difficulty of estimating the time spent in some areas of the curriculum or in certain types of educational activity.

(ii) The problem of finding an appropriate language for describing ordinary classroom practice. Distinctive features of the curriculum get reported and discussed while day-to-day activities tend to be taken for granted.

(iii) The question of how far it is meaningful to describe a curriculum for a whole school or a whole department, as opposed to a curriculum for each teacher or even a curriculum for each pupil.[1]

The first two are capable of being resolved as teachers gain experience in preparing curriculum accounts. The third is more fundamental as it presents a clear challenge to teacher autonomy. Some schools have developed a tradition of regular staff meetings to discuss their teaching, while others have a tradition of personal privacy. There is a delicate balance between teacher autonomy and a coherent school policy. If teacher autonomy is overemphasized, it ceases to be meaningful to talk about a school curriculum as opposed to a separate curriculum for each teacher, and school self-reporting becomes impossible. But if accountability is used to create more central control by the head, the relationship between the report and the reality may become increasingly tenuous as teachers find ways of disguising their departures from detailed prescriptions to which they feel little commitment. On the positive side, we found that detailed curriculum accounts were useful in maintaining internal coherence and in encouraging the exchange of experience between schools, as well as for communicating to external audiences such as parents, governors and advisers. If a curriculum account clarifies and sharpens the boundary between shared policy and what is left to the discretion of individual teachers, this too can be of benefit.

Accountability for maintenance, however, requires more than school self-reporting. There is an obligation to review policy, performance and procedures. In the context of school-based accounting, this can only be undertaken by the school staff. Institutional self-assessment can take a number of forms. We shall explore the three which have hitherto attracted most attention: the self-assessment checklist, monitoring by indicators, and a programme of focused reviews.

The simplest approach is probably the self-assessment checklist, of which the best known is that produced by the inspectorate of the Inner London Education Authority (ILEA, 1977). The primary-school section of this document contains over a hundred questions, many of them subdivided. The introduction emphasizes that the document is not intended as a blueprint and that it would be impossible for any school to examine all aspects in a single year. The questions do not carry any implicit view of the curriculum but do present a strong picture of how the authority expects a school to be managed and organized. A similar checklist could be developed from an inspection schedule such as that used in the HMI Primary Survey (DES, 1978). The main difficulty with the checklist approach appears to be the lack of guidance on evaluation strategy. Important issues of focus and methodology are glossed over. Yet that is where, according to most experienced evaluators, the real difficulties start. To the external world, checklists appear to offer an interesting compromise between external guidance and authority and internal choice and responsibility. But within the school itself their strong management orientation can seem to belie their declared purpose of guiding self-evaluation. The questions tend to be imposed from above with the result that school self-assessment comes to be seen primarily as a management problem. The consequent lack of participation may reduce the likelihood that the conclusions will be generally accepted by staff; and this in turn may make it difficult for the school as a whole to respond in the way that its management would wish.

The approach to monitoring by indicators is similarly managerial, but more technical. Though traditionally associated with external rather than internal review, it has been advanced by Shipman as the proper approach to in-school evaluation. He advocates returning to "the traditional position that evaluation has to start with a broad set of aims and a progressive specification of these until one has a set of working objectives whose attainment can be judged by qualitative or quantitative indicators". The focus on standards of performance is unequivocal. Shipman is prepared to work pragmatically, with indicators which range from standardized tests to teacher ratings, but is in no doubt about their prominence and significance:

> The in-school evaluation programme will eventually consist of a selection of indicators, collected as routine every year. Collectively they should give an idea of how well the school is running in every aspect of its work. This means that indicators have to cover the academic work in the school, but also the social, the behavioural, the sporting, the cultural, the extra-mural, the relationships with parents, employers and the public (Shipman, 1979).

Several authors have asserted that it is impossible to devise objectives from aims, as Shipman proposes, and there is little empirical evidence to suggest that his claim is feasible.[2] Devising suitable indicators is more difficult still: it has defeated the combined efforts of a large section of the research community for the last twenty years. Shipman tries to avoid the narrowness of a system of indicators based on standardized tests but fails to recognize that less reliable forms of data collection have little value as indicators. Teacher opinions, for example, can be an important element in any evaluation which has a specific purpose and allows for cross-checking of evidence, but they are unsuitable as indicators for comparing one school with another or even one year with another within the same school. Because comparison is an important element in self-evaluation, Nisbet (1978) recommends using indicators as a form of external calibration. However, he also emphasizes the narrow range of aims for which suitably reliable indicators are available. Even within that range their role is limited: although qualitative indicators may suggest that something needs examining, they cannot of themselves provide much information about what if anything is wrong or suggest any means by which it might be put right.

A further possible approach to school self-assessment, in contrast with both checklists and indicators, is a programme of focused reviews, each comprising a small evaluation study of a particular aspect of the school's provision. The task is formally assigned to individuals or working parties, who are then expected to report back to the rest of the staff. A three-year or five-year rolling programme of reviews can ensure that all aspects of school life are regularly examined. The advantage of focusing on one area at a time is that a wide range of evidence can be collected and constructive suggestions for improvements considered without imposing an impossible workload or causing teachers to feel that everything they do is being scrutinized all the time. This approach has also been advocated by Nisbet (1978) and by Hoyle (1979), but has yet to be adopted by schools on a systematic rather than occasional basis. Hoyle points to the need for teachers to develop the necessary skills, while Nisbet talks of the need for reorientation.

There is still relatively little experience in school-based evaluation, and existing styles and methods are likely to benefit from further development. The experience of incorporating curriculum evaluation projects into part-time and full-time MA courses has confirmed that they can be of considerable benefit to schools and that internal political problems are usually surmountable. But it is also clear that if such evaluations are to be productive, the teachers involved will need to develop relevant knowledge, skills and experience.

Procedures and techniques for conducting school-based evaluations are discussed by Eraut (1976, 1978a, 1978b, 1980) and by Simons (1979), both of whom suggest using a mixture of methods for collecting information and argue for careful negotiation with all the staff involved. Checklists and indicators present too simple an approach, in that they tend to assume a consensus that rarely exists in practice. Divergent views have to be incorporated if maximum participation is to be achieved; and processes as well as outcomes must be studied if sufficient understanding is to be generated to allow for subsequent constructive action. Given that the development of school-based evaluation is still at an early stage, it would be counterproductive to implement it too rapidly. A phased introduction would allow schools gradually to acquire the necessary skills and experience, and avoid some of the more obvious pitfalls.

The next question to be asked is how school self-assessment might most appropriately be reported. At the simplest level a school might report only its procedures – whether it had a programme of reviews, whether it was using indicators for monitoring its performance, whether it was using a self-assessment checklist, and who had access to the resultant information. At the next level brief summaries of the findings might be presented, together with some note of any consequent action being taken. The third and fullest level of reporting would involve the presentation of fairly lengthy evaluation reports on a regular basis. A cautious advocate of school self-accounting might suggest that the first level was appropriate for reporting to parents, and that it might also be used during a warm-up period while the school was gaining confidence. The second level would normally form the basis of regular reporting to governors and advisers, but both these groups might reasonably be able to request access to the full reports. The school should not perhaps move to this higher level of reporting until it felt fully confident to do so.

MacDonald (1978) argues that the whole process will be jeopardized unless there is a cautious beginning, because teachers will take up defensive and non-co-operative positions. The critics of self-evaluation argue that this will happen anyway, and that self-evaluation is bound to be anodyne, if not vacuous. Its advocates argue that in the long run self-evaluation is the only form of accountability worth pursuing because – leaving aside extreme cases such as William Tyndale – other forms of accountability will only increase external control over schools without being able to translate that control into improvements in the quality of teaching.

Audited self-assessment has been proposed as a means of enhancing the credibility of school self-accounting without destroying its advantages. The school could benefit from an external professional opinion, while governors should feel more confident about a school's reports if they have been independently examined. The essential difference between auditing and inspection is that auditing is based on the school's own account and has to relate to, if not agree with, the school's analysis of its own situation and its evaluative criteria. Suggestions for the auditor's role range from his being a full participant in an evaluation study to his reading completed reports and commenting upon them. In either case, he would be expected to visit the school, talk to the teachers concerned, look at children's work and possibly observe some teaching. According to the agreed role and to locally negotiated conditions of appointment, the auditor could be another teacher, an adviser, a lecturer or even a visiting panel of teachers. Several types of arrangement have been discussed (Becher and Maclure, 1978; Elliott, 1980a; Hoyle, 1979), but few have been tried out in practice. CSE moderation is probably the closest analogy (Cohen and Deale, 1977) but it serves a rather different purpose.

The Taylor Committee's proposals on the role of governors in keeping the life and activities of a school under review come close to suggesting that the governors themselves should act as auditors. Taylor (DES, 1977) recommends that the governors should establish the school's aims, review the school's policy for achieving those aims, get regular information of a statistical kind and receive periodic evaluation reports of a more qualitative nature. Moreover, the governors should make a general appraisal of the school every four years and send it on to the LEA. Much of the controversy to which this proposal for evaluation by non-professionals has given rise could be avoided if it were acknowledged that such an appraisal would inevitably have to be based on information provided by the school itself, and that governors would have the opportunity of calling on advisers for an additional professional opinion when required.

Notes
1. The East Sussex self-accounting experiment is reported more fully in Working Paper 12 (Eraut, 1979).
2. Detailed discussions of this issue can be found in Eisner (1969), Macdonald-Ross (1973) and Sockett (1976).

References
Becher, T. and Maclure, S. (1978), 'Accounting Procedures and Educational Processes', in *Accountability in Education*, NFER Publishing.
Cohen, L. and Deale, R. N. (1977), *Assessment by Teachers in Examinations at 16+*, Schools Council Examination Bulletin 37, Evans/Methuen Educational.
Department of Education and Science (1977), *A New Partnership for our Schools* (The Taylor Report), HMSO.
— (1978), *Primary Education in England*, HMSO.
Eisner, E. W. (1969), 'Instructional and Expressive Educational Objectives: their Formulation and Use in Curriculum', in W. J. Popham (ed.), *Instructional Objectives*, AERA Curriculum Monograph 3, Rand McNally.
Elliott, J. (1980a), 'Who should Monitor Performance in Schools?', in Sockett (1980).
— (1980b), 'Educational Accountability and the Evaluation of Teaching', in A. Lewy (ed.), *Evaluation Roles*, Gordon and Breach.
Eraut, M. (1976), 'School-based Evaluation', in M. Raggett and N. Clarkson (eds.), *Teaching the Eight to Thirteens, Volume 2*, Ward Lock.
— (1978a), 'Accountability at School Level – Some Options and their Implications', in Becher and Maclure (1978).
— (1978b), 'Problems of Research Design', in Gerald Collier (ed.), *Evaluating the new B.Ed.*, Society for Research in Higher Education.
— *et al.* (1979), *An Experiment in School Self-accounting*. A working paper for the East Sussex Accountability Project. Education Area, University of Sussex.
— (1980), 'Handling Value Issues', paper presented to Ethics in Education seminar, BERA Conference, September.
Hoyle, E. (1979), 'Evaluation of the Effectiveness of Educational Institutions', address to BEAS Conference, Sheffield, September.
ILEA (1977), *Keeping the School Under Review*, a method of self-assessment for schools devised by the ILEA Inspectorate, Inner London Education Authority.
MacDonald, B. (1978), 'Accountability, Standards and the Process of Schooling', in Becher and Maclure (1978).
Macdonald-Ross, M. (1973), 'Behavioural Objectives: a Critical Review', *Instructional Science*, No.2, pp.1-52.
Nisbet, J. (1978), 'Procedures for Assessment', in Becher and Maclure (1978).
Shipman, M. (1979), *In-School Evaluation*, Heinemann Educational Books.
Simons, H. (1979), 'Suggestions for a School Self-evaluation based on Democratic Principles', *Classroom Action Research Network*, Bulletin 3, pp.49-55.

Sockett, H. (1976), *Designing the Curriculum*, Open Books.
— (ed.) (1980), *Accountability in the English Educational System*, Hodder & Stoughton.

2.2 Performance Indicators for Institutions of Higher Education under Conditions of Financial Stringency, Contraction and Changing Needs
J. Sizer

In this article Sizer draws attention to the need for reliable and valid indicators of quality by which institutional policy, performance and procedures may be judged. He proposes that they should be: relevant, verifiable, free from bias, quantifiable, economically feasible and institutionally acceptable. He then discusses the issues which arise to complicate the simplistic application of these tests of the appropriateness of indicators of institutional quality. Although his discussion is in the context of institutions of higher education, much of what he proposes applies equally well to schools.

I doubt whether it is necessary to remind this conference that many institutions of higher education have entered a period of financial stagnation, falling real income per student, and perhaps actual decline in student numbers during the remainder of this century. They are increasingly being asked to justify their activities and account for their use of resources and their performance, in terms of their effectiveness and their efficiency, not only to external financing bodies but also to other influential groups in society. Are the latter's prevailing attitudes reflected in a recent *Financial Times* editorial?

> The slogan of academic freedom does not justify the presumption that all universities are equal, when clearly they are not, or that the options chosen by school leavers are the only possible guide to the allocation of expensive resources. (*Financial Times*, 30 October 1979)

Furthermore, within institutions, consideration has to be given to the efficiency of the various academic and service departments, decisions made concerning the allocation of resources, and in some cases

A shortened version of a keynote address to the Annual Conference of the Society for Research into Higher Education. Brighton Polytechnic, 19–20 December 1979.

decisions have to be taken involving major cutbacks and reallocations of resources. Clearly managements need a sound basis upon which to arrive at, and justify such decisions; in particular they need to develop and employ appropriate methods for allocating resources and for subsequently assessing the performance of the component parts of their institutions. Inevitably there is a demand for performance indicators which will aid, and possibly oversimplify, this process.

Today, institutional performance assessment has to be undertaken against the background of the long-term trends identified in the DES documents *Higher Education in the 1990s* (1978) and *Future Trends in Higher Education* (1979), the pressure to charge overseas students' full economic fees, the letters of guidance from the UGC, and the severe short-term pressures to reduce the level of government expenditure on higher education. Within institutions there is a need to balance the pressure for increased cost efficiency and possible restrictions on student admissions in the short term with the actions that need to be taken if the organization is to be effective in the long term. One of the greatest dangers in the present situation is that the short-term pressures will become so overwhelming that many actions will be taken which will be damaging to the long-term effectiveness and efficiency of institutions. For example, will the charging of full economic fees to overseas students hit hardest the very institutions which the government may wish to support in the long term; institutions such as Imperial College of Science and Technology with an international reputation in science and technology?

What do we understand by the term "effectiveness", and should a distinction be drawn between *effectiveness* and *efficiency*? Is an organization effective if it achieves the objectives it has set itself, and should those objectives be appropriate to the needs of society? Is it efficient if it achieves those objectives with optimal use of the resources available to it in the long run? What is the relationship between effectiveness, efficiency and performance assessment? Is institutional performance assessment concerned with the measurement or observation of the effective and efficient accomplishment of the expectations of the institution's constituencies (Romney, Bogen and Micek, 1979)? Is it an examination of the objective achievement process, which consists of at least four distinct stages in which objectives are set; resources are committed for the purpose of achieving these objectives; committed resources are expended to achieve the objectives; and outcomes result (Romney, Gray and Weldon, 1978)? If it is, should we view indicators of performance in this context? Is the setting of long-term objectives for institutions the most critical stage at the present time?

We should also recognize that effectiveness and efficiency are elusive concepts in higher education, and that the process of institutional performance assessment carries with it potential liabilities which warrant careful consideration. Drawing upon their extensive experience with the National Center for Higher Education management Systems, Romney, Bogen and Micek (1979) have categorized the liabilities and disadvantages associated with the process and outcomes of institutional performance assessment under four headings: political liabilities, methodological cautions, economic concerns, and philosophical caveats. Time does not permit an elaboration of these cautions; however, every budding assessor of institutional performance or generator of performance indicators should be required to study this paper before being let loose in his institution.

Objectives for Institutions of Higher Education

Non-profit-making organizations, such as institutions of higher education, exist to provide a service. Not only are services provided more difficult to measure than profits, so is the process of identifying, quantifying and agreeing an overriding objective in such organizations; developing a hierarchy of primary and secondary objectives that flow from this overriding objective; and subsequently measuring and comparing actual performance against these objectives. These difficulties, which are central to the process of performance assessment, are particularly acute in institutions of higher education.

Is an institution of higher education *effective* if it achieves objectives which are appropriate to the economic, socio-political, technological, ecological, and educational environment in which it operates? Should its objectives be congruent with the long-term needs of society? Many of those involved in the management of institutions would probably answer such a question positively. However, would they be able to reach agreement on the long-term needs of society, the contribution their institution should make to satisfy those needs, and the objectives for their institution?

In his recent book, *The Effective University: A Management by Objectives Approach*, Norris (1978) argues that:

> Until the goal question is resolved and meaningful priorities set for institutional policy as a whole, it is impossible to say what is really important for that institution, and hence where resources should be allocated.

He asks whether the time has now arrived for setting and obtaining agreement upon objectives. A study conducted in 1976 by Romney (1978) for the National Center for Higher Education Management Systems of measures of institutional goal achievement is relevant to this question. Romney undertook a survey of 1,150 persons – faculty, administrators and trustees at 45 American colleges and universities of six different types – which surprisingly indicated that faculty, administrators and trustees largely agree on what their institution's goals should be. Respondents were asked to rate with respect to appropriateness for their institution twenty broadly stated institutional goal areas. Goal preference generally varied across institutional types, but there was a large degree of agreement among trustees, faculty and administrators within institutional types.

However, even if agreement can be reached on the broad objectives for an institution, can these be translated into agreed quantifiable goals and desired performance indicators? What weighting should be given to the different objectives, and how should conflict between objectives be resolved? If it cannot, how can more detailed objectives and performance indicators be established to measure effectiveness and efficiency for the component parts of the institution? In some academic departments, particularly multi-discipline departments, is it unlikely that agreement can be reached amongst members as to what the objectives are for the department, for the courses offered by the department, and for the research programmes undertaken within departments? Therefore, where do members of academic departments, heads of academic departments, and deans fit into the spectrum ranging from goal conflict to striving towards goal congruence within institutions of higher education? Does today's environment encourage goal congruence or goal conflict within institutions?

"Partial" Performance Indicators

Given the complexities and difficulties surrounding the objective setting and planning process, it is not surprising that there is a tendency to recognize those parts of the system that can be measured and monitored with a considerable degree of precision. While it may not prove possible to agree objectives, measure outcomes and develop performance indicators for an institution as a whole, it often proves possible to do so for parts of the organization; that is, to develop performance indicators that relate physical and monetary inputs to physical and monetary outputs and outcomes, and to build these into the planning and reporting system. However, do those who develop and employ such partial performance indicators always remember that optimizing the parts does not necessarily optimize the whole?

Sorenson and Grove (1977) have summarized the objectives and properties of various service performance indicators: availability, awareness, accessibility, extensiveness, appropriateness, efficiency, effectiveness, outcomes/benefits/impacts, and acceptability. From these, the author has developed partial performance indicators for institutions of higher education (Table 1) (Sizer, 1979a). Many of these partial performance indicators are traditional *process measures* of institutional performance, such as staff—student ratios and cost per

Focus of Measure	Conceptual Content	Tells	Examples
Availability	Amount and type of course, research facility, or central service provided.	What can be obtained.	List of services available in Careers Advisory Service; list of research facilities and opportunities available in academic department; number, capacities, and locations of lecture and seminar rooms.
Awareness	Knowledge of User Population of existence; range and conditions for entry or use of courses, research facilities, or central services.	Who knows about what is available.	Knowledge of prospective students of courses offered by an academic department. Knowledge by prospective users of services provided by central computer centre.
Accessibility	Indicates if services can be obtained by appropriate groups.	Ease of reaching and using facility.	Availability of photocopying facilities; location of car parks; average waiting time for literature search by library information service; opening hours of medical centre.
Extensiveness	Compares quantity of services rendered with capacity available and/or potential demand.	'How Much' but not 'How Well'.	Students enrolled on courses compared with course quotas; number of users of Library; clients in medical centre; % of final year students using careers advisory service; % utilization of lecture and seminar rooms.
Appropriateness	Correct type and amount of service rendered, course offered, or research undertaken.	Is quantity and/or quality of facility offered that required?	Demand for courses: number and quality of applicants: mismatch between computing facilities required and available; comparison of class sizes to lecture and seminar room capacities.
Efficiency	Compares resource inputs with outputs.	How much resource was used such as – how much did it cost per unit? – how much did it cost in total? – how much time did it take? – what grade of employee was used?	Cost per client service in medical centre. Cost per FTE student by course. Cost per literature search. Cost per meal served.
Effectiveness	Compares accomplishment with objectives (or what was intended) – Qualitative – Comparative	Characteristics Duration Content Effect Proportions served Variances from budgets, standards.	Comparison of planned with actual: % utilization of lecture and seminar rooms; number of students graduating; number of graduates employed; ratio of actual utilization to planned utilization of computer; comparison of budgeted cost of central service with actual cost; comparison of actual cost per FTE for course with planned: comparison of planned course content with actual course content; actual wastage rate compared with planned wastage rate.
Outcomes/ Benefits/ Impacts	Identifies Social or Economic Benefit.	Monetary effects Non-monetary effects.	Increase in earnings arising from attendance at/graduating from course; benefits to society of successful research into previously incurable disease; benefits to local community of cultural programme. Patents and copyrights registered.
Acceptability	Assess match of Service/Course/Research outcomes with user/participant preferences.	User satisfaction with services; student satisfaction with courses; client satisfaction with outcome of sponsored research.	Demand for courses; number of complaints to Librarian; course evaluation at end of lecture programme; repeat sponsoring of research.

Table 1: Properties of Performance Indicators in Higher Education

FTE, rather than *outcome measures* or ones that substantiate *progress* towards achieving objectives. As might be expected, traditional process measures of institutional performance were rejected by almost all categories of respondent in the Romney (1978) study. Objective measures pertaining to impacts of higher education such as satisfaction, ability to apply knowledge, publications and value added were preferred.

No doubt Romney's respondents would argue that if an effective institution of higher education is one which achieves objectives which are appropriate to the economic, socio-political, technological, ecological and educational environment in which it operates, its effectiveness should be measured in terms of outcomes/benefits/impacts of its teaching and research programmes on society. There is a danger in using short-term input indicators of performance, such as cost per full-time-equivalent student or cost per graduate, in that sight might be lost of the long-term measure of the effectiveness of institutions, that is, their contribution to the needs of society. A head of an academic department may argue that while his cost per FTE student compares unfavourably with other similar departments in his own and other institutions, the long-term impacts/benefits of the research and teaching programmes in his department compare favourably and outweigh the higher costs. Furthermore, questions concerning the quality of outcomes and their impact on society are bound to be raised ". . . by a government determined to get better value for public expenditure in higher education" (*Financial Times*, 30 October 1979). In other words, short-term quantitative input and outcome measures and performance indicators are inadequate, and quality of outcomes and long-term impacts/benefits should be assessed.

This argument is fine and logical but the difficulties involved in developing impact/benefit/outcome measures, and incorporating them into management information systems, should not be underestimated. Is it likely that highly sophisticated research designs will be required, which not only will prove expensive but involve a degree of complexity which may be regarded as impractical, probably rightly so, by administrators? Balderston (1974) has observed that the data base is not available, nor are the techniques for segregating the specific impact of one university from the other forces at work. Romney (1978) put it more strongly when he concluded:

> The art of measuring the outcomes remains in a distinctly primitive state. We have done almost no research to chart the maze of differences in value that various external constituencies of higher education assign to the range of objectives that might be agreed to within the enterprise. We do not know how to measure the quality of institutional outcomes, or research outcomes, or community-service outcomes.

Nevertheless, it may well be that the time is right to assess the quality of institutions, and the social value of different disciplines. Should this Society be initiating research in this area?

It is not surprising that to date we have tended to fall back onto quantitatively based process measures even though we know these are inadequate measures of institutional effectiveness, though many of these measures (such as staff—student ratios, and cost per FTE) are relevant to decisions regarding internal planning, control and resource allocation, and for measurement of efficiency as opposed to effectiveness. As Delany (1978) has pointed out, the function of control ". . . does not cover other aspects of the problem of policy making which deal with the quality of outputs". It is concerned with the relationship between expected and actual inputs, and expected and actual outputs. Romney (1978) suggests:

> A good many legislators are quite willing to admit that the heavily numerical, efficiency-based accountability perspective is inappropriate to higher education

and considers institutions should concentrate, for the purposes of assessing institutional effectiveness, upon the development of measures that substantiate progress towards achievement in those few goal areas that constituencies consider appropriate. At the present time there is a strong case for developing *progress measures* of performance in addition to *process measures* and *measures of outcomes/benefits/impacts*.

Despite the numerous hurdles that will have to be surmounted, I do believe that a concerted effort must be made to develop and obtain agreement within institutions on their academic policy and objectives for the 1980s and into the 1990s. You will recall the DES *1990s* discussion document examines future demand for higher education by projection of student numbers under certain assumptions, and the *Future Trends* document revises these projections downwards. Neither document fully considers the demand for outputs from the educational system. It has been argued that to be effective an institution of higher education must be responsive to the long-term needs of society; therefore in looking forward into the 1980s and on into the 1990s, should not institutions examine the environment in which they will be operating and attempt to identify what the needs of society will be, given this environment? Inevitably it will be argued that we are not very good at forecasting the future needs of society, but surely it is better to attempt to identify and satisfy future needs than to assume in a rapidly changing society that today's needs (frequently measured in terms of applications from school leavers) are the best indicators we have of future needs? [. . .]

If you [examine the] trends [which] will influence significantly the environment in which institutions of higher education will be operating, you [should conclude] that it is not simply a question of examining the impact of falling numbers on the higher education system, but it is also necessary to recognize that society is likely to require a different mix of outputs from the system than at present. New courses and research priorities will emerge. It may be necessary to meet the needs of new groups of participants, and new patterns of attendance may be required to meet individual needs. Some courses will face falling demand, others will disappear, while others will need adaptations to meet the changing demands of new technology (Sir James Hamilton, 1979). Thus, not only will the system face falling total demand, but also changing demands. Furthermore, as Sir Charles Carter (1979) has argued, these changing demands give rise to questions about the types of course of higher education provided and the institutional structure we ought to create. Should all those who reach "A" level standard be allowed to attempt a full degree course? Should degree work be removed from some polytechnics so that they can become part of a community college system? There will also be opportunities for institutions to generate alternative sources of revenue from applied research, consultancy and continuing education opportunities. Is it important that institutions recognize these factors and plan not only for declining numbers, but also recognize the need for *resource mobility* on the one hand and the need for research in anticipation of new course demands, research and consultancy opportunities on the other? *Therefore should we assess the performance of an institution in terms of its responsiveness to these changing needs of society and develop appropriate performance indicators that measure an institution's progress in responding to these changing needs?*

Unfortunately, time does not permit an examination of the planning and managerial implications of this argument. It has been proposed elsewhere (Sizer, 1979b) that institutions need to compare *strengths* in various subject areas relative to other institutions with the *future attractiveness* of subject areas to provide a starting point for internal discussions on the institution's long-term strategy. It is envisaged that such a strategy would classify subject areas into *growth, consolidation* and *withdrawal* areas. The agreed strategy would need to be translated into a detailed action plan including key result areas. Measures to assess *progress* towards implementing the strategy, particularly in these key result areas, would flow from the plan.

Tests of Appropriateness

Clearly, a whole range of process, outcome and progress performance indicators should be considered when establishing appropriate indicators for the research, teaching and central service functions within an institution of higher education. Given that higher education abounds with joint inputs and multiple outputs and outcomes, and the ultimate impact of many of the outcomes is long term and extremely difficult to measure, what tests should be applied to various possible indicators to determine whether they are appropriate for the purpose intended? The standards of relevance, verifiability, freedom from bias, quantifiability and economic feasibility have been proposed (Sizer, 1979a and c) recognizing that *trade-offs* frequently have to be made between standards. Time does not permit a detailed discussion of these standards, but it is worth highlighting briefly some of the questions that arise.

– Who determines "relevance"?

– Do we always recognize that a performance indicator may be relevant for the purpose for which it was developed, but not relevant when used for other purposes?

– Should the performance indicator be free from both *statistical* and *personal* bias?

– How important is the standard of quantifiability to performance indicators in higher education?

– How can a proper balance be struck between qualitative and quantitative aspects? As we have seen, this is a particularly relevant question at the present time.

– If the external financing bodies continue to emphasize indicators of process, rather than progress, effectiveness and efficiency when assessing institutions, will administrators and faculty begin, or continue, to function in accordance with incentive structures which are not consistent with an institution's goals and objectives?

Douglas Porter (1978) has proposed a further test, *institutional acceptability*, be added to the five standards; he argued:

> The measures of performance adopted may not themselves be the most reliable indicators of effectiveness or even efficiency but they could be justified if they lead to improved performance or decision taking even though they themselves may not be thoroughly sound intellectually. What is vital is that the people using the indicators should accept them, and the basis on which they are devised, as relevant and fair.

Is Porter recognizing the political realities of institutions of higher education? As Argyris (1970) has pointed out:

> New developments for rational decision making often produce intense resentment in men who ordinarily view themselves as realistic, flexible, definitely rational. Managers and executives who place a premium on rationality and work hard to subdue emotionality, become resistant and combative in the back-alley ways of bureaucratic politics when such technologies are introduced.

Could "heads of academic departments and units" be substituted for "managers and executives" in Argyris' statement? Thus, is Romney (1978) right to argue, like Porter, that consensus building techniques can facilitate the selection of appropriate goals and measures within institutions? Will such approaches result in economy of information by concentrating on developing performance indicators for the few highly appropriate goal areas for which a consensus exists, rather than trying to document progress in every goal area that has been accorded some degree of appropriateness?

On the other hand, should we recognize that such consensus building might be more easily achieved when resources are relatively abundant than when they are relatively scarce? A recent study of the nature of budget decision-making in a university (Hills and Mahoney, 1978) suggests that while during periods when resources are relatively abundant "subunit budgeting is a process designed in part to ameliorate conflict and to maintain apparent harmony", during periods of scarcity of resources "it is the powerful subunits that emerge to claim their resources at the expense of other subunits. Further, it is the external ties that subunits have which they can use as this power base." Under these conditions do institutional acceptability and consensus building evaporate in the "back-alley ways of bureaucratic politics"? Are the decision-makers in your institution acting rationally at the present time? [. . .]

Conclusions

I conclude with a summary of the arguments developed here and elsewhere. The changing needs of society, particularly during periods of contraction and under conditions of financial stringency, necessarily involve the development of a strategy for *resource mobility*. During such periods high-quality managers of change (Sizer, 1979 b and c), of appropriate academic standing, should be motivating their institutions to strive to become effective in the long term through attempts

— to evaluate the institution's current subject area portfolio and critical resources;

— to examine systematically the future environment in which it will be operating and to identify threats and opportunities;

— to understand and communicate the implications of this future environment to institutions' constituencies;

— to agree through consensus building techniques the goals and objectives for the institution and its constituent parts, and the *measures for monitoring progress* towards achieving these goals and objectives;

— to develop

(a) a set of alternative long-term strategies and operating plans including a strategy for long-term resource mobility;

(b) a strategy for short-term financial emergencies;

and

(c) the short-term planning and control systems based on measurable information and performance indicators, backed up by a nationally organized scheme for inter-institutional comparisons.

The greatest challenge to the managers of change is to create an environment in which members of faculty and administration, heads of departments and senior academics and administrators, and the hierarchy of committees strive to achieve goal congruence between their objectives and actions and the long-term objectives and strategies of the institution. The performance indicators developed and employed should be consistent with these objectives and strategies. However, people not performance indicators make and implement decisions. No matter how appropriate and relevant the performance indicators, they will only be effective if the decision-makers' responses and actions are positive. The "managers of change" have to create an environment which will lead to positive responses – which is easier said than done under conditions of financial stringency and possible contraction.

References

Argyris, C. (1970), "Resistance to Rational Management Systems", *Innovation*, No.10, p.29.

Balderston, F. E. (1974), *Managing Today's University*, Jossey-Bass.

Carter, Sir Charles (1979), "Not Enough Higher Education and Too Many Universities?", *Three Banks Review*, September.

Delany, V. J. (1978), "Budgetary Control and Monitoring Effectiveness", *Management Accounting*, October, p.388.

Department of Education and Science (1978), *Higher Education in the 1990s*, HMSO.

– (1979), *Future Trends in Higher Education*, HMSO.

Financial Times, "Complaining in advance", editorial, 30 October 1979.

Hamilton, Sir James (1979), "Education Priorities in FE/HE in the 1980s", *Coombe Lodge Report*, Vol.12, No.4, pp.149-60.

Hills, F. S. and Mahoney, T. A. (1978), "University Budgets and Organisational Decision Making", *Administrative Science Quarterly*, Vol.23, September, pp.454-65.

Norris, Graeme (1978), *The Effective University: A Management by Objectives Approach*, Saxon House.

Porter, Douglas (1978), "Developing Performance Indicators for the Teaching Function", a paper presented to the OECD/CERI IMHE Programme Fifth Special Topic Workshop, Paris, 5-6 June.

Romney, L. C. (1978), *Measures of Institutional Goal Achievement*, Denver, Colorado, National Center for Higher Education Management Systems Research Report.

Romney, L. C., Bogen, C. and Micek, S. S. (1979), "Assessing Institutional Performance: The Importance of Being Careful", *International Journal of Institutional Management in Higher Education*, Vol.3, No.1, May, pp.79-89.

–, Gray, R. G. and Weldon, H. K. (1978), *Departmental Productivity: A Conceptual Framework*, NCHEMS.

Sizer, J. (1979a), "Assessing Institutional Performance: An Overview", *International Journal of Institutional Management in Higher Education*, Vol.3, No.1, May, pp.49-75.

— (1979b), "Institutional Performance Assessment and Planning for the 1990s under conditions of contraction and financial stringency", an address given to a Seminar on "University Planning Techniques", University of Bath, 17-18 September.

— (1979c), "Performance Assessment and the Management of Universities for the 1990s", a paper presented to the Conference of University Administrators Annual Conference, Edinburgh, 5-7 April.

Sorenson, J. R. and Grove, H. D. (1977), "Cost-Outcome and Cost-Effectiveness Analysis: Emerging Non-Profit Performance Evaluation Techniques", *The Accounting Review*, Vol.LII, No.3, July, pp.658-75.

2.3 Keeping the School under Review

Though not first in this field in Britain, this booklet (reproduced in full below), devised by the ILEA inspectorate, has been highly influential, having been issued unchanged to schools by several other LEAs, as well as being openly copied by many others. It is intended to be used by schools, with sections for primary and secondary, as a checklist to support self-evaluation. The questions, addressed to teachers, of which this booklet is composed, in fact constitute a set of indicators of quality analogous to those proposed by Sizer in the reading which immediately precedes this one. Ostensibly these indicators are provided for use in the context of teacher autonomy, but 'outsiders' are brought into evaluations by the use of their criteria – and perhaps also by their physical presence: the last paragraph of the Foreword to the booklet stresses the value of an external viewpoint . . .

Foreword

The process of self-appraisal, of looking at what you are doing, why you are doing it, whether you are doing it well, whether you ought to be doing something different is, or should be, a continuing one in every school. Now that we have reached a point of greater stability of staffing and shortages are being overcome it is easier to take stock and plan for the future with a clearer indication of where we want to go. The idea of a checklist of questions the staff of a school might seek the answers to, giving a framework to support a more systematic form of self-assessment, originated in a discussion between the Chief Inspector and some headteachers. As a result, the Staff Inspectors for Primary and Secondary Education met with a group of headteachers to see what they could produce. This pamphlet is the result of their work and a subsequent trial run in a number of schools.

What this paper offers is not a blue-print or questionnaire to be rigorously followed or answered in its entirety every year. It is presented as a basis for the development of a school's own form of self-assessment, to be modified or extended to suit the intentions and interests of the individual school. The object of applying some form of systematic self-

---

ILEA (1977), *Keeping the School under Review*, a method of self-assessment for schools devised by the ILEA inspectorate. ILEA.

appraisal is to assist in the clarification of objectives and priorities, to identify weaknesses and strengths and ensure that due attention is given in turn to all aspects of school life. To examine all aspects in a single year would be an impossible task. Improvement of the quality of education, and that I hope is the basic aim of all of us, can only come when current practices are examined in detail, questions are asked, the answers are examined and consideration is then given to appropriate action. This is a time-consuming task, not to be undertaken lightly. It will involve many and at times the whole staff. If a school undertakes this kind of course it must plan to proceed at a pace that is reasonable and within its resources. It must decide what are the areas that most need attention and deal with these first.

There is a danger in any form of self-assessment that people do not always see themselves as others see them. To overcome this it is hoped that schools who take into use a form of self-assessment such as is outlined in this paper will be prepared to discuss the outcomes with colleagues in the inspectorate so that they may have the benefit of an external viewpoint to put beside their own. Additionally, the possibility of some form of cross-moderation through linking at departmental or school level in relation to different aspects of assessment might be worth considering.

Guy Rogers
Deputy Chief Inspector
Summer 1977

The Primary School

This self-assessment paper is designed to assist a school to examine its organization, its resources, its standards of achievement and its relationships. It suggests facts to be sought and questions to be discussed. It does not attempt to be comprehensive or detailed, and it is for individual schools to elaborate upon any of the suggested sections that are of particular relevance and to work out their own priorities.

An exercise in self-assessment must take into account what in the school's view the primary stage of education is about. This view is usually put in the form of a series of broad aims concerned with the growth and personality of the child and generally makes reference to aspects of intellectual, physical, emotional, social, spiritual and moral development.

Further aims normally reflect the way in which the school functions as a community.

In most schools there is a continuing dialogue about aims which are understood and accepted by the staff although they may not always be set down in precise terms. It could be that they may need to be redefined and that from them will grow a set of more detailed objectives relating to the everyday working of the school.

Although this paper is essentially concerned with practical issues relating to the smooth running of a school it is hoped that the ensuing discussions will take account of those deeper issues that reflect fundamental principles, aims and objectives.

A   THE CHILDREN

1. In considering the needs and interests of individual children what provision is there for:
- gifted children?
- children who are slow to learn?
- children with behaviour problems?
- children for whom English is a second language?
- children from different ethnic backgrounds?
- children who have a specific skill or talent?

2. What opportunities are given for the development of initiative and responsibility?

3. What initiatives does the school take about getting to know the children coming to the school for the first time?
i.e. from home?
    from a nursery?
    from another school?

4. Who is responsible for promoting continuity for individual children and in the areas of the curriculum
(a) from home to school (including reference to play groups, etc.)?
(b) from class to class?
(c) from one school to the next (from nursery to infants; infants to junior; junior to secondary)?
(d) from a different school?

5. What attention is given to
(a) the children's previous experience at home and school?
(b) the records of the programmes of work and whatever tests may have been made?
(c) the use of individual apparatus and materials?
(d) differences in learning and teaching styles?

6. What records are passed from stage to stage
e.g. folders of work?
    children's books?
    annual records?

7. In the school are there any serious obstacles to achieving continuity?
What are they?
How are they being tackled?
What further steps might be taken to promote educational development

at each of the above-mentioned stages?

8. Does the school have adequate information about children's health and physical development?

9. What use does the school make of agencies such as the Educational Welfare Service and the Schools Psychological Service?

B PARENTAL AND COMMUNITY INVOLVEMENT

1. What initiatives are taken to introduce the school to parents?

2. How is the school developing links with the neighbourhood?

3. What opportunities are made to give parents an understanding of what the school is trying to do and of their child's part in it?

4. How are parents helped and encouraged to be interested in helping their children to learn?

5. What opportunities are there for parents to discuss their children's development and progress with the teacher and the headteacher?

6. Are there any prepared leaflets of explanation or information for the parents to consider?

7. Is there a parent/community association?
Is it effective?

8. Is there a parents' room in the school?
How is it used?

9. How are non-English-speaking parents helped to participate in the life of the school and community?

10. How and for what purpose does the school co-operate with:
   (a) secondary schools (preparation for parenthood/community studies)?
   (b) adult education service?
   (c) colleges of further education?
   (d) neighbouring special schools?
   (e) colleges of education?
   (f) other primary schools?
   (g) the teachers' centres?

11. In what way and how often does the school account to the parents for the child's progress and development:
   (a) by interview?
   (b) by interview preceded by letter/report?
   (c) by standard report?
   (d) other ways?

C MANAGERS

1. What are their contacts with the school?

2. How are they informed of what the school is trying to do?

D PROGRAMMES (SCHEMES) OF WORK OR GUIDELINES

1. Has the school programmes of work or guidelines in all or any of the following areas of the curriculum:
  (a) physical education?
  (b) language and literacy?
  (c) mathematics?
  (d) aesthetic developments, e.g. music, art and crafts?
  (e) environmental studies, e.g. geography, history, social studies, physical and natural sciences?
  (f) religious and moral education?
2. When were the programmes drawn up?
By whom were they made?
When were they last revised?
What advice was sought from any learning support agencies?
Which programmes now need revision?
3. Do all members of the staff possess copies of all of the school programmes?
4. Do new teachers receive copies of the school programme as a matter of course?
5. What help is given to teachers to help them to understand and follow the programmes of work? For example, is there staff discussion on the content and pattern of the work?
6. In which programmes of work is it of particular importance to stress continuity of development in teaching methods throughout the school?
7. Has there been an opportunity for teachers to attend appropriate in-service training courses?
Are there opportunities for them to comment on these courses on return to school?
8. To what extent is the headteacher involved in implementing the guidelines and in the development of work within the school?
9. Do the teachers keep a regular record of their plans of work?
At what intervals are these compiled?
10. Are visits and school journeys a normal part of the curriculum?
Are they designed to fit in with children's interests and stage of development?
Is there a review of the number and types of visits undertaken during the past year?
Is the distribution of resources balanced so that all classes of children have a suitable opportunity for participating in these visits?
11. What opportunities are there for children to develop talents and interests beyond the normal curriculum?
What clubs and societies have been organized?
12. In what way does the school assembly contribute to the children's development?

E CLASS ORGANIZATION

1. On what basis are children arranged in classes or home base groups?
2. Are children grouped within a class? If so, on what basis and for what purpose?
What degree of flexibility is there in this grouping?
When are revisions made?
What degree of freedom has the teacher in organizing or arranging these groups?
3. In a given period (e.g. a week or a month) how much of the teacher's time is given to each of the major areas of the curriculum?
In a similar period approximately how much time is given to class teaching, group teaching and work with individuals?
4. Are any children extracted from their classes?
For what reasons?
Does the class teacher know what work they do?
Is there consultation between teachers to ensure general educational development of the children?
5. Do the children experience a range of activities over a period of time?
How much choice does an individual child have?
What guidance is given to him?
6. Does the organization of the day and the grouping of the children enable the programme of work to be effectively interpreted and the needs of the individual children sensitively met?
If not, what changes are needed?

F ATTAINMENT

1. Do teachers make their own continuing record of children's progress in physical, intellectual, social, emotional and aesthetic areas of development as a basis for completing the authority's annual records?
2. Does the school have a common basic pattern for this recording?
3. To what extent are the school's current methods of recording successful:
    (a) in guiding a teacher's observation of children in the different areas of their development?
    (b) in identifying needs of individual children?
    (c) in assembling information that is relevant to another school or for discussion with parents?
4. In assessing progress in literacy and mathematics is any use made:
of standardized attainment tests?
of a published diagnostic test or procedure?
of internally devised tests and procedures?
5. Are tests and/or recorded observations made of other aspects of the

curriculum in order to ascertain standards of attainment?

6. Who is responsible for judging the validity and value of the testing/ diagnostic procedures?

7. When was the nature and timing of these last reviewed?

To whom are the results available?

G   STAFFING

1. What human resources are available?

Full-time teachers

Part-time teachers

Technicians

Ancillary helpers

Other adults

2. Are there any vacancies?

3. If any full-time teachers do not have regular responsibility for a class how is their teaching strength used?

4. How are the part-time teachers used?

Do their responsibilities relate to their particular skills and interests?

Do their responsibilities and those of the teachers without classes meet the stated needs of the school?

When was their deployment last reviewed?

5. What are the duties of those teachers who have posts of responsibility?

Does the staff generally know of these duties?

Are these duties revised from time to time?

Do they meet the needs of the school?

Is there a policy for training and developing the skills of post holders?

Who is responsible for the care of probationary teachers?

6. What are the duties of the ancillary staff?

(a) Around the school?

(b) In the classroom?

(c) With the children?

Who is responsible for training the ancillary staff in their duties and for reviewing their relationships within the school?

H   STAFF MEETINGS

1. What meetings of the full-time staff (all sections) have been held during the last three terms?

Why were they held?

Who initiated them?

Who attended them?

Did anyone seem to be left out for any reason?

2. Was an agenda produced in advance?

How was it originated?

3. What matters were discussed at these meetings?
Were the decisions minuted?
4. What procedure was adopted when matters could not be agreed?
5. Is there general satisfaction with the variety of the timing and mode of staff meetings and the implementation of decisions reached?

I SIMPLE STATISTICS

The following details may be of importance particularly if they represent a trend or a marked difference from the previous year's figures.

At the end of the academic year:

1. What was the number of full-time staff that left the school for:
retirement?
promotion?
family reasons?
other?
2. How many teacher-days absences due to sickness were recorded?
3. Other than normal nursery/infant transfer and statutory enrolment how many children joined the school from another school?
4. Other than the normal infant/junior or junior/secondary transfer how many children left the school?
5. How many accidents to pupils were recorded?
6. What were the results of the comparability tests in the last three years?

J GENERAL ENVIRONMENT

1. Who is responsible for ensuring that the school is kept in a state of workmanlike tidiness?
Can the storage arrangements be improved?
Are there displays of material and work to stimulate interest amongst the children, adults about the school, parents and visitors?
2. Who ensures that displays in the halls and corridors are well mounted and frequently changed?
3. Is the school in good repair?
e.g. in the classrooms?
     in the halls?
     in the cloakrooms?
     on the staircases?
     in the playgrounds?
Do the schoolkeeper and his staff make a satisfactory contribution to the maintenance of the school?

4. Is the way to the head's room and the secretary's room clearly indicated?

5. Can anything more be done to improve the use of the outside play areas?

6. What procedures are there for a regular review of the provision of materials and resources in all of the major areas of the curriculum?
   This is to include a review of past expenditure on various items,
e.g. consumable art and craft materials
   consumable stationery
   textbooks, library and resource materials
   musical instruments
   physical education apparatus
   maths and science apparatus
   school visits
   AVA apparatus and software.

7. How is waste of materials and resources avoided?

8. How are decisions about AUR reached?
Is there full staff consultation?

K ACTION

1. Are we clear what we have been trying to do? How far are we meeting those intentions?

2. What are the priorities for action
(a) next term?
(b) in the coming year?

3. Who will initiate this action?

4. Do we need any outside support and advice? If so, what?

L QUESTIONS FOR THE HEADTEACHER TO ASK HIMSELF OR HERSELF

The head will, of course, be involved in the answers to all the other sections. It may also be helpful for heads to keep a detailed diary for a given period, say a fortnight, and then to ask themselves the following questions:

Time

1. How often did I
(a) go into all classes on one day?
(b) greet parents at the beginning or end of the school day?
(c) teach?

2. What time did I give to meeting staff individually or in groups?

3. How much time did I spend out of school
(a) at County Hall?
(b) at Divisional meetings?

(c) in other schools?
(d) at conferences or in-service courses?
(e) elsewhere?
  Was this time
(a) necessary?
(b) useful to the school or to the service?
4. How much time did I spend on administration?
5. How much time did I give to visitors including parents, inspectors and ILEA officers?
6. Do I need to try to change the time distribution revealed by the answers to questions 1-5?

Objectives and Organization
1. What do I see as the priorities for the school in the next term/year/five years?
2. To what extent is my view shared by others?
3. What constraints exist?
4. Am I satisfied with the curriculum?
5. Which areas of the curriculum need attention and who can give it?
6. How do I ensure that resources are distributed in a balanced way?

Staffing
1. How available am I – formally and informally?
2. Do the staff feel that I am interested in their professional development and advancement and their personal welfare?
3. How accurate is my awareness of the load carried by different individual teachers
(a) on the timetable?
(b) in voluntary activities?
(c) in helping pupils and colleagues?
4. How accurate is my awareness of the load carried by non-teaching staff?

M   QUESTIONS FOR THE INDIVIDUAL TEACHER TO ASK HIMSELF OR HERSELF

1. My Work in the Classroom
Do I prepare adequately? What do I think of the presentation of my work? What improvements can I make in class organization? How satisfied am I with my class control and relationships? Do I spend enough time in talking to children about their work? What kind of comment do I make on it?

2. Knowledge of the Children
Do I really know all the children in my class including those who do not make obvious demands on me? Do I take account of individual

differences between children in my relationships with them and in making educational provision for them? How successful am I in keeping records of children's development and progress? In what ways do I try to ensure continuity between my stage and the one before and the one after?

3. General

How do I contribute to the development of good relationships with children, colleagues, parents and other adults connected with the school? Do I contribute to discussion in staff meetings?

N   THE ACID TEST!

Each member of staff asks the following questions:
   1. Would I recommend a colleague to apply for a post in the school?
   2. Would I recommend the school to friends for their children?

The Secondary School

Any attempt at self-assessment must take account of what, in the school's view, the secondary stage of education is about. In coming to a view, the head and his or her colleagues will be affected by the general climate of opinion in society at large, by their contact with governors, parents, fellow teachers, educational journals and other professional influences. The act of self-assessment will help to clarify what it is the school is attempting to do and whether it is satisfied that what it is attempting is right. It should be preceded by an attempt to identify short-term and more distant objectives. It may, indeed, lead to changes in some of these. This guide should help schools to make explicit some principles and practices of their work which have not always been consciously appreciated, to question them and to establish priorities for the future.

In presenting the guide, the inspectorate is aware of a dilemma. In order to be acceptably brief, the questions posed may seem superficial and inadequate. Yet, if an attempt be made to deal fully with all the issues which a school might wish to consider, the document becomes intimidatingly complex. It has been decided to try to keep the guide reasonably brief, in the expectation that a school attempting an assessment will speedily realize that one short question will itself suggest a whole set of others. In the appendix, we show how a school might take a simple question – on the timetable – and subdivide it into a more useful series. The guide assumes that a school assessment will inevitably contain both fact and opinion. It is hoped that colleagues will attempt, wherever possible, to separate factual statements and judgements upon those facts. The following sections are suggested as useful headings for a school engaging in the task.

A SIMPLE STATISTICS

It would be wrong to draw oversimplified conclusions from any one or all of the following statistics, without examining the context in which they occur. Nevertheless, taken together and viewed in the light of the local circumstances of the school, they provide useful factual information which may be borne in mind when answers are sought to later questions. They may also form a basis for comparison from year to year.

1. A curriculum analysis of the kind recommended in the ILEA Inspectorate pamphlet "Curriculum analysis and planning". This displays the deployment of staff teaching and non-teaching time. It enables one to discuss the educational implications of the arrangements and to cost the consequences of proposed changes.

2. Numbers of parents choosing the school at first and second choice, and the actual recruitment.

3. Number of primary schools from which first-year pupils came, together with schools from which a substantial number of pupils came, i.e. main intake schools.

4. Number of pupils joining the school during the year other than at secondary transfer stage.

5. Number of pupils leaving the school during the year other than at the completion of secondary education.

6. Number of pupils receiving free lunches.

7. Number of pupils receiving uniform grants.

8. Attendance rates for pupils, by year-groups and by individual classes.

9. Results in public examinations, related to the intake at 11-plus if possible.

10. Number of pupils continuing in full-time education beyond the statutory leaving-age, whether this be at school or at a college of FHE.

11. Facts about leavers' first employment.

12. Cost of furniture replacement and repair during the year.

13. Cost of repairs to windows etc. during the year.

14. Number of accidents to pupils recorded.

15. Number of staff leaving the school for (a) retirement (b) promotion (c) family reasons (d) other reasons.

16. Number of teacher-days absences due to sickness during the year.

B THE SCHOOL ENVIRONMENT

Some aspects of this can be evaluated subjectively by staff.

1. What is the general appearance of the school like – playground, corridors, classrooms, lavatories, etc.? What arrangements are made for ensuring that the school is kept in a state of good working order?

2. What visual evidence is there of the quality of pupils' work and school activities? Are there displays of work to stimulate interest among

pupils, parents and visitors? Who ensures that displays in halls, corridors and other communal spaces are well-mounted and regularly changed?

3. How would one describe the manner in which pupils move around the school between lessons, during breaks and in the playground?

4. How would one describe the noise level, and the kind of noise, at various times and places?

5. Are the appearances and use of the hall, the various common rooms, the library, the resource centre(s) satisfactory? In what ways could they be improved?

6. Is the reception of visitors by staff and pupils friendly, courteous and helpful, especially for unscheduled visits? Is the way to the school office clearly indicated?

7. What comments have we on the appearance and care of pupils' work books, our class registers, school equipment?

C RESOURCES

1. In addition to teaching staff, what other staff are available: technicians, ancillary workers, MROs, librarians and so on?

2. To whom are the various non-teaching staff responsible? Who is responsible for developing their skills and reviewing their relationships within the school?

3. Are there any staff vacancies, teaching or non-teaching? If so, for how long have they remained unfilled? Why? Is there any resulting distortion of the curriculum?

4. Do the numbers of teachers in various specialisms match the curriculum the school believes to be appropriate?

5. In what respects is the school poorly equipped? Can these deficiencies be made good?

6. Are there any minor works needed to improve the accommodation? What priority do they command in our consideration of the AUR scheme?

7. What procedures are there for a regular review of the provision of materials and equipment?

8. Does the school have a Resources Committee? If so, what is its membership? Are its terms of reference defined? Does it publish its recommendations?

9. How is waste of materials and other resources avoided?

10. How are recommendations made to the Head on the AUR scheme?

11. Is the school's Library/Resources Centre meeting our needs?

D DECISION-MAKING AND COMMUNICATIONS

1. What is the consultative structure used to help arrive at policy

decisions?

2. Are there adequate opportunities for all members of staff to express their views?

3. What steps do senior staff take outside the formal consultative structure to keep in touch with the views and hopes of their colleagues?

4. How are decisions recorded and communicated?

5. What methods are used for making clear who is responsible for seeing that decisions are carried out?

6. What steps are taken for reviewing the effects of decisions?

7. Is there a staff bulletin? Who compiles it? Who produces it? Is it effective?

8. Is there a Staff Guide? How often is it reviewed? How is this review conducted? Is the Guide worth the trouble taken to produce it? If not, should it be altered or abolished?

9. Is there a tannoy system? If so, is it used usefully and without irritation to staff and pupils?

10. Should pupils have a part to play in the consultative structure? If so, do our arrangements work well? How might they be improved?

E STAFF

1. What is the structure of responsibilities? How does a new member of staff learn about it? Does this structure reflect the importance attached to various aspects of the school's work?

2. What arrangements are made for applicants for posts to acquaint themselves with the school prior to interview?

3. What are the arrangements for integrating new members of staff, both teaching and non-teaching, and ensuring that not only are they involved but feel themselves to be involved in the school's life and decision-making?

4. What is the policy for staff deployment among teaching groups?

5. How effectively are non-teaching staff consulted about decisions affecting them, e.g. librarian, media resources officer, school-keeping staff, technicians, secretary, clerical staff?

6. What are the school's arrangements for staff development? What procedures are followed for induction? How are decisions made about appropriate in-service courses or conferences for individuals, for groups of staff or for the whole staff? What "reporting-back" arrangements are made on return from courses or conferences?

7. What are the arrangements for covering classes for short-term staff absence? Can they be improved?

8. How does the school help student teachers?

9. What links are there with colleges of education, university and polytechnic education departments?

10. What use can we, and do we, make of various support services – the

inspectorate, advisory teachers, teachers' centres, the learning materials service?

F   PUPILS

1. How are new pupils welcomed to the school, particularly those who do not join at the secondary transfer stage?
2. What is the system of personal and individual attention to pupils? How well is it working and are there any ways in which we can improve it?
3. What are the systems of careers education, careers guidance and educational guidance? Are any weaknesses apparent in these areas? How might they be rectified?
4. To what extent are pupils fully informed about further and higher education?
5. What are the links with the Education Welfare Service, the Medical Service and the Schools' Psychological Service?
6. Praise, rewards and sanctions – what do we use and why? Are any improvements feasible?
7. If the school has any form of special unit, what are the arrangements for allocation to it, what happens to pupils while they are there and what are the ways by which they return to the mainstream?
8. Are our registration arrangements satisfactory? What is the procedure for checking lateness and absence? What measures are taken to check attendance at lessons?
9. What opportunities are given for the development of initiative and responsibility?

G   PARENTAL AND COMMUNITY LINKS

1. How is a parent first introduced to the school? Is this satisfactory? Is there a prospectus for new parents?
2. Do parents of new first-formers meet personally the members of staff most responsible for their child, e.g. form teacher/house tutor and year head/house head?
3. Is there any form of parents' association? What are its functions? Is it effective?
4. What opportunities are there for parents to see staff (a) as a matter of routine (b) at their own or the school's request?
5. What are the various kinds of meetings held for parents? What proportion of parents come to each kind? How do we get in touch with non-attenders?
6. What is done to give parents an understanding of what the school is trying to do?
7. How are parents helped and encouraged to be interested in helping

their children to learn?

8. Have we looked at the language in which we couch letters to parents?

9. Are arrangements made to help non-English-speaking parents to participate in the life of the school?

10. How are complaints and difficulties dealt with?

11. How are parents/pupils consulted about curriculum choices at various stages in the pupil's career? Does the school issue pamphlets about fourth-year and sixth-year courses? Are they comprehensible to parents?

12. What reports go home to parents? What form of assessment is used? Can parents comment on the reports?

13. Does the school have any contact with external voluntary or local government agencies?

14. How fruitful is our association with the Adult Education Institute, the Youth Service, the Careers Service and employers?

15. To what extent is the school concerned with the local neighbourhood?

16. How do we ensure good relationships with local residents and traders?

17. Are pupils involved in any way with local community service?

18. What are our relationships with other users of the building?

H ARRANGEMENTS FOR LEARNING

1. (a) What initiatives does the school take about getting to know children at the school for the first time?

(b) Who is responsible for assisting continuity:

(i) from primary school? (ii) from class to class? (iii) from school to work, to further education, to higher education?

(c) What records are passed from stage to stage?

(d) Are there any serious obstacles to achieving continuity? How are they being tackled?

(e) Do we, while using the benefits of continuity, allow for the possibility of change in a pupil's motivation and relationships?

2. How are curriculum and syllabuses determined? How do they relate to the ends we have in view?

3. How and when is the timetable constructed and presented to staff? (See Appendix.)

4. What provision is there for pupils of all abilities? What is done to diagnose and remedy learning deficiencies and to extend the most able? Have we considered any special needs of pupils of varying ethnic backgrounds?

5. How do we assess the quality and quantity of work produced?

6. What is the policy about homework? Is it being followed? Does it need changing?

7. What range of subjects and levels are we offering at 14-plus and

16-plus? Are these appropriate?

8. Are we aware of information about courses in colleges of FHE in the area and in London generally? Have we, or have we considered, links with FE for older pupils?

9. Do we need to make arrangements to co-operate with other institutions to broaden the range we offer, or to release staff time to effect other improvements to the curriculum?

10. What is the school's language policy? How is it effected in practice? What arrangements are made to improve the language skills of pupils of all abilities?

11. Have we examined the question of mathematics across the curriculum?

12. Have we examined the success of curriculum changes made in the last five years?

13. On what basis are pupils arranged in classes? Are we satisfied with it?

14. If pupils are extracted from classes:
   (a) for what reasons are they extracted?
   (b) how are they enabled to fit in with the class when they return to it?

15. What does the school regard as a "balanced" curriculum in the fourth and fifth years? Does it include a common core? Does this common core need a review?

16. Who is responsible for seeing that a given pupil receives a balanced curriculum as a result of any option system?

17. Are departments sufficiently aware of the educational standards demanded for employment? How could we ensure that all our pupils have reached an adequate level of attainment in basic skills to meet the needs of employment?

18. What part do educational visits and journeys play in the curriculum? How are decisions made about frequency and timing? Who assesses their effectiveness? What checks are there on their conduct?

I DEPARTMENTAL (OR FACULTY) SELF-ASSESSMENT

1. Is communication and consultation within the department efficient? Do the staff feel effective members of a departmental team?

2. When are departmental meetings held? Are minutes kept?

3. How are responsibilities other than class teaching distributed within the department?

4. How is it decided which teacher takes which classes?

5. Who makes the syllabuses? When were they last revised? Do all members of the department have copies? Do new teachers receive copies in advance as a matter of course?

6. Do members of the department discuss together syllabuses, books, materials, equipment, pupils' work, examination entries?

7. Do staff keep regular records of their plans of work? At what intervals of time are these compiled?
8. What do we know about schemes of work and attainments in feeder primary schools? What steps do we take to assess and record progress? What do we do about (a) setting homework (b) setting work for classes when teachers are absent (c) marking work (d) testing? Can we make improvements?
9. What is done to prevent loss of materials, books and equipment while yet ensuring they are used?
10. What use is made of the school's resource centre?
11. Are pupils' standards capable of improvement? What improvements are we aiming at in the next twelve months?
12. How do we ensure continuity in a pupil's work as he or she moves up the school?
13. Is everyone aware of relevant safety precautions and carrying them out?

J QUESTIONS FOR THE HEADTEACHER TO ASK HIMSELF OR HERSELF

The head will, of course, be intimately involved in the answers to all the other sections concerning resources, the academic programme, the care of the individual and the general organization, and with the strategies to adopt in order to maintain strengths and improve weaknesses. He or she will want to consider whether the school's policies are appropriate to the actual conditions obtaining. The following questions are more concerned with style and modus operandi and, because of this, most of them are equally applicable to deputies and other senior staff.

Time
1. Keep a detailed diary for a fortnight on two occasions separated by at least a month.
2. How often did I
(a) tour the school?
(b) talk to people in the playground?
(c) go to a school gate at the beginning or end of school?
(d) go into classrooms to see pupils at work?
(e) teach?
(f) observe pupils during lesson changes?
3. What time did I give to meeting staff individually and in groups?
4. How much time did I spend out of school
(a) at County Hall?
(b) at Divisional meetings?
(c) at other schools?
(d) at conferences or in-service courses?
(e) elsewhere?

Was this time
(a) necessary?
(b) useful to the school or the service?
5. How much time did I spend on administration and meetings in school?
6. How much time did I give to visitors, including parents, inspectors and ILEA officers?
7. Do I need to try to change the time distribution revealed by the answers to questions 2-6?

Objectives and Organization
1. What do I see as the priorities for the school in the next term/year/ five years?
2. To what extent is my view shared by others?
3. What constraints exist?
4. Are any organizational changes desirable or necessary?
5. Am I satisfied with the rolling programme of meetings? Are the necessary preparatory documents forthcoming? Are agendas well prepared? Are minutes well done?
6. Am I satisfied with the curriculum?
7. Which departments are flourishing, acceptable, needing attention?
8. Does every person in the school know to whom he or she is immediately responsible and for what?
9. Am I confident that there is a system for looking after the interests of every child?
10. How do I ensure that resources are distributed in a balanced way?

Staffing
1. How available am I – formally and informally?
2. Do staff feel I am interested in their professional development and advancement and their personal welfare?
3. When, for example, did I last speak to:
   (a) the part-time teacher in so-and-so department?
   (b) a cleaner?
   (c) the new teacher in such-and-such department?
   (d) the senior lab. technician?
   (e) the second in charge of department X?
   (f) the head of department Y?
4. Who needs promotion?
5. How accurate is my awareness of the load carried by different individual teachers (a) on the timetable (b) in voluntary activities (c) in unostentatiously assisting pupils and colleagues?
6. How accurate is my awareness of the load carried by non-teaching staff?

External Relations
1. What is the first impact of the school on visitors?
2. Do I know what impression is given to telephone callers?
3. Have I satisfied myself that parents know to whom they can turn for help and that it will be forthcoming?
4. Are relationships with governors positive and fruitful?
5. Have I a sufficient knowledge of the ILEA administrative structure and inspectorate to ensure the school is properly supported?
6. Do I make good professional and personal relationships with (a) local primary-school heads, (b) nearby secondary-school heads (c) principals of local college of FHE?
7. Do I know, and am I known by
(a) local community leaders?
(b) police and welfare agencies?
(c) local shopkeepers?
(d) neighbours of the school?

General
When did I last follow a class round the school for a day?

K QUESTIONS FOR THE INDIVIDUAL TEACHER TO ASK HIMSELF OR HERSELF

1. My Lessons
Do I prepare properly? What do I think of the presentation of my work? Am I using appropriate materials and teaching aids? What improvements can I make in class organization? Am I evaluating my lessons? How satisfied am I with my class control and relationships? Do I convince the pupils I am interested in the work they produce? What kind of comments do I make on their work?

2. Knowledge of the Pupils
How much do I know about the work done in the top classes of feeder primary schools? To what extent am I aware of, and do I take account of, individual differences in the members of the class? Do I "label" pupils prematurely? Why is it that some of my colleagues get good work from pupils with whom I fail and why do I succeed with some that some of my colleagues find difficult? Am I aware of pupils with particular problems? How do I cope with them? How successful is my writing of reports?

3. General
Whose responsibility is it to help my professional development? What help do I need? Who am I going to ask for it? What contact have I with (a) the Divisional Teachers' Centre (b) a specialist centre for my subjects?

What contribution do I make to my department/faculty and to my year group/house group? What part do I play in various levels of staff meetings? How do I contribute to the development of good relationships with pupils, colleagues and parents?

4. Administration
Am I punctual in arrival at school and at lessons? Do I keep records of pupils' attendance and progress? Do I keep lesson and evaluation notes? Do I read the day's notices and act on them?

L   THE ACID TEST!

Each member of staff asks the following questions:
1. Would I recommend a colleague to apply for a post at the school?
2. Would I recommend the school to friends for their children?

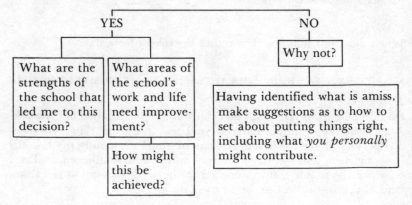

M   ACTION

1. Are we clear what we have been trying to do? How far are we meeting those intentions?
2. What are the priorities for action
(a) next term?
(b) in the coming year?
3. Do these priorities imply any re-distribution of our resources?
4. Do we need any outside support and advice? If so, what?

Appendix

Section H.3 poses the question: "How and when is the timetable constructed and presented to staff?"

This question immediately suggests a further set of questions:
1. What discussions with departments precede timetabling?

2. What consultation within departments precedes the allocation by the head of department of his or her staff to forms or sets for the ensuing year?

3. Is the present process of timetabling effective and satisfactory to those concerned?

4. In what ways could it be improved?

5. Is the timetable presented to staff at the right time and in the right form?

6. Are the arrangements for giving the pupils their timetables satisfactory?

7. Is the sixth formers' timetable arranged in good time? If not, how can the process be speeded up?

2.4 Second Thoughts on the Rutter Ethos
R. Doe

In contrast with the aspects of school process represented by the questions which comprise Keeping the School under Review, *which are included solely because they are considered to be important by ILEA inspectors, those cited in* Fifteen Thousand Hours *(Rutter et al., 1979) owe their inclusion to the statistical relationship they bear to four 'outcome' measures: attendance, pupil behaviour, examination success and delinquency. Their inclusion is thus* empirically *rather than* pragmatically *justified.*

In this article, Bob Doe summarizes what Rutter et al. *reported concerning the roots of effectiveness of schools, then reviews some of the more important criticisms of this work, illustrating the difficulty of achieving a widely accepted set of indicators of quality. All the aspects of school process examined by Rutter (i.e. including those which subsequently proved to be unrelated to outcomes) appear as Appendix E of his report, which is included in the next reading.*

Rutter says:
- Academic and behaviour standards vary dramatically between schools with similar intakes.
- Successful schools are punctual, clean and well ordered and set homework and discipline standards.
- This "tight ship" ethos partly caused their success.
- Less able pupils do better in schools with more able pupils than in those where there are few clever children.
- These results apply to other schools.

Critics say Rutter:
- Failed to take into account major differences in intakes.
- Wrongly analysed some statistics so school factors seemed more important than they were.
- Wrongly assumed differences in school styles and achievements were "cause and effect".

Doe, R. (1980), 'Second Thoughts on the Rutter Ethos', *Times Educational Supplement*, 13 June.

- Over estimated the extent to which schools can overcome social influences.
- In effect, blamed teachers for social inequalities.
- Used twelve untypical inner London comprehensives.

When *Fifteen Thousand Hours*, the book of the research of Professor Michael Rutter and his team, was published last year (Rutter *et al.*, 1979), it was widely acclaimed as justifying many practices of local authorities and schools. It seemed to give the lie to the suggestion that schools could do nothing about low intelligence or poor social backgrounds.

But since its publication the research has run into a barrage of complaints and criticisms that has led some to question whether any reliance can be placed on the Rutter findings.

Slowly emerging from the research journals is a catalogue of technical and philosophical objections. Some are serious and some nit-picking, and some are so vituperous as to verge on the libellous. Stung, it seems at times by the publicity given to *Fifteen Thousand Hours* and the questionable conclusions drawn from it by others more than by the shortcomings in the work itself, some have called into question the motives of the researchers in attacks that have even brought serious critics of the research to its defence.

Using verbal reasoning tests as an indication of the intellectual abilities and fathers' occupations as a measure of social differences, the Rutter research team found behaviour and academic achievement

Table 1: Rank orders of attendance, behaviour and exam success in Rutter's twelve schools (one equals best, twelve equals worst). Schools with best attendance levels had best academic success and best behaviour of pupils. But the school with the worst attendance, while almost at the bottom of the academic league, had the second best behaviour.

Attendance	Academic	Behaviour
1	1	1
2	2	4
3	6	3
4	5	5
5	8	10
6	4	6
7	10	11
8	9	9
9	3	8
10	7	7
11	12	12
12	11	2

varied markedly between twelve inner London comprehensives even when the IQ and background differences of their intakes were allowed for (Table 1).

Pupils in the lowest ability group (band three) in the best school did as well as pupils in the top-ability band one in the worst. After allowing for Rutter's versions of social and intelligence differences the exam score of the best school was 70 per cent above the average, while that of the worst was 50 per cent below.

The researchers also claim to have shown that schools varied considerably in rates of attendance, delinquency and in standards of behaviour in school even after differences in intake were taken into account (Table 1).

Coinciding with higher standards of attainment and behaviour were "certain characteristics of schools as social institutions". They say these amounted to a successful school "ethos" typified by punctual and well-organized teachers; agreed standards of discipline, though not harsh ones; regular homework and checks that teachers set it; policy decisions made by the heads and senior staff; clean and tidy classrooms with little grafitti or damage; and a system of rewards and recognition for good pupils [see the next reading, which gives details of these characteristics].

"We may conclude that the results carry a strong implication that schools can do much to foster good behaviour and attainments and even in a disadvantaged area, schools can be a force for the good", the final sentence in their book says.

But all this assumes the team were able to balance statistically the differences in intakes between the schools; an assumption strongly doubted by many of their critics.

Professor Harvey Goldstein (1980), Professor of educational statistics at the London University Institute of Education, says many other things besides IQ scores and fathers' jobs affect pupil performances.

Writing in the next *Journal of Child Psychology and Psychiatry* he says this, and other technical deficiencies in the adjustment of intakes, "indicates that much is left to be desired and they do not encourage the reader to place a great deal of confidence in the author's results".

Two Oxford academics, Mr Anthony Heath, sociologist, and Mr Peter Clifford, mathematician, in the *Oxford Review of Education* claim that on the evidence of *Fifteen Thousand Hours*, the school attended makes very little difference (Heath and Clifford, 1980).

They point out that only 6.5 per cent of the variation found between schools was explained by school differences, whereas 27 per cent was explained by differences in pupils' verbal reasoning scores and two thirds of the variation remained unexplained.

Rutter failed to take any account of parental interest and encouragement. "He has not controlled for all the non-school factors which are well known to affect children's school careers." Factors that might well have wiped out the 6.5 per cent influence attributed to the secondary schools.

"It is surely quite reasonable to speculate that voluntary aided schools attract more interested and educationally ambitious parents and that they also tend to run a 'tighter ship' with more emphasis on uniforms, homework, lessons, starting on time and the like.

"If this were so it would be quite wrong to attribute their success to the 'tight ship' style of management; the quality and motivation of the intake might simply provide them with the conditions under which a tight ship can be run without mutiny."

Heath and Clifford also criticize the "crude" measures used by the Rutter team. Fathers' occupations were split into three categories: (1) professional, management and clerical, (2) skilled manual, and (3) semi-skilled, unskilled and unemployed. They say Rutter should also have considered the effects of different primary schooling.

Other critics attack the researchers for assuming that the "ethos" discovered in the "good" schools was the source of their success. Though *Fifteen Thousand Hours* contains warnings that such coincidences are not proof of cause and effect, these did not satisfy the critics.

With such sensitive political and social issues it was important to put the caveats sufficiently prominently "so that even the reader who wants to believe the conclusions has to take pause for thought," say Heath and Clifford.

In the latest *Educational Research*, Mr T. A. Acton (1980), a sociologist at Thames Polytechnic, accuses the researchers of "cheating" by putting in the statistical cautions and then "blandly ignoring them".

Acton's main complaint is that the results have been used to refute the "pessimistic" views of the American, Christopher Jencks, that educational policy in modern capitalist societies can do little to lessen social inequality. Mr Acton describes as "statistical hubris" the Rutter team's claim that these results applied to all schools.

"The 'success' of these schools is extremely relative," writes Mr Acton. In the early 1970s when the work was being done "knowing middle class parents were sending their children anywhere but to these (comprehensive) schools.

"For most of these schools the mere *fact* of attending them means their pupils have already failed to make the grade for social mobility. We are not really dealing with variations in the success of these schools but with small gradations in the degree of their failure."

He also questions the researcher's judgement of the facts. Rutter claimed that in the accompanying table of rank orders that good or bad attendance, academic performance and behaviour went together consistently.

"It could be described like that;" says Acton, but to him "apart from one consistently bad and one consistently good, the rankings look thoroughly jumbled up."

Professor Ted Wragg (1980) of Exeter University also questioned whether the Rutter schools were typical. In an occasional publication from that university called *Perspectives*, which was devoted to several critical views of the Rutter research, he wrote, "Rutter's research relates to twelve schools in the Inner London Education Authority with 28 per cent of mothers handicapped by some psychiatric disorder, 28 per cent of fathers carrying convictions for criminal offences, 51 per cent of children in overcrowded homes, a pupil–teacher ratio of 14.5 to one, 43 per cent of teachers in posts for three years or less, very few children of high intelligence and a mean score of 92 for non-verbal intelligence (average 100) even after immigrant children have been excluded."

He also thought some of the "cause and effect" claims "go over the top".

Professor Rutter and his team are unrepentant about their major conclusions. In the latest *Educational Research*, in reply to Mr Acton's critique they say that their considered judgement is that this evidence, and that from other studies, give good reason to suppose they had uncovered cause and effect.

Only studies of planned changes in schools could make certain of this, but they stood by their view, and the final statement about schools being "a force for good", as a "fair appraisal of the state of the art".

They complain of misinterpretation and mis-statements of their work, false innuendo, and unwarranted implications.

Their work was not an essay on the relationship between educational policy and social inequality but a research report.

"We did not set out to find solutions to present problems of schooling and society but merely to follow the progress of 2,000 London children through their secondary schooling and to describe some aspects of their life at school."

On the question of whether schools can alleviate inequality, the authors of *Fifteen Thousand Hours* say: "Raising the quality of education will not and could not have the effect of making all pupils the same.

"Unlike Jencks, our study was concerned with the question of whether raising the quality of education could have an impact in raising overall standards of attainment (i.e. an effect on *levels* and not on *variance*). The findings suggested that it could."

In a reply to the Exeter *Perspectives* criticisms, one of the research group, Mr Peter Mortimore, says any worthwhile research in real-life is difficult.

Mr Mortimore, now Director of Research and Statistics for the ILEA, says the adjustments for intake differences was done on the best data available. He acknowledged that some of the technical objections to the statistical basis for the "ethos" were "fair comment".

So where does all this leave *Fifteen Thousand Hours?* Unfinished, tendentious, incoherent and should never have been published, is the verdict of Mr Acton.

Heath and Clifford say it provides no basis for teachers and administrators to change their practices.

"No doubt it is desirable in itself to finish lessons on time, to put pictures on the wall, to organize one's teaching so that more time is spent on the topic rather than on giving out equipment, but teachers are not entitled to use Rutter's book as proof that this will improve outcomes."

Not all teachers had the compliant pupils that made a tight ship feasible. They got poorer results, less satisfaction, and then, to add insult to injury, were told by Rutter that it was their fault.

Professor Goldstein says the results should be treated with caution if not scepticism.

"Nevertheless, the basic *idea* behind the study is a useful one and there is some *prima facie* evidence that genuine school differences may exist."

Professor Wragg warns, "Like all published investigations which receive publicity it is open to sniping and nit-picking, sometimes from people who have not themselves published empirical research".

The work raised important and fundamental questions about life in schools and the more effective use of people and resources. "It would be quite wrong for anyone, no matter what reservations he might have about methodology or ideology to dismiss the work in its entirety."

References

Acton, T. (1980), in *Education Research*, June.

Goldstein, H. (1980), *Journal of Child Psychology and Psychiatry*, Vol.21, No.4.

Heath, A. and Clifford, P. (1980), in *Oxford Review of Education*, Vol.6, No.1.

Rutter, M., Maugham, B., Mortimore, P. and Ouston, J. (1979), *Fifteen Thousand Hours*, Open Books.

Wragg, E. C. (1980), in *Perspectives 1*, Exeter University School of Education.

2.5 Fifteen Thousand Hours
M. Rutter, B. Maugham, P. Mortimore and J. Ouston

[*This appendix is in two parts, general process items (I) and those relating teachers' conditions (II)*].

Appendix E

Details of Process Items

I PROCESS ITEMS

1. Homework in the First Year
From lesson observations. One point given for homework either set or returned in each of the four lessons observed. Each school given a score which constituted an average for all lessons (0 = no homework, 1 = set or returned in that lesson, 2 = set and returned in that lesson). Range: 0.3 to 1.3 with a mean of 0.70.

2. Homework in the Third Year – Teachers' Questionnaire
Maths and English teachers of the classes we observed were asked how many minutes of homework they gave the class each week. Range of school scores 0-3 hrs. Mean 1 hr 10 mins.

3. Homework
Teachers' questionnaire: 'Is there any check on whether staff set homework?' Coded 0 = No, 1 = Yes. School score is the percentage of teachers saying 'Yes'. School scores varied from 10 per cent to 100 per cent with a mean of 52.3 per cent.

4. Expected 'O' Levels
The same teachers as Item 2 were asked what percentage of the third-year class they expected to pass either 'O' level or CSE grade 1. The average of these two teachers' estimates was used as the 'school score' and these range from 2.5 per cent to 45 per cent. Mean = 17.3 per cent.

Rutter, M., Maugham, B., Mortimore, P. and Ouston, J. (1979), *Fifteen Thousand Hours*, Open Books.

5. Work on Walls
As observed during the administration of the pupil questionnaire and the third-year lesson observations (N = 239). Each room was assessed on a five point scale: 0 = nothing on walls, to 4 = all possible areas covered. The average score for each school was calculated and used as the 'school score'. This measure was highly reliable between observers, agreement being obtained on 92 per cent of observations. School scores range from 0.25 to 1.75. Mean = 1.00.

6. Total Teaching Time
Calculated from the timetable of the third-year class we observed. School scores range from 21.9 to 24.2 hours/week. Mean = 22.9 hrs.

7. Head's Reported Pastoral Emphasis
From interview with head of school. A scale constructed from the replies of the headteacher to ten questions on the pastoral emphasis of the school. The items included are:
1. Use of special units. 0 = none, 1 = one, 2 = more than one.
2. Regular meetings with pupils. 0 = none, 1 = informal (e.g. lunch hour), 2 = school council.
3. Arrangement of free dinner confidentiality. 0 = none, 1 = some, 2 = positive attempt.
4. Topics discussed at last cabinet meeting. 0 = not pastoral, 1 = pastoral.
5. Allocation of form teachers. 0 = reasons other than to maintain continuity, 1 = continuity.
6. Reasons for class changes. 0 = reasons other than social or at pupils' request, 1 = social or pupils' request.
7. Topics discussed at last staff meeting. 0 = not pastoral, 1 = pastoral.
8. Stability of teachers from year to year. 0 = not school policy, 1 = class teachers only, 2 = class teachers and tutors.
9. Scale points allocated to pastoral heads. 0 = none on scale 4, 0.5 = some on scale 4, 1 = all on scale 4.
10. Role of pastoral care in school. 0 = minor emphasis, 1 = to support curriculum, 2 = a high priority in school.

School scores ranged from 2.5 to 11.0, with a mean score of 6.5.

8. Library Use
From pupil questionnaire: 'In the last week, have you taken any books out of the school library for enjoyment rather than work?' Coded no = 0, yes = 1. School score is the percentage of children saying 'Yes' and this ranged from 17 per cent to 56 per cent with a mean score of 33.3 per cent. Reliability of school means, $r_s = 0.73, p < 0.01$.

9. Course Planning

From the teachers' interview: 'How much freedom did you have in planning the first-, second- and third-year courses you are teaching this year?' Coded 0 = complete freedom, 1 = planned with others. The school score was the percentage of teachers who said that they planned their courses with others. The school scores ranged from 33.3 per cent to 100 per cent with a mean of 73.4 per cent.

10. Subjects Taught

From teachers' interview: 'Which subjects are you teaching?' Coded 0 = specialist subject only, 1 = general subjects. (A teacher who helped with sports as well as his own subject would *not* be considered a 'general' teacher.) The school score was the percentage of general teachers and this ranged from 0 per cent to 50 per cent with a mean of 22.4 per cent.

11. Per cent Teachers' Time on 'Topic'

Calculated from our third-year lesson observations. Defined as: uninterrupted interactions focused on the subject matter in hand, or earlier or related work, and the children's acquisitions of the skills necessary in executing the work, including methods of using equipment, laying out work etc. NB. Topic can also be scored alone, without any of the interaction categories, if the teacher is clearly engaged in work related to the instructional context of the lesson, but is not interacting with the children, e.g. marking their books, watching films, listening to tapes etc. Positive comments on a child's work should be scored as 'Topic' and 'Praise'. Negative comments on a child's work should be scored as 'Topic' and 'Punishment'. Scores on this measure ranged from 64.9 per cent to 86.0 per cent, mean = 74.8 per cent, and inter-observer reliability was significant at the 0.01 level.

12. Per cent Teachers' Time on 'Equipment'

Calculated from the third-year lessons. Defined as: setting up of equipment, writing on board, distributing and collecting materials etc. or instructions to children on distribution of resources – but not imparting of skills and use of equipment which would be coded 'Topic'. This category can be used without interaction categories if appropriate. Scores on this measure ranged from 3.2 per cent to 13.6 per cent, mean = 9.1 per cent, and inter-observer reliability was significant at the 0.01 level.

13. Per cent of Lessons Ending Early

From our observations of third-year lessons. Range of school scores 0 per cent to 44 per cent. Mean = 15.3 per cent.

14. and 15. Teachers' Interventions in the Classroom

(First- and third-year academic lessons, 3rd yr. N = 312, 1st yr. N = 96.)

Percentage of teacher observation periods when teacher dealt with pupils' behaviour. This excluded 'management' of behaviour (i.e. instructions as to how the class was to behave, such as 'Everyone be quiet now', but did include subsequent actions such as 'John Smith, do stop talking'). The definition used by the observers was: directions initiated to ensure compliance with previous management instructions which have failed to produce the desired result, or to curb unacceptable behaviour — i.e. score only when the directions given are contingent upon the children's behaviour. This measure was reliable between observers at the 0.01 level.

16. Silence
The percentage of observation blocks when the teacher expected complete silence. A block was a five-minute observation period and 'silence' would be coded if that was the predominant expectation for the whole period. Relates to third-year academic lessons only (N = 312). Scores ranged from 12.9 per cent to 63.5 per cent, mean = 37.2 per cent.

17. Teacher Interaction Style
The percentage of the observation periods where teacher was interacting with the whole class (as opposed to interacting with individuals). The definitions used by the observers were: '*Individual*': score when the teacher interacts specifically with one individual, either by e.g. calling the child out to his desk, or by positioning himself next to the child, or speaking in a way which is clearly primarily directed to one individual. '*Class*': for use in all other instances of interaction with the children, i.e. for all chalk and talk sessions directed to the whole class, for question and answer sessions only involving individuals as representatives of the class, and when the teacher is going round the class, or looking at the class, whilst they are working. Scores on this measure ranged from 22.4 per cent to 60.2 per cent with a mean of 48.8 per cent, and inter-observer reliability was significant at the 0.01 level.

18. Told off by the Headteacher
From pupil questionnaire. 'Have you been told off by the head since September?' Coded No = 0, Yes = 1. School scores are percentage of pupils saying 'Yes' and this ranged from 12.0 per cent to 51.3 per cent with a mean of 32.5 per cent. Reliability of school means, $r_s = 0.90$, $p < 0.01$.

19. Discipline
From teachers' interview: 'Are there any general standards of classroom discipline which are expected at this school?' This was coded 0 = No/Personal to teacher, 1 = Dept., Year/House or school based. The school

scores ranged from 30.0 per cent to 100 per cent, with a mean score of 66.7 per cent.

20. Detentions

From pupil questionnaire: 'Since last September, how many times have you been kept in detention?' Coded $0 =$ none, $1 =$ once or twice, $2 = 3$-5 times, $3 = 6$-10 times, $4 = 11$-15 times, $5 = 16$-20 times, $6 = 20 +$. Range of school scores 1.02 to 2.81, mean score $= 1.75$. Reliability of school means, $r_s = 0.94$, $p < 0.01$.

21. Punishment – Lines

From pupil questionnaire: 'Since September, how many times have you been given lines or extra work to do?' This was coded: $0 =$ never; $1 = 1$, 2; $2 = 3$-5; $3 = 6$-10; $4 = 11$-15; $5 = 16$-20; $6 = 20 +$ and the school score was the average score for the pupils. This ranged from 0.26 to 2.83 with a mean score of 1.04. Reliability of school means, $r_s = 0.93$, $p < 0.01$.

22. Corporal Punishment

From pupil questionnaire: 'Since September, how many times have you received corporal punishment, either in or out of class?' Coded $0 =$ none, $1 =$ once or twice, $2 = 3$-5 times, $3 = 6$-10 times, $4 = 11$-15 times, $5 = 16$-20 times, $6 = 20 +$. Range of school scores 0.13 to 2.26. Mean score $= 0.64$. Reliability of school means, $r_s = 0.99$, $p < 0.01$.

23. Punitive Action – Ten Naughty Children Scale

A sample of teachers in each school ($N = 55$) was asked how they would deal with ten different problems with the children's behaviour at school. These replies were then coded on a five-point scale ranging $0 =$ positive 'welfare' approach, $1 =$ no action. $2 =$ minor disciplinary action. $3 =$ major disciplinary action. $4 =$ suspended or expelled. The school scores ranged from 0.59 to 1.88 with a mean score of 1.13.

24. Named for Work

From pupil questionnaire: 'Since September, have you had your name read out at assembly or at any other school meeting for doing well in work?' School score is the percentage of children saying 'Yes'. Range 3.7 per cent to 36.2 per cent. Mean $= 17.4$ per cent. Reliability of school means, $r_s = 0.88$, $p < 0.01$.

25. Topic Praise

From third-year lesson observations. Recordings of teacher praise to either individuals or groups for good work, defined as: all positive remarks including e.g. 'That's good' and 'That's right', which do not simply seem to be confirming the correctness of a statement. Score also for the distribution of any formal or tangible rewards, and enter details of these in the checklist on the initial sheet. This occurred very rarely, the range being 0.2 per cent to 2.9 per cent of observation periods, mean = 1.28 per cent, and inter-observer reliability was significant at the 0.05 level.

26. Prizes for Sport
From pupil questionnaire: 'Since September, have you been presented with anything (for example a prize, badge, or certificate) for doing well in sport?' School score is the percentage of children saying 'Yes'. Range from 10.1 per cent to 46.9 per cent. Mean = 29.4 per cent. Reliability of school means, $r_s = 0.93$, p <0.01.

27. Prizes for Work
From pupil questionnaire: 'Since September, have you been presented with anything (for example, a prize, badge or certificate) for doing well in work?' Coded 0 = No, 1 = Yes. Range of school scores 1.3 per cent to 63.7 per cent. Mean score = 30.3 per cent. Reliability of school means, $r_s = 0.93$, p <0.01.

28. Potential Consultation
From pupil questionnaire: 'If you had a serious personal problem, which of these people would you discuss it with at school?' Choices were: form teacher or subject teacher, head of year or house, counsellor, priest or other adult at school. Each child was given a score from 0 to 3 and then the average school score was calculated. Range of school scores 0.67 to 0.34. Mean = 0.51. Reliability of school means, $r_s = 0.66$, p <0.05.

29. Outings
From pupil questionnaire: 'Please write the names of any places you have been to with the school on outings or journeys (and put the number of outings in the total box)'. School score was coded: 0 = 0, 1 = 1, 2; 2 = 3-5; 3 = 6-10; 4 = 11-15; 5 = 16-20; 6 = 20 + . Range of school scores from 0.6 to 2.9. Mean = 1.6. Reliability of school means, $r_s = 0.97$, p <0.01.

30. Pupil Conditions
A checklist of fourteen items which describe ways in which schools might be considerate of their pupils' needs – e.g. tuckshop, clean and well kept WCs, open building at break and dinner hour, good meals, school has a counsellor, no hair regulations, no sixth-form uniform, school pets, etc. Each school given a score from 0 to 14. Range of school scores 1-13. Mean = 6.0.

31. Decorations of Classroom
A score of 0 to 5 given to each classroom visited during administration of pupil questionnaire and during third-year lesson observations – one point being given for each item: clean room, tidy room, plants, posters and pictures. Range of school means from 2.0 to 4.4. Mean = 2.8. Agreement obtained between observers in 96 per cent of observations.

32. Pupils' Problems
From teacher interviews: 'If an individual child in your form/set was worried about a school/personal problem, when could he/she come to talk to you about it?' Coded 0 = any time, 1 = fixed time. Schools' scores were the percentage of teachers saying they would see a child at any time; this ranged from 0 per cent to 100 per cent with a mean of 64.47 per cent.

33. No. of Children with Problems Seen
Teachers' questionnaire: 'How many children (with personal or school problems) did you see in the last two weeks?' The school score was the average number of children seen, and ranged from 0.50 to 5.63 with a mean score of 2.49.

34. Form Captain
From pupil questionnaire: 'Have you ever been a form captain or monitor?' School score was percentage of children answering 'Yes'. This item has high split half reliability. Range 7.3 per cent to 50.4 per cent. Mean = 32.1 per cent. Reliability of school means, $r_s = 0.90$, $p < 0.01$.

35. Pupils Caring for Resources
From third-year lesson observations of whether pupils brought and took away their own resources (i.e. books, folders, exercise books, etc.). School score is the percentage of academic lessons where this was observed. Range 2.5 per cent to 78.5 per cent, mean 42.6 per cent.

36. Assembly Participation
From pupil questionnaire: 'Have you ever taken a special part in an assembly or school/house/year meeting?' Coded 0 = never, 1 = 1 or 2, 2 = 3-5, 3 = 6-10, 4 = 11-15, 5 = 16-20, 6 = 20 + . School score – the average for children at each school. Range 0.11 to 1.43, mean = 0.57. Reliability of school means, $r_s = 0.99$, $p < 0.01$.

37. Charity Contributions
From pupil questionnaire: 'This term, have you contributed to any collection for charity which has been organized by the school?' School score is the percentage of children saying 'Yes'. Range from 41.8 per cent to 94.7 per cent, mean = 74.4 per cent. Reliability of school means $r_s = 0.93$, $p < 0.01$.

38. Stability of Maths and English Teachers of Third-year Pupils

The school score was the average number of terms the observed third-year class had been taught by their present maths and English teachers. School scores varied from 2 to 6 with a mean of 3.5 terms.

39. Continuity of Teachers of Fifth-year Pupils only

From pupil questionnaire: 'How many form tutors/set tutors have you had at this school?', and 'How many English teachers have you had?'. School score was the average number of each reported by the fifth-year pupils. Range 5.45 to 9.16, mean 6.85. Reliability of school means, $r_s = 0.92$, $p < 0.01$.

40. Same English Class

From the pupil questionnaire. The children were asked 'Have you been in the same class for English since you started at this school?' The school score was the number of children saying 'Yes', and ranged from 40 per cent to 89 per cent with a mean of 68 per cent. Reliability of school means, $r_s = 0.98$, $p < 0.01$.

41. Same Form

From pupil questionnaire: 'Have you been in the same form/set/tutor group/class since you started at this school?' Score is percentage of children checking 'Yes'. Range 52 per cent to 98 per cent, mean 77.3 per cent. Reliability of school means, $r_s = 0.92$, $p < 0.01$.

42. Friends in the Same Year

From pupil questionnaire. The children were asked 'How many people in your year, but not in your class/English set have you visited at their homes, or arranged to meet out of school, since last September?' The number of friends was coded $0 = 0$, $1 = 1, 2$; $2 = 3-5$; $3 = 6-10$; $4 = 11-15$; $5 = 16-20$; $6 = 20 +$. School scores ranged from 0.99 to 3.74 with a mean of 2.21. Reliability of school means, $r_s = 0.96$, $p < 0.01$.

43. Decision-making

From teachers' questionnaire: 'Where do you see the most important school decisions being made?' Coded: $0 = $ at senior staff level, $1 = $ at ordinary staff level. The school score is the percentage of teachers saying that decisions are taken at the senior staff level. School scores varied from 33.3 to 100 with a mean of 81.7.

44. Representation of Views at Decision-making

From teachers' questionnaire: 'How are your views represented?' Coded $0 = $ through representative, $1 = $ personally. The school score is the percentage of teachers saying that they are represented by another teacher. School scores varied from 0 per cent to 100 per cent with a mean of 41.6 per cent.

45. Late Arrival at School

From teachers' questionnaire: 'Is anyone aware if staff arrive late for school?' Coded 0 = No. 1 = Yes. School score is percentage of teachers saying 'Yes'. School scores varied from 55.6 per cent to 100 per cent with a mean of 87.9 per cent.

46. Clerical Help

From teachers' questionnaire: 'Do you have adequate clerical help?' Coded 0 = definitely not, 1 = doubtful, 2 = yes. School mean scores were calculated which ranged from 0.45 to 2.00 with a mean of 1.04.

II ITEMS IN TEACHERS' CONDITIONS SCALE

1. No timetable problems reported.
2. Eight or more free periods/week (i.e. above mean for whole sample, mean = 7.84).
3. Guaranteed free periods.
4. Three or less free periods lost in previous two weeks (mean = 3.26).
5. Has own teaching room.
6. Has own storage space.
7. Has adequate equipment.
8. Has adequate technical help.
9. Has clerical help.
10. Clerical help adequate.
11. Has departmental office/room.
12. Has space for marking books.

2.6   Self-assessment at a London Comprehensive

G. Varnava

George Varnava is Headmaster at Norwood School, South London. Formerly Head of Modern Languages at Holland Park School and First Deputy Head at Pimlico School, he has been fully involved in mixed-ability teaching and comprehensive organization. Here he comments on how one school has responded to the challenge of self-assessment (using the ILEA self-evaluation scheme).

Two years ago, ILEA's *Keeping the School Under Review* invited schools to undertake a systematic exercise in self-assessment; in the Secondary section, to clarify what it is the school is attempting to do and whether it is satisfied that what it is attempting is right. Those courageous enough to answer its direct, practical questions with complete honesty found, no doubt, clear directions to areas of necessary or desirable improvement.

The Secondary section of the document directs its questions to facts, people, policies and procedure, concluding with an 'acid test': 'Would I recommend a colleague to apply for a post at the school?' and 'Would I recommend the school to friends for their children?' It is tempting to apply the ultimate test: Would I send my own children to the school? A final note on 'Action' is designed to ensure that the exercise is constructive.

This proposed method aims to stimulate the kind of enquiry and discussion necessary to any re-definition of the school's objectives and the general educational principles by which it functions. As the introduction points out, each question is likely to suggest others. Under Resources, for example, a separate count of male and female staff, the number of teachers who have children themselves, length of service, etc., may go some way to explaining staff attitudes to their work and their professional development. Similarly, a count of 'problem' children or one-parent families will show whether or not a shift of resources is necessary. It is worthwhile, too, to take into account any additional use

Varnava, G. (1979), 'Self-assessment at a London Comprehensive', *Forum*, Vol.22, p.1.

of the school premises and identify any particular architectural features that affect organization and working conditions: a main hall too small for full assemblies; specialist rooms that cannot be used for general teaching; dark, secret corners that invite delinquency, and as many more examples, surely, as there are schools. Even the school roll deserves careful analysis: at Pimlico, a roll of 1,591 constitutes only 1,156 families.

The entire process of self-assessment, nevertheless, can easily remain a bureaucratic exercise if not conducted with the determined intent to make changes where changes are necessary, in both particular aspects of school life and in standards of efficiency. At Pimlico, the exercise was conducted partly through a full staff conference, neatly entitled 'The Common Task', aimed at identifying areas of concern and involving staff in solving problems and, subsequently, by a complete revision of the *Staff Handbook*, a document of over 60 pages covering policy, organization, resources, curriculum and daily routines – a combination of reference book, standing orders and a statement of intent.

Apart from bringing factual detail up to date, major changes were necessary in the areas of staff responsibilities – following the evolution of the role of the form tutor and a general shift of responsibility for class-room discipline from pastoral to academic staff; in regulations regarding security in the light of the Safety at Work Act; in school uniform – resulting from prolonged discussion involving staff, School Council and Parents' Association, and finally, in the areas of the assessment of pupils where both mixed-ability grouping and setting by ability occur. This last change, subject of a working-party's discussions lasting almost two years, is perhaps the focal point in any exercise of self-appraisal, for it is ultimately the criteria by which children are judged that determine the school's philosophy and objectives, its policies and organization, and its performance.

Here is Pimlico's instruction to staff:

ASSESSMENT (GRADES AND REPORTS)

General
Continuous assessment of the individual pupil is made by awarding two grades for each subject. These are recorded in the form grades book prepared by the form tutor, and on twice-yearly reports. Each child is awarded a double grade in each subject on a five-point scale, the first digit being for the quality of the work (attainment) the second for effort.

1 – for excellent; 2 – good; 3 – average; 4 – below average; 5 – poor. For example, a child who is given in English an assessment of 2.1 is judged to have produced work of good quality and have worked very hard to achieve it. The continuous assessment of attainment and effort provides the school record of the individual pupil's academic progress throughout his school career.

Progress may be seen as competition against oneself and this simple, regular form of assessment aims to give each pupil the incentive to compete against his last performance. A combination of both mixed-ability grouping and setting occurs within certain departments and within years. To ensure, therefore, a correct scheme of assessment recording, involving the use of a letter code which precedes the grades, is used throughout the school from years one to five.

Procedure for Assessment

GRADES — attainment
           — effort   } both on five-point scale

awarded for all pupils and recorded in grade books
Grades preceded by letter A, B, C or M
A, B or C denoting level of group as fixed department; M denoting mixed-ability.
(NB: A, B, C, M *not* used for 6th)

REPORTS
1st/2nd Years:
(a) Effort grade only, preceded by M (NB: A, B or C for Latin or sets in 2nd Year);
(b) Exam mark where appropriate;
(c) Comment (explanatory and advisory);
3rd/4th/5th Years:
(a) Both grades, preceded by A, B, C or M;
(b) Exam mark where appropriate;
(c) Comment (explanatory and advisory);
6th Year:
(a) Both grades (no A, B, C or M);
(b) Exam mark where appropriate;
(c) Comment (explanatory and advisory)

Here, an attempt has been made to reconcile the fundamentally different approaches in assessing children in mixed-ability groups and those set by ability. In mixed-ability groups, co-operation between pupils is more appropriate to the learning situation than the encouragement of keen competition. Any objective assessment of ability, therefore, should not hinder the motivation of the individual pupil. In sets, assessment of attainment is progressively related to potential in public examinations.

A conventional statistical approach to examination results normally gives no more than a crude picture of a school's performance. Marten Shipman's very useful 'The Presentation of Examination Results' in *Contact* (24 November 1978) indicates how important it is to assess performance in terms of the school's intake characteristics and its examination policy. The following table shows how a school's achievement might be interpreted if the question asked is not 'how many passed?' but 'who passed?' – a question, surely, that is of much greater interest to those directly concerned.

Table 1

1st year Predicted ability		Streams	5th year Actual provenance of each category	
A	GCE	1 2 3 4 5 6 7 8 9 10 11 12	GCE	A
B	CSE			CSE
				B
C	NON-EXAM		C	

Parallels between the assessment of individual children and of the school as a whole are obvious, whether the assessment is made by comparison with others or with previous performance. In the Secondary section of *Keeping the School under Review* two brief questions only refer to the assessment of children: H5 (Arrangements for learning) 'How do we assess the quality and quantity of work produced?' and I[8] (Department Self-assessment) 'What steps do we take to assess and record progress?' The Primary section gives greater importance to 'Attainment' with fuller, more searching questions.

For the school, as with its individual children, assessment of all aspects of 'physical, intellectual, social, emotional and aesthetic areas of development' is valid and necessary. A full, regular review is essential in order to identify strengths, weaknesses, particular needs and to explain any fall in levels of achievement; to stimulate dialogue between teachers, pupils and parents, and, above all, to ensure that the individual and the school know just where they stand. Since the school must be accountable for standards to its public and its clientele it must be ready to initiate change for the sake of progress.

2.7 Process Evaluation in Schools
H. Simons

In this edited version of her article, Helen Simons advocates a process model of school self-evaluation, arguing that it is the processes of education, rather than its products, for which schools should be held accountable. She also makes a case for insulating school self-evaluation from accountability demands while skills and confidence in these procedures build up. In the long term however, she believes that school self-evaluation, committed to professional development, may be the most effective model of accountability.

In the current accountability debate process models of evaluation have been advanced as alternatives to accountability models that are based on product efficiency criteria (MacDonald, 1978, Elliott, 1978a). In order to provide an appropriate model of accountability, it is argued, evaluation should aspire to reflect the processes of teaching, learning and schooling. We need to know not so much what pupils can be demonstrated to have learned (the focus of product models) rather what transpires in the process of learning and teaching, the outcomes we could reasonably expect from such transactions and the strengths and weaknesses of educational provision. We need, in other words, to educate our judgements about the adequacy of provision for learning and the quality of experience pupils have.

One of the best ways to improve these judgements is to study the processes of teaching, learning and schooling in order to be able to compare practice with intention, opportunities with aspirations. And one of the best ways to represent and promote understanding of these processes is to accumulate and make available detailed descriptions of teaching and learning and the values and effects of curriculum policies within the context of particular schools and classrooms. Such an approach could take into account actual as well as intended practice and indicate the range of ways achievements might be demonstrated.

Product models emphasize measurable learnings, teaching intentions, and how efficiently the intentions have been achieved. The concept is an economic one and fits best within a system where resources

---

Simons, H. (1981), 'Process Evaluation in Schools', in C. Lacey and D. Lawton (eds), *Accountability and Evaluation*, Methuen (in press).

can be allocated and assessed directly in relation to outputs by measures such as achievement tests. Such an approach has an appealing logic, but its defence rests upon a dangerous oversimplification of education and evaluation.

The worth of educational experience, as Stake (1978) has pointed out, can rarely be demonstrated by such measures:

> The worth of a program is seldom indicated by the achievement of students. That is partly true because our measurement instruments are narrow and crude. They indicate only a small part of the impact of a lesson or a program. (We should continue to refine and redesign our objective measures of attainment, but we should not design evaluation studies now as if satisfactory instruments existed.) It is also partly true because the worth of a program is dependent on its relevance to other courses and programs, on its effect on teacher morale, on its compatibility with community ideology, etc., etc. . . .

The adequacy of the product efficiency model for educational purposes is often not questioned before it is invoked. And it is often invoked when questions are being asked about the value of money spent or when a society, or groups in society, wish to stress specific outcomes for instrumental purposes. Testing programmes based on this model, some argue, are a most powerful instrument of curriculum control and social engineering. (See, for example, House, 1973a.) The multi-purpose nature of education and backwash effects of such schemes are overlooked in the adoption of product-efficiency models. It is partly to redress this imbalance (but also for other reasons associated with the deficiencies of such approaches discussed below) that process evaluation is now being strongly advocated by some educationalists.

This paper presents a case for process evaluation in the context of evaluating the whole school. Process, as already indicated, can refer to the teaching/learning interface and several authors have written extensively about the need for evaluation of these processes. (See, for example, Elliott, 1978b, Stenhouse, 1975.) Others refer to the whole process of schooling (MacDonald, 1978, Simons, 1978). Both kinds of evaluation have been suggested as alternatives to current accountability models. Both have been closely linked to self-evaluation, thereby challenging the political as well as the content assumptions of orthodox thinking.

These evaluations can take different forms. The particular stance towards school self-evaluation advanced here is one which encourages a high degree of participation in the conduct of the evaluation and the sharing of knowledge.

Three main arguments are presented. First it is argued that the major justification for school self-evaluation is enhanced professionalism and that it is best introduced as a continuing part of professional practice, not as a short-term response to political pressures. Secondly, it is suggested that, in the short term, development of the process model needs to be insulated from accountability demands. Thirdly, and in the long term, it argues that such evaluation will provide a more effective and constructive model of accountability than many of the current models in use. [. . .]

One of the springboards for the surge of interest in school self-evaluation over the past five years has been reaction to the setting up of the Assessment of Performance Unit (APU) by central government. Doubts have been cast on the capacity of the APU testing programme to provide an adequate picture of the achievements of our schools (MacDonald, 1978, Harlen, 1979b) and concerns have been expressed about the constraints such a centralized monitoring programme might impose on the curriculum. The dangers associated with externally imposed schemes have been highlighted to encourage schools to respond by undertaking their own school evaluations, producing evidence of the quality and worth of what they are doing in ways determined by them.

Whilst encouraging such initiatives myself, I have also argued (Simons, 1980) that the most important justification for undertaking school self-evaluation is to enhance the professional image and practice of teachers and schools. The current accountability climate may provide a context and impetus for the development of forms of evaluation but not a stable underpinning. Schools may be tempted to respond to externally imposed schemes by producing whatever is required without themselves using the data for review of the professional practice of the school. Even if the activity does affect practice in positive ways, it may cease when the external demand fades.

If schools initiate evaluations in response to their own needs (and these may include producing accounts for outside audiences) these efforts are likely to be more sustained, to reflect the actual experience of schools and to lead to a quality control which is in the hands of those who have the prime responsibility for educating children and running the schools. It is primarily for these reasons that I wish to emphasize that the most appropriate justification for school self-evaluation is educational and professional and to suggest that it should be established as an integral part of professional practice.

Now that the era of national curriculum development projects seems to be over, the time is especially right for schools to evaluate themselves. Over the past two decades evaluation has become a highly specialized activity — the end of a chain of central development and diffusion invoked to see whether such central investment has been worthwhile. It has generally been costly, technical and specialized. Results and learnings from project evaluations have not been easy to apply to the varying circumstances of individual schools and classrooms.

What I am suggesting here is:

(a) that the sequence be reversed — evaluation should precede curriculum development and not follow in its wake;

(b) that the style of evaluation more closely reflect the ways in which schools do evaluate the quality of education they provide;
(c) that the evaluation be undertaken and managed by the schools themselves;
(e) that the evaluation focus on intra-institutional issues.

In making these suggestions I do not imply that little evaluation currently takes place in schools. Heads, teachers, pupils are continuously making judgements about teaching, the curriculum and the school. Policies are changed and decisions made implicitly drawing upon these judgements. But such evaluations are informal, frequently non-systematic and private to individuals or groups within the school: they are not part of a shared, co-ordinated and public tradition.

In the current climate pressure is being put upon schools by parents, politicians and employers to demonstrate their worth. But many of the indices being sought focus solely on pupil outcomes. These are only one measure of the worth of a school. Much more needs to be evaluated including curriculum policies, learning opportunities, the interrelationships between levels (pupil, classroom, school) and forms of provision and achievements. The specific case for such a broader evaluation is outlined below. The emphasis is on evaluation of the school as a whole, or a policy issue which concerns the whole school. Information on pupil achievement or teacher performance may form part of the evaluation if relevant to the issue chosen for study but is not focused upon directly. (For a discussion of the evaluation of pupil learning and teacher performance, see, respectively, Harlen, 1978, 1979, and Elliott, 1978b, 1979.)

The Case for School Self-evaluation
The case for studying the school as a whole is based on the following assumptions:
1. that better understanding of the organization and policies of the school could improve the opportunities and experiences provided in classrooms;
2. that systematic study and review allows the school to determine, and to produce evidence of, the extent to which they are providing the quality of education they espouse;
3. that a study of school policies can help teachers identify policy effects which require attention at school, department or classroom level;
4. that many policy issues (remedial education, for example), cut across departments and classrooms and require collective review and resolution;
5. that there are many learning experiences (field work and extra-curricular activities, for instance), which do not take place in the classroom and which require the co-operation and appraisal of the whole school;

6. that participation in a school self-study gives teachers the opportunity to develop their professional decision-making skills, enlarge their perspectives, and become better informed about the roles, responsibilities and problems of their colleagues.

Description of Process Evaluation

It is perhaps important before proceeding further to describe some of the characteristics of school process self-evaluation. What distinguishes it from other forms of evaluation? In what ways can it contribute to our understanding of education?

Studies of the process of learning and schooling will tend to be descriptive/analytic, particular, small scale. They will record events in progress, document observations and draw on the judgements and perspectives of participants in the process — teachers, pupils, heads — in coming to understand observations and events in a specific context. Close description both of practice and the social context is an important part of the study. Such descriptions provide opportunities for interpretations that elude other models of assessment or evaluation based on assumptions of comparability and elimination of variation. Such descriptions also provide opportunities for more of the complexity of educational experience to be grasped and articulated.

While the process could start with an examination of information that already exists in the school (see below), process evaluation differs from reports to school governors, information given to parents or the school prospectus in going beyond the information given to examining the assumptions and values underlying this information. Descriptions of practice, examples of outcomes, observations and analysis of different perspectives on issues may all form part of the process.

Reports to governors and parents are changing in many schools with the giving of more detailed information, and that provides, of course, a basis for outside evaluation to begin to take place. The evaluation process described here emphasizes that evaluation should start within the school in a context of informing the school's policy-making and improving educational practice. Reports with this aspiration are likely to be more interpretative than factual, to focus on particular policy issues, to expose different value positions, to provide evidence for decision-making and to raise options or alternatives for action.

Subjective judgements are an important part of the process. This needs to be emphasized, so undervalued are such judgements in many approaches to educational research and evaluation. Professional judgements are an integral part of classroom transactions and policy decisions. The subtlety of judgement may be difficult to capture but in evaluating the process of teaching, learning and schooling, the judgements of people are an important source of data which it would be foolish to ignore if understanding of the complexity of these processes is sought. There are difficulties, of course, in relying solely on judgement or, rather, any one person's judgement, but in an evaluation utilizing a range of different methods and different people as sources, cross checks on the accuracy of information can be established, and the validity of judgements assessed.

While the focus may be particular, the data base is broad and may include quantitative and qualitative indicators of progress or events; and evidence of the outcomes as well as the processes of teaching, learning and schooling. Both may be needed, if relevant to the issue under review. But what is also important here, whatever kind of data is selected, is that it be considered within the context of the particular school. This point has been made so often but is nevertheless worth stressing again that our understanding of schooling is likely to be more complete if we try and capture more of the detail of what actually transpires in classrooms and schools and more accurate if we interpret findings in context, be they examination results, achievement scores, qualitative judgements or observations.

Cronbach (1975) has made the point before:

> Instead of making generalization the ruling consideration in our research, I suggest that we reverse our priorities. An observer collecting data in one particular situation is in a position to appraise a practice or proposition in that setting, observing effects in context. In trying to describe and account for what happened, he will give equally careful attention to uncontrolled conditions, to personal characteristics and to events that occurred during treatment and measurement. As he goes from situation to situation, his first task is to describe and interpret the effect anew in each locale, perhaps taking into account factors that were unique to that locale or series of events.

It is also important to stress here that process approaches to evaluation (emphasizing description and interpretation, dynamics and context) do not reject quantitative data nor suggest that, in paying more attention to the process, outcomes be neglected. (See, for example, Stake, 1967, Parlett and Hamilton, 1972.) The case for process evaluation and more qualitative observations has sometimes been overstated, I believe, as a reaction against the narrowness of product evaluations. The strength of the advocacy is also in direct proportion to the degree to which mechanistic models are being adopted compared with more qualitative approaches. Like any different approach the case may need to be overstated to be noticed at all. But it should not be taken to entail a neglect of outcomes. Indeed, it is likely that part of the evidence for evaluating the processes of learning and schooling will be outcome data. But there are many outcomes of schooling (qualitative and quantitative), and these need to be related to the aims of teaching, the opportunities provided for learning and to the transactions which occurred in the classroom and school. The objection to product-efficiency criteria measures is to the narrowness of the measure, and the use that is frequently made of such measures.

The provision of relevant information is a third characteristic. Part of the argument against existing models of accountability rests on the fact that they do not, as Stake has pointed out, provide *relevant* information on the *quality* of educational practice and provision (Stake, 1976.) Descriptions of classroom practice and the ways in which policies are determined and translated within particular school contexts are likely to yield more relevant information for local decision-making, particularly if they utilize a range of information and judgements in describing and analysing the values, implicit or explicit in the policies and practice. An understanding of different attitudes and values towards the policy issue under discussion is essential if modification or a change in policy is to be an outcome of the evaluation. It need not be, of course. Evaluation is undertaken initially for the purpose of reviewing current practice and coming to understand some of the strengths and weaknesses in present provision. Change is a possible outcome but a next stage decision. The decision may be to leave things as they are. If the decision is to change, hopefully the evaluation would have provided insights or leads as to how this might be done.

The question is sometimes raised as to the relevance of specific studies of schools for national accountability. They may not be relevant, except indirectly. And not in the short term. But that does not detract from their value. In a decentralized system where many of the decisions are in the hands of local authorities and schools, development of forms of evaluation appropriate to the schools and local settings is needed. Locally is where many of the decisions affecting the *quality* of provision are made.

A fourth characteristic is the utilization of information and skills already available. Much information which can form a data base for analysis already exists in the school. It includes, for example, information on examination results, the academic and pastoral structure, the option system, the qualifications and allocation of staff to subjects, the resources available and their allocation to departments. A more extensive list is offered by MacDonald (1978) in outlining the first of a three-stage process of school self-evaluation. Implicit in such information are questions of value. Even a brief analysis will provide a basis for the elucidation of policies, priorities and assumptions.

Where evaluation of a policy issue is sought for the explicit purpose of review, additional data may have to be collected. Useful methods which need not take a lot of time and which utilize skills teachers already have include questioning, listening, observation, and the noting of critical incidents and dialogue between different members of the school. Data collected in these ways does not in itself, however, provide evidence: it has to be related to the issues and cross-checked for accuracy. Similarly, data will not provide information to inform decision-making unless the issues are presented in a form that is easily assimilated, a mechanism exists for the discussion of such evaluation and a commitment is undertaken by the whole school to considering the evaluation as a basis for decision-making. Written reports are economical and the most usual way of presenting information. But if they are to be used as a basis for discussion they need to be evocative rather than prescriptive, i.e. to raise questions, options, alternatives. Reports which are closed – tendentious, argumentative or conclusive – are rarely helpful for collective decision-making purposes. Written reports can, of course, be supplemented by recordings, examples of pupils' work, photographs. But in general, these take more time both to produce and assimilate.

How any particular school sets up the appropriate procedures to evaluate the policy issue chosen and utilize the evaluation to inform decision-making can only be determined in the particular context of each school in relation to the time available, the personnel who will undertake the evaluation and the ethos of the school, but some general principles necessary to ensure that the evaluation has a reasonable chance of being taken seriously and is instituted as part of a continuing process are indicated in a related paper (Simons, 1980).

My second argument – that in the short term school self-evaluation needs to be separated from accountability demands – is adopted for several reasons. The first concerns the nature of the exercise itself. Opening one's policies and practices to critique in a system characterized by privacy for so long can be a challenging but threatening exercise. What was once implicit now becomes explicit. What was once informal or the province of one or two staff now becomes an accepted part of the school's agenda for study. Even the most commonplace events and policy statements can raise controversy when the assumptions underlying such events and statements are discussed.

It is also the case, of course, that maintaining fictions about practice or the institution may be functional in preserving its stability and this is a stability that many may not want to see disturbed at least without some control over how and to what extent. For this reason I have, elsewhere (Simons, 1978), suggested a set of principles and procedures which give participants some control over the process and some protection from the risks of self-evaluations while they gain experience in documenting their own work.

Secondly, it seems important that school self-evaluation be protected for a time from public scrutiny to allow schools to build up the necessary evaluation skills to produce self-accounts. Some evidence for this point of view is presented in the final section of this paper. The ability of teachers to engage in this activity is not in doubt. One of the major premises on which school self-evaluation is based is that teachers and schools are self-evaluating all the time and have the skills to hand and the knowledge to describe and analyse their policies and practices in a relevant context. It is however, not common practice at the moment (although the trend is growing) and a certain amount of time is needed for schools to produce self-accounts and for teachers and outsiders to become familiar with the kind of data which is offered and the criteria by which self-accounts should be valued.

Given this situation it would be unfair at the present time to use a school self-evaluation as a school audit. Reflecting on one's practice can be disturbing in itself as those who have been through the process testify. Support is needed to sustain the exercise. Honest accounts of one's practice could be construed as evidence of weakness and possibly used as a basis for alleging incompetence. With so many highly qualified teachers on the market, it is not inconceivable that some heads and LEAs might want to use self-evaluation for this purpose.

A third reason, not unconnected with the second, is the use to which these accounts may be put. Pressures to go public too soon, particularly in a context of threatened closure of schools and teacher unemployment may simply result in window dressing or positive, glowing accounts. After all, what school is going to open itself to critique if that critique, undertaken in a genuine spirit of self-examination, has any chance of being used to arm its critics or put individuals at risk? Given the changing nature of governance and management of school and the increasing interest by parents and employers about what goes on in schools such an outcome is a possibility. One hopes, of course, that LEAs would not put the schools in such a position should they decide to undertake school self-evaluation; that they would respect their need for time to experiment with the process and production of such accounts and not expect to use them as an accountability mechanism before an appropriate time.

There seems little doubt that LEAs are increasing their interest in gaining more information about schools; some by taking up the DES's initiative to undertake parallel local testing to APU testing; others by strengthening the nature of the adviser's role to include an assessment of evaluation component. In several authorities LEAs have changed the name of their advisers to inspectors in preparation for the role they, or the elected members, think advisers should assume. Some advisers have undertaken their own surveys of schools. In one authority where this occurred, while objecting to the intrusion, teachers nevertheless recognized that advisers were also under pressure to justify their existence. That LEAs should have more information about schools is not at issue. What may be at issue is the kind of information sought, the means by which it is gathered and the purpose for which it is used. Ideally, schools and LEAs would have a consistent and mutual agreement on the position to be taken with regard to each of these questions.

A fourth related reason which is the core of the main argument concerns the structure of the educational system. Given the way the system is structured at present more information about the schools means more information in the hands of those who have the power to control resources; the heads get more information about their staff and pupils. Those in a hierarchical, and usually more powerful position, in short, get more information about those who are less powerful in the system. What is more, they may use their power, as already implied, to get access to evaluations undertaken by other sectors of the service for one purpose (e.g. self-reflection of school policies and practice) and use these for another purpose (e.g. resource allocation, employment decisions). If schools are to be more open to public scrutiny and be called to account for what they are responsible for it does not seem unreasonable to suggest that the other sectors of the education service do the same. Information flows one way at present – upwards.

The introduction of the APU monitoring does little to counteract this view if House (1973a) is right about the control assumptions underlying the hierarchical nature of most accountability schemes.

> In most schemes the goals are formulated by the higher levels of authority so that accountability becomes a strongly hierarchic matter. Teachers formulate goals for students, administrators for teachers, school boards for administrators, etc. Even where goals are formulated by lower levels, the accountability data are reported to those above. Students report to teachers, teachers to administrators, local agencies to state agencies, etc. Education is organized like a gigantic corporation in which each subordinate is strictly accountable to his boss. Few schemes suggest that the teacher be accountable to the student, to the parent, to his peers, or even to his own conscience. In essence, the individual is accountable to the institution, but the institution is not accountable to the individual.

Local authority accountability schemes which propose to follow the APU testing initiative are based on similar assumptions, but have an even more dangerous potential effect. Since LEAs have more direct control over resource allocation in the local environment, teacher employment and promotion, it is possible that the results could be used not simply to establish the state of overall pupil achievement but for decision-making. Those LEAs which have indicated their intention to undertake testing parallel to APU testing have also announced their intention to test all schools and not adopt the plan of light sampling adopted by the APU. Schools could be identifiable and resource decisions made in response to test achievements. Local authorities which choose to test are being offered assistance in this process by the setting up of the item bank project for local authorities at the NFER funded by the DES.

The point raised by House has a further implication in the context of encouraging schools to produce self-accounts. It concerns the openness and flow of information. How fair is it in the current climate to encourage schools to produce self-accounts detailing their practice and school policies, grounds on which decisions are taken and achievements reached if other institutions to whom they report are not to do the same? It would seem reasonable to expect that if schools are being asked to produce self-accounts of their practice and achievements, other sectors of the service should do likewise. In a democratic society the principles of openness and sharing of knowledge cannot be confined to particular groups.

It is perhaps important to point out here that in suggesting that schools control the availability of self-reports to outside audiences, I am not advocating that they become less open to public scrutiny. Quite the contrary. The issue is one of timing, confidence and credibility. I believe teachers and schools should be accountable and report upon the work of the school to parents and the community. But in order to demonstrate accountability they must be given autonomy. External imposition of accountability schemes may not produce a self-reflective teaching profession but simply engender defensiveness and hostility. This is partly because of the nature of external schemes – which emphasize measurable outcomes to the exclusion of other criteria – and partly because of the imposition itself. The most effective way of ensuring accountability is not to restrict people's autonomy but to make them accountable for it.

Giving control to schools over the timing of release of self-accounts is compatible with the concept of autonomy and is necessary for the reasons stated [earlier], concerning the production and criteria of self-accounts. The argument is not one for greater secrecy on the part of schools but quality control as the first stage in a process of gradually making information more accessible.

The third argument of this paper is that a process model of school self-evaluation can provide a more positive form of accountability than the current models in use. The dominant mode of accountability, House argues (1973a), is mechanistic, having 'productivity' as its ethic and power, not professionality, at its core.

> Most accountability schemes – whether they be performance contracting, cost-benefit analysis, performance-based teacher education or whatever – apply a mechanical solution, a power solution, to reform complex social organizations.

They are often, he goes on to say, punishing on individuals – who fail to achieve the pre-specified outcomes – and distorting of reality – since a single measure of output of precisely defined objectives is often the only indicator of value.

Evaluation on process lines allows schools to demonstrate and to account for what they can reasonably be held to be accountable for, i.e. creating the opportunities for children to learn and for the quality of provision. Given the wide range of factors affecting pupil learning (home influence, social factors, individual differences, interest and motivation, relationships between pupils and teachers), in the last analysis teachers cannot be held to be entirely accountable for what pupils actually learn or fail to learn. There is no accounting for the fact that some children may choose not to learn or not to tell what they have learned. The indicators of learning that are often used in accountability schemes are also limited, if not simplistic: they reveal what pupils did learn or did not learn on one measure but fail to indicate pupil achievement on other dimensions of learning. They also fail to indicate what contributed or did not contribute to the learning.

Pupil achievement, in short, is too narrow a dimension on which to base the case for accountability. Accountability should be related to responsibility and autonomy. Teachers should be held accountable not for the precise learning gains of pupils but for providing the appropriate opportunities for children to learn and for demonstrating the ways in which they have learned. Similarly, the LEAs should be held accountable for the adequacy of educational provision and for justifying their spending priorities. The DES likewise should be held accountable for national provision, policy priorities and administration. All sectors of the service, in other words, should be accountable for those parts of the service they are responsible for and over which they have autonomy of decision-making.

When one considers the weight of educational evidence against accountability schemes based on mechanistic models, and America provides us with lots of examples (see, for instance, Read in House, 1973b, and House, 1979), it seems surprising that in England at the present time a testing programme is being mounted by the DES with the same in-built assumptions that have dominated the American testing movement for years and which have increasingly been challenged by leading American educationalists, including those strongly associated with the test industry in the past (Cronbach, 1975). One is tempted to conclude that the exercise is only a political response to anxiety over standards and that those in power find a technocratic, rather than an educational, approach towards assessing achievement more useful in placating their own critics.

But that may be unfair. It is hard to disagree with the aspiration of central government to monitor national standards of performance. What one can disagree with, and what is at issue here, is the mode of assessment adopted to reflect standards, the specific measurement models used and the back-lash effects wide-scale testing may have on the curriculum. Particular difficulties with the Rasch model of item banking adopted by the NFER for the mathematics and language teaching have been well articulated elsewhere (Goldstein and Blinkhorn, 1977, Goldstein, 1979). The constraining effects on the curriculum are reflected in the American 'back to basics movement'. Even if teachers do not teach to the test, those subjects or areas in the curriculum that are not tested may become extraneous or be given less attention.

Here it is enough to counsel caution on the side effects of testing and to suggest that evaluation which takes a broader view of pupil achievement and pays more attention to process may lead, in the long term, to a form of accountability that reflects the quality and breadth of learning and teaching. [. . .]

Conclusion

The initial difficulties experienced by teachers in conducting self-evaluations for public scrutiny, whether that public be professional colleagues or the outside community, plus the need to build up confidence in the process both within and outside the school constitute a strong case for separating the development of school self-evaluation on process criteria from accountability demands on a traditional model. One form of evaluation cannot serve the purposes for which the other form is invoked. It is inappropriate, in fact, to compare the two since they operate on completely different assumptions. And it would be inappropriate to use a form of process evaluation as an accountability mechanism before the criteria for the production and acceptance of such evaluations were widely shared. Had school self-evaluation been initiated ten years ago, or even five, schools might be in a position to use it as a form of accountability now. As it is, it has taken the threat of external accountability to raise interest in systematic school self-evaluation (a fact that has not gone unnoticed by many teachers now concerned about the testing initiatives of central government (*TES*, 15 February 1980) and encourage teachers to assert the autonomy granted to them in rhetoric and, to a considerable degree, in reality.

External support, in the form of in-service courses and release time on and off site, now seems necessary if schools are to evaluate their practice to a point where it can become a viable form of accountability. The process will take time. But it will only begin to take place at all if the system becomes more, not less, open and demonstrates a commitment towards the sharing of information between different sectors of the service.

References
Cronbach, L. (1975), 'Beyond the two disciplines of scientific psychology', *American Psychologist*, February, pp.116-27.

Elliott, J. (1978a), 'Who Should Monitor Performance in Schools', paper first presented at ASC (Association for the Study of the Curriculum) Conference, March, 1978, in H. Sockett, *Accountability in the English Educational System*, Hodder & Stoughton.

— (1978b), 'Classroom Accountability and the Self-Monitoring Teacher', in W. Harlen (ed.), *Evaluation and the Teacher's Role*, Macmillan.

— (1979), 'The Self-Assessment of Teacher Performance', in *Classroom Action Research Network*, Bulletin 3, Spring, Cambridge Institute of Education.

Goldstein, H. and Blinkhorn, S. (1977), 'Monitoring Educational Standards—an inappropriate model', in *Bulletin of the British Psychological Society*, Vol.30, pp.309-11.

— (1979), 'The Mystification of Assessment', in *Forum*, Vol.22, No.1, pp.14-16.

Harlen, W. (ed.) (1978), *Evaluation and the Teacher's Role*, Macmillan, Ch.1.

— (1979a), 'Pupil Assessment', in *Classroom Action Research Network*, Bulletin 3, Spring, Cambridge Institute of Education.

— (1979b), 'Accountability that is of Benefit to Schools', in *Journal of Curriculum Studies*, Vol.II, No.4, pp.287-97.

House, E. R. (1973a), 'The Price of Productivity: Who Pays?', University of Illinois, mimeo.

— (ed.) (1973b), *School Evaluation: The Politics and the Process*, McCutchan Publishing Corporation.

— (1979), 'The Objectivity, Fairness, and Justice of Federal Evaluation Policy as reflected in the Follow Through Evaluation', in *Educational Evaluation and Policy Analysis*, Vol.1, No.1, Jan./Feb.

MacDonald, B. (1978), 'Accountability, Standards and the Process of Schooling', in T. Becher and S. Maclure, *Accountability in Education*, NFER.

Parlett, M. and Hamilton, D. (1972), 'Evaluation as Illumination: a new approach to the study of innovatory programmes', in D. Hamilton *et al.* (eds) (1977), *Beyond the Numbers Game*, Macmillan Education.

Read, L. F. (1973), 'An Assessment of the Michigan Assessment', in E. R. House (ed.) (1973b), *School Evaluation: The Politics and the Process*, McCutchan Publishing Corporation, Ch.6, pp.60-73.

Simons, H. (1978), 'School-Based Evaluation on Democratic Principles', in *Classroom Action Research Network*, Bulletin 2, January, Cambridge Institute of Education.

— (1980), 'The Evaluative School', in *Forum*, Vol.22, No.2, pp.55-7.

Stake, R. E. (1967), 'The Countenance of Educational Evaluation', in *Teachers College Record*, Vol.68, No.7, pp.523-40.

— (1976), 'Making School Evaluations Relevant', in *North Central Association Quarterly*, Vol. 50, No.4, pp.347-52.

— (1978), 'More Subjective!', paper submitted as part of an invited debate at AERA, Division D, March 1978, 'Should Educational Evaluation Be More Objective or More Subjective?', University of Illinois, mimeo.

Stenhouse, L. (1975), *An Introduction to Curriculum Research and Development*, Heinemann Educational Books, Ch.10.

2.8   A Year of Evaluation
A. R. Delves and J. Watts

Writing for a British audience, the Principal of Huntingdale Technical School, Melbourne, Australia and John Watts, Principal of Countesthorpe College in Leicestershire collaborated in presenting this report of the audited self-evaluation process in which both were involved at Huntingdale.

The conventional British approach to school assessment is patrician. The Full Inspection requires a team of Her Majesty's Inspectors to investigate all aspects of the school, to go away and after due deliberation to present a confidential report to the governors of the school and the Secretary of State. In practice there is likely to be a lot of valuable discussion between individual inspectors and classroom teachers, but in principle this is not part of the process. As the reporting inspector told the staff at Countesthorpe in advance of their Full Inspection of 1973, the inspectorate cannot at one and the same time report and enter into discussion.

It might be thought that such procedures ensure objectivity, free from favouritism. Unfortunately, that view turns on the assumption that in every aspect of schooling, from organization to pedagogy, from examining to counselling, the inspectorate knows best and the teachers will be judged on the extent to which they have 'got it right'.

Indeed the desire for accountability has often led politicians to call for a local inspectorate that would check whether a school was doing things 'the right way', on the analogy of industrial safety inspectors who can check conformity to regulations. It is of course a vain hope.

There are no regulations that add up to a prescription of how a school should be run, and in our changing times, there is no certainty that a team of Her Majesty's Inspectors have got all the answers for the teachers. Sometimes things will have moved on to a point where the HMIs have not even got the questions.

Many HMIs have acknowledged a change in role from that of judge-and-jury to one of counsellor, guide and friend. Many must prefer to sit

Delves, A. R., and Watts, J. (1979), 'A Year of Evaluation', *Forum*, Vol.22, No.1, pp.27-9 and 25.

down with the teachers and jointly tease out a problem together. Unfortunately, their own machinery for inspection and report has not undergone comparable re-designing. What schools desperately need is help in the techniques of self-evaluation and consultation, a totally different mode of giving account of themselves.

Teachers are amateurs in self-evaluation where they should be professionals, able to carry out mutual assessments and able to teach the techniques to their students. And to avoid complacency and insularity, they need to learn how to seek and take external counsel. To accomplish this may entail serious revision of our present procedures and of the function of the governing body. That it would be worthwhile, may be seen from the experience of Huntingdale Technical School in its evaluation of 1978.

In Australia, government primary and secondary education is controlled by the six states, with the Commonwealth government assuming direct control only in the various Territories. In the State of Victoria, school assessment was, as in Britain, the province of Boards of Her Majesty's Inspectors who reported their findings to the State Education Department and to the school, although without the element of confidentiality which surrounds British practice. Some eight or ten years ago this situation began to alter dramatically as a result of a series of fundamental changes. At the secondary level there was a significant move towards school-based decision-making in a number of areas and this inevitably led to a great diversity in curriculum across that state. At the same time, the teacher unions adopted strong policies of opposition to the system of inspection, chiefly because the promotion of teachers depended almost entirely on inspectorial reports. In addition, the inspectors, finding themselves often unwelcome in – and even locked out of – schools, sought for themselves the role of 'counsellor, guide and friend'.

These changes greatly altered the quest for accountability of schools. In the secondary high schools, the Education Department instituted a process of School Review Boards. Schools seeking assessment of their work ask for such a Board, which is then set up as a joint venture between the school and the Education Department. Control of this process, however, remains firmly in the hands of the latter. These Boards report to the school and the Department, as did the Inspectorial Boards of old, and there has been, to put it mildly, a mixed reaction to their work.

A further important recent change by the Victorian Government has been in the field of school government. In 1975, the Education (School Councils) Act significantly altered the role of the advisory Councils which had operated in all schools for some years. Firstly, each school community – parents, staff, students and interested people from the neighbourhood – determined the composition of its own Council. (In

Victoria, School Councils have never been *political* bodies in the way School Boards are in the United States, or Boards of Governors in Britain.)

The powers of the Council are wide, and include responsibility for buildings and grounds, for cleaning and maintenance, for all finance coming in to the school, for the employment (and payment) of non-teaching staff and for ensuring maximum community use of the school and its facilities. Councils may enter into contracts (for example, for building extension) on behalf of the school. Each Council is asked to *advise* (but may not *direct*) the Principal and staff on curriculum, and it has little or no role to play in the appointment of teaching staff who are placed by the Education Department.

In the case of the secondary technical schools, however, the Councils have by law a strong advisory role to play in the appointment of senior staff. In addition, the technical schools have had, by long tradition, control over all their operating finances except for teacher salaries. The importance of this power may be gauged by the fact that Huntingdale Technical School Council controls funds in excess of 150,000 pounds per annum.

The composition of The Huntingdale Council also gives a clear indication of the way in which the major groups in the school community is reflected in the overall government of the school. There are four elected parents, four elected staff, four elected students, four members nominated by a voluntary community group – the school is used extensively by the community at large – one representative of the local government authority and one of the Education Department, the principal, and up to four others co-opted by the elected and nominated members. It should also be noted that the term 'staff' is used in the school to include all employees at the school, both teaching and non-teaching.

When Huntingdale began in February 1972, the Education Department asked the school to examine alternatives for curriculum facilities and the development of community relationships. In return for this chance to innovate across a broad spectrum, the school was also asked to conduct an assessment of its work after the first five or six years of operation.

Self-evaluation

The process of evaluation began in September 1977, when individuals and groups within the school began to look at the positive and negative aspects of their work thus far. The School Council, at the same time, set up an *ad hoc* Committee to oversee the whole process, taking the view that it was the Council's special responsibility, acting on behalf of the whole school community and of the Education Department.

By early 1978, the criteria for the evaluation had been determined and agreed upon, and it was broadly decided that there was a need not merely to review what the school had already done but also to plan for the next five to ten years.

The evaluation included a range of activities, beginning with the internal evaluation mentioned above. The school also commissioned a 'Community Needs and Response Survey' which was conducted by staff and students of a College of Advanced Education, assisted by Huntingdale staff and students. Students who left the school in 1976 and 1977 were followed up to look at their job or tertiary education situations. A survey of the parents of Year 6 students in feeder primary schools was taken to establish why they would choose (or reject) Huntingdale for their children in 1979.

The School Council conducted an evaluation of its own work late in 1977, as did the Community Involvement Group which had an important role both as a committee of Council and as the management group for the community use of the school's facilities.

The major documents which had been written in and about the school since its beginning were also collected and published in a large volume entitled 'The Evaluation Book'. The Council also commissioned a Planning and Review Board of seven well-known educationists, including two from the Department of Education, to come and assess the school for a week at the beginning of August 1978. There was again emphasis on forward planning as well as on review. The Board was financed from school funds, supported by special Education Department grants, and its task was to report to the school community and the Council, and thence to the Education Department and the Minister of Education. In a very real sense, this procedure turned completely upside down the traditional school accountability process.

Council determined that the composition of the Board had to be such that the members were widely regarded in Australian education with a clear reputation for independence of spirit. At least one member of the Board was, at the very least, uneasy about the school and its work when the Review began.

This was not, however, to be the end of the evaluation, even if it was in a way the high point. The climax was a three-day live-in conference for members of the school community at a government-owned residence some 150 km from Melbourne. At this conference (The 'Lorne Seminar') *all* of the evidence of the various components of the evaluation (including the Review) would be considered and planning for the next five to ten years would take place.

In July 1978, the seven members of the Planning and Review Board (PARB) came together under the chairmanship of Ray McCulloch, Associate Professor of Education, Monash University, and chairman of the School Council of Huntingdale Technical School. The six other members were Jean Blackburn (Australian Schools Commission), John Mayfield (Director of Educational Facilities, South Australia), Barry Fitzgerald (Head of the School of Education, Ballaret College), Bill Johnson and Noel Watkins (both Assistant Directors of Technical Education, Victoria) and John Watts (Principal, Countesthorpe College). As their backgrounds show, they represent a broad coverage of the educational fields in which Huntingdale operates.

The terms given to the PARB by its chairman made clear that it was to be a part of the evaluation process and an aid to forward planning over the following years. The PARB was to spend a week in the school and to present a critical appraisal of the work of the school. All members of the Board were familiar with the school from earlier visits (even John Watts had spent the previous week in the school), and each of them had studied the recently compiled Evaluation Book, the extensive documentation of the school's six years of existence. Some members of the Board had had close contact with the school ever since its inception, and one member, Noel Watkins, had already seen his own daughter pass through the school.

It was made clear to the Board by its chairman that we would be reporting in the first instance to 'the school community'. The report would be public and it would be immediate, delivered on the last day of our visitation. It was, however, also clear that there was a wider interest and that our report would be presented to the Minister of Education for Victoria State.

In spite of initial announcements made to the school there was a tangible suspicion on the part of some staff, that the PARB had been convened to assess individual teacher performance. To establish good faith therefore, the Board announced on arrival that all its deliberations would be open, and that we would given an interim report at the end of each day. The PARB members were introduced to staff on the Sunday evening, and to the whole school on the Monday morning.

Open Dialogue

The daily report-back-sessions, starting on the Monday after school, took an increasing significance. All through the day members of the Board, singly or in pairs, would accompany staff and students, listening, questioning, and then at 3.30, would each comment on their experience, posing new questions, inviting comment, announcing their intentions for the following day. Once it was seen on Monday that the Board was being as good as its word, that an open dialogue was being created, the attendance grew from some forty or so to the two or three hundred who packed the long session of the final Friday afternoon.

The only session that became limited to members of the Board was that of the Thursday night, during which the final reports were hammered out, agreed and drafted. Not that the meeting was exclusive: very pertinent contributions were made by the Principal, who sat it out, and the Caretaker, whose perceptive and optimistic summary heartened us all round about midnight.

The PARB was given access to all records and personnel, but this access was reciprocal (in contrast to a British Full Inspection which is not open to reports or comments from parents or governors). Between them, members of the PARB saw teaching in progress, students in unsupervised study, pastoral meetings, staff meetings, curriculum discussions, a meeting of the School Council, and adult students, they examined equipment and resources, explored the site and the new buildings under construction.

The PARB had agreed initially that it would try to consider the ways in which the school saw itself serving its community, and the feasibility of the proposed use of its resources over the next five to ten years. The Board also felt it should comment on the ways in which Huntingdale's unique features might or might not be contributing any useful model for wider application. The task was therefore no mean one, and well comparable to a Full Inspection by HMI.

The climax of the week was Friday afternoon's presentation. Each member of the Board read a report, agreed in draft the night before, each covering one particular aspect so as to make a coherent whole. The presentation was public, and subsequently edited into a final document of some forty pages. Probably what is more significant procedurally is that what the Board had to say collectively was delivered before departure. There was no prolonged deliberation behind closed doors and no final anonymous and confidential document delivered to the Principal and governors. It is also significant that the conclusion of this intensely busy and stressful week came *after* the PARB's delivery and all the votes of thanks, with a satirical masque performed by students and a celebratory buffet supper for everybody. They may well have been celebrating the PARB's summary statement which concluded by saying that their school 'already ranks among the most prominent and promising break-throughs in the present world-wide quest for new and more appropriate forms of popular education. . . .'

111 members of the school community attended the Lorne Seminar for three days in November. Seventy-one of those were staff, twenty-two students and eighteen parents and other interested people. Sixteen of the total were also members of the School Council.

Prior to the Seminar, agenda items were proposed by anyone who wanted to put something forward, and these were distilled by the Agenda Committee into five main Topics: (a) A Caring Community; (b) Curriculum; (c) Beyond a Secondary School; (d) School and Community; and (e) HTS 1984.

Each Topic was introduced by a 'lead' speaker who helped to set the parameters for the subsequent discussion which took place in groups of about eight to ten people. At general sessions motions previously committed and new motions proposed by groups were debated and adopted only if a broad consensus was reached. Over forty resolutions were approved by this process.

One important outcome was the setting up of a Curriculum Steering Committee to recommend an overall curriculum policy to the whole school community. The need for this committee arose directly out of concerns about curriculum planning raised by PARB. The CSC is at present examining the relationship between the curriculum practices of the school, the principles on which the school operates and the general assumptions made by educationists about the nature of the curriculum process. It includes three or four advisers from outside the school, including one member of the PARB.

What did become obvious at Lorne was the strength of the consensus about the positive aspects of the school. There was an overwhelming re-affirmation of the principles on which the school operates, and of the need for Huntingdale to be both a learning *and* a caring community.

Without the Lorne Seminar, the Planning and Review Board would have been an end point rather than simply one (important) point in a continuing process. One suspects, indeed, that much of the value of the PARB Report would simply have been dissipated in an aura of self-congratulation without the hard-headed follow-up which placed the whole exercise much more firmly into context.

In any short list of implications for the UK must stand consideration of alternatives to the Governing Body and the role of the inspectorate. Huntingdale's extensive re-appraisal was effective as a spur to development because it was a corporate venture. Changes will be undertaken because the conclusions reached at Lorne were those of the staff, the students, their parents and the school's own Council. Nobody was acting under duress or made to feel they were responding to correction. And in the end, only those working in continuous contact with a school can decide what will and what will not work for it. A review, call it what we will, has to find a way of being both critical and creative: it has both to reveal possibilities hitherto unrealized and to inspire those on the job to devise the strategies appropriate to realizing them. We would claim that in these respects, Huntingdale's review system was highly successful.

2.9 The North Central Association of Colleges and Schools
J. W. Vaughan and T. E. Manning

At the time of compiling this reader, there are few British examples of externally audited self-evaluations or peer evaluations of educational institutions. The only notable exception is the CNAA procedure for course validation. Arguably however this approach is 'ripe' for development as a response to accountability. Drawing on experience elsewhere, the following extracts offer an account of an external audit operating in the United States.

The North Central Association was founded in March 1895 when thirty-six school, college, and university administrators met at Northwestern University in Evanston, Illinois, to consider the desirability of forming an association of educational institutions. Those present endorsed the concept and drafted a constitution stating that the object of the association was to be "the establishment of closer relations between the colleges and secondary schools of the North Central States".

That other educators shared an enthusiasm for the idea of a voluntary association focusing on the common concerns of school-level and collegiate education was evidenced at the first NCA annual meeting held the subsequent year. Eighty-two institutions sent representatives, demonstrating the professional interest in cooperation that presaged well the subsequent growth and vigour of the association.

The two published histories of the North Central Association (cited below) trace the decisions and actions taken throughout the past eighty-two years of the association's efforts to provide leadership in education. The books document the fact that although the Commission on Schools and the Commission on Institutions of Higher Education have for the most part been absorbed in their own work, there has always been a sufficient residue of goodwill to maintain the association structure that serves as bond within and as proof without that the overarching purpose of it all is truly "the establishment of closer relations between the

Vaughan, J. W., and Manning, T. E. (1978), 'The North Central Association of Colleges and Schools', in *North Central Association Quarterly*, Vol.52, No.3, pp.395-8, 399, 400-1.

colleges and schools of the North Central States".

This article describes briefly the two NCA accrediting commissions. Supplementing the work of each with their own institutions (each is autonomous in procedures and in accrediting actions) are the co-operative activities that constitute the association in action. These association activities are subsidized by equal contributions from the two accrediting commissions and are overseen by a board of directors to which each of the commissions elects representatives. Chief among the association efforts are: the annual meeting which draws several thousand educators to discussion sessions and business meetings; the publications of the association (the *NCA Quarterly* and the *NCA Today* newsletter speak to all educators); and the Council on Research and Service that funds research projects of value to the NCA membership, as well as develops common programs for colleges and schools at the annual meeting to support "closer relations".

The Commission on Schools: The Past as Prologue

The history of the Commission on Schools since its inception in 1901 may be viewed as an evolution through two phases: first, the decades-long effort toward the development of standards descriptive of quality education at the school level; then, second, the decades-long effort to help schools to utilize those standards (and the evaluation imperatives implicit within them) as bases for the development of programs serving the unique needs of the individual students being served by the school.[1]

At first glance the objectives of the two phases may appear to be contradictory — the earlier activities tending to nourish uniformity and commonalities among schools, the latter seeking diversification and particularity. But the fact is that only consequent to the development of prototype standards could the commission and its member schools learn to use those standards as tools and not totems. The two published histories of the North Central Association (Davis, 1945 and Goiger, 1970) recount the ways in which the commission has at various times in the past served as either agent of change or as safe harbor — whichever reflected society's greatest need of the moment.

Purposes

The commission's charge to itself is presented simply and clearly in the first article of its rules of procedure:

> The function of the Commission shall be to encourage and assist schools in the development, maintenance and continued improvement of a program of education that will satisfy the needs, interests, and abilities of individual students. It also shall be the intent of the Commission to encourage the member schools to adapt their programs and procedures to the evolving needs of society and of children and young people.

From those overarching goals, the commission has derived a program of activities centering around two major foci: accreditation and evaluation. Because other accrediting agencies sometimes use those two terms synonymously, the commission has defined their use for its purposes:

School accreditation is fundamentally a system of voluntary self-regulation. Decisions concerning accreditation are based on the degree to which a school meets discrete threshold standards that have been established as preconditions for all schools seeking or maintaining membership in a specific membership category. The process of school accreditation encompasses the totality of activities and functions of the Commission on Schools of the North Central Association.

School evaluation involves the relentless and continuous quest for school quality. It is the self-study and visiting team process that a school undertakes for the purposes of reviewing its present purposes, goals, and activities, and for planning future activities that will enable the school to improve the quality of service to its clientele.

The relationship between accreditation and evaluation within the work of the commission may be described as follows and an understanding of the interplay is necessary context in discussing the work of the commission:

The primary purpose of the requirement for a visiting team and the preparation of the visiting team's report is school improvement and is not to provide information upon which decisions are made concerning continued accreditation; however, if following a review of the Visiting Team's report by the State Chairperson and/or the State Committee a possible discrepancy is noted, additional follow-up information may be requested from the school so that an informed decision may be made concerning initial or continued accreditation. Accreditation is dependent upon the degree to which the school meets the Commission's policies and standards and not on the extent to which the school meets or exceeds its established goals and objectives. After all data relating to the operation of the school are examined, a determination is made by the State Committee whether or not to recommend the school for initial or continued accreditation.

As bases for its accreditation services, the commission has developed a set of standards for each of the constituencies it now serves: elementary schools, junior high/middle schools, secondary schools, independent college-preparatory schools, adult high schools, vocational/occupational schools, and optional/special function schools. These sets of standards (unique among the regionals) represent the commission's current consensus on the minimal preconditions necessary for a quality school program. Both quantitative and qualitative statements are included in the standards, and although the quantitative standards are subject to all the criticisms that may with justification be levied against any effort to "quantify quality education", nevertheless the standards seem to serve schools well in many contexts. Proposed revisions of individual standards may be presented to the commission at each annual meeting and it is an unusual year in which no revisions are made.

To provide structure for its evaluation services, the commission has delineated in its publication *Directives and Guidelines for School Evaluation* those essential elements required in all commission evaluations (for example, that the site visit be at least two full days in length exclusive of team organization time). The most common evaluation format is the total school survey consisting of a self-study, external team visit, then development of a school improvement plan evolving from the first two phases. However, the commission encourages schools to tailor evaluations to meet unique school needs and the *Directives* brochure offers for consideration a dozen alternative evaluation formats. Among the other publications developed by the commission to assist schools in their evaluation activities is *The NCA Guide for School Evaluation: A Workbook for the Self-Study and Team Visit,* which is applicable to all levels of schooling and may be adapted to numerous formats. Its use is not mandated; the *Guide* is offered as yet another option among the manuals available nationally.

Organization and Structure of the Commission on Schools

Because of the large number of schools encompassed within the nineteen states served by the North Central Association, the Commission on Schools has chosen to supplement the regional office with an NCA agency in each state. Some of the costs of these state offices are underwritten by the sponsoring agency (which may be either the state department of education or an NCA college or university); the remaining funding is from a subvention of member school dues. The sponsoring agency usually provides the services of the professional educator designated as State Chair, plus office facilities and support services. Among these state chairpersons the percentage of time devoted to NCA activities range from 25 to 100 per cent, depending upon the educator's other assigned responsibilities.

The State NCA Office administers the evaluation and reporting activities of schools within that state and serves as headquarters for the state committee which is composed of NCA educators elected to three-year terms by the member administrators within the state. One of the major responsibilities of the state committee is to forward to the central/regional reviewing committees convened during the annual meeting an accreditation recommendation for each school within the state. During the central review, the decision of the state committee is appraised by NCA educators from states other than the one under review. It is then the recommendation of the central reviewing committees that is forwarded to the commission for official action.

The governing body of the commission is the congregate of the nineteen state committees plus the Overseas Dependants' Schools Committee[2] plus the Administrative Committee. This group of about 200 educators convenes each spring at the annual meeting of the association in order to act upon business items presented to it and to determine the accreditation status of member and newly-applying schools, subsequent to the work of the central reviewing committees.

The Administrative Committee is composed of twenty-one educators elected by the commission to represent it between its annual meetings and to make proposals for the welfare of the commission and its member schools. To carry out that function the Administrative Committee meets at least five times each year.

The Unending Quest for Quality School Education

For the commission to "encourage the member schools to adapt their programs and procedures to the evolving needs of society and of children and young people" implies (1) a continuous monitoring and reevaluation of commission activities and (2) a willingness to accept a leadership role in education. [. . .]

That voluntary regional accreditation of schools has survived since its inception at the turn of the century is a tribute to the persistence and devotion of the many educators who hold it to be a valuable and necessary adjunct to the kind of educational system Americans prefer. Given the precariousness of its base of financial support, such longevity borders on the astonishing. Whether the regional accrediting associations can continue to be viable education-enhancing agents given the increasing activity of the federal government in this area and given the host of counter-forces cannot be known at this time. The North Central Association Commission on Schools is cautiously optimistic.

Commission on Institutions of Higher Education[3]

[. . .] The Commission now has on its accredited list over 800 postsecondary institutions with another over 100 in candidate status. Its work of evaluation (over 150 institutional evaluations each year) is administered by a staff of five full-time professionals. The pages of the *NCAQ*, as well as those of other journals, show that this staff not only provides for the day-by-day workings of the commission, but also is actively contributing to the development of accreditation procedures and theory.

From the beginning of accreditation the commission has relied on faculty members and administrative officers from other accredited institutions to make its site visits and review the accreditation recommendations. This emphasis on peer evaluation continues strong, with some 500 persons from member institutions now serving in this capacity. With the growth in numbers of member institutions the association and the commission have turned to new ways to maintain peer review: the original pattern of an annual meeting at which an official delegate from each member institution would be able to cast informed votes on accreditation and policy decisions does not work when there are over 800 members. But the Executive Board of the commission, which now makes those decisions, remains a group of persons, serving without pay, largely drawn from the member institutions – peer representatives of the members, now supplemented with persons representative of the public interest in accreditation.

Active cooperative among all the accrediting commissions for higher education of the several regionals is high. In 1964 these commissions formed the Federation of Regional Accrediting Commissions of Higher Education (FRACHE). [. . .] Through FRACHE the regionals began to develop common policies and public postures, without losing the desirable regional accents which keep them close to their member institutions. This cooperation continues today, broadened through the formation of the Council on Postsecondary Accreditation (COPA) to include other institutional accrediting agencies and also the program accrediting agencies.

Notes
1. The introduction and section on the Commission on Schools are written by John W. Vaughan.
2. The United States Department of Defense has chosen the NCA Commission on Schools to evaluate and accredit its overseas schools maintained for the dependants of military personnel.
3. Thurston E. Manning wrote the section on the Commission on Institutions of Higher Education.

References
Davis, C. O. (1945), *History of the North Central Association of Colleges and Schools, 1895-1945*, North Central Association of Colleges and Schools.
Goiger, L. C. (1970), *Voluntary Accreditation: A History of the North Central Association 1945-1970*, George Bania.

2.10   Evaluation and Advisers
J. Dean

In this paper the author, herself an LEA Chief Inspector, discusses the benefits and difficulties of advisers functioning as inspectors, a transmutation which (she suggests) is marked by a change in title in only some LEAs, but a change in function and spirit in almost all: a change in emphasis which is ". . . difficult to reconcile with the idea of teachers as professional people. . . ." We have added our own headings.

During the last ten years many teachers have developed considerably in the skills of self-evaluation. This development has stemmed partly from CSE and from teachers' involvement in curriculum development, particularly where this has involved Schools Council projects in which evaluation has been built in, but also from a growing demand from the public that schools should be accountable for the work that they do.

These two starting points lead to very different kinds of activity. On the one hand there is a move to get objective examination/inspection into a proper perspective and this has led to the development of forms of evaluation which take many more things into account and perhaps shape action and to a growing literature of evaluation and considerable development in techniques. There is also a greater consciousness on the part of teachers of the need for self-assessment and for looking at their work more broadly and critically and from more varied view points.

This professional view contrasts with a lay view which is beginning to be expressed more frequently by councillors, employers, parents and others. This view suggests that it should be possible to take the temperature of a school or education system without too much difficulty, by putting an educational thermometer in here and there. Those who hold this view believe that taking the temperature and letting people know what it is, will enable them to make judgements and comparisons and will give children and teachers something to aim for. This, they believe (with some justification), may lead to higher levels of achievement and may also lead to the view that test and examination

Dean, J. (1979), *Evaluation and Advisers*, paper presented at the annual conference of the British Educational Research Association, Brunel University, September.

results are a direct indication of the work of a school irrespective of the abilities and background of the children and the policies of the school over testing and examination entry. Explanations of the complexities of assessment may be dismissed as excuses for poor achievement and tend to lead to a mistrust of the professionals. There may also be considerable doubt about the value of non-traditional forms of assessment and evaluation, mode 3 approaches and forms of continuous assessment which are not external and objective.

The advisory service, standing somewhat uneasily between the schools on the one hand and the administration and elected members on the other and at the receiving-for-action end of parental complaints to the authority, tends to be very conscious of the gap that can exist and has to be concerned both to help teachers to extend their evaluative skills and to satisfy lay demands for information.

The changes in lay thinking over the past four or five years are clearly reflected in the changed role of the advisory service in a number of authorities. Some authorities have changed the title of their advisers and now call some or all of them inspectors, and although the title adviser remains in the majority of places, there is for most advisory services a greater emphasis on the evaluative and inspectorial role and more time than formerly is spent in this kind of activity.

This change of emphasis can seem difficult to reconcile with the idea of teachers as professional people although many advisory teams try hard to create a situation in which teachers are partners in the evaluation process. This view is evident in some of the titles chosen to describe a process which might once have had the unequivocal title of 'inspection', but which is now more likely to be called a 'co-operative review' or an 'appraisal' or something similar. Teachers also feel uneasy about possible changes of role for advisory staff as can be seen from statements made by a number of teachers' organizations about 'inspection'. It is, nevertheless, wise to accept a need for some external assessment of the education service and it may be that the professional observations of a good advisory team, which can take a number of things into account, is preferable to some alternatives.

Reporting on this kind of activity, especially in writing, is full of pitfalls for the unwary. There is also a change in the demands being made. Not only are far more reports of all kinds being called for, but there is a much greater demand than formerly for statements about levels of achievement which enable the layman to make judgements. This is not easy to do in ways which ensure adequate interpretation of what is said and many a Chief Adviser finds himself steering a careful course between the Scylla of the teachers' associations and the Charybdis of the elected members.

Advisers have, of course, always had an evaluation role. You cannot advise adequately without first inspecting to assess the situation and inspection which does not lead to advice for someone seems an unnecessary activity. Evaluation is thus an integral part of the process of advising both the schools and the authority. What has changed is the emphasis and demands made upon advisers which now cover a much wider range of aspects of the education service.

Part of the problem which advisers face is that the professionals and the non-professionals often work from differing frames of reference and this is not always appreciated by either group. There are often differences in view between teacher and teacher, teacher and head, adviser and teacher or headteacher, but the differences between advisers, teachers and headteachers on the one hand and parents, elected members and employers on the other are often considerably greater.

In any evaluation, an adviser needs to discover the frames of reference of those involved and arrive at some common view of what is being assessed and how the assessments are to be judged. Advisers need to be particularly sensitive to the frames of reference of the schools and teachers whose work they assess, if they are to be able to help and support them. This does not mean that an adviser should evaluate only in the light of the school's aims and the frames of reference of its staff, but that he should know what they are and make some attempt to see how far teachers are meeting their objectives, as well as evaluating against his own aims and those of his authority. He also needs to consider the ideas a given community may hold about the role of the school and the function of education and to look at how far the school meets the expectations of parents and employers.

We have already seen that a particular danger of the current 'outside' view is to count as evidence only that which is measurable or to regard it as superior evidence. It is easy to forget that however carefully we make judgements we can never do more than sample a small part of another person's thinking and behaviour. Moreover, people are not always consistent in what they do. All tests and judgements are therefore fallible however carefully constructed and there are many situations where the human mind is able to make a wider variety of judgements and take more into account in a given time than any testing procedures yet available to us. This is elementary to the professionals but is often not appreciated by others. An LEA wishing to get a broad picture of what is happening in its schools may get the most complete picture by using the professional observation skills of a good advisory team complemented by carefully planned testing. In this context testing will provide a yardstick for an adviser and may help him to identify the schools which most need his help and support.

Those of us who are professionally concerned with making judgements about what is happening in schools sometimes tend to forget that what we are doing is no more than an extension of the everyday practice of observing and making judgements in order to predict. We extend the ordinary human behaviour in various ways in order to make the judgements more valid. This may involve making criteria for judgement more explicit, and it must certainly involve thought and care in sampling whether this is a matter of looking at the progress of an individual student, the effectiveness of a way of teaching or a form of organization or the professional development of a teacher. It involves not only considering whether the sampling is representative, but giving thought to when sampling is done and how often and balancing the work involved in different types of sampling against the information they yield.

A problem about this for advisers is that of time. An adviser may set out to look at enough to make a valid sample but is called away to fight fires elsewhere. Or the report which was scheduled for the Spring committee cycle is suddenly needed in the preceding Autumn. Local government is not generally geared to long-term planning and there is often a lack of appreciation of the work involved in providing valid reports. [. . .]

Another aspect of advisory work seen as a problem by some, though not usually by advisers, is that an adviser who advises on work in school also has an involvement in the promotion of teachers. This, it is said, can make teachers feel threatened and perhaps less ready to reject advice which seems to them to be inappropriate. What is needed, it is suggested, is a consultancy service or evaluation teams whose views teachers may accept or reject without fear of the consequences. This is rather similar to the view that those who train teachers should not also assess their performance and it has the same attendant problems. It is, nevertheless, a view to be considered carefully.

The advent of the professional evaluator makes available for some purposes, an independent assessment of a situation, and this undoubtedly has value, if the LEA can afford it, not least in providing the occasional opportunity to evaluate an activity in greater depth than any advisory team can hope to do.

An alternative possibility is that the advisory service should divorce itself from promotion activities and thus from some of the ill effects on teachers which result from this. This is the case in at least one LEA. It would not wholly meet the critics since an adviser still would be seen as the agent of the employer, but it would go some way towards it. The effect of doing this would be to make those concerned with appointments turn to other sources for their information. The most important of these would be the heads of schools. A head must undoubtedly be the most important single source of evidence on the work of a teacher at the present time, but what happens to the teacher who is at odds with the head? It also means that heads might well find their own work assessed on much more limited evidence than at present, at a time when we are all conscious of the crucial importance of the quality of those holding senior posts in schools.

If appointments are to be made on real evidence of the way teachers work and are developing, then each school needs to be known well by someone in the authority who is in a position to advise those concerned with the appointment. The only way in which such a person can know the school and its teachers well is in being involved in helping them with the work they do and the day-to-day problems. This must involve evaluation if an adviser is to do anything useful. If evaluation is divorced from this, then it is unrealistic to expect to have a large enough group of people to know each school well, since this is clearly a problem at present staffing levels. At the same time, it is important to guard against the possibility that the head or teacher who is at odds with his adviser is at a disadvantage and this means that advisers need to be careful to check each other's views and that an LEA should seek more than one view of the work of any teacher or head.

One further danger of the independent evaluation team is that they do not have responsibility for the long-term outcome of their evaluation. The LEA as employer has responsibility for what goes on in its schools. The work of an advisory service must in some measure at least be judged by the quality of work in the schools of the authority.

We must, nevertheless, recognize that the role of the adviser enables him to do some things more easily and effectively than an outsider, because there can be an edge to the argument, and other things less effectively. There are occasions when an independent evaluation may help an advisory team to clarify its own views and convince teachers that its advice is disinterested. [. . .]

Whatever the specific function of a particular adviser, it will incorporate a number of evaluative tasks. He must also work to help schools and teachers to develop the ability to evaluate their own work, drawing on the skills of the advisory service. The tasks normally involved include some or all of the following:

1. Evaluation of the work of individual teachers in order to advise
(a) The teacher on the quality of his work or on particular aspects of it, in order to help him to maintain it at a high level, improve it, or use it as a basis for new developments.
(b) Heads and senior staff on the professional development of the teachers for whom they are responsible, and on the deployment of staff.
(c) The authority on the completion of a teacher's probationary period.
(d) The authority on the service of a teacher who is a candidate for promotion.
(e) The authority on the work of a teacher who gives serious cause for concern.
2. Evaluation of the work of a school or a department of a school in order to

(a) Advise the authority, governors or the head, head of department or other teachers on any aspect of the life and work of the school.

(b) Provide a base for new development.

(c) Find a way of solving specific problems and difficulties.

3. Evaluation across the institutions of the authority or a part of the authority in order to

(a) Advise the authority on levels of attainment, needs, effects of policy etc.

(b) Advise the institutions concerned of ways of working together.

(c) Discover the most effective ways of doing some things.

(d) Advise the authority on in-service needs.

4. Evaluation of the design of buildings in order to

(a) Devise briefs for new and remodelled buildings.

(b) Consider the implications of existing buildings for providing resources in staffing and equipment.

5. Evaluation of the authority's in-service programme.

6. Evaluation of its own performance as an advisory service.

Evaluation of the work of individual teachers is a major part of advisory work. A great deal of advisory staff time is spent observing teachers at work and talking with teachers and headteachers with the adviser continually assessing and making judgements in order to support and advise as well as for the specific purposes listed above. He is in this way contributing to the professional development of teachers and headteachers, sometimes directly, sometimes by considering the way forward with the head and senior staff.

There is a tendency to think of evaluation as something separate from the professional development of teachers. In a similar way professional development and in-service education are sometimes seen as separate from the teacher's work in school, though complementary to it, and if successful affecting it. Yet in a very real sense, they are all part of the same process. Much of the most effective professional development takes place because a teacher or group of teachers has identified a problem, assessed the situation and the possible ways forward, tried out a solution and evaluated the effect. New skills and knowledge may be acquired through this activity, sometimes by trial, error and practice, and sometimes by using resources inside or outside the school. More formal in-service training is at its most effective in this context, as is personal reading and study and observation and study of children and their learning.

Evaluation takes place at points throughout this activity; the situation and the problem needs to be explored before progress can be made; solutions need assessing for their suitability and the chosen solution which is put into action also needs to be evaluated during and after the activity though there is a tendency to stop short at this stage if the solution tried appears to work. It is as part of this process that much of an adviser's most effective work may be done, though it may not be regarded as evaluation. An adviser will, in the process of visiting a school and observing and talking with people, identify problems and points of possible development. There may be problems already discussed with the head and staff or problems not yet formulated. An adviser may thus be involved with the initial evaluation process and may start off or contribute to the search for possible ways forward. He may be used by head and staff as a sounding board for ideas and may suggest other schools which have found solutions to similar problems or books, in-service courses or other resources relevant to the situations and help the school to assimilate and make judgements about them. He may then follow up what has happened as a result of all the discussion and help the teachers to make judgements about their success, assess what worked and what has failed and how further progress might be made. [. . .]

Teachers and Self-appraisal

A very important part of an adviser's task is to help teachers to develop their own skills of evaluation. This may mean working with the staff of a school or an individual teacher to devise ways of assessing how well something is working or offering them evaluative tools, such as checklists or questionnaires and discussing their findings with them.

Education differs from many other forms of employment in having no pattern of regular review and appraisal of those who work in it. A teacher can still qualify, pass his probationary period and then spend all his days behind a closed classroom door, virtually unseen by any but his pupils and not seeing any of his colleagues at work. This is a great loss to his development and is something now changing rapidly.

If teachers are to become good at self-assessment, they need to be open to assessment by colleagues. Much progress is sometimes made where someone in a more senior post is ready to allow his colleagues to look critically at a piece of his teaching and discuss it with him. An adviser can sometimes be the catalyst in a situation of this kind or he may be the person starting off such an exercise. It helps if it is possible to video tape work done in this context, so that it can be viewed again and discussed. It is useful, though often salutory, simply to see oneself on video tape and to have a private opportunity to play over work recorded in such a way.

Many organizations build in a regular review of each person's work in which he meets with a senior colleague to discuss his progress towards his objectives. This can be a rather negative process if it is too formal, but properly used it can be a powerful tool for professional development. An advisory service can do much to encourage heads to provide this kind of support for their senior staff who may in turn provide it for their juniors. In this context, an adviser can well offer a head an opportunity to review his work with a professional peer who knows and understands its context. This would seem to be an area where there is much scope for development, particularly since it can help the head to think about how he is evaluating the work of the school. It also provides encouragement for long-term planning, which tends to be neglected in education. If this is a service offered regularly to all heads in a professional way, it makes it easier to spot at an early stage the head who may be failing and to support him without appearing to behave in ways which seem threatening.

It is often in the process of working with an advisory group which is looking closely at a school, that its staff themselves become more evaluative. It helps if the school is asked for such things as statements of aims and if teachers are involved in working out some aspects of the appraisal although if this is taken too far, the benefits of having an outside view may be lost.

The advisory service should be able to offer a school and the authority a global view of the school's activities, a view of what their work adds up to for the children they teach. It should be possible to make judgements about how effectively a school is catering taking into account its problems and strengths. Such judgements are valuable to the head and staff of a school who may find it helpful to have outside assessment from time to time and are also needed by the authority, particularly where shortage of resources makes it necessary to decide how some scarce resources can best be used. An advisory team may be called in to advise on the best use of one or two additional teachers in an area, for example, and a global view of the schools is needed to decide on the most profitable use of this resource which cannot be equally distributed.

Techniques

The development of this type of global review has led advisory teams to think carefully about ways of controlling observation in order to increase its accuracy and objectivity, so that the hunch of the experienced observer can be checked and verified.

There are various ways of doing this. For example, observations can be planned against some form of checklist or structured interview and one observer can be required to check his observations against those of another. Observations at different times of day, term or year may also give a fuller picture. This is not to suggest making observation too formal a process, because this could result in an adviser seeing only what he expects to see. What is needed is a disciplined checking of one person's reactions against those of others and a deliberate attempt to include certain observations or to see from a particular vantage point. The task of making a checklist of things to look for has considerable value as an individual or group activity in its own right for the professional development of an adviser or teacher making it, even if the list is put to one side and not used. Checklists of this kind are also particularly useful to those new to the service.

In a similar way, analytic tools, such as those put forward in the Cosmos courses, offer new insights, and an advisory team with mathematicians and others who can devise tools of this kind is fortunate. The information these tools give needs interpreting in each situation, but it offers a basis of comparison which is difficult to provide in other ways.

Where assessment is needed for a report which will be used to make comparisons or to select, there is a good deal to be said for having a list of the observations needed. Confidential reports on the work of teachers, for example, should be planned so that essential ground is covered. Written reports on the work of a school need to have something of a recognized format and an agreed style if a number of people are to contribute and this means listing the necessary information and observations in advance and agreeing on such matters as the use of teachers' names and whether the report should be written in the third person.

It is valuable to check how things are seen from different viewpoints. It is interesting, for example, to talk at some length with different groups of people within a school about how they view such things as consultation, communication, record-keeping etc. It is very likely that the views of the head and senior staff will differ from those of the more junior staff and that the pupils' views will be different again. Indeed, many things in a school look different when you attempt to stand where an individual child stands and try to see through his eyes and those of his parents. Much can be learned by spending a day in a secondary school following the timetable of a particular child or group of children.

The views of other parts of the advisory service are sometimes informative. Psychologists, in particular, more often see the school through the eyes of individual children. Careers officers and youth officers offer their own special insights. [. . .]

Other Demands on Advisers

Recent years have seen considerable development in the demands made of advisory services for evaluation of some aspect of work across the institutions of an authority. A specialist adviser may be asked to report on the state of his specialism. Reports may be requested on the effects of falling rolls, the in-service needs of teachers or the needs of a particular area or age group, the results of financial stringency and so on. Part of the task of a chief adviser and the administration is to anticipate such requests sufficiently to allow time for the necessary studies to be done. However well an advisory service knows its schools it is nearly always necessary to make some further study in order to give a valid answer to a request for information of this kind. Specific questions usually require specific study to produce specific answers.

This development has meant that advisory services have had to develop skills of a slightly different order from those used in looking at an individual teacher or institution. Some statistical knowledge is needed and some knowledge of techniques for gathering information, together with an awareness of the kinds of errors which are likely and the ways of countering them. Most advisory teams have among their members people who have this kind of knowledge and skill, but others have had to acquire it.

Part of this process depends upon the way in which a team records and exchanges information. Here again, there has been considerable development in recent years. Most teams now have much more systematic ways of recording visits and maintaining information than were usual in the past. These systems, like records in schools, need to be sufficient to provide the necessary information for reports and studies.

Records of this kind will also identify good practice and provide an advisory service with information about ways in which particular schools are tackling and solving problems.

Falling rolls are the normal situation now in many authorities. Consequently the role of the advisory service in advising on the design and equipping of buildings has changed from one of advising mainly on new or extended buildings to advising on remodelling and refitting buildings for different purposes. Skill in doing this pre-supposes careful evaluation of the effects of different kinds of school design and different sorts of equipment. This careful evaluation has always been important and must remain so in a climate of diminishing resources. When you can only afford to spend a little, the way you spend it is crucial. [. . .]

Self-evaluation of Advisers

All advisory teams need to practise what they preach. If advisers are to be credible as evaluators in schools, they need to submit themselves to various kinds of assessment. This is not easy and the pressures on most advisory services seem to leave little time for evaluation. It is all too easy to be so completely absorbed in dealing with the problems as they arise that there is little opportunity to assess overall needs, set objectives and plan to meet them. This should be a particular function of the chief adviser and senior members of the advisory team, but individual members of the team also need to set objectives and plan in the light of them, even if the pressures of fire fighting may mean that objectives must mainly be met informally in the course of dealing with problems as they arise. If the advisory team, or groups within it, also assess needs and set objectives, the individual activity of each member may reinforce that of other members and the process of planning provides some criteria by which progress may be assessed especially if the planning includes some consideration of how the achievement of objectives will be identified.

Advisers need to draw on each other's skill and knowledge to make judgements about their own work. An advisory team can set up the same kind of review process for itself as is suggested for schools. Advisers can provide for each other situations in which one looks critically at another's skill in lecturing, leading discussion, interviewing, questioning heads and teachers about their work, dealing with complaints and so on. Advisers can record their own performance on video tape and view it individually or with others.

In addition, it is important to try to get feedback from heads and teachers and from the administration, both about what they expect from the service and about the extent to which they feel they are getting it. There is also a sense in which advisers often check their observations by feeding them to those they observe and asking for their views. This often results in on-going modification of work, as well as giving an adviser feedback on how what he says is seen by others – though it should be noted that observations are not necessarily more or less accurate because they accord with the views of those being observed.

The advisory service recruits from experienced teachers. Each adviser brings with him from his teaching experience a range of knowledge and skills. He will need to extend these very considerably as an adviser, so that he gradually sees more widely and from more points of view. He needs particularly to develop his skills of observation in looking at the inter-actions between people at all levels in the school. He also needs skill in questioning and interviewing others to gain information, if he is to be able to take part in the evaluation of the work of teachers. There are considerable extensions of the skills he needed as a teacher though similar in kind. Experienced advisers too will need to check their observations from time to time in order both to maintain their frame of reference and to be sure that they are not becoming limited in what they are seeing or in the judgements they are making. These skills may be developed as part of a deliberate training programme or more informally through working with colleagues. There is much to be said for an organization in which advisers work in teams doing some work together and thus getting the benefit of other people's observation, skill and knowledge. A new adviser gains particular benefit from being part of such a team especially if the team leader has a training role which involves visiting schools with his new colleague and discussing work with him regularly. There is also benefit in a pattern of review meetings of individual advisers with their senior colleagues which enable members of the advisory team to assess what they are achieving.

It is often difficult to assess the effects of advisory work, partly because the good adviser may make people feel they did it all themselves. One important criterion of the success of an advisory service may be the extent to which its members have helped teachers to become skilled at self-assessment and have fostered thinking schools. In theory, this may seem to suggest that advisers should work to make themselves redundant. In practice it is usually the schools which have developed the highest levels of autonomy in their capacity to analyse their needs, evaluate and plan, which make the heaviest and perhaps the most rewarding demands on advisers.

2.11 Local Authority Monitoring of Schools: A Study of its Arithmetic
J. Pearce

In this article John Pearce calculates the problems and possibilities of LEA inspections in the effective monitoring of schools. John Pearce is a senior inspector with ten years' experience in the Cambridgeshire LEA, and from 1978 to 1981 he was Education Secretary of the National Association of Inspectors and Educational Advisers. The views expressed in this article are his own.

The 1944 Education Act empowers local education authorities to make inspections, but the great majority have rarely if ever exercised that power. While some have sought to do so recently, just as many have explored alternative approaches such as self-assessment and collaborative forms of evaluation. Many authorities, however, probably the great majority, have done neither of these things – because when elected Members have examined the case for setting up such new machinery to monitor their schools they have nearly always found that the work was already being done. The routine monitoring of schools does not make headlines: part of its purpose is, precisely, to avoid the disasters that do that. For the same reason, it seeks to be as continuous and as unobtrusive as water in the mains.

The typical LEA in England and Wales is managed by a professional staff of remarkably small proportions. Authorities with budgets running into a hundred millions a year are led by managerial staffs of twenty rather than thirty, with clerical and administrative support of a scale that industry would dismiss as laughable. This management works with the 'on site' management of schools and colleges, the headteachers and their deputies, whose establishments may range from hundred-teacher comprehensives costing up to £1m a year to run to two-room rural primaries. This partnership is distinctive, because the headteachers are professionals who cannot be 'managed' in the conventional fashion. Rather, the need is for a sensitive network of contact which enables schools and authority alike to be alert to each other's messages and condition. The needs on either side may range from the humbly

First publication.

practical like repairs to a thermostat to the deeply personal like emotional breakdown in a teacher. It is as important for the health of a school that its condition be known and understood in 'the office' as it is for the health of the authority that it possess up-to-date professional knowledge of its schools and their work. There is no universal wisdom about how this network should be provided. In the smaller education authorities which predominated before the 1974 reorganization, many education officers were their own field staff, and the deficiencies in specialist expertise which became apparent were fully explored by the Maud Commission. One of the best-known examples was the widespread installation of language laboratories in schools, which many specialist advisers in language work have regarded as unwise (and costly) investment. Larger education authorities had in some cases inherited well-developed inspectorates from the School Boards which had developed before the 1902 Act, and a few have retained them ever since. Other local authorities took advantage of special grants to appoint, between the wars, advisers for subjects thought to be important but in danger of neglect in elementary schools, notably home economics and physical education. After the Second World War there was a widespread but very uneven growth of advisory appointments in specialist subjects such as music or drama, but it was not until the 1970s that a majority of local education authorities had advisers for the 'basic' subjects. The spread of the comprehensive reform gave them a particular if transient role, but the titles 'inspector' and 'adviser' had become almost indistinguishable in most areas. A very few teams conducted formal inspections as routine; almost all other advisers saw their role in mainly supportive terms; and in most authorities inspection had the status of a regrettable necessity when all else failed.

This evolution was rarely a product of conscious thought about the needs of the LEA. A peripatetic force of professional officers occupying the complex interface between schools and 'the office' was partly a result of 'ad hoc' decisions, partly a product of the cross-fertilization whereby Chief Education Officers are usually appointed from other authorities. This movement naturally generates variety, not least in the scale, duties and remuneration of advisory staffs. The uneven nature of the pattern can be seen in the extent to which advisers have (or lack) what is known as a 'general' role over and above their subject (or 'specialist') one. In practice this may range all the way from being a deeply valued counsellor of headteachers to uncertain trespass on territory in which the adviser is simply not competent. Even so, in spite of all the diversities which make advisory work so difficult to explain to those unfamiliar with it, advisers/inspectors are now an essential part of LEA administration, and this paper now sets out to show how that works in practice.

The layman tends to see 'inspection' as an event, usually traumatic: the dreaded visitor arrives, tours the school, catechizes the pupils, berates the teacher (not always in private), and departs, sending a report to 'the office' which the teacher may never see. It is a picture fitting for the pages of *Billy Bunter* or *The Beano*. Reality is otherwise, not least in time-scale. For inspection is a process which need not be an event. Hence, the term 'monitoring' is more appropriate, and in this paper the term 'inspection' will refer to formal processes where the routine visiting of advisory staff is concentrated in time and directed to the writing of a report. Routine monitoring is a two-way process of contact. It may be supplemented by analysis of examination results or social data or test scores, but the heart of it is the individual inspector visiting individual classrooms.

There is no way in which this visiting can escape an inspectorial element. It may be viewed as mainly supportive, by the teacher as well as by the adviser, and the teacher is entitled to the visitor's help. But the authority is entitled to his information and his judgement. There is no uniform way of achieving the balance between the two roles: every adviser has to strike his own. One reason for this is the diversity of the local authorities themselves: the Isle of Wight and Hampshire are adjacent authorities, but the population of the one would just about fill the sixth-forms of the other. With some variations in manning levels and especially in curriculum coverage, local authorities maintain roughly one adviser for every 25–28 schools. (The London Boroughs have fewest but enjoy the best ratios, the rural counties have most advisers but with the worst ratios, and the metropolitan districts fall in between on both counts.) The least well-provided county has roughly one inspector for every eighty schools while the best-staffed metropolitan district has one for as few as fourteen.

For the LEA to monitor its schools adequately requires a definable minimum of routine visiting. For example, a subject inspector who already knows the teaching staff in a secondary school department, and has visited them in the classroom before, would expect to update his knowledge of the department with two full-day visits each year. If the department were a large one (and some English and mathematics departments number fifteen or sixteen teachers), or if the adviser or head of department were new to the authority, the time required would be much greater. An inspector has other sources of information, of course: public examination results, discussion with the headteacher, apparently casual meetings at professional functions and courses, participation in staffing interviews and career counselling of teachers seeking advice. Even so, on this general basis an average secondary school of some 50–60 staff and a normal set of departments calls for about 25 working days of routine visiting each year. Primary schools' needs would range from three to eight days a year, since the more isolated the school the more necessary a termly visit may be. These figures are rarely attained in practice: to most advisers/inspectors they are impossible ideals. Why?

Let us consider a medium-sized education authority with a population of about 420,000. If it is typical (and this one will have to be mythical as well) it will have approximately 220 primary schools, between 36 and 45 secondary schools, and six or so special schools. If the advisory staff did nothing else but routine visiting, they could sustain the frequency outlined in the previous paragraph with a team of sixteen. That would leave them no term-time hours for guiding probationary teachers, planning and running in-service short courses, formal advice to the LEA, taking part in staffing interviews, and above all providing close support to schools and teachers found to need more sustained and specific help. Moreover very few LEAs of the size suggested would have advisory teams more than twelve or thirteen strong, and they would certainly have most of these additional duties. The routine visiting thus becomes a balancing of calculated neglect of schools known to be in good heart against undue attention to schools needing help but able or willing to respond to it only very slowly. In these circumstances it is quite natural that schools already of fine quality should be visited less often than others.

There is some merit in the view that well-run schools do not need such intensive coverage, and in most LEAs they would not receive it anyway. That is not quite the same thing as saying that good schools do not need routine visiting at all, a position taken in the past by some teaching associations. To go on to suggest that advisers/inspectors duplicate the work of headteachers is distortion by overstatement: advisory staff supplement, support and strengthen the work of headteachers because heads themselves vary, the challenges facing them change, and isolation is almost as serious a threat to a good school as complacency. Given that the LEA is obliged to monitor, its assurance that particular schools are in good heart cannot be taken on trust from visits a year or more in the past: it has no option but to see for itself if it has the manpower. A good example of the problems of managing advisers' time occurs in their involvement in redeploying teachers as a consequence of falling rolls: many LEAs have found them ideally suited to the work, and some teaching associations much prefer advisers to undertake it; but its cost in advisory time is high, and the scale of the work hard to predict.

The quality of routine visiting matters quite as much as its quantity. The layman who has latched firmly on the idea of formal inspection may underestimate how routine observation may reveal the quality of a school. Advisory staff are by experience and training quickly sensitized to variations between schools which laymen and teachers alike may overlook or take entirely for granted. Advisers see many schools and hundreds of classrooms every year, and have an acute sensitivity to how pupils move in and out of classrooms; how their body-language speaks when a teacher arrives in a classroom; how long the class takes to fall silent or start work; how they behave when the teacher's back is turned. These can be observed without asking a question or looking at an exercise book, and advisers ask many questions and study many books.

When the routine visiting reveals weakness that needs to be remedied, how do advisers/inspectors set about the task? Let us take an example. Halley Lane Primary School lies between a pleasant suburban area and a decaying inner-city zone. It was opened in 1955 as a six-class school, but now has a staff of fourteen and 360 pupils on roll. The headmistress was appointed in 1967 and is now 54: she has recently returned to work after a serious internal operation. The deputy head, appointed to the school in 1959 and promoted deputy in 1964, is not the most energetic of men. Over the past two years the primary adviser has gradually won the confidence of head and deputy, and with the headmistress now fit again proposes some needed improvements. He briefs the head about disciplinary procedure, and she calls in three members of staff for private interviews with each: one is advised to improve her punctuality, one is warned that he has been found asleep in the classroom on several occasions after lunch, and one is invited to attend properly to marking pupils' work. No disciplinary action is suggested, but the possibility of it is indicated. Head and adviser agree about the poor standard of display in the school, and arrange for the head to take each class in turn while the staff, one by one, spend a full day visiting other schools. Unsure of her success in making teaching appointments, the head asks the adviser for help in some interviews due shortly. The structure of special responsibility posts is reviewed, some changes are agreed with the staff concerned, and each holder of a major post is offered systematic help — reading lists, other schools to visit, participation in local groups developing schemes of work. Schools vary, as do their weaknesses and the causes of them. The remedies also will vary, but they will have this in common: much more progress is to be made by slowly establishing mutual confidence and providing steady professional support than by any kind of disciplinary or inspectorial action. This reality explains why most LEAs have had so limited a place for inspection in the last few decades. At the same time, work as intensive as this with one school, which may absorb ten times its normal share of routine visiting, cannot be available to more than a very few schools at a time, and requires specialist primary advisers that some LEAs still lack: Halley Lane was comparatively fortunate.

Secondary schools are less tractable because of their greater size and complexity, but at departmental level similar approaches may offer considerable progress. Once again the critical element is the relationships between professionals whose standards are in question or have fallen and those whose duty it is to tell them so. However, a secondary school where several departments and the overall management share similar weaknesses is unlikely to yield to the kind of remedies outlined above. It is in these circumstances that an authority may well resort to formal inspection. A practical example will illustrate the process and problems involved when it does so.

Mount Wells High School is a 7/8-form entry 11–18 comprehensive school, whose sixth form also draws on two neighbouring 11–16 schools. It has a total roll of 1,266, a teaching staff of about 70, and works a 40-period week. There are in all 2,310 entries in the weekly timetable. The school has had an enviable reputation for music, but that is in decline, and in the past two years there has grown up a large body of criticism from parents and others in the locality. The complaints have alleged bullying, theft of pupils' belongings, refusal to use cloakrooms, some classroom disorder, laxity about homework, and plain bad teaching in several departments. The Director of Education, after consultations with members of the Education Committee, directs that a full inspection be made. A senior adviser is designated Reporting Inspector and eight others constitute with him the inspecting team. Discussion with the headmaster secures agreement to seven working days at the beginning of November.

Nine inspectors working for seven days at eight periods a day will have a total of 504 periods in which to observe lessons. The Reporting Inspector will have to resolve many questions, including these:
(a) Since each teacher is entitled to an inspector's comment on his work, is that discussion to take place after each lesson (when all concerned are under pressure) or after school in what some teachers may see as their 'own' time?
(b) With nine inspectors for fourteen subject departments, is he to leave five departments without cover, or to depute colleagues to cover work not strictly within their competence?
(c) Will each inspector choose what teachers and lessons to observe, or should he plot a complete timetable for all of them?
(d) Will the inspection's coverage of the general life of the school (such as discipline or pastoral care or curricular guidance) happen incidentally, or should each inspector be assigned a specific aspect to study?
(e) Will each inspector go away to ponder his report and write at leisure for the Reporting Inspector to edit into the full report, or will the team seek to reach a consensus before they disperse with tight deadlines for the writing?
(f) Will any serious inadequacies found in the teaching become direct grounds for disciplinary action, or would such action be postponed until after a more thorough study of the individual teacher's work?

These issues are typical of those which arise in practice, and every inspection will raise others peculiar to the local scene (e.g. how to cope with a split site or a ten-day timetable). Almost all LEA teams which have undertaken inspection have found it helpful to codify their solutions to such questions. This certainly avoids a constant re-invention of the wheel, at the cost of formalizing the inspection process still further. In practice, the first of the issues listed above is the only one on which individual inspectors retain much freedom. On the other issues, practice tends to move firmly towards the second of the options proposed above, and it is not hard to see why this is so. Thus, consider the arithmetic of 504 periods to observe 70 or more teachers, discuss their work with each, assess the management, timetable and organization of the school, monitor its ethos and pastoral care and sample its supply and use of teaching resources. To observe any teacher for more than five lessons might well be thought oppressive; to observe for less than four might well leave most teachers feeling themselves only rather superficially studied; but to achieve more than the latter at Mount Wells High School would be very difficult. Hence, even if an inspection is as tautly planned and managed as experience suggests is necessary, it is almost bound to disappoint the teaching staff. To do otherwise calls for a longer and more searching exercise than any *general* inspection could provide and remain manageable. Thus, a general inspection is not a disciplinary weapon. A factual assessment it must be, but for it to be factual to the exclusion of assessment is futile.

The structural differences between formal inspection and either routine visiting on the one hand or other forms of evaluation on the other are thus two. The first is in respect of finiteness: an inspection needs to have clear termini and a distinctive process. Curiously, however, the great majority of the individual contacts between teacher and inspector will closely resemble those which occur during routine visiting – a brief exchange in which the inspector indicates his approval, perhaps inserts reference to a better way of doing something, hears the teacher comment on the way the lesson plan's intentions went awry or were fulfilled. In conversation over lunch the inspector may relate how a teacher in another school solved the problem which he and teacher have agreed has defeated her that morning. It is the other structural difference which may show sharp contrasts with routine visiting: the report. This will be addressed to the Director of Education, but in most authorities is in reality written for the Education Committee. The nature of that audience poses professional problems to the writer: how technical should the report be? How long? How should he treat deficiencies which have already been put right? How should he attribute responsibility for faults? (Some LEAs insist on naming teachers individually, but most LEA inspectors would view that as unprofessional practice.)

These issues touch in turn on the central argument pertaining to inspection by the LEA, which is the suggestion, first made by teaching associations in 1975, that inspectors employed by the LEA are thereby not professionally independent. From the inspector's point of view such an argument is redolent of special pleading, since an inspection report which appears unduly independent and severe can be impugned as prejudiced or politically inspired or even influenced by prejudgement by the inspectors. On the other hand, inspectors are experienced teachers, and they and the teachers are alike servants of the same authority for the good of the same children. Inspectors do not need to be told that their presence may change the very classroom behaviours they are there to observe, although they may not be chiefly interested in the teacher's 'performance' when there are so many other aspects to observe which the teacher cannot change for the occasion. Behind the procedures and formalities an inspection is about competent specialist teachers watching teachers at work. The rarity of such an event is bound to put the teachers on their mettle, to make some of them very nervous and inhibit others – facts which the inspectors well know and make full allowance for. Inspection is also about comment – laudatory if possible, constructive always, geared to the improvement of the teacher's work with his pupils. But inspection is a cumbersome method of generating professional development and extension in the individual teacher. As an exercise in professional development self-assessment seems full of potential, but it would be incautious to suppose that it can replace an authority's need to be able to inspect. Self-assessment needs to be viewed as assembling inspection and routine monitoring as one of a range of approaches to accountability which complement and supplement one another.

References

Becher, R. A. (1978), 'Ends, Means and Policies', in Becher and Maclure (1978).
– and Maclure, S. (1978), *Accountability in Education*, NFER.
Craddock, J. (1979), 'Looking at Schools in Hillingdon', *Journal of National Association of Inspectors and Educational Advisers*, No.10, Spring, p.8.
Elliott, J. (1979), 'The Case for School Self-Evaluation', *Forum*, Vol.22, No.1, September.
Fiske, D. A. (1979), 'The Adviser's Skills', *Journal* of NAIEA, No.11, Autumn, p.9.
Lello, J. (ed.) (1979), *Accountability in Education*, Ward Lock.
ILEA (1977), *Keeping the School under Review*, London County Hall.
Oxfordshire Education Department (1979), *Starting-points in Self-evaluation*, Oxford County Hall.
Wilcox, B. (1978), 'An LEA Perspective on Evaluation', *Journal* of NAIEA, No.8, Spring, p.7.

PART 3: STRATEGIES AND TECHNIQUES

Editors: John Bynner and Caroline Morrow Brown

3.1   The Politics of Curriculum Evaluation
D. Lawton

This overview provided by Lawton, in an abridged chapter from his book, Politics of the School Curriculum, *emphasizes the political context of evaluation and describes the evolution of evaluation strategies through six overlapping models. These display the shift of focus from the effects of success in the achievement of pre-specified educational performance goals, via the "illumination" of the classroom processes of teaching and learning; to eclectic case study of educational processes and products in a particular educational setting. One of these models – illuminative evaluation – is examined in more detail in the articles by Parlett and Parsons which follow.*

[. . .] Ernest House at the beginning of his book on evaluation in the USA (*School Evaluation: the Politics and Process*, 1973) makes the point that evaluation is inevitably a political enterprise:

> The major theme of the book is the political nature of evaluation. Contrary to common belief, evaluation is not the ultimate arbiter, delivered from our objectivity and accepted as the final judgement. Evaluation is always derived from biased origins. When someone wants to defend something or to attack something, he often evaluates it. Evaluation is a motivated behaviour. Likewise, the way in which the results of an evaluation are accepted depends on whether they help or hinder the person receiving them. Evaluation is an integral part of the political processes of our society.

This statement is no less true in the UK than in the USA. Evaluation is becoming a very important political issue in education in at least two ways. First, there is a growing recognition that more evaluation needs to take place at various levels within the schools themselves as an answer to demands for accountability. Second, there is a need to evaluate the expensive curriculum projects financed by the Schools Council or other financing bodies.

Evaluation has often been seen simply as a process of measuring the success of teaching in terms of pupils' learning. More fundamental

Lawton, D. (1980), 'The Politics of Curriculum Evaluation', in *Politics of the School Curriculum*, Routledge & Kegan Paul.

questions about the value of that particular teaching—learning process have frequently been ignored. But evaluation should be concerned not only with how well a group of students have learned a particular set of skills or kind of knowledge, evaluation must also be concerned with questions of *justification* (why should they learn X?) as well as the unintended consequences of learning (what else do they learn?; by learning X what else do they fail to learn?).

In England, and to some extent in the USA and Sweden, curriculum evaluation developed as a by-product of curriculum development projects. In some cases the evaluation came almost as an afterthought. Those who had financed the innovation wanted to know whether it worked — simply in terms of how much did the pupils learn, or how much more did they learn than they would have with a more traditional approach. By contrast, today it is usually thought that evaluation must be concerned with the total context of an educational situation: its causes and its results.

Evaluation is much wider than *measurement*. Although evaluation does not necessarily exclude the use of assessment, or measuring techniques, or examinations, it must necessarily invoke attention to other aspects of the learning process in a wider context. For example if we decide that it would be a valuable experience for a group of students to learn some history, we may want to test what history they have learned as a result of a particular programme. It may, however, be much more important to know whether they will still be interested in history ten years later, long after they have left school. Such long-term effects are rarely tested, although they are clearly more important than short-term memorization. One of the paradoxes in education and one of the major difficulties of evaluation is that teachers are unable to find out what they would really like to know about long-term learning processes. So teachers tend to settle for something else — something easier to test, such as short-term recall of specific facts. But this gives a false importance to certain kinds of tests. House (1973) defines evaluation in this way:

> At its simplest, evaluation is the process of applying a set of standards to a programme, making judgements using the standards, and justifying the standards and their application. But there are many standards, especially in a pluralist society: which to apply? There are many ways of using standards. Often the initiator of the evaluation determines the standards: if a school superintendent wants to defend a programme, he usually chooses the ground on which it is evaluated; if a school critic wishes to attack a programme, he chooses different standards. Whichever side the results favour will use them to gain political advantage. Evaluation becomes a tool in the process of who gets what in this society (p.3).

It is clearly too naive to see evaluation in terms of a neutral evaluator who applies certain objective standards to the project and then produces an evaluation answer, preferably in the form of neat percentages. The reality is much more complex. An evaluator will use (consciously or not) a model of some kind with certain built-in assumptions, advantages and disadvantages. Another difficulty is that evaluators are often not clear about the role they are expected to play. Are they scientists testing a hypothesis by a curriculum experiment? Or are they technologists starting with a specification on which they base an evaluation design to assess the efficiency of the product? Or are they indulging in some kind of art form?

If evaluation tends to be biased because evaluators have certain positions, it may be useful to be aware also of different models of evaluation so that certain kinds of presuppositions can be detected and guarded against.

Six overlapping models will be examined below. They are overlapping in two senses: chronologically and in terms of content and methodology. To some extent it is true that the one model has arisen from the ashes of an old model, but this is by no means wholly true. Many evaluators have no desire to depart from either model 1 or model 2. The six models to be examined (in semi-chronological order) are:

1. The classical (or agricultural–botanical) research model.
2. The research and development (or industrial, factory) model.
3. The illuminative (or anthropological, responsive) model.
4. The briefing decision-makers (or political) model.
5. The teacher as researcher (or professional) model.
6. The case study (or eclectic, portrayal) model.

1. The Classical (or Agricultural–Botanical) Research Model

The classical experimental model of evaluation treats the problem of evaluating the success of any particular learning programme, or curriculum project, or new textbook as a simple matter, essentially the same as an experiment in agriculture or botany. An educationist measures success just as an agriculturalist might test the efficiency of a new fertilizer by: (i) measuring the height of a plant; (ii) applying the fertilizer for a given amount of time; then (iii) measuring again comparing the growth of the 'experimental' plants with that of plants in a control group (which have not received the benefit of the fertilizer). Much of the reaction against applying that kind of experimental design to children's learning rests on the argument that the teaching–learning situation is much more complex. For example, human beings perform differently when under observation, cabbages do not; the unintended consequences of human interference are likely to be much more important in any situation involving human beings.

Apart from that very fundamental objection to the use of that particular experimental model, there are more technical difficulties. For example, with a class of children there are usually far too many variables to produce a nice, neat experiment such as the agricultural one quoted above. Either very large samples are needed or very strict controls are required which raises difficult ethical questions. There is also a tendency in this kind of experimental model to concentrate on the *average* differences between the control group and the experimental group, and to ignore the important *individual* differences.

Another objection is the alleged tendency for experimenters to measure what is easily quantifiable, rather than, for example, much more important long-term results. An important technical difficulty, or perhaps it is a fundamental one, is that the tests which are used (before and after the educational treatment) in this kind of experiment tend to assume that the same thing is being taught to the experimental group as to the control group. But this is not necessarily so: it is not possible to evaluate new mathematics teaching by traditional mathematical test or vice versa. Applying a new teaching programme is much more complicated than applying fertilizer to some plants. However, the tests are often used and interpreted as though they were not problematical at all. They are used politically, even if the researchers/evaluators believe they are completely neutral.[1]

2. The Research and Development (or Industrial, Factory) Model

This model might be considered to be simply a variation of the classical research model, but I think there is enough to distinguish it from that mode to consider it separately. The research and development model sees the problem of evaluation not as a classical agricultural experiment but more like the industrial process of improving upon or testing out a product. According to this model all curriculum development should begin with *research*, one result of which would be a clear statement of goals. The industrialist must know exactly what he is trying to produce. The school should know what kind of difference in pupil behaviour will be achieved by a particular programme.

With this model the evaluator's task is:

1. To translate general aims into specific, measurable, behavioural objectives.
2. To devise a battery of tests to assess the student performance (before and after the programme).
3. To administer these tests with a sample of schools adopting the innovative programme.
4. To process results to yield useful information to the team who are producing the new programme (formative evaluation)[2] or to the sponsors and potential adopters of the project (summative evaluation).[3]

A control group may or may not be considered necessary, partly according to the views of the evaluator, partly according to the precise nature of the project.

There are a number of objections to this kind of evaluation model, some of them overlapping with the criticisms of the classical experimental model.

1. There are theoretical as well as practical difficulties in translating aims into *behavioural* objectives. It is possible for an evaluator to do this when dealing with simple skill-learning such as typing, early reading or basic arithmetic, but impossible in fields such as English literature, art, music or social studies. The translation of aims into objectives rests on the false atomistic, assumption that education can be reduced to a checklist of learned responses.

2. If education cannot be reduced to a list of specific behavioural responses, then the task of testing is made much more difficult – in some cases impossible. Even within their own terms of reference, evaluators of the objectives school have greater difficulties than they admit: changes in *behaviour* cannot be measured sufficiently accurately to enable valid judgements to be made.

3. Samples are rarely found to be representative: schools are a nightmare world for the statistician: variables cannot be held constant.

4. Another problem is that this kind of measurement-based study, involving pre- and post-testing, allows little or no modification to the teaching programme. Formative evaluation, which is the most important kind in a development project, is sacrificed for accuracy in terms of summative evaluation.

Perhaps more important than all of these is that such a testing programme fails to see the organism of the school or the class as a whole: it is essentially reductionist.

Several Schools Council projects have started on the basis of objectives, but have moved away from that model during the course of evaluation. The Schools Council Classics Project is one example; 'Science 5-13' is another, and has the advantage of being written up in considerable detail (see Schools Council, 1973). Perhaps the most systematic example of this model was, however, the Swedish IMU mathematics project. The purpose of this project was to produce self study materials for secondary pupils: it was based on the idea of a common mathematics curriculum with three levels. A change in level from one module to the next was made on the basis of diagnostic tests. In this project the teacher became much more a manager and tutorial adviser to individual pupils rather than a didactic classroom performer. The evaluation study was very carefully planned beforehand: the evaluation deliberately excluded any subjective reactions of the teachers and the pupils and deliberately excluded any 'political' context from parents and others. The measured results seem to be extremely impres-

174 Calling Education to Account

sive: they indicated that the project was a considerable success in terms of pupil learning. The evaluation did not however indicate a number of other factors which were eventually considered to be even more significant: (a) pupils' boredom; (b) the dissatisfaction of the teachers who did not like their new role; (c) the political use of the project (i.e. to justify mixed ability teaching in comprehensive schools).

3. Illuminative Evaluation

Alternative models of evaluation have developed partly to meet objections to the Classical and Industrial models but also for more positive reasons. Parlett and Hamilton's 'Evaluation as Illumination' (1972) was a seminal paper in this respect. Much of the interest in the new evaluation is that it shifts the style of educational research generally as well as curriculum evaluation in particular. This is of considerable political interest. Another motive was the comparative lack of success, or failure of 'take-up', of many large and expensive curriculum projects (partly for reasons discussed in connection with the Swedish IMU project). Teachers in both the USA and the UK, when they were free to make a choice, appeared to resist the supposed advantages of innovatory programmes even when there was 'evidence' to show that the new programmes were better than the traditional alternative. Teachers seem to be unconvinced by the kind of evidence produced by Classical or Industrial models of evaluation.

Clearly other kinds of evidence were also necessary in addition to the test results obtained from a handful of picked experimental schools. Another aspect of experimental and industrial evaluation which has received considerable criticism was the emphasis on size: a necessary feature of traditional experiments was the large sample capable of showing differences that could be measured and seen to be statistically significant. But many evaluators have come to the conclusion that large samples were not only unnecessary and costly, but had other disadvantages. Bob Stake, for example, has suggested that what was needed at that stage of evaluation was a panoramic view finder rather than a microscope. Stake was not criticizing the use of empirical methods, but simply asserting that many evaluators had moved to detailed measurement much too soon: they should have first acquired a better means of describing the full picture of an evaluation situation.

Many evaluators would agree with criticisms of the old models but are uncertain about the alternatives being proposed. In December 1972 the conference of the 'new wave' evaluators was held in Cambridge at which the reasons for the shift away from the experimental model to qualitative forms of evaluation were explored. The participants were not in agreement about all the issues under discussion but they managed to produce a statement which indicated some major shifts in concern.

They suggested, for instance:

1. that traditional methods of evaluation had paid too little attention to the whole educational process in a particular milieu, and too much attention to those changes in student behaviour which could be measured;
2. that the educational research climate had underestimated the gap between school problems and conventional research;
3. that curriculum evaluation should be responsive to the requirements of different audiences, illuminative of complex organizational processes, and relevant to both public and professional decisions about education (MacDonald and Parlett, 1973, pp. 79-80).

More specifically the conference recommended that: (a) observational data should be carefully validated and used for evaluation; (b) evaluation designs should be flexible enough for response to unanticipated events (progressive focusing not pre-ordinate design); and (c) the value position of an evaluator should always be made explicit.

There was however no agreement among the evaluators on whether evaluation should consist of observations being interpreted by the evaluator himself or whether the evaluators' role was simply to present data. These problems are, to some extent, familiar problems of social anthropology and the method known as participant observation. Illuminative evaluation is much more than participant observation, of course, but it has sometimes been suggested that whereas the traditional methods of evaluation (classical, experimental and research and development) were heavily influenced by behaviouristic and industrial psychology, illuminative evaluation is similarly indebted to the methodology of social anthropology.

A number of doubts have been expressed about the so-called anthropological or illuminative paradigm of evaluation:

1. Although there are established rules of procedure for anthropologists working in unfamiliar societies, and participant observers working within organizations of various kinds in advanced societies, these procedures themselves are still somewhat controversial, and it does not necessarily follow that they can be carried over into the field of curriculum evaluation or educational research.
2. The rules of procedure for non-traditional evaluation are insufficiently clear, and the skills, both professional and personal, needed by evaluators should be specified more clearly. There is, as yet, no tradition comparable to the established standards in historical and anthropological research.
3. There is a danger of personal, subjective impressions being put forward as objective data.
4. The problem of role conflict is very great for evaluators and may place them under conditions of intolerable strain.

5. There is a danger that because these difficulties exist, evaluators will develop esoteric methods and language which will make curriculum evaluation just as remote from teachers and administrators as conventional educational research.

4. Briefing Decision-makers (the Political Model)

Barry MacDonald, who has had much to do with the development of the political model, would probably object to being called an illuminative evaluator since he prefers to use a mixture of methodologies in his evaluation projects. He was very much concerned with the evaluation of the Humanities Curriculum Project (HCP) which rejected the idea of objectives, but which used measurement and conventional tests as well as more holistic approaches.

Cronbach (1963) suggested that evaluation should not simply be concerned with providing information about the success of teaching or learning, but with information about which decisions have to be made. Cronbach suggested that there were three main types of decision which evaluators would provide information about:

1. Course improvement: deciding what materials and methods are satisfactory and where change is needed.
2. Decisions about individuals, identifying the needs of pupils and judging pupil merit and deficiencies.
3. Administrative regulation: judging how good the school system is, how good an individual school or individual teachers are.

According to MacDonald (1976) evaluation is inevitably concerned with attitudes to the distribution of power in education. Outlining three 'ideal types' – bureaucratic, autocratic and democratic evaluation – he suggests that the style of an evaluation study is related to a particular political stance. He maintains that much research, including educational research, is closely related to ideology; evaluators should stop pretending that they are value-free and be explicit about what the values in question are. For MacDonald evaluation is not a simple task of making a judgement about the success of an educational programme and passing it on to decision-makers; it is a complex process of collecting information (including judgements) which will enable the decision-makers to make a more rational choice. The evaluator is concerned with making judgements, but the final choice is not his. This does not mean that the evaluator simply passes on information which the decision-makers will find acceptable; it does mean that the evaluator has to recognize the value stance of the decision-makers. The evaluator has to be aware of the total context of the educational programme. To illustrate this point MacDonald quotes an American researcher who had been asked to evaluate a state's 'bussing' policy. On educational grounds she strongly recommended the continuation of the policy of bussing pupils from one area into schools in another area; but the decision-makers ignored her recommendation, and the bussing was discontinued. MacDonald remarked that it was a good piece of educational research but an inadequate evaluation since it had ignored the political context in which the educational decision had to be made.

Against this political background of evaluation for decision-making, MacDonald describes his three ideal types. The implication is that evaluators ought to know what type of evaluation they are likely to be involved in and negotiate a contract accordingly, or possibly decide to withdraw from the field.

BUREAUCRATIC EVALUATION

Bureaucratic evaluation is an unconditional service to those government agencies controlling educational resources. The evaluator accepts the values of those holding office and provides information to help them accomplish their policy objectives. His role is that of a management consultant. His criterion of success is client satisfaction. The report is owned by the bureaucrats. His attitude must therefore be 'You pay me a fee; I will give you information and advice; and you can do whatever you like about it.' This might be described as the 'hired hack' role. The key concepts in this style of evaluation are, according to MacDonald: service, utility, and efficiency. The justificatory concept in bureaucratic evaluation is the reality of power.

AUTOCRATIC EVALUATION

This style of evaluation involves a conditional service to those agencies which control educational resources. It is a system of external validation by the evaluator in exchange for strict compliance with the recommendations of the evaluator. The values are derived from the evaluator's perception of the constitutional and moral obligations of the bureaucracy. In this style of evaluation the focus is upon issues of educational merit; the role of the evaluator is that of expert adviser. The techniques of study must be seen as yielding scientific proofs because the evaluator's power base is the academic research community. His contract must guarantee complete non-interference by his bureaucratic clients or whoever the clients are. The evaluator retains ownership of his evaluation report. The position of the evaluator is autocratic in the sense that he says 'I will give you advice which you *must* take!' He is the evaluator king. The key concepts in autocratic evaluation are: principle and objectivity. The justificatory concept is responsibility of office.

DEMOCRATIC EVALUATION

Democratic evaluation attempts to be an information service to the whole community. Sponsorship by one particular group, such as the bureaucrats, does not give them a special claim to advice or secret information. The assumption behind this style of evaluation is 'value pluralism', i.e. that there is no consensus about basic values and basic educational issues. The only value which can be assumed is the desirability of an informed citizenry. The role of the democratic evaluator is that of an 'honest broker'. An essential requirement is that the data collected by the evaluator must be accessible to non-specialists. Another aspect of this style of evaluation is that the evaluator must offer confidentiality to his informants and he thus gives them control of the data, or at least partial control. The evaluator's report must be non-recommendatory. The criterion of success with this style of evaluation is the range of audiences served: the information provided by the evaluator must be understood by a wide range of the citizenry and enable them to make better decisions. The position of the evaluator would seem to be 'you pay me, but I owe you no more than any one else in this community!' The key concepts in democratic evaluation are: confidentiality, negotiation and accessibility. The justificatory concept is the right to know.

In the USA the bureaucratic style of evaluation still appears to be dominant despite vigorous counter-attacks. In 1973 thirteen states had passed legislation which related teacher tenure and dismissal to the achievement of performance-based objectives. The long-term effects of such evaluation is inevitably increased power and control by the administrative decision-makers.

Autocratic evaluation has also had an interesting history in the USA. Experts have been hired *to make decisions* about the relative merits and disadvantages of various curriculum programmes; by this method administrators can effectively get what they want without taking the blame for ultimate decisions (provided that they choose their evaluator carefully).

Democratic evaluation is still at an early stage of development. In the USA Robert Stake has advocated that evaluators should be responsive to a range of different audiences and interests. He has suggested more openness in evaluation to reflect pluralistic values. Stake suggests that, rather than make recommendations, the evaluator should make public the nature of the problems on a range of issues, decisions on which would have to be taken by the informed citizenry. In the UK the Ford Safari project, directed by Barry MacDonald, is exploring the democratic model in a study of the medium-term effects of curriculum development projects.

5. Teacher as Researcher (the Professional Model)

Lawrence Stenhouse (1975), partly as a result of the evaluation of the

Humanities Curriculum Project, suggested that evaluation should move away from the product and process models of curriculum towards a research model. Stenhouse did not accept the distinction between evaluation and development and preferred to cast the teacher—developer—researcher not:

> in the role of creator or man with a mission but in that of the investigator. The curriculum he creates is then to be judged by whether it advances our knowledge rather than by whether it is right. It is conceived as a probe through which to explore and test hypotheses and not as a recommendation to be adopted. (Stenhouse, 1975, p.125)

This is clearly a political stance, and has something in common with the democratic model described by MacDonald. Stenhouse's recommendation about evaluation came after the evaluation of the Humanities Curriculum Project and at a time when research was projected into teaching about race in schools.[4] Stenhouse suggested that the race project started from two premises: (1) that nobody knows how to teach about race; (2) that it is unlikely that there is any *one* way of teaching about race which could be recommended in all schools.

The teacher thus becomes a professional indulging in 'research-based teaching' changing the emphasis from independent evaluation to *self-evaluation*. This would help to destroy the strange mystique about evaluation which has previously been referred to, but there are still a number of difficulties in accepting this view of the teacher as researcher. The first is that of role conflict: the teacher has to be both someone who is trying to bring about learning and is also the participant observer trying to assess successes and failures in the classroom; the second difficulty is the related one of objectivity.

Another by-product of the Humanities Curriculum Project evaluation was the research project directed by John Elliott (who had been one of Stenhouse's colleagues on HCP). Elliott developed the Ford Teaching Project which was in the tradition of 'the teacher as researcher' but was concerned to develop certain techniques and rules of behaviour appropriate to this model of evaluation. It is necessary for certain rules to be laid down for teacher behaviour in this situation (these are also discussed in Stenhouse (1975), chapter 10). As part of the process of self-evaluation it had been found helpful for teachers to invite an observer into their classrooms – often another teacher. This is one of the techniques developed by John Elliott in the Ford Teaching Project under the title of 'Triangulation'. The teacher's view of the classroom is compared with that of his pupils and also that of the independent observer (teacher). This has proved to be significant in developing teachers' professionalism and their expertise in the classroom; but here again there are methodological problems.

This kind of evaluation is getting closer to the kind of educational research described as 'action research'. Halsey (1972) has defined action research as the kind of research where it is frankly accepted that the purpose of the project is *not* merely to observe and to describe, but to produce change during the course of the research programme. In Halsey's project an attempt was made to improve the learning of the children in educational priority areas; in Elliott's Ford Teaching Project it was an attempt to help teachers to become aware of their own teaching methods and to narrow the gap between their attempts and their achievement.

6. Case Studies (the Eclectic Model of Evaluation)[5]

Many of the 'new wave' evaluators have been anxious to point out that they do not wish to reject all traditional methods of measurement, survey, questionnaire, etc. But they do want to develop methods of describing the whole context of the subject under evaluation, and also where appropriate to use conventional 'hard data'. This eclectic approach is sometimes referred to as the case study model, which is not in itself a method of evaluation but a whole approach which encapsulates certain ideas and values.

In December 1975 there was a 'second Cambridge Conference' on the subject of 'rethinking case study'. A report was written by Adelman, Jenkins and Kemmis (1976) which concluded in this way:

Possible advantages of case study
Case studies have a number of advantageous characteristics that make them attractive to education evaluators or researchers:
(a) Case study data, paradoxically, is 'strong in reality' but difficult to organize. In contrast, other research data is often 'weak in reality' but susceptible to ready organization. This strength in reality is because case studies are down-to-earth and attention holding, in harmony with the reader's own experience, and do provide a 'natural' basis for generalization. A reader responding to a case study report is consequently able to employ the ordinary processes of judgement by which people passively understand life and social actions around them.
(b) Case studies allow generalizations either about an instance or from an instance to a class. Their peculiar strength lies in their attention to the subtlety and complexity of the case in its own right.
(c) Case studies recognize the complexity and embeddedness of social truths. By carefully attending to social situations, case studies can represent something of the discrepancies of conflicts between the viewpoints held by participants. The best case studies are capable of offering some support to alternative interpretations.
(d) Case studies, considered as products, may form an archive of descriptive material sufficiently rich to admit subsequent re-interpretation. Given the variety and complexity of educational purposes and environments, there is an obvious value in having a data source for researchers and users whose purposes may be different from our own.

(e) Case studies are 'a step to action'. They begin in a world of action and contribute to it. Their insights may be directly interpreted and put to use; for staff or individual self-development; for within-institutional feedback; for formative evaluation; and in educational policy making.

(f) Case studies present research or evaluation data in a more publicly accessible form than other kinds of research report, although this virtue is to some extent bought at the expense of their length. The language in the form of the presentation is less esoteric and less dependent on specialized interpretation than conventional research reports. The case study is capable of serving multiple audiences. It reduces the dependence of the reader upon unstated implicit assumptions (which necessarily underlie any type of research) and makes the research process itself accessible. Case studies, therefore, may contribute towards the 'democratization' of decision-making (and knowledge itself). At its best, they allow the reader to judge the implications of a study for himself.

An interesting early example (pre-dating the second Cambridge Conference) was the evaluation of the Keele University Integrated Studies Project. The project is even more interesting from an evaluation point of view because it was evaluated twice: once by David Jenkins (summarized in Schools Council, 1973), and once more by Marten Shipman who was financed by the Nuffield Foundation to make an independent evaluation of the whole project. Shipman's book *Inside a Curriculum Project* (1974) is a fascinating 'outsider' view which is made more interesting by his giving the 'insiders' (i.e. Jenkins and his colleagues) an opportunity to comment on his judgements.

The project was set up in 1968 to examine the problems and possibilities of an integrated approach to humanities teaching in secondary schools. The first concern was to investigate patterns of curriculum organization that might promote greater interrelation between the subjects. The evaluation process that developed was more analytical and judgemental than conventional approaches. Since the team wanted to take account of the individuality of schools, a simple process of pre-testing and post-testing was not seen as meaningful:

> This virtually dictated a reliance on participant observation; this meant that, as in social anthropology, the observer entered and shared the sub-culture being investigated. Not only did the participant teachers become observers, but the observing project members became participant. (Jenkins, 1973, p.76)

There were three kinds of data: first an objective description of the aims, objectives, environment, personnel, methods, content and outcomes, as these were apparent in individual schools; second, there were personal judgements about the quality and appropriateness of materials; third, there were process studies of the programme in action.

Apart from this evaluation made by David Jenkins and team members, there was also an independent panel of local advisers, teachers and lecturers. They devised their own questions and attempted to get answers to such questions as 'how far do the materials help schools to develop integrated work or how far do they restrict them?' or 'what deficiencies in resources did the use of the project expose?' etc.

Shipman's book was subtitled 'A Case Study in the Process of Curriculum Change'. As a case study it illustrates some of the difficulties in the case study methodology as well as some of the difficulties of evaluating subjectively. Shipman showed that the various participants — Director, Deputy Director, co-ordinators and teachers — had quite different views on the purpose of the project, the methods that were employed, and it was not even clear whether some schools were in the project or not. This confusion was not due to the incompetence or inefficiency of the project team, but was probably a normal feature of curriculum development of this kind.

The study is an illustration of the fact that it is very difficult to establish what is the 'truth' about the success or failure of a project or even to establish exactly what happened. The Director and evaluator were invited to give their accounts in separate chapters:

> The inevitability of such gaps in the knowledge of the history of a project that lasted over four years makes the contributions by Bolam and Jenkins to this book so important. Everyone sees a different moving picture of an event in which all are involved. There are differences in interpretation and disagreement about what actually happened, but these are not necessarily right or wrong. The accounts differ because we all played a different part in the same ball game. (Shipman, 1974, p.x)

Open Government

All six models of evaluation are necessarily political, but some are more appropriate for democratic societies than others. Even in supposedly democratic societies there is often much less openness than is desirable — especially in such fields as education. The work of House and others in the USA, and MacDonald and his colleagues in the UK is very important in this respect.[. . .]

Conclusion

In recent years evaluation has moved away from the objectives model and the classical approach based on testing and post-testing. It would, however, be a major error to think of evaluation in terms of two clear-cut alternatives: classical or experimental on the one hand and non-traditional qualitative or illuminative on the other. Although the six models overlap considerably, they have been outlined in order to show the complexity of the world of evaluation. The impression sometimes given in discussions about evaluation is that the two styles are now far apart and are forging ahead in quite different directions. This is clearly not the case. Non-traditional evaluation has evolved gradually out of dissatisfactions with the rigid experimental model, but the overlap has always been considerable, and at the moment the two models appear to be converging. When the Schools Council Research Study *Evaluation in Curriculum Development: Twelve Case Studies* was published in 1973, it was possible to label some of the twelve projects as traditional and others as being more non-traditional. But even then there were many difficulties. The Cambridge School Classics Project was identifiable as experimental, whereas integrated studies was regarded as illuminative. However, both the Nuffield 'A' level Biological Science and the Humanities Curriculum Project had characteristics of both kinds of evaluation. The 'Science 5–13' Project evaluated by Wynne Harlen was not a pure example of the classical model.

By 1973 it seemed that the best kind of evaluation for such projects was a mixture of styles – the eclectic approach. Getting the balance right was the major difficulty, and also knowing when to use one kind of procedure and when another. it is also true that a major problem remains in the form of working out details of the methodology of the eclectic approach.

It is ironic that at a time when the main stream of educational opinion has moved away from the objectives approach to curriculum and away from a narrow view of evaluation based on testing, that the DES appears to be moving quietly in that direction, devoting large sums of money to the APU and commissioning tests from the NFER and others.

It will not be the first time that the central authority (Ministry/DES) has been a generation out of date in its educational theory[. . .]. This is part of the price paid for secret decision-making rather than open discussion.

Summary

1. Any form of curriculum evaluation is potentially political.
2. Evaluation is not simply a question of applying objective standards to an innovatory project or school.
3. Six models of evaluation were outlined, each possessing a distinctive set of political assumptions about education and society.
4. The evaluation of the dissemination of innovation is also essentially political.
5. The eclectic, case study approach is emerging as a very useful model, but many unsolved methodological problems remain.
6. The DES/APU is moving towards a dangerously obsolete model of evaluation.

Notes
1. It should be noted that this debate is not confined to curriculum evaluation: it is a familiar problem in the social sciences – especially sociology and psychology.
2. 'Formative' and 'summative' are useful adjectives to describe evaluation processes but are often used imprecisely. 'Formative' evaluation is the kind of 'on-going' evaluation received by members of a team during the lifetime of a project so that materials etc. can be improved before the final stage is reached.
3. 'Summative' evaluation comes at the end of a project as a final measure of success/failure.
4. Originally there was a section on Race in the Humanities Curriculum Project, but the Schools Council refused to authorize the publication of the materials. The result was a separate project specifically concerned with teaching about race.
5. 'Case study' as a term is not without its ambiguities. It is sometimes used to denote an eclectic approach, combining test data with illuminative techniques; on the other hand, case study is sometimes identified wholly with the 'soft-data' approach of observation etc. Adelman, Jenkins and Kemmis (1976) appear to be using case study in the more limited sense, but I would prefer to include the use of hard data within the bounds of case study.

References
Adelman, C., Jenkins, D., and Kemmis, S. (1976), 'Rethinking Case Study: Notes from the Second Cambridge Conference', *Cambridge Journal of Education*, Vol.6, No.3.
Cronbach, L. J. (1963), 'Evaluation for Course Improvement', in R. Heath (ed.), *New Curricula*, Harper & Row.
Halsey, A. H. (1972), *Educational Priority*, Vol.1, HMSO.
House, E. R. (ed.) (1973), *School Evaluation: The Politics and Process*, McCutchan Publishing Corporation.
Jenkins, D. (1973), 'The Keele Integrated Studies Project', in Schools Council (1973).
MacDonald, B. (1976), 'Evaluation and the Control of Education', in D. Tawney (ed.), *Curriculum Evaluation Today*, Macmillan.
– and Parlett, M. (1973), 'Rethinking Evaluation: Notes from the Cambridge Conference', *Cambridge Journal of Education*, Vol.3.
Parlett, M., and Hamilton, D. (1972), 'Evaluation as Illumination', in D. Tawney (ed.), *Curriculum Evaluation Today*, Macmillan.
Schools Council (1973), *Evaluation in Curriculum Development: Twelve Case Studies*, Macmillan.
Shipman, M. (1974), *Inside a Curriculum Project*, Methuen.
Stenhouse, L. (1975), *An Introduction to Curriculum Research and Development*, Heinemann Educational Books.

3.2 The New Evaluation
M. Parlett

The Criteria to be Met?

Evaluation is on the move. Not only is there a steady expansion in the amount going on, but as a field of education research it is coming under increased critical scrutiny. The level of interest and discussion is high. Curriculum evaluators have met; committees have been formed and funds set aside. Arguments centre in what evaluation aims to do and how best to go about doing it. What has precipitated this rapid spate of activity?

There seem at least three major factors. First, there is the official enthusiasm, both at government and at other levels, for increased accountability and attention to cost-effectiveness. Second, there is an abundance of innovations and alternative curricular schemes in circulation. Increasingly it is troublesome to choose between them: it is like choosing a new refrigerator before the days of *Which?* Both factors encourage and promote evaluation: how do you 'measure benefits' to weigh against the costs? How can you decide on a 'best buy'? The third, and major reason for the new initiatives and questioning stems from a worrying realization about evaluation studies in the past: namely, that they have often been hopelessly inadequate as aids to practical decision-making of any sort. In other words, a situation exists in which there is both demand for the services of evaluators, and scepticism about what they have done in the past.

The Churchill College Conference

This is precisely the climate in which new ideas can germinate and grow rapidly. And this is what is happening. One of the most significant recent developments was a Nuffield-supported conference at Churchill College, Cambridge, in December 1972 at which a small group of 'non-traditional' evaluators, from Britain, the USA, and Sweden, sat down and pooled their experiences. Each was sharply critical of traditional,

Parlett, M. (1974), 'The New Evaluation', in *Trends in Education*, Vol.34, pp.13-18.

orthodox evaluation. Each had tried to develop radical alternatives. But before the Churchill meeting, each had worked in isolation. It had been a case, we discovered, of multiple simultaneous discovery.

The conference (organized jointly by Barry MacDonald – evaluator of the Schools Council Humanities Curriculum Project – and by the author) concentrated both on new developments in research method and theory, and also on how evaluation relates to educational policy. 'Decision-makers' were there in force: representatives from the Centre for Research and Innovation in Education of OECD, from the DES, and from the Nuffield Foundation took an active part. They addressed the problems of evaluation as seen from their perspectives, and intervened whenever the evaluators' constructions began to look too well-oiled and smooth-running.

What characterized the Churchill discussions? What is 'non-traditional' evaluation? What was wrong with 'traditional'? And what sort of evaluation is, in fact, useful for educational decisions, varied and complicated and politically sensitive as so often they are? There were many differences in detail and a lot of constructive argument at the conference. But there was a strong agreement about the basic issues.

The Need for Change

First, we agreed that conventional styles need to be radically changed: that the predominant evaluation model is inappropriate. It has centred on the idea of 'testing educational effects under controlled conditions': a laudable ambition perhaps, but one that is probably impossible ever to achieve technically, given the nature of educational practice. So many random, unpredicted, and human factors intervene that neat experimental designs cannot contain them all. For this reason, results from such studies rarely carry conviction: they present an emaciated and artificial picture of real-world educational life. The results are usually numerical in form, difficult to mesh with the 'qualitative' view of the world held by most of us. Moreover, differences are often negligible or hedged about with statistical qualifications. To interpret such findings sensibly often means going beyond the formally reported data – using the very type of information that was excluded from the design (because it 'could not be tested scientifically' or because it 'cropped up too late for inclusion in the study').

This basic, experimental model I have referred to elsewhere is the 'agricultural-botany paradigm': appropriate for testing fertilizers on carefully tended fields of crops at agricultural research stations, but inapplicable and incongruous for monitoring how innovations become absorbed and adapted in a diversity of school settings, by teachers with different perspectives, teaching separate and distinctive groups of children.

Second, we found ourselves in substantial agreement about what an alternative model or paradigm should look like. The first obligation upon it was that it should be applicable to situations that actually exist; and that no artificial arrangements (such as 'balanced control groups') should have to be incorporated. The second obligation was that it should be reality-based: that it should do justice to the complex and to the atypical, review the curriculum or innovation not in isolation but as it interacts with its context, and study unexpected and unintended consequences as well as those that were planned. The third, and most severe obligation, was that the new model or paradigm should lead to studies that are useful and interesting – what's the good of research reports that are never read?

The view of evaluation we settled on, therefore, had certain characteristics. It should set out not to 'test' so much as to 'understand and document' an innovation – examining its background, its organization, its practices, and its problems, in addition to its outcomes. It should constitute a thoroughgoing and detailed exploration of the innovation-in-action. It should provide, for all concerned with the curriculum or programme, as well as for outsiders, an informed and accurate description of the operation of the scheme, summaries of the various points of view expressed by those associated with it, and a detailed historical-type account of the development of the innovation over time – its teething troubles, success stories, and the improvements devised.

Studies along these lines, we considered, were likely to provide a far more effective and realistic means of helping decision-makers than did evaluations of the old type. They could assist, for instance, in deciding whether a particular innovation is what they want; whether it has done what it set out to do and what aspects of it could be improved, curtailed, modified, or reassessed.

'Illuminative' Evaluation

What exactly is entailed in such a type of study? Perhaps this can best be portrayed by referring in greater detail to one of the particular approaches discussed at the Churchill meeting: 'illuminative' evaluation. To quote from a paper describing the mode,[1] the aims of illuminative evaluation are to study an innovatory programme: how it operates; how it is influenced by the various school situations in which it is applied; what those directly concerned regard as its advantages and disadvantages; and how students' intellectual tasks and academic experience are most affected. It aims to discover and document what it is like to be participating in the scheme, whether as teacher or pupil, and, in addition, to discern and discuss the innovation's most significant features, recurring concomitants, and critical processes. Generally speaking, there are five different phases of an illuminative evaluation study:

STAGE 1: SETTING UP THE EVALUATION

Illuminative evaluation constitutes a general strategy, not a detailed research blueprint. Each study evolves separately, uses a different combination of techniques, and serves different functions. The evaluator has to clarify, at the outset, what type of study is being commissioned, and what type of report is envisaged. He has to ensure that there is no ambiguity in the range, scope, character, and status of the study, that those who will be most directly concerned (e.g. head teachers, LEA officials) are properly consulted and informed of the plans; and that the message is got across clearly that the illuminative evaluator is not going to 'inspect' or 'pass judgement on' the scheme, but study it with a view to understanding it as a working system, its processes and its impact. Decisions are made about the size, duration, and overall plan of the study. But there is no detailed pre-specification of 'variables to be included': no closing of research doors before discovering what lies behind them.

STAGE 2: OPEN-ENDED EXPLORATION

This phase is usually one of the longest and most significant. The researcher must familiarize himself thoroughly with the day-to-day reality of the scheme in schools. He gets his feet well and truly wet. He spends a lot of time visiting the participating schools, observing what is going on, listening to teachers and pupils, getting to know each school's particular circumstances, and generally behaving somewhat like a social anthropologist on location – though here he is studying not a village community but a group of schools. During this phase the researcher is receptive to a mass of different information: he listens and observes and becomes 'knowledgeable' about the total scheme. He notes, for instance, how teachers use it, how it fits into long-term departmental curriculum plans, what resources and hidden costs are involved, and what activities and intellectual tasks pupils are asked to perform. His enquiries are not confined to the schools themselves: he will also trace the background, rationale, and history of the curriculum or innovation, how it was set up, accepted by the LEA, and introduced into the schools. He will meet not only teachers and pupils, but advisers, LEA officials, and the originators of the scheme. He will want to know how they see the innovation from their respective points of view. In short, he tries to build as comprehensive a picture as possible.

STAGE 3: FOCUSED ENQUIRIES

There is no sharp cut-off between Stages 2 and 3. During Stage 2 the researcher is constantly sifting through his experiences, spotting the similarities and differences between viewpoints expressed (by participating teachers, say, about the suitability of resource materials provided), noting the issues and problems most frequently raised (e.g. possible timetabling difficulties arising from adopting the innovation on a greater scale), and observing recurring classroom events and trends (e.g. the evident enthusiasm of pupils for a particular type of instructional material). Stage 3 begins when these phenomena, occurrences, or groups of opinions become topics for more sustained and intensive enquiry. The study takes on a more directed and systematic look. Interviews become more focused, observation in classes more selective. Certain forms of pencil-and-paper enquiry may also be introduced. Questionnaires have many faults (e.g. they are impersonal, expensive and difficult to produce, and most people find them a frustrating and trivializing medium for communicating their views); but on occasion they can be useful – e.g. to provide an independent check on findings from interviews. Useful sometimes, too, are conventional tests of achievement and attitude – but, if used, they occupy no privileged position; they represent merely another source of data.

STAGE 4: INTERPRETATION

Illuminative evaluation sets out to clarify and interpret: in short, to 'illuminate'. Detailed, accurate, and sensitive reporting is an essential component. But extensive description is not enough. The investigator must organize and order his description, adding interpretative and explanatory comment. By Stage 4 of an illuminative evaluation, the researcher is busy organizing and arranging his data, going back to fill in gaps in his knowledge, weighing alternative interpretations, and already structuring his report. To quote from the same paper: 'The transition from stage to stage, as the investigation unfolds, occurs as problem areas become progressively clarified and redefined. The course of the study cannot be charted in advance. Beginning with an extensive data base, the researchers systematically reduce the breadth of their enquiry to give more concentrated attention to the emerging issues. This 'progressive focusing' permits unique and unpredicted phenomena to be given new weight. It reduces the problem of data overload, and prevents the accumulation of a mass of unanalysed material'.

STAGE 5: REPORTING THE STUDY

The outcome of an evaluation study is usually a report. A weak, dull, over-technical, or sloppily written report can sabotage what has gone before, however skilfully the study was conducted. The illuminative evaluator is conscious, throughout his investigation, of his audience or readership. He will ensure that he provides the information that they want to have at their fingertips, that he addresses the issues that concern them, and that he presents his findings in an appropriate format and style. This sensitivity to the needs of the audience must not undermine his autonomy, of course, nor cause him to censor what he has discovered. A safeguard against doing so is that rarely is there a single constituency or audience: the report is likely to be read and to be used by widely different groups, e.g. by administrators, teachers, and the public at large. What is 'uncomfortable' for one group is likely to be a happy vindication for another, and vice versa. It is important to remember, however, that while straight reporting is certainly called for, so is tact and humanity.

First encounters with illuminative evaluation prompt several different types of question. Some refer to the 'lack of objectivity' and the possibility of research bias. These, of course, are hazards in all social research, however numerical and statistical: take, for instance, how statistical findings are selected for public presentation. The illuminative evaluator finds himself in a similar position methodologically to the anthropologist, historian, or psychiatrist. There is the same necessity for the careful exercise of intelligent human judgement in handling the complex material and evidence encountered. Like them, he makes no apology for doing so. But counter-checking his findings (against the opinions of others or with data accumulated from other sources) for accuracy and consistency, is a crucial part of his activity. If his readers can spot factual errors, he is unlikely to retain their confidence.

A second question is whether such an intensive style of research is suitable for evaluating large-scale curricula or programmes. It certainly can be so adapted, though a good part of any larger sample research will still compromise close-up study of specific school situations. Appropriate enquiry methods and shorter visits can be used for studies in the remainder of the schools.

Third, there is often concern at the supposed lack of emphasis on finding out about 'educational effects'. This is a mis-reading. In fact, finding out the innovation's effects on pupils necessarily lies at the very centre of an illuminative evaluation of a curriculum scheme. It is important to remember that 'learning' is a highly complicated set of experiences, of which 'assimilating content' is only part. People develop habits of study which may become habits of mind; they acquire 'experience'; they are introduced to 'legitimate' knowledge, to conceptions of 'what is stupid' or 'bright' and what constitutes 'good work'. In short, they respond to a total 'learning milieu'. An innovatory scheme does not exist in abstract. Its adoption entails its being absorbed into a pre-existing milieu or context. The scheme and the milieu interact together: pupils respond to both together. Illuminative evaluation aims to elucidate the interaction, and to demonstrate how pupils' educational experiences – widely conceived – are affected by the total learning milieu. It is for this reason that a major portion of the research effort is directed towards exploring the milieu.

The foregoing constitutes a brief, summary introduction to one particular model discussed at the Churchill conference. Like others proposed there, it is still evolving rapidly. There is no shortage of ideas, research opportunities, or problems to grapple with. Before such models can be widely applied we need more experience and more skilled research workers. But as a new direction for curriculum evaluation the portents are good. Not only is the new evaluation likely to contribute to increased understanding of educational innovations – it can also serve as a signpost towards a more pertinent and intellectually exciting educational research.

Note
1. Parlett, M. R., and D. F. Hamilton, *Evaluation as Illumination: a New Approach to the Study of Innovatory Programs*, Occasional Paper 9, Centre for Research in the Educational Services (University of Edinburgh).

3.3   The New Evaluation:
A Cautionary Note
C. Parsons

To want to know how good an innovation is and whether it is better than what it is designed to replace is almost a cultural imperative. If the dimensions along which improvement is sought and the criteria by which improvement may be known are largely accepted, then the task of those responsible for providing information relevant to such judgements is that much easier. Until fairly recently there has been considerable agreement in these areas amongst those involved in curriculum development in schools. Evaluators attached to curriculum development projects have concerned themselves with the effectiveness of particular materials and teaching strategies or, more broadly, with whether the aims of a project are being realized; the criteria for success/ effectiveness have been seen in terms of changes in pupil competence, attitude or behaviour.[1] It can be argued that such a role will always be of some importance, though contributions to the Schools Council's *Evaluation in Curriculum Development: Twelve Case Studies* (1973) do not suggest that evaluators had a great influence on either the development of the projects in which they were involved or on the course of the wide-scale implementation which followed.

Both in Britain and the United States there is a growing body of work which argues that such evaluation exercises are too narrowly conceived, taking no account of the multitude of other factors in the school situation that affect the fate of an innovation, either in the trial stage or, more importantly, when it goes on 'general release'. The way in which an innovation is used and the setting in which it is used are as important as the nature of the innovatory package itself. Furthermore, the full range of outcomes, beneficial or otherwise, are often neither predictable nor, in the event, examined by evaluators, though they may be of considerable importance to the innovating schools and may

Parsons, C. (1976), 'The New Evaluation: a Cautionary Note', *Curriculum Studies*, Vol.8, pp.125-38.
The author is indebted to the following for comments made on an earlier draft: Douglas Barnes, Helen Charlton, George Hudson, Rob Walker and Brian Walsh.

usefully inform those schools contemplating implementation of the innovation.

Concern that, in the medium and long term, expensive curriculum development projects may be having significantly less impact on schools than originally hoped has also led to demands that a wider range of factors should receive attention and that other methods besides formal testing should play an important role in evaluation studies.

Intensive studies of a small number of innovating schools are recommended on the grounds that a multi-faceted representation of the experience of innovation may be made available. Certainly, the processes at work in innovating schools and classrooms are crucial to the outcome of any innovation; any worthwhile summative evaluation must surely deal with this area.

With this in mind, Scriven (1967) advocates 'process studies', Stufflebeam (1969) describes four interlocking evaluation models – context, input, process and product – while Stake (1967) recommends the use of 'a panoramic viewfinder' rather than a microscope. Many have pointed to our lack of understanding of the teaching process and the questionable assumptions upon which much of educational research has been based. (See contributions to Wax, 1971, and Young, 1972.)

This upsurge in the more flexible, comprehensive, sensitive, 'understanding' approach to evaluation is closely related to the anthropological or ethnographic styles of classroom research now being advocated (Hamilton and Delamont, 1974, Walker, 1972). It would be worthwhile, elsewhere, to reflect on the scarcely challenged dominance of psychometricians in earlier educational research and to consider fully the cultural conditions which have provoked the present debate. With hindsight it can be argued that the relative absence of social psychologists, sociologists and anthropologists from the field of formal learning and teaching is a perplexing phenomenon, as is the complementary situation whereby this area was the preserve of psychology oriented educationists who focused on the individual and were not equipped to take account of anything beyond measurable, individual pupil response. Forbearing to speculate too far on this issue, I would suggest that there is as much sentiment as sense in this emerging orientation, underlying which is the belief that the human state cannot be adequately represented by ticks on an observation schedule or scores and quotients derived from standardized tests. This humanism acknowledges the intentionality of human action, the importance of subjective opinions and perspectives, and the possibilities and implications of multiple realities within an institution. In curriculum change we are also now predisposed to look beyond the 'rational' stance of earlier research and development projects which had sufficient faith to believe that 'instructional systems' or new curriculum packages would sell on merit. Commentaries on curriculum innovation are replete with statements concerning barriers to change, the lack of lasting impact, and the need for more research into the 'chalk-face' of education.

In this situation, the 'new wave evaluators', as Stenhouse (1975) has dubbed them, are concerned with not merely, 'How good is it?' but with, 'What is happening?'

New Modes of Evaluation in Britain

Barry MacDonald (1971, 1973 and 1974a), Malcolm Parlett and David Hamilton (1972) have been the foremost exponents of the new evaluation. At the University of East Anglia two investigations are underway which represent developments from MacDonald's earlier work as evaluator for the Humanities Curriculum Project;[2] both UNCAL[3] and SAFARI[4] rely heavily on studies in the field which aim to depict more broadly the circumstances surrounding an innovation. These studies and the style of evaluation advocated by Parlett and Hamilton (1972) in 'Evaluation as Illumination: a new approach to the study of Innovatory Programs' have many common attributes and may be justifiably presented as in the van of the New Evaluation movement. Parlett and Hamilton on a number of counts indict the product centred, 'learning effectiveness' psychometric tradition which has dominated evaluation studies. They delineate the shortcomings of the traditional approach in terms of its methodology, the narrowness of its concerns and the utility of its results. They claim that the approach is questionable in terms of the standards of objectivity to which it aspires but, more importantly, that its results have had little significance for action. Further, the authors suggest that reports often have little relevance to, or congruence with, the experience of those actively engaged in the innovation. This point is acknowledged by Elton (1973), commenting on the results of traditional evaluations reporting minimal differences stemming from an innovation, he says:

> And yet, we often feel it in our bones that there are beneficial changes of a less tangible kind if we could only pin them down. The feeling is far too general to be ascribed solely to the euphoria of the innovator and it is, therefore, fortunate, that evaluation methods more suitable for detecting such changes than the orthodox 'agricultural–botany' ones are being developed.

Parlett and Hamilton, to whom Elton was referring, see traditional evaluation as lying within an 'agricultural–botany paradigm'. This 'paradigm', involving large samples, control groups and an emphasis on measurement and quantification, is contrasted with the 'social anthropology paradigm' which proceeds through small sample studies, taking account of the wider context in which the educational pro- grammes are to function. Data are gathered from a number of sources by a number of methods, thus 'illuminating' the situation; the methods of participant observation are particularly prominent. The authors say, moreover, that 'illuminative evaluation need not be confined to innovation', but would be of service in studies of traditional teaching.

Many of these criticisms of traditional evaluation are to be found in MacDonald's ideas. Despite different terminology and his concern with specific evaluation problems, similar recommendations for flexible holistic approaches emerge. (MacDonald, 1971 and 1973.)

Research and Evaluation

In many ways however, illuminative evaluation is not merely a style of evaluation, but fits more comfortably beneath the broader title of educational research. It recommends flexibility in method, and breadth and variety of data sources, aiming for 'description and interpretation' and a 'comprehensive understanding'. In presenting itself with such a wide brief, such research is similar to that carried out into the workings of other institutions – the medical school (Merton, 1957), the hospital (Becker *et al.*, 1961), the gypsum mine (Gouldner, 1965), the college (Becker, 1968).

By addressing the question, 'What is happening?' in relation to an innovative enterprise in the curriculum rather than 'Are we having the effects we wanted to have?' illuminative or holistic evaluators have abandoned the narrow criteria of success ordinarily operative in conventional evaluation. These criteria have not been explicitly replaced by others, the object being that diverse audiences may make their own judgements on the basis of the results of the reported investigation.

MacDonald has developed this in his conceptualization of the role of the educational evaluator. It is instructive to review his definition of evaluation and the criteria by which he distinguishes it from research. He sees evaluation as an inescapably political activity which is 'the process of conceiving, obtaining and communicating information for the guidance of educational decision making with regard to a specified programme' (UNCAL, 1975). The evaluator 'has to decide which decision makers he will serve, what information will be of most use, when it is needed and how it can be obtained' (MacDonald, 1974a).

MacDonald argues that the evaluator is constrained in a number of ways which do not apply to the researcher; the evaluator does not choose his problems – these are derived from an assessment of the information needs of his audiences; his problems direct his methodology; diverse audiences must be catered for; reports must be speedy enough to inform action and be in a form accessible to the audiences; where non-specialist audiences are concerned this last aim may necessitate devising new techniques which will enable the report to 'respond to the ways of knowing that his audience uses' (MacDonald, 1974a).

On reflection one can argue for the 'continuity thesis' which MacDonald rejects and claim that the researcher and evaluator are in the same camp. Ambition and opportunity often combine to prompt a researcher to work on problems not amongst his favourites; similarly, his methodology may be defined by his problem (equally the evaluator may be sought for, or seek for himself, contracts where his methodology may best be applied), research too aspires to utility and it is inexcusable if research reports are so presented that they are beyond the understanding of those whose work they might inform. The need to address complex issues and report in haste raise procedural and practical difficulties in the exercise of the research function where specific and immediate audiences are concerned, but they are not a logical condition as to why such studies, in seeking to enhance understanding, should be outside the research field. Some audiences have less urgent information needs than others. While SAFARI has no deadlines beyond which the research would not serve decision-makers, UNCAL, as part of its task, must provide information at specified points in time on the individual projects within the National Programme to the Programme Committee so that decisions on the continuation of funding may be informed.

As for methods of research and presentation which are more compatible with the modes of understanding of lay audiences, perhaps research is as much in need of these as the new evaluation. In their search for them MacDonald and co-workers cannot hope to be excused from 'a research critique'.

These ideas constitute penetrations beyond the basic challenge to traditional evaluation contained in the earlier works of MacDonald and Parlett and Hamilton, and, as such, deserve separate treatment.

The main point is, despite MacDonald's elaboration, that such evaluation, if it forbears either to make judgements or to specify the criteria upon the basis of which judgements may be made, is not easily distinguishable from educational research in general. Such broad-based research is potentially more informative than the narrower psychometric approaches, but serves relevant audiences no differently than studies within the established research tradition. I cannot accept that specifying audiences, being subject to political pressures, confronting problems not of the researcher's own choosing, and the requirement to report relevantly and effectively, are sufficient reasons for distinguishing this mode of evaluation from educational research in general.

'Illuminative evaluation' taken as one authoritative statement of the 'innovative evaluation paradigm' must be commended for its beneficial, bracing effect on the research and evaluation establishment. It urged the admissibility of a wider range of data and the use of a fuller repertoire of methods.

While SAFARI and UNCAL are, in many senses, enactments of the sort of research advocated in 'Evaluation as Illumination', their publications are, to an extent, justificatory, defensive and situation specific. Both MacDonald's paper and that of Parlett and Hamilton are not available to a wider audience and, while the former is likely to provoke more debate than action, the latter is open and recommendatory.

For these reasons I think it important to review this particular work with the intention that the weaknesses to which attention is drawn will be apparent in other variations on the theme of illuminative evaluation. Little discussion of the ideas in this paper has appeared in print and citations in the literature suggest that illuminative evaluation has come to be seen as a base from which such studies may reliably proceed. Much remains to be done in pointing out the shortcomings and limitations of what was surely intended as a seminal paper.

The deficiencies to which I wish to draw attention relate to the research tradition which is inadequately represented; to the skills of the field worker which receive insufficient emphasis; to the role of extant theories and conceptualizations which is scarcely considered, and to the possibility that the widened context of such research studies is not wide enough.

With Roots in Rich Soil

This research orientation, though only emergent in education, has a distinguished history in the United States; the investigations of the Chicago School of Sociologists into communities and organizations are numerous, ranging from Whyte's 'street corner society' (1965) to Becker's (1961) work on medical school and college. In this respect, Illuminative Evaluation and variants stemming from it are open to criticism on the grounds that to foster the belief that such research designs are only now being conceived is to divert attention from the sound practice, useful conceptual models and potentially rewarding theoretical frameworks made public in investigations of social institutions elsewhere. Parlett and Hamilton, through their references, *draw parallels* with much that has gone before in sociological case study work; however, by not *integrating* their approach with this tradition, they fail to emphasize the point that researchers in sociology, e.g., Becker (again) and Cicourel (Cicourel and Kituse, 1963), in their investigations of facets of institutions, have marked out fairly rigorous standards: (1) for the collection and validation of data; (2) for hypothesis generation and testing; (3) for the construction of descriptive models and conceptual frameworks which best explain the assembled data; (4) for ways of displaying data to support conclusions, in order that others may judge the credibility of these.

The validation of findings and interpretations is an area of critical importance; critical in the sense that those using what are ostensibly more objective instruments – questionnaires, structured observation, standardized tests – claim that their conclusions are not so heavily dependent on subjective interpretations; this acknowledges the role and angle of the conventional research community in defining what is 'critical' but, in any social science undertaking, reliability and validity must be maximized.

Parlett (1972) lists five approaches to serve as checks on the 'personal' interpretation of the researcher: (1) multiple observers or interview material coded by someone not directly engaged in the research; (2) major conclusions checked by information from several sources and with separate techniques; (3) note down negative evidence; (4) carefully separate 'established fact from cheerful speculation'; (5) there should be no pig-headed reaction against quantitative data.

The list is incomplete and, on the whole, unobjectionable, though to suggest that some speculation might be 'cheerful' could lend support to those who claim that case study work is unsystematic or the tool of the non-specialist. It is, unfortunately, a pale reflection of the methods and safeguards proposed by sociologists such as Becker (1958), Denzin (1970), and Webb (1966). This is not to imply a lack of scholarship on the part of the authors, nor that these issues remain unexamined. These problems are, no doubt, aired in informal gatherings or conferences[5] but it is important that, for the benefit of those who draw on the experiences and ideas of those at the forefront of the new evaluation movement, the weaknesses, uncertainties and experimental nature of such approaches are articulated more publicly.

In certain circumstances, the need to provide information quickly, comprehensively and in a digestible form, may appropriately override demands for rigour. This invites, however, misconceived penetration, poorly substantiated insights and misleading conclusions provoking misguided recommendations for action. Still, even 'non-rigorous' probes may be an improvement on ignorance and hunches, or data from standardized tests and structured questionnaires, and may be of some utility in school-based investigations, or as preliminary or supplementary strategies for the curriculum project evaluator. But the possibilities of this mode of research go far beyond this and promise hope of a definite advance in our understanding of schools and schooling. It is to the role of illuminative evaluation in relation to these wider possibilities that my criticisms are intended to apply.

Perhaps it is unfair to hold the 'New Wave' evaluators responsible for the misuse by others of a potentially productive style of research; the Open University course on Research in Education deals with the case study in a few short paragraphs – 'it can . . . be used by students to gain the flavour of research *without being involved in unnecessary complications'* (Open University, 1973). Some myopic psychometricians are alive and well and sojourning in some corner of Milton Keynes![6]

It is interesting to see that some members of the 'new wave' are exceedingly intolerant towards misuse of methods, faulty reasoning and, particularly, ethical standards; Barry MacDonald (1974b) begins his review of Roy Nash's *Classrooms Observed* with the words: 'This is shoddy research.'

Despite this, a failure on the part of Parlett, Hamilton and their sympathizers to spell out the complexity, sophistication and rigour of previous field studies has led to a misinformed view as to the facility with which this sort of research can be carried out. MacDonald, in his proposal to the National Development Programme in Computer Assisted Learning (UNCAL, 1975) outlining the evaluative study, indicates the difficulties of pursuing such a study by his reference to the need for 'a team of able and experienced evaluators'; he thought it appropriate to name those who would serve on the team should the proposal be accepted and one feels that David Tawney and David Jenkins should meet his requirements.

A conflicting illustration derives from a Schools Council Evaluators' Group Meeting where, following a brief description of case study possibilities in project evaluations, it was suggested (by myself) that if an evaluator intended to proceed illuminatively, much was to be gained from surveying the practices and conceptualizations of field workers in the social sciences; subsequently, a member of a project team addressing the meeting on his evaluation strategies, began by saying that he had not the time to read Becker and academic sociology. Such an outlook can only be deleterious to the conduct of meaningful, reliable and useful enquiry. It is not uncommon to hear of people who plan (which might not be the right word) 'to adopt the Parlett and Hamilton approach'.[7]

Intellectual Requirements of the Field Worker

To compound the foregoing point, one can turn to the skills needed by the researcher in the execution of such an investigation. Placing, as they do, such emphasis on the collection of 'everyday knowledge' of the situation by participants, Parlett and Hamilton unwittingly imply the ease with which the eager, intelligent novice can embark upon such an investigation.

Parlett, in another article (1972), states that the anthropologist aims 'to understand and portray the cultural setting he is in' and that in relation to Illuminative Evaluation 'the chief connection with social anthropology is the emphasis on interpreting; on building up explanatory models of particular systems; on discovering patterns of coherence and interconnectedness that usually go unnoticed'. This involves, however, the need to break out of conventional frameworks of thought, to strive for a mental *tabula rasa*, far more easily attainable when dealing, as anthropologists more commonly are, with other cultures. The suspension of one's own understanding and pre-conceptions in observation and interview carried out in one's own culture is an ideal which can only be fought towards through dedicated, conscious effort. Much may be lost through accepting unquestioningly the metaphors and conventional terms of participants ('the bright kid', 'a good lesson', 'good staff esprit'). In classroom observation it takes a considerable effort of will and imagination to stop seeing only the things that are conventionally there to be seen. The problem of the researcher of developing the most open perspective and holding in check preordinate and, possibly constricting suppositions is considerable; and yet it is inherent in the anthropological approach that the 'deep structure' — the nexus of underlying perspectives and valuations — be elucidated. Whether by training or experience in the field, it is important that this sensitivity and receptivity be fostered in the researcher if the data, rather than relatively unreflective interpretations of them, are to command the generation of useful hypotheses in the 'grounded sense' (Glazer and Strauss, 1967). A tightly controlled, systematic approach to data analysis is needed if progressively more adequate hypothetical accounts of the situation are to be achieved. Subjective accounts, imaginative, insightful reporting may well 'strike chords' with those who are readily able to identify with the events described and interpreted; but where audience impact (and remember that 'democratic evaluation' — SAFARI and UNCAL, presumably — aims that its reports should aspire to 'best seller' status) displaces thoroughgoing checks on validity and reliability the accounts may be more convincing than accurate. The possible consequences for decision-making are clear.

Without going into the additional problems that the researcher has — in terms of presentation of self in the research situation, maintaining appropriate relationships with respondents, minimizing reactivity, etc. — I would emphasize that the pronouncements of Parlett and collaborators have dealt insufficiently with the problem of generating the necessary 'intellectual orientation' in the case study researcher and paid too little attention to the rigour and systematization which could add to the value and credibility of the investigation.

The Role of Theory

A third, and possibly more serious criticism of illuminative evaluation is also related to omission and under-reporting; though billing itself as a new paradigm, with all its world view and supra-theory connotations, illuminative evaluation dwells almost exclusively on method — it concentrates on information gathering; we are told that the new approach 'involves new suppositions, concepts and terminology', yet we are given little more than a vague notion of 'holism' and two key terms (which are not indispensable) – 'instructional system' and 'learning milieu'. Maybe the absence of any theoretical model, any conceptual scheme or set of interrelated propositions is excusable in that the investigator is to be eclectic, responding to the contingencies of the empirical setting.

Reports should serve as inputs to the decision-making process. Parlett and Hamilton (1972) suggest that they may best do this if they convey a 'recognizable reality'. This argument has been more extensively developed within the UNCAL and SAFARI projects; Stake (1972), upon whom these projects draw approvingly, writes that many clients need a 'credible, thorough representation', 'a comprehensive portrayal', and that theory, as a simplifier, draws attention away from the complexity and reality of what teaching and learning is. Walker (1974) points out the difficulty teachers have, inferring from generalized, theoretical statements to their specific circumstances. He suggests an alternative form of educational research could remain close to the 'commonsense knowledge of practitioners and support the process by which professional judgement is gained from personal experience'. The possibilities of theory development have been set aside in SAFARI in favour of practice-related research. This is, as Walker makes clear, an alternative – and one which has yet to substantiate its claim to superior utility. There remains still a strong case for recognizing the role of theory as both a guide and a goal in such research, and failure to clarify this is a serious omission in the presentation of illuminative evaluation. Illuminative/holistic evaluation implies a different concept of the subject matter from that current in most evaluation exercises; the main focus is on man (in this case the school man) interacting intentionally in a complex scene, wherein he and other participants attribute meanings. People act on the basis of their interpretation of the social environment. In this respect, one can argue that preliminary observation proceeds from a vague base of theory about the location and character of factors which constitute considerations important to the actor in the empirical situation and that there are notions from social interaction theory, role theory, organization theory, and the work on sub-cultures and professions and their development which might act as broad points of reference.[8] There is also work on the school itself (Davies, 1973, or Bidwell, 1965) and on the roles and tasks of the teachers (Hilsum and Cane, 1971, Taylor, 1970, and Gibson, 1973) which might usefully be drawn upon. This list is but suggestive; combined with the researcher's own experience of social life and that gained from his initial sortie into the empirical situation, these areas of theoretical, conceptual or descriptive development can be held at the ready to help make sense of the data as they are accumulated.

Certainly it can be detrimental to the conduct of the research to enter the field in the grips of a particular theoretical model, through which attention is directed to certain issues and problems rather than allowing these to be generated through close analysis of the practical scene; but to enter the field in ignorance of the accumulated wealth of conceptual and theoretical schemes available is culpable. One can begin with the necessary openness and receptivity, holding constricting assumptions and presuppositions in check, but having already assembled on the sidelines resources, in terms of available theoretical orientations, which might prove useful in 'making sense' of the situation being investigated.

Deriving from, and reacting to the psychological tradition in education research, illuminative evaluation draws heavily on methods and contexts common to variants of sociology and social psychology, and on the vague 'holistic' and interaction orientations found in these fields. The theoretical perspectives in these fields are neglected, giving the impression that evaluation and research along these lines will be *ad hoc*, if not atheoretical. Case studies or small sample studies can be seen as not simply descriptions of particular places at one time to be added to a bank of similar ones which might (or might not) aid a slow accretion of knowledge, but as instances, both representative and unrepresentative, of the class from which they are drawn. They offer the opportunity of testing and generating theories; abstraction and generalization are respectable goals, but realistically attainable only by building on, drawing from and relating to theoretical perspectives currently available: the disciplines of sociology, social psychology and social anthropology provide such perspectives. Referring to Schwab's (1969, 1972) recommendation of an 'eclectic approach', Elliot (1975) writes, 'The eclectic mode consists of the use of theories for the purposes of practical deliberation. It therefore wrenches them out of their normal context of use within a theoretic mode of enquiry and subordinates them to the purposes of practical reflection. This requires the use of many theories and types of theory to avoid the limitations of both "incompleteness of subject matter" and "partiality of view".'

Becker (1958) makes a similar point about the role of theories as tools; in the preliminary stage a phenomenon might be observed or its relationship with another noted. 'By placing such an observation in the context of a sociological theory, the observer selects concepts and defines problems for further investigation. He constructs a theoretical model to account for that one case, intending to refine it in the light of subsequent findings.'

The contribution that extant theories can make to the conduct of case study research is not discussed in writings on illuminative evaluation and yet the continual interaction between theory and data is central to productive case study work. MacDonald and Walker (1975) touch briefly on this two-way relationship between the case study and theory in a recent article.

The presentation of a new 'paradigm' does not, perhaps, require a cataloguing of theories, models, etc. which fall within its broad territory. Parlett and Hamilton (1972) say of illuminative evaluation that 'the task is to provide a comprehensive understanding of the complex reality (or realities) surrounding the program' (p.30), and that 'its primary concern is with description and interpretation rather than measurement and prediction.' Interpretation, explanation and understanding in social science contribute to prediction – they are not at odds with it. If one understands, one can attempt prediction and hopefully thereby plan better for the future. Theory organizes description, explanation and prediction in a multi-symbiotic process, the like of which is not touched upon by Parlett and Hamilton.

The Cul-de-sac of Conservatism

The Ford SAFARI research project exhibits many features in common with the illuminative evaluation approach, in particular the aim to be responsive to the knowledge needs of the variety of decision-makers who comprise their ultimate audience, and also the prominence given to participants' views in data collection, in the context of multiple realities. MacDonald (1974a) and Walker see evaluation research as inevitably political and they seek to abide by certain ethical and practical guidelines through the application of a 'democratic' mode of evaluation (distinguished from bureaucratic and autocratic modes). The aim is to portray reality and communicate participants' perceptions of it. No greater claim to validity attaches to the interpretations of researchers who are to act as 'brokers in exchanges of information between groups who want knowledge of each other. Democratic evaluation is an information service to the whole community'.

This research moves away from the 'abstract, relativistic and generalizing' aspects of social science that Everett Hughes talks of, towards a practical art of portrayal for the benefit of laymen involved in decision-making.

At a conference in Cambridge (1972) the aim was to explore 'non-traditional modes of evaluation'. MacDonald and Parlett (1973) report that three evaluation studies of this type were described which had major features in common. 'Each evaluation (1) featured naturalistic, process-oriented field studies of educational experiments which attempted to portray the innovation in the context of a recognizable social reality; (2) documented a full range of phenomena, perspectives and judgements that might have relevance for different audiences and diverse interest groups; (3) utilized observational and interview techniques extensively, and gave less than usual prominence to measurement procedures; (4) followed a flexible rather than a predetermined research plan, thus enabling the investigation to be responsive to unpredictable and atypical phenomena, and to sudden changes of direction in the form of the experiment, as well as to the planned and the typical'. Implicit in this and explicit in the SAFARI approach is the element of conservativeness; Walker (1974b) acknowledges this, writing of the SAFARI approach that 'it offers support, perhaps even unthinking support, to the *status quo.*'

It is a critical shortcoming of such research that perceived relevance to decision-makers here and now should occupy such a central position in the rationale of the work. Seeking to inform decision-makers of the whole scene from which they may select features amenable to short-term remedial action may foreclose consideration of more fundamental possibilities. One can go some way along the road with MacDonald in agreeing that 'it is no use providing answers to questions that no one is asking.' But it is surely as relevant to provoke questions other than those customarily asked by practitioners and decision-makers. There is no basic necessity for the researcher to shackle himself within the confines of the everyday understanding of practitioners. SAFARI has chosen to do so but we should not be so easily convinced as to immediately follow on.

The ineffectiveness of research and evaluation in serving decision-makers may have been because the former focused on an area of interest too restricted and too far removed from everyday realities; but to overcome problems in the management of communications, the case study method does not have to be emasculated to the extent that the qualities of the journalist and negotiator should win out over those of the social scientist. The variant of illuminative evaluation manifest in SAFARI gives prominence to the role of negotiation, both as an ethical necessity to achieve publication and as a central procedure in validation of reports (Walker, 1974b). There is a crucial difference between gaining acknowledgement of the accuracy of descriptive accounts and more intensive procedures aimed at corroborating casual relationships, inferences and implications. There is a need to do more than 'mobilize response', as Walker puts it, and this takes us into the realms of educating one's respondents, almost.

Multiple realities can be handled without recourse to the notion of truth and objective realities and, furthermore, the autocratic approach whereby the researcher's interpretation dominates, can be mollified; participants in the research setting can be brought into the process of analysing and interpreting findings, helping to validate and generate hypotheses, collaborating in a number of ways in the final phase of the research. If, in the social relationships out of which the research grows, participants can come to see themselves, not as unique individuals under study, but as representatives of a class, then the possibilities of social science case studies are enhanced. The problems of publication and ethics with which Becker (1964) deals need not reduce the field worker to the role of jobber in the information market.

A further conservative feature of the new evaluation, consequent on this position of acquiescing in perceived political demands and minimizing ethical problems, is that one of the foremost sources of data is the participants' views: Parlett's enactment of this research strategy in one case dealt almost exclusively with this aspect (Parlett and King, 1971). However, one major criticism of traditional evaluation was that its view of the empirical situation was constricted and inappropriate, ignoring as it did, the contextual pressures inherent in it. One can argue that in the 'new evaluation' the dominance of the participants' views, which are not necessarily examined within a much wider context, can again lead to a reified and disembodied sort of reasoning. The opinions of participants or groups are themselves context-bound, not just with a contemporary situation or vis-à-vis a particular innovation, but within a personal developmental and experiential field, within organizational, cultural and professional fields which have histories. George Hudson (1975), in pointing out the convergence of the traditional and new evaluation modes, indeed touches on the difficulty of defining the limits of the context (see also contributions in Wax *et al.*, 1971). A school 'ideology' may have particularly prominent historical antecedents (e.g. a comprehensive born out of a selective school with relatively unchanged staffing). There may be certain idiosyncratic features of the local authority which sustain certain ways of thinking (e.g., advocacy of external examinations for all pupils regardless of ability). Furthermore, there is the influence of the teaching 'profession', from unions to staff groups, and that arising from, and sustained by, the professional socialization process both through formal training and on-site experience and interaction. That attention be given to the historical component in these areas is vital to a full *understanding* of the context in which an innovation functions.

Illuminative evaluation does not draw sufficient attention to this. It offers only the scantiest conceptual framework in terms of the complex, interactive nature of the school situation. The meanings and evaluations given by participants in an innovatory programme are themselves situated in a wider social structural and historical context, to which illuminative evaluation hardly alludes. The 'holism' of anthropology, which proved most productive in the study of relatively static pre-industrial societies, has been imported into educational research in industrial society without appreciating anthropology's failure to deal with continuous change which is an inescapable feature of the modern condition.

Hudson (1975) suggests that, if our understanding is to be greatly increased, 'all the features of education — its organization, examination system, power relationships, descriptive concepts and so on — will have to be located in the historical and social network that creates, maintains and controls it.'

Conclusion

In pointing to new areas of data and new methods which would be more relevant (and enlightening!) for those concerned with innovation in schools, the 'new evaluation' has served a very useful purpose. However, pronouncements made by Parlett and Hamilton four years ago refer insufficiently to the large body of work on participant observation research in institutions (mostly American) which demonstrates good practice. The pedigree of the 'new evaluation' is not acknowledged – we, none of us, should be trying to reinvent the wheel, and there are very real dangers in importing the spokes alone. Illuminative evaluation is certainly very liberating but there is insufficient guidance about how this new-found freedom may best be used.

The difficulty in suspending our own cultural understanding in order, for instance, to see schools as social institutions rather than exclusively agencies of formal education (Wax, 1971) is underestimated.

The limited role given unconsciously to theory, in order that portrayal and communication should better serve decision-makers, is a more crucial shortcoming; theory and service to the community need not be mutually exclusive. Though there is, as yet, little evidence to go on, I would suggest that, just as traditional evaluators has an over-simplified view of the innovation process and a denuded concept of the innovation context, those adhering to the 'new evaluation' have a similarly deficient conception of decision-making in education. It will be interesting to see if the community avails itself of these research reports. What action follows Parlett's studies at MIT and Edinburgh? How will the community respond to the tapestry to emerge from SAFARI?

A greater blight on our attempts to advance our understanding of issues in educational change would result if this emergent style of research should become the new orthodoxy because of the conservative assumptions it embodies, because of its limited 'holism' and because of its ahistorical nature. Inherent in the situation of 'taking' problems for study is the taking of concepts and conventional modes of understanding the phenomenon; the problems 'taken' are framed in terms of the established reality definers – curriculum developers, teacher-training institutions, LEAs, DES and research bodies who depend for their existence on these.

The foregoing criticisms are not intended to imply that people should not embark on research of this nature without, at least, a diploma in sociological field technique, but to argue strongly that, in a good many situations where research is likely to proceed along these lines, we do have the right to demand that researchers proceed reflectively from the substantial basis of other work.

Sufficient homage has been paid to the lead given by Parlett and Hamilton, but it is not improper to demand a re-evaluation of the way forward along the lines set out by these authors and others. There is the need to highlight the limitations inherent in this style of research as it has, hitherto, appeared in print. It is salutary to look upon SAFARI, and similar work which aims for respondability, as valuable explorations of new ground in education in Britain but nonetheless as questionable and tentative. Illuminative evaluation and the further developments within SAFARI should be viewed as sticks (or carrots) to encourage us to reconsider, elaborate, justify and develop our research intentions, rather than as staffs upon which the uncertain or unwary may feel safe to rest. Similarly, one can acknowledge the merit of the work of Stake and fellow Americans who are critical of conventional evaluation studies – they point the way but much needs to be done in charting the territory and working out modes of transportation across it.[9]

Finally, it is chastening to see new approaches, methods, 'paradigms', as superseding older ones for ideological as well as technical reasons. Similarly, their later demise may be due to other than technical reasons alone. Our methods, concerns and conceptualizations can be viewed, to an extent, as cultural artefacts; such a perspective may be of value in maintaining a critical awareness of new orthodoxies.

Notes

1. This 'classical' model has been applied most enthusiastically in the United States, where a body of criticism has suggested this has not been successful in even its own terms; there has indeed been a plethora of equivocal and contradictory findings. See Cronbach, 1963, and Walker and Schaffarzick, 1974.

2. The Schools Council/Nuffield Humanities Curriculum Project, 1967-72, directed by Lawrence Stenhouse. The project eschewed any statement of specific objectives. The case study method formed a significant part of MacDonald's approach to evaluation; reprinted in Tawney, 1976.

3. UNCAL (Understanding Computer Assisted Learning) University of East Anglia. Evaluation Team: B. MacDonald, D. Tawney, D. Jenkins and S. Kemmis. £94,000 over three years to provide information on individual projects to decision-makers within the national programme, highlight issues generally, and make accessible to a wider public the work of the national development programme.

4. Ford SAFARI Project (Success and Failure and Recent Innovation) Centre for Applied Research in Education, University of East Anglia. Project Director: Barry MacDonald; Senior Research Associate: Rob Walker. An

investigation of the 'Medium term' effects of four recently concluded development projects.

5. Such a 'closed' conference was held at Churchill College, Cambridge, 15-19 December 1975, to discuss Methods of Case Study in Educational Research and Evaluation. Howard Becker was amongst those attending.
6. Course E341 has now been replaced by DE304, *Research Methods in Education and the Social Sciences*, which includes a very detailed description and evaluation of ethnographic methods (Editor's note).
7. Quoted from personal correspondence received.
8. The references for 'armchair theorists' and for more empirically-based work in sociology and social psychology are too numerous for listing here.
9. Several very recent and forthcoming publications may well be of service in articulating more fully the character, variety, strengths and weaknesses of this emergent style of research. The authors are, however, from within the New Evaluation Cohort rather than 'critical friends': Dockerell and Hamilton (forthcoming), Hamilton, 1976, Hamilton *et al.* (forthcoming), MacDonald and Walker, 1976.

References
Becker, H. S. (1958), 'Problems of Inference and Proof in Participant Observation', *American Sociological Review*, No.3, pp.652-9.
— (1964), 'Problems in the Publications of Field Studies', in A. J. Vidich *et al.* (eds.), *Reflections on Community Studies*, Wiley.
— *et al.* (1961), *Boys in White*, University of Chicago Press.
— *et al.* (1968), *Making the Grade*, Wiley.
Bidwell, C. E. (1965), 'The School as a Formal Organization', in J. G. March (ed.), *Handbook of Organizations*, Rand McNally.
Cicourel, A. V. and Kituse, J. I. (1963), *The Education Decision Makers*, Bobbs-Merrill.
Cronbach, L. J. (1963), 'Course Improvement through Evaluation', *Teachers College Record*, No.64, pp.672-83.
Davies, B. (1973), 'School Organization', in R. Brown (ed.), *Knowledge, Education and Cultural Change*, Tavistock.
Denzin, N. K. (1970), *The Research Act in Sociology*, Butterworth.
Dockerell, W. B. and Hamilton, D. (eds) (forthcoming), *Rethinking Educational Research*, Hodder & Stoughton.
Elliott, J. (1975), *Preparing Teachers for Classroom Accountability*, Paper written for the Curriculum Development in Teacher Education Seminar: Council for Research into Teacher Education Conference, September.
Elton, L. R. B. (1973), reported in the proceedings of the Society for Research into Higher Education, European Symposium.
Gibson, T. (1973), *Teachers Talking: Aims, Methods and Attitudes to Change*, Allen Lane.
Glazer, B. and Strauss, A. (1967), *The Discovery of Grounded Theory*, Aldine.
Gouldner, A. W. (1965), *The Wildcat Strike*, Harper.
Hamilton, D. (1976), *Curriculum Evaluation*, Open Books.
— and Delamont, S. (1974), 'Classroom Research: A Cautionary Tale', *Research in Education*, No.11, pp.1-15.
—, Jenkins, D., MacDonald, B., King, C., and Parlett, M. (eds) (forth-

coming), *Beyond the Numbers Game: A Reader in Educational Evaluation*, Macmillan.

Hilsum, S., and Cane, B. S. (1971), *The Teacher's Day*, NFER.

Hudson, G. (1975), *Two Paradigms of Educational Research*, Paper given at the BERA Conference, Stirling, published in Research Intelligence, BERA Bulletin No.2.

MacDonald, B. (1971), 'Evaluation of the Humanities Curriculum Project: A Holistic Approach', *Theory into Practice*, No.10, pp.163-7.

— (1973), 'The Humanities Curriculum Project', in *Evaluation in Curriculum Development: Twelve Case Studies*, Macmillan.

— (1974a), 'Evaluation and the Control of Education', in *SAFARI Innovation, Evaluation Research and the Problem of Control: Some Interim Papers*, SAFARI Project, CARE, University of East Anglia, pp.3-19, reprinted in D. Tawney (ed.), *Curriculum Evaluation Today: Trends and Implications*, Macmillan.

— (1974b). Review Article in *Journal of Curriculum Studies*, Vol.6, No.2, pp.80-1.

— and Parlett, M. (1973), 'Rethinking Evaluation: Notes from the Cambridge Conference', *Cambridge Journal of Education*, Vol.3, No.2, pp.74-82.

— and Walker, R. (1975), 'Case Study and the Social Philosophy of Educational Research', *Cambridge Journal of Education*, Vol.5, No.1, pp.2-11.

— and — (1976), *Changing The Curriculum*, Open Books.

Merton, R. K. (1957), *The Student Physician*, Harvard University Press.

Open University (1972), *The Curriculum: Context, Design and Development*, Unit 6, Open University Press.

— (1973), *Educational Studies: Methods of Educational Enquiry*, Course E341, Block 1, Open University Press, p.20.

Parlett, M. (1972), 'Evaluating Innovations in Teaching', in H. J. Butcher and E. Rudd (eds), *Contemporary Problems in Higher Education*, McGraw-Hill.

— and Hamilton, D. (1972), *Evaluation as Illumination: a new Approach to the Study of Innovatory Programs*, Centre for Research in the Educational Sciences, University of Edinburgh, Occasional Paper 9.

— and King, J. G. (1971), *Concentrated Study: A Pedagogic Innovation Observed*, Society for Research into Higher Education, Monograph.

Schools Council (1973), Research Studies, *Evaluation in Curriculum Development: Twelve Case Studies*, Macmilan.

Schwab, J. (1969), 'The Practical: A Language for Curriculum', *School Review*, Vol.78, No.1.

Scriven, M. (1967), 'The Methodology of Evaluation', in AERA Monograph No.1, *Perspectives on Curriculum Evaluation.*'

Stake, E. R. (1967), 'The Countenance of Educational Evaluation, *Teachers College Record*, No.68, pp.523-40.

— (1972), *An Approach to the Evaluation of Instructional Programs, (Program Portrayal vs Analysis)*, Paper delivered at AERA Annual Meeting.

Stenhouse, L. (1975), *An Introduction to Curriculum Research and Development*, Heinemann Educational Books, p.116.

Stufflebeam, D. (1969),'Evaluation as Enlightenment for Decision Makers', in *Improving Educational Assessment*, Association for Supervision and Curriculum Development.

Tawney, D. (1976), *Curriculum Evaluation Today: Trends and Implications*, Macmillan.

Taylor, P. H. (1970), *How Teachers Plan their Courses*, NFER.

UNCAL (1975), *The Programme at Two*, University of East Anglia.

Walker, R. (1972), 'The Sociology of Education and Life in School Classrooms', *International Review of Education*, No.18, pp.32-43.

— (1974a), 'Classroom Research: A View from SAFARI', in *SAFARI Interim Papers,* SAFARI Project, CARE, University of East Anglia, reprinted in Tawney (1976).

— (1974b), 'The Conduct of Educational Case Study: Ethics, Theory and Procedure', in *SAFARI Interim Papers*, op. cit.

Walker, D. F. and Schaffarzick, J. (1974), 'Comparing Curricula', *Review of Educational Research*, Vol.44, No.1, pp.83-111.

Wax, J. L. *et al.* (eds) (1971), *Anthropological Perspectives on Education*, Basic Books.

Webb, E. J. *et al.* (1966), *Unobtrusive Measures – Non-reactive Research in the Social Sciences*, Rand McNally.

Whyte, W. F. (1965), *Street Corner Society*, University of Chicago Press.

Young, M. F. D. (ed.) (1972), *Knowledge and Control*, Collier-Macmillan.

3.4 Evaluation Techniques
S. Steadman

This article is an abridged and modified version of one he wrote originally for a Schools Council publication, Curriculum Evaluation: Trends and Implications, *edited by D. Tawney. The focus of the original article was on methods used by 'an outsider' entering a school specifically for the purposes of curriculum evaluation. The new version covers only those techniques of direct use to schools engaged in self-evaluation, including teachers evaluating their own curriculum. Two techniques of particular relevance for in-school evaluation are examined in further articles by Delamont and Hamilton and Simons (pp.224 and 239).*

Introduction

An earlier review of the techniques available for evaluation was written with large-scale national curriculum development projects very much in mind (Steadman, 1976). Since then the move to school-based curriculum development has been pronounced. And with this move, teachers themselves are more likely to have to become evaluators. It is not that teachers have suddenly all become curriculum developers, but there is now a greater expectation that, in contemplating changes and introducing new ideas and materials, and meeting demands for accountability, teachers will attempt to evaluate their procedures.

From one point of view evaluation provides evidence for decision-makers: i.e. for the teacher attempting something new, for colleagues whose co-operation is required, or for the headteacher or local education adviser from whom future resources are required. Thus an evaluative technique should provide information which is valid, reliable, relevant to the concerns of the decision-makers, and available in time to help the decisions.

In the following pages the techniques have been considered under five major headings: the provision of formative feedback – of interest

Steadman, S. (1981), 'Evaluation Techniques', adapted from S. Steadman (1976), 'Techniques of Evaluation', in D. Tawney (ed.), *Curriculum Evaluation Today: Trends and Implications*, Schools Council Research Studies, Macmillan.

particularly to anyone writing materials or introducing new approaches; the measurement of attainment – of general concern; the assessment of attitudes and non-cognitive factors – often as equally important as attainment; the description of the curriculum context and processes; and the analysis of curriculum materials. This broad schema has obvious overlaps. However, it reflects current concerns and blurs the distinction between 'objective' and 'subjective' techniques – a distinction now outwearing its usefulness. The final section considers some recurring problems in evaluation: the problems of time, sampling and the question of the reliability and validity of the techniques used.

A brief overview, such as this account is, cannot dwell upon particular techniques. But recently the School of Education, Nottingham University, has published a series of inexpensive booklets called 'Rediguides'. Each booklet focuses upon a research technique and many of the titles would prove useful to a 'trainee evaluator'. They provide an invaluable supplement to what follows.

Formative Feedback

Using data for feedback on the effects of a curriculum change implies that such data arrives in time to allow remedial action to take place, even if this means that sometimes the data will be crude and highly selective. It is also important to confine the provision of data to those problems which are likely to lead to changes in materials or methods. And the evidence produced must also be psychologically convincing if changes are to result. One crucial factor in deciding between the success and failure of a curriculum development is the opinion participants (principally teachers and children) come to hold of its aims and activities. Therefore feedback giving details of such opinion, is vital if there is to be any interaction. The methods used to provide such feedback are simple and direct, commonly employing *questionnaires, checklists, teacher diaries, group discussions* and *personal interviews*.

QUESTIONNAIRES AND CHECKLISTS

It is when teaching materials are being produced that these instruments are most often employed. Because it is usual to supplement any questionnaire responses by interviewing at least some recipients, many of the questions are heavily structured – rating and ranking scales being freely used. Precoded responses help in collating replies, an essential matter when dealing with many respondents.

Key questions arise from three sources: the writers of new materials will have certain issues requiring clarification; previous interviewing will have spotlighted certain facets that teachers seem worried about; there may also be additional questions raised by other interested parties such as LEA advisers, or anticipating requirements at a later stage. Writers' queries usually centre upon the effectiveness of the materials; estimates of the time it takes to cover a unit of work; whether the level of language is appropriate to the age group being taught and other similar matters closely tied to the teaching materials. Teachers trying out the materials share these concerns but may also want to indicate problems of classroom and child/pupil management.

Ideally, opinion questionnaires and checklists should be constructed with the same stringency that is expected in the construction of attitude scales and attainment tests. The realities of available time often make this impossible. To minimize the inevitable shortcomings of using checklists or questionnaires it is advisable to observe the following guides:

(a) Be sure that the questions you ask are ones that the informants can answer.

(b) Observe the same kind of rules which govern the construction of an attitude scale; e.g. at its most simple, don't use four grades A-D for the expression of approval. Everyone will answer B.

(c) Consider carefully the sample of teachers from whom you draw opinion.

(d) Arrange to cross-check opinions against the opinions of one group with another, e.g. teachers' with pupils'.

(e) Use more than one method of collecting information.

For guidance in design and use see Youngman (1978) and Oppenheim (1966).

TEACHER DIARIES

Because it is important to know how much time has actually been spent on a new teaching approach, it is useful for teachers to keep a diary. At their simplest, diaries provide spaces for pupils' progress to be monitored in terms of how many units have been completed. Usually there is also space for comments on difficulties experienced with equipment, preparation time, etc. If teachers can be persuaded to complete them regularly, they offer a quick indication of slowing down in the work, which signals the possible loss of pupil or teacher motivation, errors in the level of difficulty of materials, or other causes for concern. Diaries also offer a gauge of the involvement of a teacher, and clues as to the teacher's degree of objectivity about his or her own methods. Drawbacks can lie in the sporadic way in which some are completed and in the heavy demands they can make on a teacher's time.

Instead of supplying a separate work progress sheet and diary, teachers can be encouraged to make jottings in the margin of trial texts, recording little more than the date and their reactions as the work progresses. It is important to know about these spontaneous reactions which new forms of working evoke, and a teacher's rough contemporary notes provide a record which is easily amplified in later discussion.

GROUP DISCUSSIONS

If teachers are working as a group on a development, at an early stage in a series of discussions teachers should have the opportunity to describe their circumstances to each other, and then have time to discuss these accounts among themselves and digest the meaning before being asked to formulate any critical opinions. A group discussion provides teachers with the group identity that is often needed to evolve seriously critical comments.

A second advantage is that teachers can take account of the differing experiences of their colleagues and unconsciously modify their criticisms. Not that they cease to offer genuine opinion; rather, they tend to disregard those critical opinions of their own that they now see to be peculiar to their own special circumstances. Extreme pressures for change on the basis of individual experiences are therefore toned down. It can also be useful to draw a sharp distinction between sessions designed to evoke all shades of criticism, and constructive sessions at which the repetition of purely negative stances is discouraged.

A major difficulty is that of recording the opinions that emerge. Tape recording seems an obvious method, but technical problems can arise and transcription is expensive. Furthermore, it is not always the case that a monolithic opinion emerges, and recording to supplement a written record of someone acting as a secretary is probably the best compromise.

INTERVIEWS

The uses of the interview are manifold, from guiding the construction of attitude scales to being the foremost means of gathering opinions. It is worth emphasizing that most objective tests and observation schedules are based upon early interviewing and discussion, and that the survey by interview is a research methodology in its own right. But in the interview's very versatility lies a danger, for the same person often has to interview the same informant in order to achieve different purposes; sometimes to organize, sometimes to evaluate. Inevitably, a definable relationship will emerge which inexorably and imperceptibly colours every dialogue. And when a teacher is the informant there are always difficulties if he or she feels their competence is being questioned.

Nonetheless, it should not be assumed that an entirely subjective opinion is all that an interview can provide. The dangers of interviewer bias, failure to accept the aims of the interview, leading questions, etc. are thoroughly documented in the literature of sociology. By adopting the correct procedures, structuring the interview, establishing the necessary rapport, defining the information required, presenting the questions in a neutrally worded, standard fashion, supporting with non-committal cues, and cross-checking whatever information is obtained against other sources, contact with a general view of the reality of the situation may be maintained. However, the view of a teaching scheme's effects differs markedly as the viewpoint changes from that of the central activist, to half-enthusiastic colleague, to headteacher, or to outsider, let alone the children. It is misleading if data gathered from these differing – yet valid – viewpoints is merged and an unreal consensus then sought.

PUPIL OPINION AND REACTION

All the techniques described above mainly in the context of ascertaining teacher opinion are equally valuable in soliciting pupil opinion of materials and methods. In addition, the *review of selected samples of pupil work* offers feedback data to confirm or deny hypotheses about the content and methods used by teachers nominally following a new programme of work. The general tendency is to weigh pupil opinion less heavily than teacher opinion and sometimes, regrettably, to rely solely upon *teacher assessment* of pupil opinion, the safeguard of some cross-checking of pupil opinion being ignored.

The worth of pupil opinion is limited by restricted experience and often by the pupil's inability to express himself freely. The younger the child, the less his opinions can sensibly be sought – understandably so. Teacher assessment of the reactions of children under eleven is heavily relied upon unless methods of direct observation are used. In contrast, at secondary level, in working through mathematical packages, guides to experimentation or language booklets, the pupils' responses on difficulty, interest levels and time taken can easily be obtained and are a particularly valuable addition to the evaluation.

Attainment Testing

ATTAINMENT TESTING IN GENERAL

Attainment testing in the form of public examinations is an accepted evaluative measure for a large section of the population. But today the results of attainment tests ought to be set in a context of other information, and it is usually wise to do so if some explanations are required for the results obtained. For example, if a group of pupils does badly, it may be the pupils who are lazy, the teaching which is bad, both, or neither – because the attainment test itself is faulty.

When a new course is introduced it is very unlikely that an existing standardized attainment test is going to be entirely appropriate for assessing pupil progress in learning a new content, or new skills. And often new styles of teaching cause problems. There is now a deal of experience in a variety of methods of continuous assessment using: pupil profiles; percentile progress within a year group; and rank ordering of pupils. Criterion referenced, or mastery tests, which refer a pupil's attainment to pre-specified criteria of performance – rather than referring to the norms of the age group – are now being widely used in the teaching of French. See Deale (1976) for advice on assessment in secondary schools.

Testing attainment can clearly be a complex business, but potentially it offers the chance to monitor changes in pupil attainment after 'exposure to the new course'. However, to show any comparative gains or losses one must first have a suitable test and then think about the use of control group procedures and pre- and post-testing.

A SUITABLE TEST

In science, mathematics and modern languages, where the subject area admits of definable items of knowledge, skill, evaluation, synthesis, etc., it is comparatively easy to form a pool of items from which a test may be drawn. Each test should be recognized as a sample of items, however. And the pool of items must be adequately representative of the particular aims of the work under examination as well as adequate in size, if the test is to present a fair sample. This involves heavy time commitments for the construction of a test frame and the necessary content analysis and item analysis for two parallel tests to take place. At least two parallel tests are needed for pre- and post-testing. Tests which are readily available are listed in Buros (1972) and the regularly issued NFER catalogue. But often the information required by teachers does not justify the fine discrimination that standardized tests are constructed to supply. Crude levels of discrimination are often perfectly adequate for inter-group comparisons. And a wealth of untapped comparative information may be uncovered by asking pupils, with proper guidance, to assess themselves, their abilities and the progress they have made on the course being investigated.

CONTROL GROUPS AND PRE- AND POST-TESTING

The basic difficulty in setting out to compare methods of teaching is that of supplying a control group which truly matches the teaching group which is being exposed to the new style of teaching. While matching on variables such as attainment levels, socio-economic background and school status may be achieved somewhat roughly in practice, the real difficulty lies in reproducing the enthusiasm factor and adequate similarity of aims in the control group. The enthusiasm, or innovative excitement, engendered by working with something new is likely to produce the well-known Hawthorne effect (that improvement occurs in response to anything new) within the teaching group. This should not necessarily be regarded as a *defect*. In part, the aims of curriculum development include the exploitation of such enthusiasm effects throughout the teaching system. However, it is very difficult to obtain a control group which exhibits a similar enthusiasm.

It was at one time feared that pre-testing altered the situation, thereby invalidating any movement of scores shown in post-test results. Research designed to test this possibility has not invariably supported this fear. So the use of this technique, whether merely to reassure developers that their work is having some measurable effect – in which case careful controls are usually omitted – or whether in control group situations, has been freely adopted.

Attitudinal and Non-cognitive Measures

The measurement of attitudes has traditionally involved the use of *attitude scales* on which individuals indicate their degree of agreement with various statements. Different kinds of scale have been evolved. Details of how such scales as those of Likert, Thurstone and Guttman may be constructed are given in standard texts such as Oppenheim (1966). If such scales are to be adequately reliable, the initial pool of items required is very large, and the process of item refinement by judges or by analysis of internal self-consistency is very lengthy. The validity of a scale needs to be demonstrated as a separate exercise. This is always difficult, when it is possible at all.

As with attainment tests, it is unlikely that available attitude scales will be suitable for use in the context of a particular piece of curriculum development. The problem therefore, becomes one of constructing a suitable scale in the time available. Interim solutions can involve the use of *checklists* and *inventories* as described in Oppenheim (1966). If time permits, the initial indications these give may form the basis for the construction of a Likert or Thurstone scale. Checklists and inventories are open to faking of responses and suffer from 'response sets'. Their validity is generally regarded as low. But, even with comparatively crude indicators of attitude, useful results may be gained.

Other non-cognitive approaches which have been used in schools to examine teacher and pupil perceptions include several varieties of the *'repertory grid test'* Kelly (1955); the *semantic differential*, Osgood, Suci and Tannenbaum (1957); and a range of *sociometric techniques*, Thomas (1979). The 'grid test' was originally intended for use in a clinical setting and, in its original form, asked individuals to judge and label the similarities and dissimilarities between people. Later work extended the use of the technique to objects, concepts and situations.

Kelly and subsequent workers have found that, despite the use of a variety of labels, when analysed, many labels were being used to make essentially the same distinctions. The assumption is that, underlying these labels, there exist relatively few 'constructs' which are the determinants of the pattern of a person's thinking (Fransella and Bannister, 1977; Hall, 1978). Using their own labels increases people's acceptance of the technique, and presumably the approach to a truer reflection of a personal value system is enhanced in comparison to the public dictionary meanings and common sets of constructs and objects which often have to be used in the semantic differential (scales and concepts in semantic differential terminology). But if every pupil or teacher may use his own individual scales, how may group attitudes be determined? The answer lies in using a mixture of 'supplied' and 'own' labels, i.e. semantic differential and repertory grid methods combined.

Sociometric techniques are used to investigate relationships within a group rather than the perceptions of individuals, although the distinction is not hard and fast. Friendship groupings, status, group structure, acceptance, social distance, etc. are the usual realms of investigation of sociometry. These methods provide an approach to the problem area of motivation through the possibilities they offer of investigation of the self-concept. Arguably, the pupil's self-concept is the greatest single determinant of his future progress. With the increasing interest in counselling and guidance in schools, interest in the effect the curriculum has on a pupil's self-awareness, self-concept and relationships with his peers will grow, but will be a delicate area for investigation.

Describing the Curriculum Context and Processes

There are several levels at which the curriculum context may be considered to have an effect. General staffing levels, limitations of choice within the timetable, co-operation between departments, and availability of physical facilities, etc. can have obvious effects. Furthermore, the quality of the teacher—pupil relationship, which may be recognized on a group level or in person-to-person contacts, is probably the major determining influence on effective learning, as this establishes the expectations of both parties.

School level evaluation reports can make reference to the school's setting, reflecting the socio-economic area in which the school is placed and the intake of its pupils. It is also useful to add data such as the school type, sex, size, number of examination entrants, the percentage of children applying to the school as their first choice, the sources from which the school draws its teaching staff, and accounts of how many of the school's outdoor activities involve real contact with the local community. Such information enables the reader to interpret the account, not only in a way which renders the interpretation more valid for his own purposes, but also from a standpoint which may be unique to him. The thought-provoking *Fifteen Thousand Hours* (Rutter, 1979), is a rich source of ideas for indicators and contextual measures which might be considered.

CASE STUDIES

All the levels of context mentioned above are amenable to incorporation in a case study with the great advantage of providing information about the interrelationships involved. Additionally, a case study can reflect the perceived concerns of the author(s) in a way which is often sub-conscious, but the more revealing because of this. The drawbacks to using a case study description are connected with its uncontrolled nature: at worst it may be too introspective and consequently unilluminating.

However, if the boundaries of a case study are clear, the drawbacks are minimized. The study may be longitudinal or sectional as required; it may be responsive to the demands of the situation and it could be focused on inter-personal relationships when these are important.

Close, Rudd and Plimmer (1974) provide accounts of different team-teaching situations written by actively participating teachers, who describe not only classroom matters, but also problems of teacher co-operation and organization both in and out of the classroom. It is difficult to find consistent guidelines for preparing an educational case study. The best advice before starting is to examine as many examples as possible beforehand. And it is sensible to think very deeply about any foreseeable problems with confidentiality and the release of information. From a methodological point of view a case study is easy to do badly!

OBSERVATION

Observation inside individual classrooms has moved from being based on casual observers to the use of pre-set schedules which categorize happenings on the basis of frequent sampling of activities. Commonly, an observer sits in the room and every few seconds or minutes, using a stopwatch, notes down what is happening at that time. The operation is usually repeated over several lessons, to provide a representative sample of events from which a teacher or pupil profile may be constructed. This technique has several potential uses but basically it enables changes to be registered when changes occur. This requires two things: first, adequate preliminary samples of behaviour, and secondly, categories on the schedule which reflect the changes in behaviour.

Interaction schedules aim to record sequences of behaviours. Most often it is the linking of a pair of behaviours that is recorded – for instance, a teacher asks an open-ended question which is followed by a pupil request for more information – but the 'strings' may take any length. In recording interactions, the hope is to gain understanding at a deeper level than that afforded by isolated observations, so that, in principle, more may be said about patterns of teacher and pupil involvement in learning. At this stage it is important to note the limitations of any schedule which is too concerned with spoken interchange.

The practical difficulties in preparing such schedules are the usual ones, lack of time and the heavy commitment of resources involved, for although many schedules have already been devised (see Simon and Boyer, 1967-72; Galton, 1978) users often need to devise their own.

There are additional difficulties because the interpretation of both observation and interaction schedules involves first an analysis of the structure and then a translation of the results. The analysis stage is often mathematical, and it is possible at this juncture to impose, unwittingly, a mathematical structure which need not be meaningful. Schedules may be of two types, low inference or high inference. The low inference model records unambiguous data which do not require much judgement by the observer, while high inference models demand that the observer makes judgements as to the intentions behind actions at the time of recording.

The users of observation and interaction schedules have tended to concentrate upon 'processes', and tried to establish cause-and-effect relationships in the classroom. But even when clear relationships cannot be established, the use of a schedule may still provide invaluable background description.

PARTICIPANT OBSERVATION

The onlooker, armed with interview or observation schedule, may see most of the game, but it could be just those aspects hidden by the inevitable disturbance of his presence that are the critical ones. However, there is, in all the social sciences, a long tradition of mistrusting the accounts of actors in situations. Unconscious motivations, self-justification and *post hoc* rationalizations can all operate to bias such accounts. Participant observation offers the possibility of being both participant and observer.

In a school, as Nash (1973, 1976) describes, it can involve an outsider virtually becoming one of the teaching staff: taking lessons, accompanying children on trips and attending staff meetings. On the one hand, teachers themselves in recording their observations of their own classrooms and the classrooms of colleagues may be seen as adopting a participant observation role. If the observer merely observes systematically, he has failed to test the water. If, on the other hand, he loses all detachment, that too rates as a failure, rendering suspect the data gathered.

Unfortunately readers of a report which has used this method have very little to guide them on how successfully it was judged. Some clues lie in the kinds of data obtained. If such data are purely anecdotal, the chances are that the evaluator was more participant than observer; if there are too many pencil-and-paper tests, the chances are that the evaluator was never truly accepted as a participant by the other teachers or the pupils. However, even granting these difficulties, there is little doubt that, when successful, participant observation offers unrivalled insights into the working of the curriculum and the success of methods to improve it. This is the particular strength of the teacher in undertaking self-evaluation.

Analysing Curriculum Materials

A constant problem for teachers is that of assessing new teaching schemes and publications. It is difficult to know what criteria to bring to bear upon the content and required teaching approaches, and it is important to know whether any pupil materials are pitched at the correct level for the intended teaching group.

As well as drawing upon experience – as an individual or in co-operation with other teachers – teachers can turn to *The Analysis of Curriculum Materials*, Eraut, Goad and Smith (1975). This offers several analytical schemes to help teachers pose a standard set of questions which probe the aims, content, presentation, underlying assumptions, implications for resources and management, and other relevant features.

To help judge the level of language used in supplementary readers, textbooks, or work-cards, several indices of 'readability' have been developed. Centres which specialize in reading often assign reading ages to the books in a reading scheme on the basis of a computed readability index. The trouble is that many different indices have been developed which emphasize different aspects of written prose. A recent book for teachers by Harrison (1980) gives a comprehensive review, and recommends which indices suit which needs. Harrison puts a careful emphasis upon the importance of teacher judgements, motivation of pupils, and the dangers of trying to write artificially simplified prose to gain a low index score, important when writing work-cards.

Recurring Problems in Evaluation

TIME

Time is a constant constraint, not only as a limit upon the whole operation, but sometimes as an implicit constraint upon the use of techniques. When changes are to be made, there may be insufficient time to construct measures of attitude which would be adequately valid and reliable. Or, if it is left too late, it may be impossible to apply a pretest *before* development begins.

SAMPLING

The notion of what constitutes an 'adequate' sample in the context of curriculum evaluation is a tangled one. Whenever the intention is to ascertain numerical levels, obtained by tests or scales, and supply statements about the attendant error, the requirements of classical sampling theory apply. The samples have to be quite large if the accuracy is to be sufficient for useful conclusions to be drawn, because of the need for randomness in the sampling procedure. Formulae exist for calculating the required sample size in these circumstances. On the other hand, curriculum evaluation focuses upon the quality of interactions between teachers and pupils, and it is not always necessary to quote numerical levels or give standard errors within the population. The need is usually for information which is generalizable, and reveals cause-and-effect relationships. The question of how many instances should be considered before being able to draw reliable inference is not then answerable by statistical theory alone. Educational experience and judgement must be brought to bear.

If adequately selected large samples are required for involved purposes, the unskilled should seek the advice of experts. Useful primers are provided by Butcher (1966), Selkirk (1978) and Barnett (1974).

RELIABILITY AND VALIDITY

Reliability and validity have technical meanings. Crudely summarized: a reliable technique is one which – if we could go back in time and use it again – would give the same result; a valid technique supplies the answer to the question we believe we are asking – not a similar but different question. However, when data have been obtained informally, it is not always possible to offer reassurance of adequate reliability even in the technical sense. It is best to admit this and offer instead the amalgam of reliability and validity data which inquirers often have in mind. The validity of even informally obtained views is open to confirmation if a proper programme of cross-checking has been incorporated into the evaluation and the context of events is adequately delineated.

DISTORTION

A few closing words of warning are also due on the possibly distorting effect which choice of evaluation techniques may have on the curriculum being evaluated. This danger is not so real now that evaluation is generally acknowledged to be more than attainment testing, but distortion of aims is possible if the evaluation is too firmly restricted to certain methods. Evaluation is a service industry — and should remain so.

References

Barnett, V. (1974), *Elements of Sampling Theory*, English Universities Ltd.

Buros, O. K. (ed.) (1972), *The Seventh Mental Measurements Year Book*, Gryphon Press.

Butcher, H. J. (1966), *Sampling in Educational Research*, Manchester University Press.

Close, J. J., Rudd, A. W. G., and Plimmer, F. (1974), *Team Teaching Experiments*, NFER.

Deale, R. N. (1976), *Assessment and Testing in the Secondary School*, Examinations Bulletin 32, Evans/Methuen Educational.

Eraut, M. R., Goad, L. H., and Smith G. E. (1975), *The Analysis of Curriculum Materials*, Education Area, University of Sussex (Occasional Paper 2).

Fransella, F. and Bannister, D. (1977), *A Manual for Repertory Grid Techniques*, Academic Press.

Galton, M. (1978), *British Mirrors: a Collection of Classroom Observation Systems*, School of Education, Leicester University.

Hall, E. (1978), *Using Personal Constructs*, School of Education, Nottingham University (Rediguide 9).

Harrison, C. (1980), *Readability in the Classroom*, Cambridge University Press.

Kelly, C. A. (1955), *The Psychology of Personal Constructs*, Vol.1, Norton.

Nash, R. (1973), *Classrooms Observed*, Routledge & Kegan Paul.

— (1976), *Teacher Expectation and Pupil Learning*, Routledge & Kegan Paul.

Oppenheim, A. N. (1966), *Questionnaire Design and Attitude Measurement*, Heinemann Educational Books (reprinted 1973).

Osgood, C. E., Suci, G. J. and Tannenbaum, P. H. (1957), *The Measurement of Meaning*, University of Illinois Press (new edition, 1968).

Rutter, M. *et al.* (1979), *Fifteen Thousand Hours*, Open Books.

Selkirk, K. E. (1978), *Sampling*, School of Education, Nottingham University (Rediguide 4).

Simon, A. and Boyer, E. G. (eds) (1967-1972), *Mirrors for Behavior: an Anthology of Classroom Observation Instruments*, Vols.1-6, Philadelphia, Pa: Research for Better Schools.

Steadman, S. D. (1976), 'Techniques of Evaluation', in D. Tawney (ed.), *Curriculum Evaluation Today: Trends and Implications*, Macmillan Education.

Thomas, K. C. (1979), *Sociometric Techniques*, School of Education, Nottingham University (Rediguide 18).

Youngman, M. B. (1978), *Designing and Analysing Questionnaires*, School of Education, Nottingham University (Rediguide 12).

3.5 Classroom Research: A Critique and New Approach

S. Delamont and D. Hamilton

This is a shortened version of the introductory chapter for the book Explorations in Classroom Observation *by M. Stubbs and S. Delamont. It parallels Parlett's attack on traditional 'psycho-statistical' evaluation methodology (in a previous reading, see pp.185-191), in comparing and contrasting, for use in classroom study, structured versus unstructured observational methods. The structured methods, of which Flanders's* Classroom Interaction Analysis *is taken as a typical example, require the location of observations over a fixed time period in predetermined categories such as 'types of teacher talk' and 'types of pupil talk'. This is compared with anthropological observational methods, favoured by the authors, in which the categories are allowed to emerge during the process of field work itself.*

[. . .] The form of this chapter is as follows. First, there is a brief section which explains why we feel that there should be discussion about classroom research in Britain at the present time – there are clear signs that research effort is about to be concentrated on the classroom, but that this will be only one restricted kind of research. Second, we deal with the position in America, where classroom studies have been funded for over ten years – the present position in America is a cautionary tale for Britain. Third, we contrast the two major types of classroom observation which do exist, to show how they are in fact designed to do very different things and how they carry implicit assumptions that are not usually appreciated by their practitioners. Finally, we make a plea for a more eclectic approach to the study of the classroom and for tolerance of different perspectives. [. . .]

The Classroom – a New Research Area

Educational research in Britain is currently entering a new phase. As its preoccupations with mental testing, the results of streamlining and cur-

Delamont, S. and Hamilton, D. (1976), 'Classroom Research: a Critique and New Approach', in M. Stubbs and S. Delamont (eds), *Explorations in Classroom Observation*, John Wiley.

riculum development gradually diminish, a variety of other research interests seek to achieve pre-eminence. One area in which all the funding agencies are becoming increasingly active is classroom research.[1]

To anyone outside education it may seem paradoxical that such a central area of educational life has previously been a peripheral area for research. But it remains the case, overall, that the classroom has been a 'black box' for researchers, providing merely a vehicle for 'input-output' research designs or a captive audience for psychometric testing programmes. Even research on *teaching* has been carried on outside the classroom settings where the teaching occurs! While reviewing this field ten years ago, Medley and Mitzel (1963, p.247) commented that:

> The research worker limits himself to the manipulation or studying of antecedents and consequents . . . but never once looks into the classroom to see how the teacher actually teaches or the pupil actually learns.

Even today this comment could be applied with justice to most educational research in Britain.

Morrison and McIntyre highlight the doubtful origins of this disregard for the classroom in their remark that 'it is *almost a cliché* of modern educational thinking that pupils' behaviour in the classroom derives largely from their lives outside it' (1969, p.119, emphasis added).

One consequence of this neglect of classroom life is that teachers have remained largely indifferent, or even antagonistic, to the claims made for educational research. For insight into their daily lives they turned elsewhere, to 'travellers' tales' (e.g. Holt, 1969), to 'non-fiction novels' (e.g. Blishen, 1955), or to the compounded folk-tales, myths and mores of the staffroom.

Unquestionably, however, there is now a shift in research interests, with the classroom as the new focus. It is not difficult to find reasons for this shift. From various quarters more and more recognition is being paid to the fact that an appreciation and understanding of classroom events is essential to any analysis of educational processes. Thus, for example, problems found with certain new curricula at the classroom stage (see MacDonald and Rudduck, 1971), the 'ineffectiveness' of much teacher training (see Stones and Morris, 1972) and the survival of 'streaming attitudes' among teachers in unstreamed primary schools (see Barker Lunn, 1970) all point towards the classroom as a relevant, indeed essential, field of research.

Basically, classroom research aims to study the processes that take place within the classroom black box. Hitherto such research in Britain has been small-scale, pursued largely by isolated individuals using *ad hoc* methods and theory. In the USA, however, classroom research has been extensively funded and vigorously promoted for over a decade.

Like the better known curriculum reform movement, it grew from a concern with the quality of educational practice.

Despite such widespread attention, classroom research in the USA has not been without its problems. While results have grown to voluminous proportions, their contribution to *understanding* has been disproportionately small. Gage, summarizing several decades of research on teacher effectiveness, could only damn with faint praise:

> . . . here and there, in research on teaching methods, on teacher personality and characteristics, *and on social interaction in the classroom* it might be possible to come up with more sanguine judgements about the meaning of research findings! (1971, p.31, emphasis ours).

In America, therefore, a decade of classroom research has not produced the revolution in educational understanding which its proponents expected. In this chapter we argue that this 'failure' is due to an overemphasis on one type of observation, 'interaction analysis', at the expense of other kinds, which we will call 'anthropological'. In the following section we contrast the main American traditions – interaction analysis and anthropological classroom research – in the American context. By contrasting interaction analysis (the dominant tradition) with anthropological classroom research, we hope to demonstrate the reasons for our argument that a wholesale and uncritical adoption of the former in Britain is premature if not misguided.

The American Traditions

INTERACTION ANALYSIS

In this section, the American experience with interaction analysis is discussed and certain issues are raised that we feel are relevant to the successful development of classroom research in Britain.

Interaction analysis[2] is a research tradition true to the behavioural core-assumptions of American psychology. Characteristically, research of this type involves using an observational system to reduce the stream of classroom behaviour to small-scale units suitable for tabulation and computation. *Mirrors for Behavior* (Simon and Boyer, 1968 and 1970), the interaction analyst's 'pharmacopoeia', details seventy-nine different systems. These various systems cover slightly different kinds of small-scale units – some provide lists of pre-specified categories (e.g. 'teacher asks question' or 'student replies'), others give the observer a checklist of events to watch for (e.g. 'teacher leaves room' or 'pupil talks with visitor'). The best known system [is] that of Flanders (1970). Table 1 shows the categories which make up the system.

Table 1 Flanders's Interaction Analysis Categories* (FIAC)

Teacher Talk		
	Response	1. *Accepts feeling.* Accepts and clarifies an attitude or the feeling tone of a pupil in a nonthreatening manner. Feelings may be positive or negative. Predicting and recalling feelings are included.
		2. *Praises or encourages.* Praises or encourages pupil action or behaviour. Jokes that release tension, but not at the expense of another individual; nodding head, or saying "Um hm?" or "go on" are included.
		3. *Accepts or uses ideas of pupils.* Clarifying, building, or developing ideas suggested by a pupil. Teacher extensions of pupil ideas are included but as the teacher brings more of his own ideas into play, shift to category five.
		4. *Asks questions.* Asking a question about content or procedure, based on teacher ideas, with the intent that a pupil will answer.
		5. *Lecturing.* Giving facts or opinions about content or procedures; expressing *his own* ideas, giving *his own* explanation, or citing an authority other than a pupil.
	Initiation or	6. *Giving directions.* Directions, commands, orders, to which a pupil is expected to comply.
		7. *Criticizing or justifying authority.* Statements intended to change pupil behaviour from non-acceptable to acceptable pattern; bawling someone out, stating why the teacher is doing what he is doing; extreme self-reference.
Pupil Talk	Response	8. *Pupil-talk – response.* Talk by pupils in response to teacher. Teacher initiates the contact or solicits pupil statement or structures the situation. Freedom to express own ideas is limited.
	Initiation	9. *Pupil-talk – initiation.* Talk by pupils which they initiate; expressing own ideas; initiating a new topic; freedom to develop opinions and a line of thought, like asking thoughtful questions; going beyond the existing structure.
Silence		10. *Silence or confusion.* Pauses, short periods of silence and periods of confusion in which communication cannot be understood by the observer.

*There is *no* scale implied by these numbers. Each number is classificatory; it designates a particular kind of communication event. To write these numbers down during observation is to enumerate, not to judge a position on a scale.

(From N. Flanders (1970), *Analyzing Teaching Behavior*, Addison-Wesley. Reproduced by permission.)

The categories of Table 1 appear in slightly different versions in Flanders's various publications. For convenience, the version reproduced here is from Flanders's main book (1970). In this version the terms 'response' and 'initiation' replace the terms 'indirect' and 'direct' influence with respect to teacher-talk. See Flanders, 1970, p.102, for discussion of this slight alteration. Flanders (1970) still uses the concept of I/D ratio (indirect to direct) in his discussion of teaching styles.

Some try to tackle more complex phenomena – in one scheme, ideas expressed verbally as 'thought units' are coded according to their 'thought level' and their 'function'. The majority (sixty-seven) of the seventy-nine systems in *Mirrors for Behavior* are described as suitable for use in classrooms; fifty-nine as suitable for any school subject; and fifty-two as suitable for coding 'live'. (Some kind of audio-visual device for recording the events is essential for the remainder.) Although all the systems in *Mirrors for Behavior* were developed for research purposes, perhaps their most successful application has been as teacher-training tools. In fact, according to Simon and Boyer (1970, p.27), 'forty-seven of the seventy-nine systems have been transferred from research to training instruments'.

The interaction analysis tradition has, of course, both strengths and weaknesses. On the credit side can be placed the simplicity of most of the observation systems. They are well-tried, reliable and easy to learn. In addition, they can be used to study large numbers of classrooms and readily generate a wealth of numerical data suitable for statistical analysis.[3] The data produced with such systems tell one something about life in an average classroom and allow one to 'place' a teacher in relation to his or her colleagues – the data are therefore numerical and normative. Like the results of a survey or of a psychological test, they refer to samples and populations.

In the debit column, however, must be placed factors which impose certain restrictions upon the use of these systems:
1. All but ten of the interaction analysis systems ignore the temporal and spatial context in which the data are collected. Thus although this is not made explicit in the description of the schedules, most systems use data gathered during very short periods of observation (i.e. measured in minutes and single lessons rather than hours or days); and the observer is not expected to record information about the physical setting.[. . .]

Divorced from their social and temporal (or historical) context in this way, the data collected may gloss over aspects relevant to their interpretation.

2. Interaction analysis systems are usually concerned only with overt, observing behaviour. They do not take directly into account the differing intentions that may lie behind such behaviour. Where intention is relevant to the observational category (as in Flanders's Category 2, 'Teacher praises or encourages') the observer has himself to impute the intention, making no attempt to discover the actor's actual or self-perceived intention. In such cases only the observer's interpretation is considered relevant. Thus by concentrating on surface features, interaction analysis runs the risk of neglecting underlying but possibly more meaningful features. A comprehensive understanding of classroom life may, for example, depend upon the translation of 'silent languages' (Smith and Geoffrey, 1968) or the uncovering of 'hidden curricula' (Snyder, 1971).[. . .]

3. Interaction analysis systems are expressly concerned with 'what can be categorized or measured' (Simon and Boyer, 1968, p.1). They may, however, obscure, distort or ignore the qualitative features which they claim to investigate, by using crude measurement techniques or having ill-defined boundaries between the categories. (The distinction between 'accepting student's feeling' and 'using student's idea' to take an example from Flanders's system, cannot, by its nature, be clearly defined, yet is important if the system is to 'work' properly.)

4. Interaction analysis systems focus on 'small bits of action or behaviour rather than global concepts' (Simon and Boyer, 1968, p.1). Thus, inevitably, they have a tendency to generate a superabundance of data which, for the purposes of analysis, must be linked either to a complex set of descriptive concepts — customarily the original categories — or to a small number of global concepts built up from these categories (e.g. Flanders's 'direct/indirect ratio' built up from combinations of Categories 1, 2, 3, 6 and 7). But since the categories may have been devised in the first place to reduce the global concepts to small bits of action or behaviour, the exercise may well be circular. The potential of interaction analysis to go beyond the categories is limited.[. . .] This circularity and lack of potential necessarily impede theoretical development.

5. The systems utilize pre-specified categories. If the category systems are intended to assist explanation, then the pre-specification may render the explanations tautological. That is, category systems may assume the truth of what they claim to be explaining. For example, if a set of categories is based on the assumption that the teacher is in the same position as the leader of a T-group, any explanation of 'teaching' in other terms is not possible.

6. Finally, we feel that, by placing arbitrary (and little understood)

boundaries on continuous phenomena, category systems may create an initial bias from which it is extremely difficult to escape. Reality frozen in this way is not always easy to liberate from its static representation.

All these limitations inherent in interaction analysis systems are implicitly or explicitly acknowledged by their originators (e.g. Flanders, 1970, chapter 2). However, they are not usually acknowledged by other researchers and soon slip from view even in the writings of the originators themselves. We believe that if such systems are to be used, these limitations must not be allowed to become implicit, but must be openly acknowledged all the time. The methods must not be seen as something they are not. To be valid as methods of studying the classroom, the techniques must be constantly scrutinized, not once accepted and then taken for granted.

In spite of the 'credits' which we accept for interaction analysis, its proponents make other claims which we dispute. First, interaction analysis claims to be objective. Its proponents argue that, compared to other forms of observation, interaction analysis systems provide unambiguous data uncontaminated by observer 'bias'. However, the price paid for such 'objectivity' can be high. We believe that by rejecting, as invalid, non-scientific, or 'metaphysical', data such as the actor's ('subjective') accounts, or descriptive ('impressionistic') reports of classroom events, the interaction analysis approach risks furnishing only a partial description. Furthermore, in justifying the rejection of such data on operational rather than theoretical or even educational grounds, the interaction analysis approach may divert attention from the initial problem towards more 'technocratic' concerns such as the search for 'objectivity' and 'reliability'. (In the instructional handbook of the Flanders system, ten pages deal with observer reliability, but only two with how to understand classroom phenomena (see Flanders, 1966).) All of us would question the exclusion of so-called subjective data in favour of a striving for superficial objectivity.

Another preoccupation which can be seen in all the papers in the present collection is a consideration of the role of the observer. With one exception, all the systems in *Mirrors for Behavior* make a rigid distinction between the observer and the observed. The former is considered a 'fly on the wall', detached from the classroom events. For example, in an observational study of English infant classrooms, Garner (1972) devotes no discussion to the impact of the observer. More particularly, his checklist makes no reference to infant behaviour directed towards the observer, though it is reasonable to assume that it did (or could) occur.

By maintaining a strict 'distance' from those being observed, interaction analysis may again promote an incomplete appraisal. As Louis Smith has pointed out, teaching must be viewed as an intellectual, cognitive process:

The way (the teacher) poses his problems, the kinds of goals and sub-goals he is trying to reach, the alternatives he weighs . . . are aspects of teaching which are frequently lost to the behavioural oriented empiricist who focuses on what the teacher does, to the exclusion of how he thinks about teaching. (Smith and Geoffrey, 1968, p.96.)

In much of interaction analysis these aspects are rarely considered. They too are labelled 'subjective' and placed beyond the bounds of the empirical world. In contrast [we] believe that rigid distances between the observer and the teacher and pupils can be maintained only in certain circumstances, and so have generally opted for participant observation.

Finally, in the interests of objectivity, many interaction analysis research studies feel compelled to survey large numbers of classrooms. It is argued (correctly) that small samples may fail to provide statements relevant to the population at large. Such an approach (even if it can achieve true randomness) may however fail to treat as significant local perturbations or unusual effects. Indeed, despite their potential significance for the classroom or classrooms to which they apply, atypical results are seldom studied in detail. They are ironed out as 'blurred averages' and lost to discussion.[. . .]

In addition to our reservations about the use of interaction analysis, we have doubts about the historical tradition from which the research is derived. We feel that interaction analysis is plagued by a number of deep-rooted theoretical and ideological constraints. Most of the American classroom research is ethnocentric — based on a model of the classroom and a conception of education that is not always relevant in Britain. Many of the systems assume the 'chalk and talk' paradigm and focus predominantly upon the teacher. (Flanders's interaction analysis system has ten categories, seven devoted to 'teacher-talk' and two devoted to 'pupil-talk'. The tenth is a 'junk' category, 'silence or confusion'.)[4] They imply a classroom setting where the teacher stands out front and engages the students in some kind of pedagogical or linguistic ping-pong (teacher asks question/pupil replies/teacher asks question/. . .).

Interaction analysis systems frequently have built in to them outdated assumptions about teaching and learning. Flanders's system concentrates upon the 'affective' domain and *Mirrors for Behavior* classifies techniques according to their 'affective' or 'cognitive' focus. This split between affective and cognitive domains, dating at least from Bloom (1956),[5] is no longer accepted without question by educationalists in general. Certainly none of us would want to use such a simplistic dichotomy when talking about the complexities of classrooms in Britain.

Interaction analysis may also involve ideological assumptions in more subtle ways. Like much of the social-psychological and educational research conducted in the USA since the Second World War, it has developed from certain premises concerning 'democracy', 'authoritarianism', 'leadership' and 'mental hygiene'. Ned Flanders is expressly concerned to encourage 'indirect' teaching and, as a result, there is a latent evaluative residue in his observational system. It can be seen, for example, in Flanders's operational statement:

> Direct influence consists in those verbal statements of the teacher that restrict *freedom* of action, by focusing attention on a problem, interjecting teacher *authority* or both. (Flanders, 1965, p.9, emphasis added.)

This fact may not always be appreciated when the system is used in other, less experienced, hands.

These then are some of the major objections which [we] have to interaction analysis, the classroom research method which has dominated the American research scene for ten years and now threatens to be adopted wholesale, and without critical thought, in Britain. The next section deals with another American tradition of classroom research which is little known in this country but which all of us feel has greater potential for Britain.

'ANTHROPOLOGICAL' OBSERVATION

Outside the interaction analysis tradition in the USA there have been certain other important but widely neglected programmes of classroom research. Often described as 'anthropological', this work has developed beyond the margins of mainstream educational psychology and relates instead to social anthropology, psychiatry and participant observation research in sociology. No satisfactory name exists for this tradition. It has been described as 'microethnographical' (Smith and Geoffrey, 1968), 'naturalistic' (MacDonald, 1970) and 'ecological' (Parlett, 1969). Unlike the interaction analysis tradition, whose origins are clearly rooted in behavioural psychology, the anthropological tradition has no established roots. Some of its members are 'straight' anthropologists (e.g. Jules Henry), some are sociologists (e.g. Howard Becker), some are psychiatrists (e.g. Zachary Gussow) and some are 'converts' from behavioural psychology (e.g. Philip Jackson, Malcolm Parlett and Louis Smith).

In the USA this tradition is perhaps better known for its work in higher education (see, for example, Becker *et al.*, 1968, Kahne, 1969, and Parlett, 1969). It contrasts strongly with interaction analysis and can be thought of as representing an alternative tradition: one that goes back to Malinowski, Thomas and Waller, rather than Watson, Skinner and Bales.

While both interaction analysis and anthropological classroom research are concerned with developing 'metalanguages' (Simon and

Boyer, 1968, p.1) adequate to the complexity of the behaviour they countenance, the latter uses an approach based on ethnography rather than 'psychometry'; and a conceptual framework which considers education in broad socio-cultural terms, rather than, say, in 'cognitive' or 'affective' terms. In each case, 'knowledge', the 'curriculum', and even 'learning' are regarded differently. Methodologically, 'anthropological' classroom studies are based on participant observation, during which the observer immerses himself in the 'new culture'. That is, they involve the presence of an observer (or observers) for prolonged periods in a single or a small number of classrooms. During that time the observer not only observes, but also talks with participants; significantly, the ethnographer calls them informants, rather than subjects. Also, the anthropologist does not make such a strong category distinction between observer and observed as the interaction analyst does. Gussow and Vidich put the anthropological case most clearly:

> When the observers are physically present and physically approachable the concept of the observer as non-participant though sociologically correct is psychologically misleading. (Gussow, 1964, p.240)

> Whether the field-worker is totally, partially or not at all disguised, the respondent forms an image of him and uses that image as a basis of response. Without such an image, the relationship between the field-worker and the respondent by definition does not exist. (Vidich, 1935, p.35)

In addition to observing classroom life, the researcher may conduct formal interviews with the participants and ask them to complete questionnaires. Usually, to record his observations, the observer compiles field-notes or, more recently, field-recordings. Compared with the results of the interaction analysis, the data of the 'anthropological' researcher are relatively unsystematic and open-ended.[6]

The 'anthropologist' uses a holistic framework. He accepts as given the complex scene he encounters and takes this totality as his data base. He makes no attempt to manipulate, control or eliminate variables. Of course, the 'anthropologist' does not claim to account for every aspect of this totality in his analysis. He reduces the breadth of enquiry systematically to give more concentrated attention to the emerging issues. Starting with a wide angle of vision, he 'zooms' in and progressively focuses on those classroom features he considers to be most salient. Thus ethnographic research clearly dissociates itself from the *a priori* reductionism inherent in interaction analysts.

'Anthropological' classroom research, like interaction analysis, begins with description. But, whereas the former is governed by pre-ordained descriptive categories (e.g. 'verbal', 'non-verbal', 'teacher', 'pupil') the latter allows and encourages the development of *new* categories. Anthropological research can freely go beyond the *status quo* and develop new and potentially fertile descriptive languages. [. . .]

Unlike ethnographic classroom research, interaction analysis is, as stated above, often concerned with generating normative data, that is, in extrapolating from sample to population. It should be remembered, however, that statistical norms (e.g. 'teacher-talk percentages' (Flanders, 1970)) apply to the population *taken as a whole*, not to its individual members. They apply to individual settings only in probabilistic terms. And since settings are never equivalent, such statistical generalizations may not always be relevant or useful. [. . .]

It is often argued against anthropological studies that their results cannot be generalized to other settings. This criticism refers only to statistical generalizations. To an anthropological researcher, the development of generally or universally applicable statements is quite a different task, one that is never achieved merely by carrying out a survey. Despite their diversity, individual classrooms share many characteristics. Through the detailed study of one particular context it is still possible to clarify relationships, pinpoint critical processes and identify common phenomena. Later, abstracted summaries and general concepts can be formulated, which may, upon further investigation, be found to be germane to a wider variety of settings. Case studies, therefore, are not necessarily restricted in scope. Indeed, unlike interaction analysis, they can acknowledge both the particulars and the universals of classroom life. In this respect, interaction analysis is akin to demography or census-taking, whereas anthropological studies are equivalent to the small-scale studies commonly reported in medical journals.[7]

Thus, interaction analysis and anthropological traditions can be seen to differ in a number of respects. In the USA they are sharply insulated from one another. Interaction analysis has largely ignored classroom research conducted outside its own territorial preserve. For example, the AERA curriculum evaluation monograph on *Classroom Observation* (Gallagher *et al.*, 1970) contains no discussion or even acknowledgement of any of the anthropological literature related to curriculum evaluation (e.g. Russell, 1969, Smith and Keith, 1967, or Hanley *et al.*, 1969). Also, *Mirrors for Behavior* fails to acknowledge that there are (or even can be) '"metalanguages" for describing communication of various kinds' (p.1) that are based on anything other than measurement or *a priori* categorization.

Anthropological research has developed outside the prestige universities of the American east coast and is concentrated in the mid- and far-west. By comparison with interaction analysis, it is poorly funded, its findings are difficult to obtain and its formal outlets (journals and conferences) are minimal. In Britain, this unenviable state has yet to come about. Dialogue still takes place: recent classroom observation conferences have included papers reflecting both interests and British literature reviews (e.g. Delamont, 1973 and Walker, 1972) have considered the merits of both traditions. This reading is intended as a contribution to this continuing dialogue. We hope that proponents of interaction analysis will admit the value of other types of study, such as those reported here, and vice versa.[. . .]

Conclusion

Although for the purposes of this discussion we have divided classroom research in two fields, we do not regard them as necessarily mutually exclusive. Indeed, in our own work we are concerned to go beyond this distinction. The task is not easy, as the differences are clear and deep-rooted, and the respective positions entrenched. For this reason we suggest that significant advances will ultimately depend, not on increased technological sophistication nor upon some kind of methodological convergence, but instead upon a reconceptualization and transformation of the dimensions which divide the two traditions.

While research awaits this advance, it is still incumbent upon researchers to treat interaction analysis and anthropological classroom research for what they are. Confusion still exists as to their aims and objectives. Too often, questions such as 'What are they for? What can (or cannot) they do?' are not considered. As different tools, they are better suited to different tasks. A knowledge of their deficiencies is as important for their successful use, as an appreciation of their potential. Neither is, or can be, a universal panacea.

Thus, for example, to criticize anthropological studies for not providing demographic information is as misplaced as it is narrow-minded. Likewise, to complain that interaction systems are not as sensitive as, say, in-depth interviews, is to forget that they were never intended as clinical devices — their focus is the *average* rather than the *individual* classroom.[. . .]

Acknowledgements
A slightly different version of our argument has appeared in *Research in Education*, 11 May 1974. The authors wish to thank the editor for permission to reproduce it here. In addition we wish to thank all those who commented on earlier drafts of this paper, particularly those at the Centre for Research in the Educational Sciences, University of Edinburgh, and to thank the Social Science Research Council, the Scottish Council for Research in Education, and the Scottish Education Department for financial support during our research and the preparation of this paper.

Notes
1. During 1972 programmes were announced by NFER (The 'Secondary School Day' project and the 'Evaluation of the Primary School'); by the OECD (The International Microteaching Unit, University of Lancaster); and by the

Scottish Education Department (The Interaction Analysis Project, Callender Park College). These projects together represent a funding commitment approaching £¼ million.

2. For the sake of our discussion, 'interaction analysis' refers to any research technique which fulfils the criteria for inclusion in *Mirrors for Behavior* (Simon and Boyer, 1970). Strictly speaking, interaction analysis is the name given to the system developed by Ned Flanders. However, as 30 per cent of the classroom systems in *Mirrors for Behavior* are expressly related to interaction analysis (referring to Flanders or his forbears Bales and Withall in their abstracts) we feel the designation to be valid.

3. It is more correct, though perhaps tautological, to say that all the *widely used* systems are simple. Of the remainder, five require four observers, one requires an extensive knowledge of psychoanalysis, and one requires a knowledge of the foreign language being taught in the classroom. A few systems are also restricted in the situations in which they can be used (e.g. a 'correctional institution for delinquents').

4. For critiques of Flanders's system see Silberman (1970, p.455 ff.) and Mitchell (1969, pp.704-10).

5. This affective–cognitive category distinction dates back to Wolff (1679–1754) when it formed the foundation of faculty psychology – now largely disregarded (see O'Neil, 1968, pp.24-5).

6. This is not, however, to imply that all anthropological research is open-ended 'pure' research. Like interaction analysis it has been used in curriculum evaluation (e.g. Smith and Pohland, forthcoming, Parlett and Hamilton, 1972) and in teacher-training (e.g. Goldhammer, 1969).

7. See Glaser and Strauss (1967) and Strodtbeck (1969) for separate discussions of theory building and case study research.

References
Barker Lunn, J. C. (1970), *Streaming in the Primary School*, NFER.
Becker, H. S. *et al.* (1968), *Making the Grade*, Wiley.
Blishen, E. (1955), *Roaring Boys*, Thames & Hudson.
Bloom, B. S. *et al.* (1956), *Taxonomy of Educational Objectives Handbook I: Cognitive Domain*, McKay.
Delamont, S. (1973), 'Academic Conformity Observed: Studies in the Classroom', unpublished Ph.D. thesis, University of Edinburgh.
Flanders, N. A. (1965), *Teacher Influence, Pupil Attitudes and Achievement*, Cooperative Research Monograph, University of Michigan.
— (1966), *Interaction Analysis in the Classroom: A Manual for Observers*, revised edition, School of Education, University of Michigan.
— (1970), *Analyzing Teaching Behavior*, Addison-Wesley.
Gage, N. L. (1971), *Teacher Effectiveness and Teacher Education: the Search for Scientific Basis*, Pacific Books.
Gallagher, J. J. *et al.* (1970), *Classroom Observation*, AERA Monograph Series on Curriculum Evaluation No.6, Rand McNally.
Garner, J. (1972), 'Some aspects of behaviour in infant school classrooms', *Research in Education*, No.7, pp.28-47.
Glaser, B. G. and Strauss, A. (1967), *The Discovery of Grounded Theory*, Weidenfeld & Nicolson.

Goldhammer, R. (1969), *Clinical Supervision: Special Methods for the Supervision of Teachers*, Holt, Rinehart & Winston.

Gussow, Z. (1974), 'The observer-observed relationship as information about structures in small group research', *Psychiatry*, Vol.27, pp.236-47.

Hanley, J. P. *et al.*(1969), *Curiosity. Competence. Community*, Education Development Centre, Cambridge, Mass.

Holt, J. (1969), *How Children Fail*, Penguin.

Kahne, M. J. (1969), 'Psychiatrist Observer in the Classroom', *Medical Trial Technique Quarterly*, Vol.23, pp.81-98.

MacDonald, B. (1970), 'The Evaluation of the Humanities Curriculum Project', unpublished paper.

— and Rudduck, J. (1971), 'Curriculum Research and Development: Barriers to Success', *British Journal of Educational Psychology*, Vol.41, pp.148-54.

Medley, D. M. and H. E. and Mitzel, H. E. (1963), 'Measuring Classroom Behaviour by Systematic Observation', in N. L. Gage (ed.), *Handbook of Research on Teaching*, Rand McNally.

Mitchell, J. V. (1969), 'Education's Challenge to Psychology: the Prediction of Behaviour from Person–Environment Interaction', *Review of Educational Research*, Vol.39, pp.695-721.

Morrison, A. and McIntyre, D. (1969), *Teachers and Teaching*, Penguin.

O'Neil, W. M. (1968), *The Beginnings of Modern Psychology*, Penguin.

Parlett, M. R. (1969), 'Undergraduate Teaching Observed', *Nature*, Vol.223, pp.1102-4.

— and Hamilton, D. (1972), *Evaluation as Illumination: A New Approach to the Study of Innovatory Programs*, Occasional Paper 9, Centre for Research in the Educational Sciences, University of Edinburgh.

Russell, H. (1969), *Evaluation of Computer-Assisted Instruction Program*, CEMREL, St. Ann, Mo.

Silberman, C. E. (1970), *Crisis in the Classroom*, Vintage Books.

Simon, A. and Boyer, G. E. (eds) (1968), *Mirrors for Behavior*, Research for Better Schools, Philadelphia.

— (1970), *Mirrors for Behavior II*, Research for Better Schools, Philadelphia.

Smith, L. M. (1971), *Dilemma in Educational Innovation: a Problem for Anthropology as Clinical Method*, paper presented to AERA symposium 'Anthropological Approaches to the Study of Education', New York.

— and Keith, P. M. (1967), *Social Psychological Aspects of School Building Design*, USOE Cooperative Research Report No.S-223, Washington DC.

— and Geoffrey, W. (1968), *The Complexities of an Urban Classroom*, Holt, Rinehart & Winston.

— and Brock, J. A. M. (1970), *'Go Bug, Go!': Methodical Issues in Classroom Observation Research*, CEMREL, St. Ann, Mo.

— and Pohland, P. A. (forthcoming), 'Educational Technology and the Rural Highlands', in AERA Monograph Series on Curriculum Evaluation No.7, Rand McNally.

— and Brock, J. A. M. (forthcoming), *Teacher Plans and Classroom Interaction*, CEMREL, St. Ann, Mo.

Snyder, B. R. (1971), *The Hidden Curriculum*, Knopf.

Stones, E. and Morris, S. (1972), *Teaching Practice: Problems and Perspectives*,

Methuen.

Strodtbeck, F. (1969), 'Considerations of Meta-method in Cross-cultural Studies', in D. R. Price-Williams (ed.), *Cross-cultural Studies*, Penguin.

Vidich, A. J. (1955), 'Participant Observation and Collection and Interpretation of Data', *American Journal of Sociology*, Vol.60, pp.354-60.

Walker, R. (1972), 'The Sociology of Education and Life in School Classrooms', *International Review of Education*, Vol.18, pp.32-43.

3.6 Conversation Piece: The Practice of Interviewing in Case Study Research
H. Simons

This paper is an extract from a much longer one directed at 'outside' researchers entering schools to study educational processes. The original article explored all aspects of unstructured interviewing as a research tool in such a situation, including the procedures to be adopted for gaining access to schools and the informants within them. It drew extensively on the author's own experience in the 'Ford Safari Curriculum Evaluation Project'. The extract presented here is taken from that section of the paper dealing with interviewing technique, and has relevance to any researcher, including teachers doing a study of their own curriculum.

1. Process

Judging from the questions asked of case study workers both by new practitioners and by interviewees, many assume that the interview is a one-way process, for the researcher to gain information for a particular research enquiry; where the interviewer asks the questions and the interviewee 'gives' the information. But the process is much more complex than that – more dynamic, interpersonal, intangible.

Both the interviewer and the interviewee bring preconceptions to the interview which will affect what they say, hear and report and which may be confirmed or changed in the course of the interview. Both are making judgements of each other's attitudes and expectations as well as considering the content or implications of the question or issue under discussion. Perceptions differ too. How the interviewee perceives the interviewer as sympathetic, critical or theatening, for example, will influence what kind of information is offered; how the interviewer perceives the interviewee, as interested, indifferent or hostile, will affect how he or she behaves. The interview, in other words, is a complex

Simons, H. (1977), Conversation Piece: the Practice of Interviewing in Case Study Research, in *SAFARI* II CARE, UEA, Norwich.

Also in Adelman, C. (1981), *Uttering, Muttering: Collecting, Using and Reporting Talk for Social and Educational Research*, Grant McIntyre.

social process in which much more than information is being sought or communicated. (It can also be an educational process as interviewees begin to reflect on their own situation and, perhaps, continue the inquiry beyond the formal interview.) The interviewer should be continually responsive to the range of social and intellectual reactions in the process of engaging the person in talk: an interview should be a conversation piece, not an inquisition.

Given this emphasis, what does the interviewing process look like in practice? The following are points I try to keep in mind. They are not meant to sound prescriptive. What will suit one person or one situation may not suit another. I am simply going to try and uncover the process of interviewing as I have experienced it – to articulate what I think are the assumptions and principles I work with, or should work with, in interviewing.

1.1   It is important at the outset to establish confidence and trust so that people will speak freely. There must be some motivation to participate other than institutional expectation. On the whole, people will treat the interview seriously if they think you can change something or if they think you accept and understand their problems. Since researchers are rarely in a position to directly influence events they have to rely on demonstrating empathy with the interviewees' concerns. What can help to secure their confidence is to indicate indirectly that you have some understanding of the problems facing them. Offering confidentiality may help if this convention has meaning for them. So might informal chat around a topic of local or personal interest to the interviewee; although informal talk is sometimes perceived to be unrelated to the formal interview.

1.2   One way to engage interviewees' involvement in the study is to encourage them to talk about what interests them much as they might in a social conversation. This also helps to break down the formality of the interview over which the interviewer is perceived to have control. Reversing expectations however takes time and may need prompting. Try and dispossess them of any notion that you are the expert. Shift the role to them in early interviews by asking questions which touch on their concerns and which are open-ended enough to allow them scope to reply fully. Respond acceptingly so they will feel free to talk without feeling anxious about being judged or not giving the 'right response'. Let them shift from topic to topic. Counter any question to the interviewer with one which shifts the onus back to them to demonstrate that you really are interested in their perceptions and judgements.

Information people offer on their own initiative is more true, some argue, than what they say in answering questions. Whether or not this is so, interviewees' unsolicited responses frequently alert the interviewer to consider the subject under discussion in a new light and in the context central to the person interviewed. Piaget (1929), in criticizing the questionnaire as a means of obtaining access to a person's mental processes, put this point neatly when he wrote:

> But the real problem is to know how he [the subject]* frames the question to himself or if he frames it at all. The skill of the practitioner consists not in making him answer questions but in making him talk freely and thus encouraging the flow of his spontaneous tendencies instead of diverting it into the artificial channels of set question and answer. It consists in placing every symptom in its mental context rather than abstracting it from its context. (*My brackets.)

1.3   In many cases where both parties to the interview share a view of the task there is no need to ask many questions; it is more important to listen. A comparison of a tape recording where the interviewer does not speak for thirty minutes with one where the interviewer asks a question every second minute may illustrate the open-ended approach better than any description. (This is not to say that the interviewer is inactive. His presence, his responses, non-verbal though they may be, and how he takes notes, contribute in quite significant ways (See point 1.8.).) Usually the issues the interviewer thought of will be raised by the interviewee if the interviewer listens carefully and refrains from asking questions too soon. Take the following example related by an interviewee:

> "It is difficult for me to hold a dialogue," he said, "someone came to interview me once and I gave a monologue for two hours . . . I liked him. He was an easy person to talk to. Then I realised the time. 'You must have some questions' I said to the interviewer.
> 'No', the interviewer replied, 'you've answered them all.'"

1.4   Listening by itself, of course, does not always lead to depth of understanding. Probing is necessary to get behind the expected response or test the significance of what you are being told. Taking up cues from the interviewee, asking them to elaborate or explain why they adopted a particular view or introducing a theme for comment are all means of extending the initial response. But these can still be pursued in a non-directed way if the aim of the research is to portray the interviewees' judgements, perceptions and theories of events.

1.5   It is evident from the emphasis given to the above points that I think one of the most common errors in open-ended interviewing is failing to listen, either by asking too many questions or interrupting to confirm one's own hypotheses. A second related error is seeking closure too soon by accepting the initial response too readily, summarizing erroneously or by asking questions which give the interviewee a plausible response without committing him to reveal what he really thinks or feels. (This is a special danger when interviewing pupils. See point 2.) Timely summarizing of course is very useful to clarify issues and shift the interview a stage further.

1.6   In summary, the kind of skill flexible interviewing calls for is what the anthropologist, Hortense Powdermaker, has called 'psychological mobility' (quoted in Walker, 1974, p.90) or, the novelist, Sybille Bedford, 'emotional intelligence' (ibid., p.91). Sybille Bedford (1968) summarizes the complex skills involved when she writes:

> "It takes two to tell the truth."
> "One for one side, one for the other?"
> "That's not what I mean. I mean one to tell, one to hear. A speaker and a receiver. To tell the truth about any complex situation requires a certain attitude in the receiver."
> "What is required in the receiver?"
> "I would say first of all a level of emotional intelligence."
> "Imagination?"
> "Disciplined."
> "Sympathy? Attention?"
> "And patience."
> "All of these. And a taste for the truth – an immense willingness to *see*."

1.7   If the study involves a series of interviews, who sets and shifts the topics may vary from interview to interview. What is appropriate at one point may not be at another, as understanding and perceptions change. At times the interviewer may want to feed in some interpretation, at other times to take up a cue from the interviewee. Towards the end of the study precisely the opposite tactic from responding to the interviewee's initiative may be appropriate, particularly if the interviewee has a habit of repeating his story over and over again. In such a case the interviewer may want to be quite assertive or exclusive about the issues he would like the interviewee to comment upon.

1.8   Interviewing encompasses more than listening, asking questions and being socially responsive. Often it is important to judge the significance of what is said by non-verbal cues such as gestures, the tone of the voice, how people dress, how they look, how and where they sit or to infer from what is not said or what is denied what the interviewee thinks or feels. At the same time acceptance of non-verbal cues may be misleading. Their significance has to be judged in relation to all the data obtained.

1.9   In what order people are interviewed affects the process and the kind of information obtained. If teachers are interviewed after the head they may assume what he has told you and be guarded in their response. If pupils are the last to be interviewed – the usual pattern – they may feel that they are expected to confirm what the teachers said. While much of the data must remain locked in confidentiality it is difficult for the interviewer to avoid using the information gained from previous interviews to sharpen and focus subsequent ones. It may also be necessary to further understanding. But it does raise a difficult ethical question if confidentiality is assured. The interviewer may breach confidentiality quite unwittingly as he asks a question which was stimulated by information he gained from previous interviews. It is not difficult to offer a defence in such a case and thus protect previous interviewees from feeling you have betrayed their confidence. The interviewer can simply deny the inference (which may not, in fact, be true) or indicate that the issue was highlighted in a previous setting. This may seem a minor point to deliberate but it does illustrate why the interviewer needs to be continually responsive to the reactions of interviewees if he wants to retain trust and obtain reliable data.

1.10 It may also be useful to note the number and kind of interruptions accepted in the interview. Does the head, for instance, take an interruption from the deputy head but dismiss one from the careers' officer? Does he differentiate between the telephone calls he takes and those he defers? Who comes into the room while you are there? What issues does he discuss with others while you are there and what does he reserve? Not only may these observations indicate how the interviewer or whole study is perceived, they offer useful clues for how to act subsequently.

2. Special Problems in Interviewing Pupils

Many of the points already mentioned apply equally to pupils but are more difficult to put into practice. Talking too much, listening too little, suggesting answers are real traps if one is aspiring to reflect pupils' thoughts and feelings. The constraints of interviewing within the school in a short time do not make the task any easier.[1]

2.1 Pupils learn to live by rules and conventions prescribed by those responsible for the running of the school and may not *feel as free* as teachers to express their attitudes and feelings. In schools which have a fairly traditional curriculum, furthermore, pupils may not have had much opportunity to talk in class or informally to teachers outside class. A stranger coming in for a few odd days may have difficulty *getting beyond institutional habits*. Some pupils appear to treat the interview as a test situation and try to give 'right' answers.

Direct questioning while providing a check on perceptions or events described by teachers rarely gets beyond conforming to what the teacher or institution expects and, therefore, often fails to reveal understanding of the pupil's experience. More inferences have to be drawn or a more indirect starting point adopted to try and free pupils from the constraints of the school environment.

2.2 Where pupils have been selected by the teacher they may associate the interviewer with teachers and the authority structure and this may restrict discussion. (This differs from the authority of the research agency which, while useful to gain access, may also inhibit interaction.) You may be seen as a spy of the establishment. It may help to indicate that you were once a teacher but now are visiting schools talking to pupils about what school is like from their point of view. Or you may appeal to status "I am from the university . . ." or to their interest in helping you with research, though this tactic appears to have low credibility. Whatever tactic is adopted it is important to try and disassociate yourself from the school establishment. At the same time to maintain credibility with staff one must avoid the opposite danger of appearing to be on the side of the pupils.

Some pupils may be reluctant to talk out of loyalty to teachers or the institution, fear of peer group or teacher reprisal, or simply lack of interest in your enterprise or the school. But others may be quite willing to vent spleen and seek your sanction and support. "Can you change things for us, Miss?" is a common request from the disgruntled or hapless fourth-year leaver.

2.3   It is not simply a problem of getting pupils to talk but to get them to talk on relevant issues. They may well chat on about school meals, assembly, uniform (which may give you insight into how the school is run) but not so easily talk about teachers, subjects or school. A common response to questions about school for a fourth-year leaver, for example, is to say, "It's boring". It is important to sort out boredom or institutional responses from what they are really saying. Sometimes one of the peer group may begin to reveal the actuality. "They say it's boring, but they don't mean that. In such-and-such a case this happened . . ." Other times the interviewer has to infer.

2.4   In section 1.5 I noted that seeking closure too soon was a special danger when interviewing pupils. Note the following instance where I interrupted a pupil in an interview on the theme of participation in class discussions to summarize what I thought she might feel. The girl was a 'non-talker' in class.

> "Did you feel . . . that you did have things to say?"
> "Yes. But often other people said them . . ."
> "And that put you off saying something another time did it?"
> "Umm. If you say something you sometimes think that if you say something wrong people are going to think it is funny."

Here the pupil dismissed my summary question in fact to go on to say why she felt diffident about talking in class. In other cases such a question effectively closes discussion having presented the pupil with an acceptable response. If pupils do associate the interviewer with teachers, 'wanting to please the teacher' may extend to wanting to please the interviewer.

2.5   Acceptance of non-verbal cues may be especially misleading when talking to pupils. The pupil who is having difficulty expressing himself for instance, frequently responds to questions by saying nothing, with gestures – shifting in his seat, shrugging his shoulders – or by how he looks. Here there is often a tendency for the interviewer to rely on non-verbal cues as indicators of what the pupil thinks and feels. If you accept them too readily you may simply be creating a problem which may end up in an interviewer's monologue or a multiple choice check-out, "Is it this, this . . . or this . . . that you think?" none of which may actually be what the pupil does think.

2.6 With pupils peer group norms may be supportive or destructive, either way quite a powerful influence. In general, if pupils know each other and have worked together in groups before, they are quite supportive in a group interview. Take the silent pupil, for instance. If she does not speak up much in a group interview other pupils will often explain what she feels or say affectionately, "She's alright, she's much better at writing than talking". Or, as in the following example, she may explain herself. Carol is the pupil in question.

Interviewer: Does the lesson help the shy ones or does it make them stand out more?
Angela: They're so quiet and then all of a sudden one of them'll speak and you think 'What's come over them?' I suppose they've got their opinion in their head and they hear everyone else talking so they think they will.
Patricia: Carol's quiet.
Interviewer: You're quiet Carol?
Angela: Not as quiet as you used to be.
Carol: I'm better than I used to be.
Interviewer: You didn't like speaking?
Carol: I'd only talk when I was asked a question.
Angela: Sort of speak when you're spoken to. I noticed that when I first met her, I thought she was quiet.
Interviewer: But now you speak when you want to put your point of view.
Carol: Yes. When I think someone's wrong, I'll say what I think.
Interviewer: And how long did it take you to get to this stage?
Carol: Well, it was more friendly, we sat in a circle and we could speak to each other. That was better and it didn't take long, only a few lessons.
Angela: I noticed after three or four lessons Carol started speaking more.
Patricia: I spoke the first lesson.
Angela: So did I.
Carol: It gets me mad when people say you're very quiet though. I enjoy other people's views as well.
Angela to Patricia: Probably the way you shout, you probably frighten them to death.

If pupils do not know each other, peer group norms may operate in a constricting way and one may get little mileage out of group interviews with pupils. The same may be true of interviewing boys and girls together.

3.   Some Continuing Problems

However experienced in interviewing one becomes there will always be situations you feel you did not handle satisfactorily. Some which remain problematic for me include:

— how to get the teacher out of the room when you want to interview students;

— how to interview inarticulate pupils;

— how to respond to the person who reveals all and immediately wishes he had said nothing;

— how to evoke pupil responses which are not just responses to the interview situation;

— how to deftly get out of the headmaster's office;

— how to get beyond the institutional response in a short time;

— how to avoid the headmaster escorting you to coffee in the staff room when you have arranged to interview a teacher immediately afterwards;

— how to deal with the unanticipated, like teachers not involved in the study wanting to be interviewed when you are working to a tight schedule;

— how to respond if the interviewee tries to reverse roles and assume the interviewer's position.

If some of these points sound trivial this is perhaps evidence of the extent to which we underestimate the importance and the delicacy of the social process which the case study worker is compelled to negotiate in the pursuit of data. There are no formulae, no prescriptions for resolving such problems. Resolution is a matter for personal judgement in the specific context.

Note

1. For those interested in interviewing pupils unconstrained by the school context and with a view to understanding their mental processes, Piaget (1929) is valuable reading.

References

Bedford, S. (1968), *A Compass Error*, Fontana.

Piaget, J. (1929), trans. Joan and Andrew Tomlinson, *The Child's Conception of the World*, Routledge & Kegan Paul, introductory chapter, 'Problems and Methods', p.4.

Walker, R. (1974), 'The Conduct of Educational Case Study: Ethics Theory and Procedures', *SAFARI, Innovation, Evaluation, Research, and The Problem of Control*, Some Interim Papers, CARE, University of East Anglia, p.90.

3.7 Problems of Inference and Proof in Participant Observation
H. S. Becker

The participant observer gathers data by participating in the daily life of the group or organization he studies.[1] He watches the people he is studying to see what situations they ordinarily meet and how they behave in them. He enters into conversation with some or all of the participants in these situations and discovers their interpretations of the events he has observed.

Let me describe, as one specific instance of observational technique, what my colleagues and I have done in studying a medical school. We went to lectures with students taking their first two years of basic science and frequented the laboratories in which they spend most of their time, watching them and engaging in casual conversation as they dissected cadavers or examined pathology specimens. We followed these students to their fraternity houses and sat around while they discussed their school experiences. We accompanied students in the clinical years on rounds with attending physicians, watched them examine patients on the wards and in the clinics, sat in on discussion groups and oral exams. We ate with the students and took night call with them. We pursued interns and residents through their crowded schedules of teaching and medical work. We stayed with one small group of students on each service for periods ranging from a week to two months, spending many full days with them. The observational situations allowed time for conversation and we took advantage of this to interview students about things that had happened and were about to happen, and about their own backgrounds and aspirations.

Sociologists usually use this method when they are especially interested in understanding a particular organization or substantive problem rather than demonstrating relations between abstractly defined variables. They attempt to make their research theoretically meaningful, but they assume that they do not know enough about the organization *a priori* to identify relevant problems and hypotheses and that they must discover these in the course of the research. Though participant observation can be used to test *a priori* hypotheses, and

Becker, H. S. (1958), 'Problems of Inference and Proof in Participant Observation', *American Sociological Review*, Vol.23, pp.652–60.

therefore need not be as unstructured as the example I have given above, this is typically not the case. My discussion refers to the kind of participant observation study which seeks to discover hypotheses as well as to test them.

Observational research produces an immense amount of detailed description; our files contain approximately 5,000 single-spaced pages of such material. Faced with such a quantity of 'rich' but varied data, the researcher faces the problem of how to analyze it systematically and then to present his conclusions so as to convince other scientists of their validity. Participant observation (indeed, qualitative analysis generally) has not done well with this problem, and the full weight of evidence for conclusions and the processes by which they were reached are usually not presented, so that the reader finds it difficult to make his own assessment of them and must rely on his faith in the researcher.

In what follows I try to pull out and describe *the basic analytic operations carried on in participant observation*, for three reasons: to make these operations clear to those unfamiliar with the method; by attempting a more explicit and systematic description, to aid those working with the method in organizing their own research; and, most importantly, in order to propose some changes in analytic procedures and particularly in reporting results which will make the processes by which conclusions are reached and substantiated more accessible to the reader.

The first thing we note about participant observation research is that analysis is carried on *sequentially*,[2] important parts of the analysis being made while the researcher is still gathering his data. This has two obvious consequences: further data gathering takes its direction from provisional analyses; and the amount and kind of provisional analysis carried on is limited by the exigencies of the field work situation, so that final comprehensive analyses may not be possible until the field work is completed.

We can distinguish three distinct stages of analysis conducted in the field itself, and a fourth stage, carried on after completion of the field work. These stages are differentiated, first, by their logical sequence: each succeeding stage depends on some analysis in the preceding stage. They are further differentiated by the fact that different kinds of conclusions are arrived at in each stage and that these conclusions are put to different uses in the continuing research. Finally, they are differentiated by the different criteria that are used to assess evidence and to reach conclusions in each stage. The three stages of field analysis are: the selection and definition of problems, concepts, and indices; the check on the frequency and distribution of phenomena; and the incorporation of individual findings into a model of the organization under study.[3] The fourth stage of final analysis involves problems of presentation of evidence and proof.

Selection and Definition of Problems, Concepts and Indices

In this stage, the observer looks for problems and concepts that give promise of yielding the greatest understanding of the organization he is studying, and for items which may serve as useful indicators of facts which are harder to observe. The typical conclusion that his data yield is the simple one that a given phenomenon exists, that a certain event occurred once, or that two phenomena were observed to be related in one instance: the conclusion says nothing about the frequency or distribution of the observed phenomenon.

By placing such an observation in the context of a sociological theory, the observer selects concepts and defines problems for further investigation. He constructs a theoretical model to account for that one case, intending to refine it in the light of subsequent findings. For instance, he might find the following: 'Medical student X referred to one of his patients as a "crock" today.'[4] He may then connect this finding with a sociological theory suggesting that occupants of one social category in an institution classify members of other categories by criteria derived from the kinds of problems these other persons raise in the relationship. This combination of observed fact and theory directs him to look for the problems in student–patient interaction indicated by the term 'crock'. By discovering specifically what students have in mind in using the term, through questioning and continued observation, he may develop specific hypotheses about the nature of these interactional problems.

Conclusions about a single event also lead the observer to decide on specific items which might be used as indicators[5] of less easily observed phenomena. Noting that in at least one instance a given item is closely related to something less easily observable, the researcher discovers possible shortcuts easily enabling him to observe abstractly defined variables. For example, he may decide to investigate the hypothesis that medical freshmen feel they have more work to do than can possibly be managed in the time allowed them. One student, in discussing this problem, says he faces so much work that, in contrast to his undergraduate days, he is forced to study many hours over the weekend and finds that even this is insufficient. The observer decides, on the basis of this one instance, that he may be able to use complaints about weekend work as an indicator of student perspectives on the amount of work they have to do. The selection of indicators for more abstract variables occurs in two ways: the observer may become aware of some very specific phenomenon first and later see that it may be used as an indicator of some larger class of phenomena; or he may have the larger problem in mind and search for specific indicators to use in studying it.

Whether he is defining problems or selecting concepts and indicators, the researcher at this stage is using his data only to speculate about possibilities. Further operations at later stages may force him to discard most of the provisional hypotheses. Nevertheless, problems of evidence arise even at this point, for the researcher must assess the individual items on which his speculations are based in order not to waste time tracking down false leads. We shall eventually need a systematic statement of canons to be applied to individual items of evidence. Lacking such a statement, let us consider some commonly used tests. (The observer typically applies these tests as seems reasonable to him during this and the succeeding stage in the field. In the final stage, they are used more systematically in an overall assessment of the total evidence for a given conclusion.)

THE CREDIBILITY OF INFORMANTS

Many items of evidence consist of statements by members of the group under study about some event which has occurred or is in process. Thus, medical students make statements about faculty behaviour which form part of the basis for conclusions about faculty—student relations. These cannot be taken at face value; nor can they be dismissed as valueless. In the first place, the observer can use the statement as evidence *about the event*, if he takes care to evaluate it by the criteria an historian uses in examining a personal document. (Cf. Gottschalk *et al.*, 1945.) Does the informant have reason to lie or conceal some of what he sees as the truth? Does vanity or expediency lead him to mis-state his own role in an event or his attitude toward it? Did he actually have an opportunity to witness the occurrence he describes or is hearsay the source of his knowledge? Do his feelings about the issues or persons under discussion lead him to alter his story in some way?

Secondly, even when a statement examined in this way proves to be seriously defective as an accurate report of an event, it may still provide useful evidence for a different kind of conclusion. Accepting the sociological proposition that an individual's statements and descriptions of events are made from a perspective which is a function of his position in the group, the observer can interpret such statements and descriptions as indications of the individual's perspective on the point involved.

VOLUNTEERED OR DIRECTED STATEMENTS

Many items of evidence consist of informants' remarks to the observer about themselves or others or about something which has happened to them; these statements range from those which are a part of the running casual conversation of the group to those arising in a long intimate tête-à-tête between observer and informant. The researcher assesses the evidential value of such statements quite differently, depending on whether they have been made independently of the observer (volunteered) or have been directed by a question from the observer. A freshman medical student might remark to the observer or to another student that he has more material to study than he has time to master;

or the observer might ask, 'Do you think you are being given more work than you can handle?', and receive an affirmative answer.

This raises an important question: to what degree is the informant's statement the same one he might give, either spontaneously or in answer to a question, in the absence of the observer? The volunteered statement seems likely to reflect the observer's preoccupations and possible biases less than one which is made in response to some action of the observer, for the observer's very question may direct the informant into giving an answer which might never occur to him otherwise. Thus, in the example above, we are more sure that the students are concerned about the amount of work given them when they mention this of their own accord than we are when the idea may have been stimulated by the observer asking the question.

THE OBSERVER – INFORMANT – GROUP EQUATION

Let us take two extremes to set the problem. A person may say or do something when alone with the observer or when other members of the group are also present. The evidential value of an observation of this behavior depends on the observer's judgment as to whether the behavior is equally likely to occur in both situations. On the one hand, an informant may say and do things when alone with the observer that accurately reflect his perspective but which would be inhibited by the presence of the group. On the other hand, the presence of others may call forth behaviour which reveals more accurately the person's perspective but would not be enacted in the presence of the observer alone. Thus, students in their clinical years may express deeply 'idealistic' sentiments about medicine when alone with the observer, but behave and talk in a very 'cynical' way when surrounded by fellow students. An alternative to judging one or the other of these situations as more reliable is to view each datum as valuable in itself, but with respect to different conclusions. In the example above, we might conclude that students have 'idealistic' sentiments but that group norms may not sanction their expression. (See further Becker, 1956.)

In assessing the value of items of evidence, we must also take into account the observer's role in the group; for the way the subjects of his study define that role affects what they will tell him or let him see. If the observer carries on his research incognito, participating as a full-fledged member of the group, he will be privy to knowledge that would normally be shared by such a member and might be hidden from an outsider. He could properly interpret his own experience as that of a hypothetical 'typical' group member. On the other hand, if he is known to be a researcher, he must learn how group members define him and in par-ticular whether or not they believe that certain kinds of information and events should be kept hidden from him. He can interpret evidence more accurately when the answers to these questions are known.

Checking the Frequency and Distribution of Phenomena

The observer, possessing many provisional problems, concepts and indicators, now wishes to know which of these are worth pursuing as major foci of his study. He does this, in part, by discovering if the events that prompted their development are typical and widespread, and by seeing how these events are distributed among categories of people and organizational sub-units. He reaches conclusions that are essentially quantitative, using them to describe the organization he is studying.

Participant observations have occasionally been gathered in standardized form capable of being transformed into legitimate statistical data. (See Blau, 1954.) But the exigencies of the field usually prevent the collection of data in such a form as to meet the assumptions of statistical tests, so that the observer deals in what have been called 'quasi-statistics'. (See Lazarsfeld and Barton, 1951, pp.346-8.) His conclusions, while implicitly numerical, do not require precise quantification. For instance, he may conclude that members of freshmen medical fraternities typically sit together during lectures while other students sit in less stable smaller groupings. His observations may indicate such a wide disparity between the two groups in this respect that the inference is warranted without a standardized counting operation. Occasionally, the field situation may permit him to make similar observations or ask similar questions of many people, systematically searching for quasi-statistical support for a conclusion about frequency or distribution.

In assessing the evidence for such a conclusion the observer takes a cue from his statistical colleagues. Instead of arguing that a conclusion is either totally true or false, he decides, if possible, how *likely* it is that his conclusion about the frequency or distribution of some phenomenon is an accurate quasi-statistic, just as the statistician decides, on the basis of the varying values of a correlation coefficient or a significance figure, that his conclusion is more or less likely to be accurate. The kind of evidence may vary considerably and the degree of the observer's confidence in the conclusion will vary accordingly. In arriving at this assessment, he makes use of some of the criteria described above, as well as those adopted from quantitative techniques.

Suppose, for example, that the observer concludes that medical students share the perspective that their school should provide them with the clinical experience and the practice in techniques necessary for a general practitioner. His confidence in the conclusion would vary according to the nature of the evidence, which might take any of the following forms:

1. Every member of the group said, *in response to a direct question*, that this was the way he looked at the matter.

2. *Every* member of the group *volunteered* to an observer that this was how he viewed the matter.

3. *Some given proportion* of the group's members either *answered* a direct question or *volunteered* the information that he shared this perspective, but none of the others was asked or volunteered information on the subject.

4. Every member of the group was asked or volunteered information, but *some given proportion said* they viewed the matter from the differing perspective of a prospective specialist.

5. No one was asked questions or volunteered information on the subject, but *all members were observed to engage in behavior* or to make other statements from which the analyst *inferred* that the general practitioner perspective was being used by them as a basic, though unstated, premise. For example, all students might have been observed to complain that the University Hospital received too many cases of rare diseases that general practitioners rarely see.

6. *Some given proportion* of the group *was observed* using the general practitioner perspective as a basic premise in their activities, but *the rest of the group* was not observed engaging in such activities.

7. *Some proportion* of the group *was observed* engaged in activities implying the general practitioner perspective while *the remainder* of the group was observed engaged in activities implying the perspective of the prospective specialist.

The researcher also takes account of the possibility that his observations may give him evidence of different kinds on the point under consideration. Just as he is more convinced if he has many items of evidence than if he has a few, so he is more convinced of a conclusion's validity if he has *many kinds* of evidence. (See Gouldner, 1954.) For instance, he may be especially persuaded that a particular norm exists and affects group behavior if the norm is not only described by group members but also if he observes events in which the norm can be 'seen' to operate — if, for example, students tell him that they are thinking of becoming general practitioners and he also observes their complaints about the lack of cases of common diseases in University Hospital.

The conclusiveness which comes from the convergence of several kinds of evidence reflects the fact that separate varieties of evidence can be reconceptualized as deductions from a basic proposition which have now been verified in the field. In the above case, the observer might have deduced the desire to have experience with cases like those the general practitioner treats from the desire to practice that style of medicine. Even though the deduction is made after the fact, confirmation of it buttresses the argument that the general practitioner perspective is a group norm.

It should be remembered that these operations, when carried out in the field, may be so interrupted because of imperatives of the field situation that they are not carried on as systematically as they might be. Where this is the case, the overall assessment can be postponed until the final stage of post field work analysis.

Construction of Social System Models

The final stage of analysis in the field consists of incorporating individual findings into a generalized model of the social system or organization under study or some part of that organization.[6] The concept of social system is a basic intellectual tool of modern sociology. The kind of participant observation discussed here is related directly to this concept, explaining particular social facts by explicit reference to their involvement in a complex of interconnected variables that the observer constructs as a theoretical model of the organization. In this final stage, the observer designs a descriptive model which best explains the data he has assembled.

The typical conclusion of this stage of the research is a statement about a set of complicated interrelations among many variables. Although some progress is being made in formalizing this operation through use of factor analysis and the relational analysis of survey data (see Gouldner 1957b—1958, Coleman 1958), observers usually view currently available statistical techniques as inadequate to express their conceptions and find it necessary to use words. The most common kinds of conclusions at this level include:

1. Complex statements of the necessary and sufficient conditions for the existence of some phenomenon. The observer may conclude, for example, that medical students develop consensus about limiting the amount of work they will do because (a) they are faced with a large amount of work, (b) they engage in activities which create communication channels between all members of the class, and (c) they face immediate dangers in the form of examinations set by the faculty.
2. Statements that some phenomenon is an 'important' or 'basic' element in the organization. Such conclusions, when elaborated, usually point to the fact that this phenomenon exercises a persistent and continuing influence on diverse events. The observer might conclude that the ambition to become a general practitioner is 'important' in the medical school under study, meaning that many particular judgments and choices are made by students in terms of this ambition and many features of the school's organization are arranged to take account of it.
3. Statements identifying a situation as an instance of some process or phenomenon described more abstractly in sociological theory. Theories posit relations between many abstractly defined phenomena, and conclusions of this kind imply that relationships posited in generalized form

hold in this particular instance. The observer, for example, may state that a cultural norm of the medical students is to express a desire to become a general practitioner; in so doing, he in effect asserts that the sociological theory about the functions of norms and the processes by which they are maintained which he holds to be true in general is true in this case.

In reaching such types of conclusions, the observer characteristically begins by constructing models of parts of the organization as he comes in contact with them, discovers concepts and problems, and the frequency and distribution of the phenomena these call to his attention. After constructing a model specifying the relationships among various elements of this part of the organization, the observer seeks greater accuracy by successively refining the model to take account of evidence which does not fit his previous formulation,[7] by searching for negative cases (items of evidence which run counter to the relationships hypothesized in the model) which might force such revision; and by searching intensively for the interconnections *in vivo* of the various elements he has conceptualized from his data. While a provisional model may be shown to be defective by a negative instance which crops up unexpectedly in the course of the field work, the observer may infer what kinds of evidence would be likely to support or to refute his model and may make an intensive search for such evidence. (See Lindsmith, 1952.)

After the observer has accumulated several partial models of this kind, he seeks connections between them and thus begins to construct an overall model of the entire organization. An example from our study shows how this operation is carried on during the period of field work. (The reader will note, in this example, how use is made of findings typical of earlier states of analysis.)

When we first heard medical students apply the term 'crock' to patients we made an effort to learn precisely what they meant by it. We found, through interviewing students about cases both they and the observer had seen, that the term referred in a derogatory way to patients with many subjective symptoms but no discernible physical pathology. Subsequent observations indicated that this usage was a regular feature of student behavior and thus that we should attempt to incorporate this fact into our model of student-patient behavior. The derogatory character of the term suggested in particular that we investigate the reasons students disliked these patients. We found that this dislike was related to what we discovered to be the students' perspective on medical school: the view that they were in school to get experience in recognizing and treating those common diseases most likely to be encountered in general practice. 'Crocks', presumably having no disease, could furnish no such experience. We were thus led to specify connections between the student-patient relationship and the student's view of the purpose of his professional education. Questions concerning the genesis of this perspective led to discoveries about the organization of the student body and communication among students, phenomena which we had been assigning to another part-model. Since 'crocks' were also disliked because they gave the student no opportunity to assume medical responsibility, we were able to connect this aspect to the student – patient relationship with still another tentative model of the value system and hierarchical organization of the school, in which medical responsibility plays an important role.

Again, it should be noted that analysis of this kind is carried on in the field as time permits. Since the construction of a model is the analytic operation most closely related to the observer's techniques and interests he usually spends a great deal of time thinking about these problems. But he is usually unable to be as systematic as he would like until he reaches the final stage of analysis.

Final Analysis and the Presentation of Results

The final systematic analysis, carried on after the field work is completed, consists of rechecking and rebuilding models as carefully and with as many safeguards as the data will allow. For instance, in checking the accuracy of statements about the frequency and distribution of events, the researcher can index and arrange his material so that every item of information is accessible and taken account of in assessing the accuracy of any given conclusion. He can profit from the observation of Lazarsfeld and Barton that the 'analysis of "quasi-statistical data" can probably be made more systematic than it has been in the past, if the logical structure of quantitative research at least is kept in mind to give general warnings and directions to the qualitative observer' (Lazarsfeld and Barton, 1955, p.348).

An additional criterion for the assessment of this kind of evidence is the state of the observer's conceptualization of the problem at the time the item of evidence was gathered. The observer may have his problem well worked out and be actively looking for evidence to test an hypothesis, or he may not be as yet aware of the problem. The evidential value of items in his field notes will vary accordingly, the basis of consideration being the likelihood of discovering negative cases of the proposition he eventually uses the material to establish. The best evidence may be that gathered in the most unthinking fashion, when the observer has simply recorded the item although it has no place in the system of concepts and hypotheses he is working with at the time, for there might be less bias produced by the wish to substantiate or repudiate a particular idea. On the other hand, a well-formulated hypothesis makes possible a deliberate search for negative cases, particularly when other knowledge suggests likely areas in which to look for such evidence. This kind of search requires advanced conceptualization of the problem, and evidence gathered in this way might carry greater weight for certain kinds of conclusions. Both procedures are relevant at different stages of the research.

In the post field work stage of analysis, the observer carries on the model building operation more systematically. He considers the character of his conclusions and decides on the kind of evidence that might cause their rejection, deriving further tests by deducing logical consequences and ascertaining whether or not the data support the deductions. He considers reasonable alternative hypotheses and whether or not the evidence refutes them.[8] Finally, he completes the job of establishing interconnections between partial models so as to achieve an overall synthesis incorporating all conclusions.

After completing the analysis, the observer faces the knotty problem of how to present his conclusions and the evidence for them. Readers of qualitative research reports commonly and justifiably complain that they are told little or nothing about the evidence for conclusions or the operations by which the evidence has been assessed. A more adequate presentation of the data, of the research operations, and of the researcher's inferences may help to meet this problem.

But qualitative data and analytic procedures, in contrast to quantitative ones, are difficult to present adequately. Statistical data can be summarized in tables, and descriptive measures of various kinds and the methods by which they are handled can often be accurately reported in the space required to print a formula. This is so in part because the methods have been systematized so that they can be referred to in this shorthand fashion and in part because the data have been collected for a fixed, usually small, number of categories — the presentation of data need be nothing more than a report of the number of cases to be found in each category.

The data of participant observation do not lend themselves to such ready summary. They frequently consist of many different kinds of observations which cannot be simply categorized and counted without losing some of their value as evidence — for, as we have seen, many points need to be taken into account in putting each datum to use. Yet it is clearly out of the question to publish all the evidence. Nor is it any solution, as Kluckhohn has suggested for the similar problem of presenting life history materials (Gottschalk *et al.*, 1945, pp.150-6), to publish a short version and to make available the entire set of materials on microfilm or in some other inexpensive way; this ignores the problem of how to present *proof*.

In working over the material on the medical school study a possible solution to this problem, with which we are experimenting, is a description of the natural history of our conclusions, presenting the evidence as it came to the attention of the observer during the successive stages of his conceptualization of the problem. The term 'natural history' implies not the presentation of every datum, but only the characteristic forms data took at each stage of the research. This involves description of the form that data took and any significant exceptions, taking account of the canons discussed above, in presenting the various statements of findings and the inferences and conclusions drawn from them. In this way, evidence is assessed as the substantive analysis is presented. The reader would be able, if this method were used, to follow the details of the analysis and to see how and on what basis any conclusion was reached. This would give the reader, as do present modes of statistical presentation, opportunity to make his own judgment as to the adequacy of the proof and the degree of confidence to be assigned the conclusion.

Conclusion

I have tried to describe the analytic field work characteristic of participant observation, first, in order to bring out the fact that the technique consists of something more than merely immersing oneself in data and 'having insights'. The discussion may also serve to stimulate those who work with this and similar techniques to attempt greater formalization and systematization of the various operations they use, in order that qualitative research may become more a 'scientific' and less an 'artistic' kind of endeavor. Finally, I have proposed that new modes of reporting results be introduced, so that the reader is given greater access to the data and procedures on which conclusions are based.

Notes

1. This paper grew out of my experience in the research reported in Becker *et al.* (1961). I worked out the basic approach in partnership with Blanche Geer and we then applied it in writing up our study of medical education and in the research reported in Becker *et al.* (1968). Our own experience has been largely with the role Gold terms 'participant as observer', but the methods discussed here should be relevant to other field situations. Cf. Gold, 1958.

2. In this respect, the analytic methods I discuss bear a family resemblance to the technique of *analytic induction*. Cf. Lindesmith (1947), especially pp.5-20, and the subsequent literature cited in Turner (1953), pp.604-11.

3. My discussion of these stages is abstract and simplified and does not attempt to deal with practical and technical problems of participant observation study. The reader should keep in mind that in practice the research will involve all these operations simultaneously with reference to different particular problems.

4. The examples of which our hypothetical observer makes use are drawn from Becker *et al.*, 1961.

5. The problem of indicators is discussed by Lazarsfeld and Barton (1951 and 1955) (the latter important paper parallels the present discussion in many places); and Kendall and Lazarsfeld (1950).

6. The relation between theories based on the concept of social system and participant observation was pointed out to me by Alvin W. Gouldner. See Gouldner, 1956 and 1957a.
7. Note again the resemblance to analytic induction.
8. One method of doing this, particularly adapted to testing discrete hypotheses about change in individuals or small social units (though not in principle limited to this application) is 'The technique of discerning', described by Mirra Komarovsky in Lazarsfeld and Rosenberg (1955). See also the careful discussion of alternative hypotheses and the use of deduced consequences as further proof in Lindesmith (1947).

References
Becker, H. S. (1956), 'Interviewing Medical Students', *American Journal of Sociology*, Vol.62, September, pp.199-201.
—, Geer, B., Hughes, E. C. and Strauss, A. L. (1961), *Boys in White: Student Culture in Medical School*, University of Chicago Press.
—, Geer, B. and Hughes, E. C. (1968), *Making the Grade: The Academic Side of College Life*, Wiley.
Blau, P. M. (1954), 'Co-operation and Competition in a Bureaucracy', *American Journal of Sociology*, Vol.59, May, pp.530-5.
Coleman, J. (1958), 'Relational Analysis: the Study of Social Structure with Survey Methods', *Human Organization*, Vol.17, pp.28-36.
Gold, R. L. (1958), 'Roles in Sociological Field Observations', *Social Forces*, Vol.36, March, pp.217-23.
Gottschalk, L., Kluckhohn, C. and Angell, R. (1945), *The Use of Personal Documents in History, Anthropology, and Sociology*, New York Social Science Research Council, pp.15-17, 38-47.
Gouldner, A. W. (1954), *Patterns of Industrial Bureaucracy*, Free Press, pp.247-68.
— (1956), 'Some Observations on Systematic Theory, 1945−55', in H. L. Zetterberg (ed.), *Sociology in the United States of America*, UNESCO, pp.34-42.
— (1957a), 'Theoretical Requirements of the Applied Social Sciences', *American Sociological Review*, Vol.22, February, pp.92-102.
— (1957b-1958), 'Cosmopolitans and locals: toward an Analysis of Latent Social Roles', *Administrative Science Quarterly*, Vol.2, December, pp.281-306, and Vol.3, March 1958, pp.444-80.
Kendall, P. L. and Lazarsfeld, P. F. (1950), 'Problems of Survey Analysis', in R. K. Merton and P. F. Lazarsfeld (eds), *Continuities in Social Research*, Free Press, pp.183-6.
Lazarsfeld, P. F. and Barton, A. (1951), 'Qualitative Measurement in the Social Sciences: Classification, Typologies and Indices', in D. Lerner and H. D. Lasswell (eds), *The Policy Sciences: Recent Developments in Scope and Method*, Stanford University Press, pp.155-92.
— (1955), 'Some Functions of Qualitative Analysis in Sociological Research', *Sociologica*, Vol.1, pp.324-61.
— and Rosenberg, M. (eds) (1955), *The Language of Social Research*, Free Press, pp.449-57.
Lindesmith, A. (1947), *Opiate Addiction*, Principia Press.
— (1952), 'Comment on W. S. Robinson's "The Logical Structure of Analytic

Induction"', *American Sociological Review*, Vol.17, August, pp.492-3.

Turner, R. H. (1953), 'The Quest for Universals in Sociological Research', *American Sociological Review*, Vol.18, December.

3.8 The Conduct, Analysis and Reporting of Case Study in Educational Research and Evaluation
L. Stenhouse

This paper was written especially for us by Lawrence Stenhouse, who for some time has been attempting to define the boundaries of case study research and to develop its methodology for use in the study of education. In this article he focuses particularly on the problems in analysing and reporting case study data, emphasizing the parallels with historical research. His distinction between narrative, vignette and analysis as forms of presentation of case study results is a particularly interesting approach to the problem of reporting. His further discussion of generalizing across cases via the historian's technique of judgement of evidence also suggests important new lines for the development of this kind of work, both in evaluation and in educational research generally.

On the road toward science, social philosophy has lost what politics formerly was capable of providing as prudence.

> Jurgen Habermas, *Theory and Practice.*

Researchers have turned to case study in the face of the difficulties which have been encountered in attempting to apply a classical scientific paradigm of research to problems in which human behaviour, action or intention play a large part. Experiment in the physical sciences depends heavily on the control of variables. As we move through the life sciences to the behavioural and social sciences, the control of variables becomes increasingly difficult. The classic response to this difficulty (Fisher, 1935) is to attempt to randomize the effects of uncontrolled variables so as to tone them down into a kind of white noise in the backgound of observed experimental effects. This process of allocating experimental treatments to subjects by chance rather than by judgement enables the researcher to use the mathematics of probability to calculate how far differences between observations of the experimentally treated subjects and the others may be 'significant'. This

First publication.

strategy is the basis of the use of inferential statistics in experimental design. (See Glass and Stanley, 1970.)

Experiments based on this logic have been powerful in improving the yield of crops and of animal proteins in agricultural research. Similar logic lies behind surveys of attributes in populations and behind attitude and opinion polls in which the samples of respondents studied are selected by random methods, i.e. each individual member of the population has an equal and independent chance of being selected for the sample. The results of such investigations are actuarial, describing trends or distributions in broad populations. We can readily calculate the distribution of heights of adult males in Britain, but that gives us little idea of how tall the man we're about to meet off a train will be. We can decide with a fair degree of probability on our side what strain of wheat, what fertilizers and what other treatments are likely to maximize the yield on an East Anglian farm, but we can say little about the fate of individual wheat plants in that field. When our need is to act or to devise a policy, such research techniques guide us only to the extent that the action, treatment or policy must be the same for every case we meet.

In all social arts, such as education, the practitioner aspires to modify his actions to meet the characteristics of particular cases. He or she diagnoses the case before treating it. In such situations practitioners need to know the broad trends which can be expected as responses to treatments but equally importantly the pattern of variation across cases. Medical practitioners and researchers have long recognized this and have reported individual cases which illuminate the incidence and treatment of particular conditions. One may say that the reporting of cases improves the practitioner's judgement by extending his or her experience and by treating experience more reflectively and more analytically. In my own experience there were within the Humanities Project, for instance, three styles of case study as applied in education which I shall call action research, evaluation and naturalistic research. All shade into each other.

The action research element is based on the close study of individual classrooms involved in the action of the project. From this study are derived hypotheses concerning the important variables in teacher behaviour which seemed to affect the quality and progress of student discussion. There is analysis across cases but the emphasis is not on extrapolating findings in the project as generalizations applying to a target population. Instead the teacher is urged to investigate his case by acting experimentally in it and monitoring effects. The research is applied by the user to his case rather than generalized by the team to a population of schools. Using research means doing research. This strand of experimental case study is developed in John Elliott's *Ford T. Project* in Jean Rudduck's *Small-group Work in Higher Education* (1978) and *Learning to Teach through Discussion* (1979) and by Robert

Wild (1973) and Stenhouse *et al.* (forthcoming) in *Problems and Effects of Teaching about Race Relations*. It is generally addressed to teachers.

The evaluation element is centrally concerned with gathering evidence which enables people to make judgements about the project in reflective or deliberative settings. Where action case studies invite action responses, the evidence gathered and presented by an evaluation supports decision-making, either by individuals or by groups. Examples can be found in the main publications from the Humanities Curriculum Evaluation Project (e.g. Hamingson, 1973, MacDonald, 1978, Verma, 1980), the first of which was called *Towards Judgement*. Other examples are Parlett and Hamilton's *Illuminative Evaluation* (1972) and an American trend characterized particularly by the work of Robert E. Stake (1967, 1972a, 1972b), who writes of evaluation in terms of 'portrayal' of cases and suggests that it should be responsive to the case rather than imprisoning the study of cases in preordinate categories. More recently Barry MacDonald has taken up again the theme of democratizing judgement which was broached in the Humanities Project and distinguished autocratic, bureaucratic and democratic styles of evaluation (MacDonald, 1974). The democratic style, clearly preferred by the author who chose those terms, rests heavily on case studies presented in forms that make them accessible to a wide public.

This general tradition of evaluation has been well publicized and widely applied at varying standards of quality. It always involves case study, and I would regard it as characteristic of evaluation as opposed to research that the case in point — be it policy, programme, institution or individual — be identified (not anonymized). The tradition of evaluation is exemplified by MacDonald's work in *Understanding Computer-Assisted Learning* (UNCAL, 1975), and *Careers Guidance Observed* (currently supported by DES and EEC).

Independently of this growth of case study work in evaluation, there is a classic case-study tradition. In Britain this includes Hargreaves's *Social Relations in a Secondary School* (1968) and Lacey's *Hightown Grammar* (1970). In America Smith and Keith's *Anatomy of an Innovation* (1971), Harry Wolcott's *The Man in the Principal's Office* (1973) and Alan Peshkin's *Growing up American* (1978) are exemplars. All of these studies are in a style that goes back to the Chicago School in sociology. A particular characteristic is the use of participant observation as a research strategy. The participant observer conducts his research by joining a social group, participating to a greater or lesser extent in its activities in order to achieve an understanding of the meanings and perceptions of its members, but retaining a degree of detachment as an observer and recording observations and conversations.

The participant observer role was forged in ethnography when

Western anthropologists studied preliterate societies by living in them. The term for this kind of case study most commonly used in America is 'school ethnography'. The term is coming to be used loosely, but at its most precise it probably implies penetration of the *culture* of a group by participant observation (Wolcott, 1980). The technique of participant observation demands aptitude, theoretical training (since theory is important to the maintenance of the observer role while participating) and long-term field work, certainly extending over months.

The characteristic nuance which evaluation contributes to case study work is caught in Walker's phrase 'condensed field work' (Walker, 1974). Evaluation runs to the pace of the events it studies and the demands of sponsorship. A portrayal of a case is needed and time allows only a few days in the field. The classic participant observer strategy is not available on such terms (though some condensed case workers do describe themselves as participant observers). The conditions of condensed field work radically alter case study and require us to rethink its rationale and validity. But that strategy also offers the possibility of bringing case study within the range of opportunity of the majority of researchers who cannot see the prospect of laborious long-term studies in the classic mould.

Case studies based on condensed field work are currently being undertaken in a variety of settings in evaluation and in research. The two fields are not always easy to distinguish. When a research is commissioned by a sponsor who asks that it provide evidence on which to judge a specific issue or policy or programme or institution, we are pretty sure it is evaluation. When a research can be seen to relate to an issue of understanding or interpretation conceived as contributing to our state of knowledge about education, we can see that it needs no name but research. However, there are many instances where the distinction is not easily drawn.

There are, moreover, common field work problems in both research and evaluation and these can perhaps best be reviewed by picturing them in a real situation, say, the study of a school.

In the tradition of condensed field work what is the researcher's task in the school? In a project on 'Library Access and Sixth Form Study' in which I am currently engaged (to take an example) he will have not more than twelve days' field work. Most of the time will be spent on interviewing – in this case teachers and students, but in some cases parents, employers or former pupils. Some time will be spent in observation. For my part I may give the librarians of the two institutions I am studying clerical assistance for a couple of days so that I can observe the activity in the library, and I shall also in one case spend time in the public library used by the students. Records will be collected of a kind called by the Webbs (1932) 'documents', that is, records made by the schools to serve their own purposes rather than the purposes of research. Some quantitative indices will be recorded: data on the library holding, borrowings, physical space, budgets and so forth.

Typically, interviews will be tape recorded. Those with staff who have their own rooms will be conducted in their rooms: those with other staff and students will be conducted in a room allocated to me for field work interviews. Rooms I have used include: a stockroom, a medical room, a librarian's sideroom, a spare lounge and a parents' waiting room. I never sit facing the interviewee: always side by side, generally angled towards each other. The interview starts with securing the right to record and undertaking to return an anonymized transcript of the interview for clearance. Its purpose is described as trying to capture a sound picture of the school in the voices of the people who work in it. The interview will be a one-sided conversation in which I speak relatively little. In the present project my purpose will be to consider with the interviewee the growth and limitations of the capacity for independent study as students move up the school and into the sixth form with some emphasis on the role of access to books and other library resources.

Observation is not in the classic sense participant observation, though superficially it has a participant appearance. Sitting working at such a paper as this in a public library, I am privy to the fact that three fourth formers, who came in to look up a reference to an author in *Who's Who*, chance upon Ringo Starr and look up and copy out the four Beatles' entries. Or I notice which boys engaged in study in the library do not look up when girls walk in, and I find I know some of them from interview.

Documents collected include prospectuses and school hand-outs, syllabuses and reading lists, library publications, perhaps minutes of staff meetings, perhaps photocopies of essays.

Quantitative indices include demographic and budgetary data on the school, library holdings and data on use, dimensions of the library, number of seats, tallies of users, and so forth. In some circumstances time series analysis or routine testing is appropriate. *Middletown* and *Middletown in Transition* (Lynds, 1929, 1937) are good stimulants to imagination in descriptive statistics: Tukey's *Exploratory Data Analysis* (1977) is thought-provoking on presentation. The statistics used in surveys and experiments conducted on samples need rethinking when one wants to apply them to cases.

These descriptions of field work practice are not meant to offer a model: on the contrary, they are intended to throw up dilemmas or problems. Among the most crucial of these are: observation versus interview; data versus evidence; explicit versus covert research; and the participant roles available.

I lean towards interview rather than observation. As has been explained above, this is partly because I feel that the conditions of condensed field work preclude classic participant observation. But that is not the whole story. The people I interview are participants and they are observers of themselves and others; my object is to provide in interview the conditions that help them to talk reflectively about their observations and experience. It is their observations I am after, not mine. There is, of course, the possibility that at some points the interviewee is out to deceive the interviewer, and we must take account of the truism that we are all self-deceiving. (That is, of course, what a major concern of historical criticism is about.) I find these problems less intractable than the dominance of the researcher's eye.

At the same time it must be recognized that interview is often dependent upon observation. When you ask: 'Do you think the siting of the library is an important factor?' or hazard to the librarian: 'I suppose you have to keep them in order from time to time', it is either observation or experience that lies behind your question. In the end, perhaps the issue is: is observation used to test interview or interview used to test observation? The first position is likely to be taken by those who see themselves as trying to establish facts: the second by those who see themselves as trying to disclose meanings.

Whether one's attitude to information will be to use it as data or as evidence (the distinction is mine rather than generally current) is an important issue. When we use information as data we hope to process it as 'comparable' or standardized. Generally this means stripping information of context and treating it analytically. When we use information as evidence, we try by critical selection to present an interpretation which we claim is tenable: the test is that we achieve a synthesis which carries meaning and rings true without violating the tendency of the larger store of information from which our selection is drawn. In both cases we reduce information and attempt to control distortion.

The choice between explicit and covert styles of research is partly a matter of ethics and partly a matter of validity. There are those who believe that research with human subjects should not be conducted without their consent and understanding and this points to an explicit approach. The urge towards more covert strategies comes from those who fear that the responses of subjects who understand the research in which they are involved will be influenced by this knowledge. Such influence will, it is claimed, distort the data they provide for the researcher and hence reduce the validity of the research. Whether this is a cogent argument or not must depend heavily on the research problem and on the style of interpretation to which the researcher aspires. My own stance is the ethical one, perhaps the more easily adopted because I am working with fellow professionals in education as subjects. In so far as this limits the problems and the modes of interpretation accessible to the researcher, those limitations are generally acceptable to me. But I find acceptance the easier because the limitations do not constrain me too much.

A problem of particular force for the researcher in schools or similar institutions is the narrow range of participant roles available. In some social situations it is relatively easy to become a member of the group being investigated, but in the classroom there appear to be only two truly participant roles available – that of teacher and that of pupil. Normally each classroom has only one teacher: normally the researcher cannot be mistaken for a pupil. Even when we include in the school community ancillary staff such as caterers, caretakers, lab technicians and secretaries the role opportunities for participant observers are strictly limited. Most observation in educational institutions is non-participant and at the same time explicit. The observer thus influences the behaviour observed, if only marginally, but does not enter fully enough into the pattern of interaction for his own experience of participation to become admissible as evidence.

Of course, with the growth of research work by serving teachers, we are finding more fully involved and natural participants turning to observation. The promise and the difficulties of this teacher-as-researcher stance in the classroom have been well explored in the Ford T Project (Ford T n.d.) and in its follow up – the Classroom Action Research Network (CARN, 1977-80). Less well-documented so far are the problems of studying, not one's own classroom, but one's own institution. A number of excellent pieces of this kind of work now exist, mostly in the form of master's theses, but it takes a good deal of discretion and power to conduct such a study successfully. The main problem is that social and political life in schools as elsewhere depends heavily on the unspoken agreement and the hidden cards. Studies which open the process in a particular school to scrutiny do not merely put personal relations at risk: they shift the balance of power.

Such important issues in field work as have just been discussed need to be taken into consideration in planning case study research and ought then to inform sensitivity in its execution. The problems of record-keeping are less a matter of sensitivity than of efficiency. It is on them that the plans of many case study researchers are wrecked.

The essence of the problem is this. Since the field worker in case study does not much simplify or attenuate the information he will gather by preordinate decisions, he will have a great deal of information to handle. His first problem is to record this information, his second to organize the record for use and his third to use the record to write a report.

So far as interviews are concerned the choice is between tape recording and taking notes. I use a tape recorder if I can: it protects the interviewee against misrepresentation, it captures the vividness of speech, it preserves a full record. Working within the context of projects which are fairly generously funded for secretarial support, I have been fortunate enough to be able to get full transcriptions of interviews. When this is not possible, tapes need to be carefully indexed, and selected portions should be transcribed and each annotated with a contextualization. When interviews are not taped, it is a good idea to make notes on paper divided into two columns – one column being used for a running contents list or minutes of points made, the other column being reserved for verbatim quotation.

Notes on observations (like interview records) should always be dated and a time record should be kept in a margin. Sketches or photographs may be useful. A considerable problem in observation is its relation to inference, and the observer should cultivate a considerable depth of insight as to the individual characteristics of his observation and the degree and style of inference involved.

My name for the total collection of information as organized for use – interview, observation and document – is the 'case record' (Stenhouse, 1977). The good organization of this record is crucial for writing up. It should be carefully indexed. Photocopies of the record can be used to cut up and sort under different topics (record the page number on each piece!). Another possibility is to colour code margins using a different colour for each section or chapter of the report. Meticulous attention to such detail makes an enormous difference when the job of writing up has to be faced.

There is not enough experience of the problem of writing up this kind of material in contemporary educational research. The examples to turn to are clearly historians. For present purposes a good starting point is to consider the use of narrative, vignette and analysis. Such styles as these can, of course, be blended.

Narrative, as a form of presentation, has two great strengths: it is simple and direct to read and it is subtle. Its simplicity and directness is partly due to its being within a convention of representing the natural world that is thoroughly established and that most readers meet in the nursery, but it is also partly because, as compared with analysis, the narrative form constrains the author from presenting his own logic in the teeth of resistance from the story. He does not drag the reader on to the territory of his own mind, but rather goes out to meet him. The subtlety of narrative lies in its capacity to convey ambiguity concerning cause and effect. In telling a story the author does not need to ascribe clearly causes and effects. Rather he may select from the record an array of information which invites the reader to speculate about causes and effects by providing him with a basis for alternative interpretations. Hexter (1972) has some interesting observations on story-telling written from the point of view of an historian. In case study of the kind we are discussing, narrative lends itself to the treatment of the history of institutions and of the biography of individuals as well as to reportage of transactions such as meetings or the course of events observed.

A vignette has the status of a sketch as compared to a fully worked picture. Inevitably interpretative, it is founded on the act of selection of a subject for the vignette which in itself constitutes an interpretation, and the illumination of the observation, situation or event by the selection of features whose meaning is determined by the author's interpretative stance. The art in the hands of a master can readily be observed in the extended scene settings in Bernard Shaw's plays. The element of interpretation in vignettes does not necessarily rule out ambiguity if the writer is skilful.

Analysis, by contrast with narrative and vignette, debates its points explicitly, wherever possible reviewing evidence. Analysis may be couched in the concepts of the people in the case, but often its conceptual framework is contributed by its author and draws on systematic theory – in our field generally from the social sciences – in which the concepts chosen by the author are anchored. Analysis is, viewed in one light, much cruder than narrative or vignette, but it is more explicit. This tends to mean that, though it is difficult to understand at times, it is also less easy than narrative to misunderstand, and also that it favours the search for precision in terminology and in theory. Whereas the words of narrative are crowded with their connotations and derivations those of analysis tend to be starker, denotative in the light of their definitions.

An important issue in all reports of case study is the conception of reality they reflect. The sort of issue involved can be illustrated by contrasting two typical viewpoints. In one of these reality is seen as factual or at least consensual. In order to establish what *really* went on we use 'triangulation' taking bearings on the issue by using evidence from different sources to cross check. From another viewpoint there are multiple realities, for the world in which reality is to be located is that of the perception of participants and the meanings they ascribe to them. The point is well illustrated in Karel Capek's novel, *The Cheat*, in which a single character is seen successively from different points of view.

Interesting problems for both the use of case records and the writing of reports are set by multi-site case study research. In the United States the National Science Foundation project, Case Studies in Science Education, directed by Stake and Easley (1978) was based on case studies of twelve different cases, each written up by the field worker who handled the case. The overview attempted to generalize across the cases. This work, though it shows some evidence of our lack of a tradition in this genre, is nevertheless of great interest. In the project on Library Access and Sixth Form Studies, mentioned above, the field workers in a twenty-four case study are contracted to produce indexed case records rather than case studies, and the overview will be based on this less refined data.

The emergence of multi-site case study as a style of research raises interesting issues. What would earlier studies based upon sampling look like if they were analysed, not within the conventions of the classical statistical tradition, but as a collection of cases? Could one look towards a national archive of case records? There is certainly much of promise in research based on interpretative case study though some of its disciplines still need to be thought through.

A crucial issue in the development of case study research is the role of theory in educational thinking. There is a sense in which no thinking is entirely free of theory, but there are types of research in which theory is seen as the crucial product – notably the sciences – and other types in which theory is a groundwork on which a different kind of interpretative effort is built – notably history and criticism.

Popper begins his *Logic of Scientific Discovery* with this simple statement:

> A scientist, whether theorist or experimenter, puts forward statements, or systems of statements, and tests them step by step. In the field of the empirical sciences, more particularly, he constructs hypotheses, or systems of theories, and tests them against experience by observation and experiment. (Popper, 1959, p.27)

The press is towards predictive generalization: the result is a hierarchy of generalizations, the more circumstantial and testable deducible from those that are more abstract and general (and consequently more difficult to test directly). Much theory in the social sciences is rather distant from this conception, but it aspires towards it and one can see that theory in social science which met the criteria suggested for the physical sciences would be accepted by most social scientists. Zetterberg (1965, p.ii) suggests that 'the quest for an explanation is a quest for theory'; and yet in half-a-dozen books concerning explanation in history (which I have consulted in the space afforded by the preceding semi-colon) I find no reference to theory in the indexes. The fact is that there is an alternative, interpretative style of explanation:

> We do explain human actions in terms of reaction to environment. But we also explain human actions in terms of thoughts, desires, and plans. We may believe that it is in principle possible to give a full causal explanation of why people think, desire or plan the things they do in terms of their past experience or training, or perhaps in terms of the working of their bodies. But, even if the latter proposition is true, it still does not follow that explanation in terms of thoughts and desires has been rendered superfluous, or that it has been 'reduced' to cause-effect explanation. (Gardiner, 1961, p.139)

This is still too simple, but it cannot be refined here. Suffice it to say that there is an interpretative, rather than theoretical style of explanation of human action, that it can at times use ambiguity as a spur to speculation and that its generalizations will contain the qualifier *often*, or *probably* (Habermas, 1974, p.45) not *other things being equal*. Thus their soundness may be the subject of discussion or discourse but their refutation will be by informed judgement and not by proof.

In history, judgement is informed by virtue of the quality of the historian's 'second record' (Hexter, 1972). This second record which he brings to the 'first record' of documentary sources in order to interpret them is a specially tutored experience: an experience of, say, eighteenth-century diplomatic practice or fifteenth-century agriculture.

In the matter of educational case study, theoretical interpretation would appear to be most applicable when the interests of the researcher are in social science rather than in education. Such an interpretative framework is alternative to a strong second record, and rests on generalizations across from other studies of human behaviour in institutions. It may, of course, contribute new insights concerning educational behaviour. An historical style of interpretation would be more open to the researcher, the richer his or her second record of educational experience, and it would in its turn offer to enrich the experience of the reader, being accessible to those who have experience of education.

There is an interesting line of thought to be followed up concerning the application of these two styles of case study to practice or action; for theory in the context of social science approximates *episteme* while interpretation in the light of a second record approximates *phronesis*. Such an identification leads us to the heart of the dilemma underlying one of the most famous recent attempts to relate theory and practice, that of Habermas, who points to Vico towards the opening of his own discussion:

> Vico retains the Aristotelian distinction between science and prudence, *episteme* and *phronesis*: while science aims at 'eternal truths', making statements about what is always and necessarily so, practical prudence is only concerned with the 'probable'. Vico shows how this latter procedure, precisely because it makes lesser theoretical claims, brings greater certainty in practice. (Habermas, 1974, p.45)

Interpretative descriptive case study of the kind which has been given centre stage in this paper is deeply concerned with practice. It appeals to the experience of participation in education rather than to technical theory and holds to the vernacular because it recognizes 'the task of entering into the consciousness and the convictions of citizens prepared to act' (Habermas, 1974, p.75). It aims to strengthen judgement and develop prudence.

References

CARN (1977–80), Annual Bulletins 1-4, Classroom Action Research Network, Cambridge Institute of Education.

Fisher, R. A. (1935), *The Design of Experiments,* Oliver & Boyd.

Ford T (n.d.), Materials from the Ford T Project (booklets) obtainable from J. Elliott, Cambridge Institute of Education.

Gardiner, P. (1961), *The Nature of Historical Explanation*, Oxford University Press.

Glass, G. and Stanley, J. C. (1970), *Statistical Methods in Education and Psychology*, Prentice-Hall.

Habermas, J. (1974), *Theory and Practice*, Heinemann.

Hamilton, D., Jenkins, D., King, C., MacDonald, B. and Parlett, M. (eds) (1977), *Beyond the Numbers Game: a Reader in Educational Evaluation*, Macmillan Education.

Hamingson, D. (ed.) (1973), *Towards Judgement: the Publications of the Evaluation Unit of the Humanities Curriculum Project 1970–1972*, Norwich Centre for Applied Research in Education, Occasional Publications No.1.

Hargreaves, D. (1966), *Social Relations in a Secondary School*, Routledge & Kegan Paul.

Hexter, J. H. (1972), *The History Primer*, Allen Lane, Penguin Books.

Lacey, C. (1970), *Hightown Grammar: the School as a Social System*, Manchester University Press.

Lynd, R. S. and Lynd, H. M. (1929), *Middletown: A Study in Contemporary American Culture*, Harcourt Brace.

— and Lynd, H. M. (1937), *Middletown in Transition: A Study in Cultural Conflicts*, Constable.

MacDonald, B. (1974), 'Evaluation and the Control of Education', in MacDonald and Walker (1974), pp.9-22.

— (1978), *The Experience of Innovation* Vol.2 of the revised edition of the publications of the Humanities Curriculum Project Evaluation Unit. Norwich Centre for Applied Research in Education. Occasional Publication No.6.

— and Walker R. (eds) (1974), *Innovation, Evaluation Research and the Problem of Control*, SAFARI, Interim Papers, CARE, University of East Anglia.

Parlett, M. and Hamilton, D. (1972), Evaluation as illumination: a new approach to the study of innovatory programmes. Occasional Paper of the Centre for Research in the Educational Sciences. University of Edinburgh. Mimeo. October 1972. Reprinted in Hamilton *et al.* (1977), pp.6-22.

Peshkin, A. (1978), *Growing up American*, University of Chicago Press.

Popper, K. R. (1959), *The Logic of Scientific Discovery*, Hutchinson.

Rudduck, Jean (1978), *Learning Through Small Group Discussion*, London Society for Research in Higher Education.

— (ed.) (1979), *Learning to Teach through Discussion*, Norwich Centre for Applied Research in Education, Occasional Publication No.8.

Smith, L. and Keith, P.M. (1971), *The Anatomy of Educational Innovation*, John Wiley.

Stake, R. E. (1967), 'The countenance of educational evaluation', *Teachers'*

College Record, Vol.68, pp.523-40.

— (1972a), *An Approach to the Evaluation of Instructional Programs (program portrayal vs analysis).* Paper delivered at the AERA Annual Meeting in Chicago, 4. April.

— (1972b), Responsive evaluation. Mimeo. Urbana-Champaign: Center for Instructional Research and Curriculum Evaluation, University of Illinois.

— and Easley, J. (1978a), *Case Studies in Science Education. Vol.I The Case Reports. Vol.II Design, Overview and General Findings,* Urbana-Champaign: Center for Instructional Research and Curriculum Evaluation and Committee on Culture and Cognition, University of Illinois, Reprint: Washington D.C.: U.S. Government Printing Office, Stock Nos. 038-000-00377-1.

— (1978b), 'Case Studies in Science Education: executive summary', in *The Status of Pre-College Science, Mathematics, and Social Studies Educational Practices in U.S. Schools: An Overview and Summaries of Three Studies,* Washington, D.C.: U.S. Government Printing Office. Stock No. 038-000-00376-3.

Stenhouse, L. (1977), 'Exemplary Case Records': a proposal to the Social Science Research Council.

— (1978a), 'Towards a Vernacular Humanism', *New Themes for Education Conference Papers,* Vol.III, The Dartington Society, The Elmhurst Centre, Dartington Hall.

— (1978b), 'Case Study and Case Record: Towards a Contemporary History of Education', *British Educational Research Journal,* Vol. 4, No.2.

— (1981), 'Educational Case Records': a report to the Social Science Research Council.

—, Verma, G. K., Wild, R. E., Nixon, J., Sheard, D. and Sikes, P. (forthcoming), *The Problems and Effects of Teaching about Race Relations,* Routledge & Kegan Paul.

Tukey, W. (1977), *Exploratory Data Analysis,* Addison-Wesley.

UNCAL (1975), *The Programme at Two,* Norwich Centre for Applied Research in Education.

Verma, G. K. (ed.) (1980), *The Impact of Innovation,* Vol.I of the revised edition of the publications of the Humanities Curriculum Project Evaluation Unit, Norwich Centre for Applied Research in Education, Occasional Publication No.9.

Webb, S. and Webb, B. (1932), *Methods of Social Study,* Longmans Green.

Walker, R. (1974), 'The Conduct of Educational Case Study: Ethics, Theory and Procedures', pp.75-115 in MacDonald and Walker (1974).

Wild, R. E. (1973), 'Teacher Participation in Research'. Conference document, project on Problems and Effects of Teaching about Race Relations.

Wolcott, Harry (1973), *The Man in the Principal's Office,* Holt, Rinehart & Winston.

— (1980), *How to Look like an Anthropologist without Actually Being One,* Paper at Annual Meeting of the American Educational Research Association, Boston. Available on audio-tape from AERA (session 28.01: Alternative Conceptions of Qualitative Educational Research).

Zetterberg, H. L. (1965), *On Theory and Verification in Sociology,* Totawa, N. J. quoted in D. Harvey (1973), *Explanation in Geography,* Edward Arnold.

3.9 The Department as a Learning Milieu

M. Parlett

Parlett's description of his studies of university departments at the Massachusetts Institute of Technology exemplifies the way in which the illuminative evaluator seeks to develop ideas through and across particular pieces of field work, to put together finally an overview of what he calls departmental orientations.

Everyday academic talk is full of statements such as 'he was a typical Balliol man', or 'he absorbed the MIT philosophy', or 'the college made me what I am'. An individual's intellectual style, working habits, personal values, and even ways of speaking and mannerisms, may all be attributed to the lasting influence of his or her former place of education. Both in reminiscence and biography one finds a preoccupation with drawing out such connections. Personal experience tends to confirm that we are profoundly affected by features of our education beyond the formal realm of the curriculum: certainly memories ten years after are often more vivid for context (e.g. place, individuals, atmosphere) than for content (of courses and texts).[1]

Although educational researchers and social scientists have in general shied away from systematic study of such long-term effects of institutions, there is no lack of awareness or conjecture of a less formal kind. For instance, at an American liberal arts college for women, interviews showed that the teaching staff were highly conscious of the college as a milieu that might have profound educational consequences over and above those deriving from the academic programme itself (Parlett, 1977). The campus (a superb country park with a lake, woods, rolling lawns and gothic style residence halls set on hills) was described by one staff member as being a 'frame of reference' for students that had a 'conditioning effect on them' – they began to take its 'country club' comfort and appointments as the norm. Another professor thought that there was a distinctive 'institutional ethic, a sort of lip-service paid to the desirability of reading old books', and that this

Parlett, M. (1977), 'The Department as a Learning Milieu', *Studies in Higher Education*, Vol.2, No.2, pp.173-81.

provided a background context that was 'absorbed' by students. An 'academic philosophy, almost a culture' characterized the college and was 'reflected in everything we do' – there was no way that students could 'fail to get the message'. Other references, e.g. to the 'humane atmosphere' and to the 'flavour of the place . . . gentility: a sort of politeness' reflected other qualities of the college and 'what it was doing to students'.

The kinds of academic impact alluded to here derive not from the focused activities related to teaching and learning themselves but from the context, or surroundings, in which they occur. There is an educational 'foreground' (of tutorials, lectures, courses, examinations, etc.) but also a relatively unchanging 'background' (of buildings, traditions, local customs, geographical features, etc.). While students are concerned – inevitably and properly – with attending to the foreground, much of what they do and think about while in the institution is governed by the background. That this is ever present, 'taken as read', and rarely examined systematically, is no guarantee it is educationally insignificant in its long-term impact.

Henry James has another metaphor for the background. In writing of the education he and William James received at the hands of their father, he mentions the 'queer educative air' full of 'humanity and gaiety, of charity and humour'; he goes on: *'what I speak of is the medium itself, of course, that we were most immediately steeped in'*. While there were numerous switches from school to school, times spent abroad, and a dazzling array of events at home, the on-going influence of the immediate family setting was sustained throughout.

Henry and William James reacted differently to the 'medium they were steeped in'. This is inevitable: while some students seem to embody their institution, others react against it. But, one suspects, the two young Jameses (like perhaps the majority of students in higher education) would have found it hard to escape altogether the influence of the medium they were subjected to: for example, 'the literal played in our education as small a part as it perhaps played in any, and we wholesomely breathed inconsistency and ate and drank contradiction . . . pedantries were anathema'.[2] The present paper has no pretensions to set about analysing the long-term results of attending particular institutions, nor does it speculate on how academic and professional identities are formed. Its aim is altogether more modest: to prompt examination of the medium in higher education in which the majority of students are most immediately steeped, i.e. the department of a university, college, or polytechnic. Starting from the position that the background may be educationally significant but – by definition – largely disregarded, it is suggested that departments might profit from reviewing the 'learning milieu' (Parlett and Hamilton, 1977) they provide for their students.

Awareness of the Milieu

'Familiar things happen, and mankind does not bother about them. It requires a very unusual mind to undertake the analysis of the obvious.' (Whitehead, 1925.) Alfred North Whitehead's dictum may usefully serve as encouragement for the kind of departmental self-study to be proposed here. Indeed, possibly the main reason why the department is rarely thought about as a learning milieu is that we habituate to our surroundings and find it hard to 'step outside' to view them in a detached way. While few would deny the importance of a supportive and stimulating working environment for both staff and students, little systematic attention is given to appraising it as such.

The concentration here is on what the department is like for students. As the operational unit of higher education, it is a 'home within the institution' for the majority of undergraduates. The department provides the human, social and intellectual milieu in which they study, pass through the developmental stages from fresher to finalist, and begin to acquire professional skills and outlooks. If we are looking at the students' educational medium, the department is a good place to start.

There are other reasons for pursuing some kind of departmental self-study. We are in a period of enforced stabilization within higher education. Compared with ten years ago there are fewer new ventures that shake departments up; expansion and mobility of staff used to bring new faces, ideas, and brooms into departmental common rooms. Now there is an obvious danger of stagnation and rigidity of outlook. As the recent Nuffield report (Becher *et al.*, 1977) argued, it is a time for departments to consider improvements in the quality, rather than in the quantity, of their endeavours.

There are obviously many different kinds of review a department might make: its curriculum, teaching methods, selection procedures, use of staff time, administrative mechanisms might all be overhauled in the process. What is proposed here, however, may be even more fundamental – an examination of the department not feature by feature but as a totality experienced by its students.

There are numerous different ways for teaching staff to conduct investigations of the department as a milieu. In the sections that follow three different approaches are briefly introduced. Each entails some human natural history or do-it-yourself anthropology of kinds that could be sophisticated but need not be. In each case, the staff members acting as the anthropological observer will be trying to look at the department as if from the outside – distancing himself somewhat, standing back to reflect on what he sees and hears. (There are, incidentally, obvious advantages in drawing on the observations of visiting staff who, present in a department for a term or two, can speak as both outsiders and insiders, often in illuminating fashion.)

Departmental Initiation Rites

Organizations attempt to put their imprints on new members as rapidly as possible. Departments do not generally have elaborate induction ceremonies but there is usually some kind of introductory meeting or address. The first suggestion for the anthropological observer is that he attends such a meeting: it can be an occasion that may reveal a surprising amount about the department as a milieu for students.

A recent study investigated what it was like for undergraduates in the first few weeks of higher education. (Simons and Parlett, 1977.) The new arrivals did not know what to expect, they felt insecure, and they underwent 'culture shock'. The department loomed large as an unknown quantity. They particularly wanted to 'get a sense of what it was like'. They remembered the first meetings at their departments in great detail for a long time afterwards.

How, then, at this critical moment, does the department present itself? What is the 'tone', the display of priorities, the weight of emphasis? What key statements are made about policy and practice within the department? More speculatively, what first impressions are students likely to carry away with them? What inferences will they draw about how the department operates on the basis of how the first meeting is conducted?

Here is a description of a first meeting in one applied science department. A senior member of the staff spoke for forty minutes:

> He outlined what would be expected of the students on the course. It sounded (according to one of the research team present) more like joining the army than an academic department: 'You will take this . . . you must tackle this . . . your course will contain . . . you are required to submit . . .' Half of his presentation was taken up with discussion of assessment, and of that amount about half had to do with academic failure. There were numerous citations from the regulations, with particular emphasis on the punitive aspects: 'If your report is late it will get docked ten per cent per diem and if it is ten days late it will be worth nothing . . .' There were statistics such as 'four per cent withdraw, fourteen per cent fail'. There was an elaborate explanation about how doubtful types were not failed early in the course but, rather, were allowed to continue; but 'those who were only a borderline pass know that they have to do better in later years . . . it's up to you that you do not fail . . . (it is) only fair to give the candidate a fair crack of the whip'. And there were bluff, joking asides such as 'some students are brighter than others, others work harder, some are simply better and that's the end of it'.
>
> The overwhelming message was that it was going to be tough, hard work; that some would fail, that there were penalties for not doing this or that, that students were ignorant and that control of all aspects of the course lay unequivocally with the department. Almost, it seemed, as an afterthought at the end of the meeting, the senior staff member added '. . . it is also our practice to hold smaller occasions to get together in the bar to get to know students . . . it's difficult to get to know students in a big department.'

Finally, two younger members of the staff addressed the students. Although they adopted a more informal approach the austere image already conveyed seemed to prevail. One said, for instance, 'Things are not as black as they may seem . . . but statistically some of you are bound to fail.' And then, describing the assessment of another part of the course, concluded with the statement: 'You won't fail unless your reports are too late or you have a very bad assessment – if you work satisfactorily you'll get it . . . we're looking for about one failure a year, so you can decide between yourselves whom it will be!' The last part provoking nervous laughter from the students assembled. (Simons and Parlett, 1977.)

For our purposes it is not relevant whether or not this was representative of applied science departments. What is significant is that a departmental style seemed to be set by the meeting. It is possible that the total picture conveyed of the course was never considered as such – that the information, asides, jokes, were all considered independently, with no regard to how they looked when assembled. It is also possible – though unlikely – that the meeting was deliberately contrived, perhaps to get students 'off to a flying start'; and that the view of the course and how the department worked were inaccurate representations.

In other departments observed, there was a dramatic contrast – as in this arts department:

> The chairman of the departmental board gave a first brief talk clearly designed to be friendly and chatty: 'University will be a time during which you should take a critical look at yourselves and rethink things . . . it should be a most stimulating time.' He then reminded the students that they ought to remain in contact with their tutors as much as possible. He made it clear the staff anticipated students might have numerous problems to cope with regarding choice of courses, and perhaps more personal problems, but stressed '*do* come and talk to us' . . . The meeting broke into small tutorial groups to discuss the course in more detail and to proffer advice about the necessity of planning their workload – 'don't let it all get on top of you'. The afternoon finished with a tour round the departmental and university libraries. (ibid.)

A third example was of a department of human biology:

> Here, the concentration was quite different. The organisers deliberately capitalised on students' keenness to begin academic work at once, by setting up a series of easy experiments in which students learned to take biological measurements on humans, using each other as subjects. . . . Students were forced rapidly into talking to each other, the atmosphere was relaxed, and members of staff circulated and instructed students in the various techniques required. The department had developed the scheme, refining it over several years, in order to provide a beginning that was genuinely intellectual rather than procedural, and designed to encourage social interaction both between staff and students and between the students themselves. (ibid.)

In making visits to introductory meetings the observer can note, for instance, whether staff—student collaboration or 'intellectual partnership' are talked about; how much weight is placed on assessment; whether the new students are being given useful departmental information or are being left in the dark, and whether they are given a foretaste of intellectual excitement or are submerged in regulations.

Talking to the Inhabitants

A second approach is to engage directly in dialogue with students, inviting them to describe their experiences and to spell out their views of departmental life. There may be difficulties: students may be uncomfortable with the 'artificial' nature of the exercise, wary of disclosing personal feelings to a staff member, self-conscious in front of other students, or incapable of expressing their perceptions at all lucidly. A shallow discussion full of generalities and stereotypes would obviously be useless; on the other hand, an unrestricted talk, seriously approached and sensitively handled by the anthropological observer, would almost certainly tell him a great deal about the student's world that was not known before.

For a start, discrepancies between staff and student perceptions are likely to be discovered. A strongly research-orientated department may be seen by staff as a milieu conducive to first-rate intellectual work, but may come across to students as a place where they feel intellectually insignificant. There will probably be some surprises — in that matters of importance to students may not seem of consequence to their teachers. For example, few staff appreciate how much students in general value any reductions made in their anonymity: 'if a tutor nods in a corridor it makes a difference'; 'If he recognizes you it helps.' In three separate studies, this dissatisfaction has appeared high in students' hierarchies of concerns; yet it seems a trivial point in the eyes of most staff and not worth making a fuss about (Parlett, 1977, Parlett and Simons, 1977, Miller and Parlett, 1974).

Discussions can also lead to hitherto puzzling reactions of students becoming more comprehensible. In many departments there is a general invitation to students to seek help when in academic difficulty. Annually, examinations may reveal such difficulty. Why, then, does the invitation go unheeded? Discussions can show that the 'ever open door' can be almost a bad joke.

First of all, many students (not just first years, but these especially) were afraid to go and knock on the study doors of members of staff, even when an ever open door had been prominently advertised. They spoke of 'summoning up courage' or said that 'raising yourself to a psychological pitch' was first necessary. The staff member's 'if you need me, I'm around' was not always sufficient to overcome the diffidence. The longer term implications were pointed out by a third year undergraduate: 'There are a lot of students who can't bring themselves to knock on the door; the longer they leave it, the more they create their own syndrome of not being able to.' A number of students commented that having overcome their reluctance to go and see a staff member, they felt let down by not finding him there. 'If you keep going and nobody is there,' said one, 'about the third time you give up.' (Parlett and Simons, 1977.)

Other kinds of discovery include the following. (1) The department's goals are found to conflict with other forces – a group of staff trying to foster increased out-of-class discussion come up against an institution-wide reluctance among students to talk about matters of intellectual substance ('There is, in fact, a taboo on it – it's quite non-U to talk about them'). (2) Students make perceptive comparative comments, pointing to differences between this departmental milieu and others they experience ('Tutorials differ in the chemistry and physics buildings – relaxed and over cups of tea in chemistry, and on the griddle, a bit of a torture in it, you are sweating in physics'). (3) Divergencies between how staff view students' priorities and what they in fact are, and how these priorities, in turn, are a response to prominent departmental characteristics. Take, for instance, the following account by an ex-engineering student:

> Staff would be appalled if they saw what their students do in order to cope with their course . . . when we were having tutorials one of the things that happened was that some students wanted to talk about amplifiers and electronics in general, while others wanted to find out specific answers on the tutorial sheets . . . I was one of the chaps who wanted the answers. We were always unhappy when other people wanted to broaden it out . . . these guys didn't realise it wasn't going to help them. You had to know these tutorial questions or you were going to fail. If the department had rewarded intellectual debate then this is what I would have done. Instead, they dictated that you had to slog, memorise, learn the material on the examination papers. So I concentrated on that. The tasks I was succeeding at – memorising, understanding esoteric mathematical tricks – weren't any use for being an engineer – the qualities that are needed to make a good engineer are not those fostered by the department . . . it was the way they set up their course.[3]

It is clear that discussions can range far. There are limitations, however. Students may be unaware of some of the most influential aspects of the department because they have insufficient basis for comparison: only subsequently, perhaps after exposure to other academic milieux, will they realize how powerfully they were affected by a particular departmental point of emphasis. As with any educational enquiries that are concurrent rather than retrospective, there is the difficulty of students' views not being their final ones; those sought long after the event may deserve greater notice. Finally, there is the difficulty that students may be responding to the milieu in ways they may not wish to disclose; and of which they may be only partially aware. They may not like, for instance, to admit semi-publicly to being thrilled about learning 'how to tear holes in other people's arguments' – say, through watching certain staff at work on visitors at seminars. Equally, they may scarcely admit – even to themselves – that they derive personal security by assuming discipleship within a powerful school of thought.

Nevertheless, despite these reservations, an appreciation of the student's outlook will almost certainly depend heavily on probing it by direct enquiry. It is surprising that such open-ended discussions do not already take place more widely. For the anthropological observer, the ease or difficulty of setting up such discussions may be informative in itself: if the prevailing climate is 'student centred' and relations with staff are relaxed, the discussion may well be easier to fix up, and win support for, than in a department where 'pandering to students' is abjured or where there is deep suspicion of innovation of whatever kind.

Attending to the Local Thinking

Organizations and social groups have formal structures and procedures for decision-making. Yet orderly functioning rests equally on a network of informal understandings between members. Working principles and traditional ways of doing things are built up over time: they provide a framework of expectations that do not need spelling out explicitly; they are taken as read.

There is another domain – beyond norms, rules, and mutual obligations – that is also a shared one. Members have a number of overlapping notions about the organization: what it is like (and not like), how it operates, and how its distinctiveness has evolved. These strands of common thinking – reflected in ordinary conversation and called here 'ideas in currency'[4] – deserve scrutiny. They make use of a local jargon and constitute an 'in-house' shorthand comprehensible often only to insiders. If a group consciousness can be said to exist, the way to exploring it might be via its ideas in currency – the common coinage of the department's talk about itself. Such talk not only reflects the organizational milieu but may help to create and sustain it.

The third approach suggested here, therefore, is that the anthropological observer might usefully collect samples of the department's ideas in currency. They come in many different forms. They include the following (all taken from interviews with staff in an environmental sciences department[5]): (1) pervasive beliefs about the direction of the department's policy ('We hope to make the department an identifiable group that students feel they belong to'); (2) summary descriptions of its character ('We are less formal here than in other departments'); (3) definitions of major problems ('with "joint" students there is difficulty in communicating . . . apparent inaccessibility of faculty . . . the feedback indicated how important it is to have a sense of place'); (4) anecdotes and reminiscences about its past ('There were too many people teaching in the first year – students didn't know who was teaching'); (5) disavowals, and statements about what the department is *not* like ('We are not like a conventional department in that so many disciplines are represented').

The ideas in currency listed here make reference to what is seen as the natural order, the departmental wisdom. Such statements do not often need full articulation for insiders – yet, when they are so cited, they have all the appearance of referring to unquestioned 'fact'. As such they may underpin, or further reinforce, a department's defining characteristics.

An example of this is provided by the same environmental sciences department: there was a pronounced set of ideas in currency, held by both students and staff, that centred on the purported 'informality' existing between them. Annual field trips to remote parts of Scotland were thought particularly effective in 'breaking down barriers' between teachers and undergraduates. However, reference was made so persistently to the informality that, one suspects, the ideas in currency may have become self-fulfilling. It was as if new initiatives had almost to be checked to see whether they accorded with the informal milieu; and, if they fell short of it, that they had to be rearranged. Thus, the system for advising students in the department had been progressively modified. When compared with similar schemes in the same university, it was striking in its flexibility: if students did not get on with the adviser first designated, they were encouraged to shift elsewhere without administrative fuss or any embarrassment to either party. The system had been deliberately changed to reduce complications that could stand in the way of good informal contact.

Clearly, one cannot isolate here the effects of ideas in currency *per se*; but their repetition and endorsement as expressions of the 'normal state of affairs' may not only reflect but further promote the characteristics which they highlight.

That ideas in currency may become normative, and therefore supportive of the *status quo*, is not surprising. Reiteration of statements of the kind 'that place is dull' can easily lead to evidence of dullness being underlined and counter-examples – of liveliness – being overlooked (or dismissed as 'untypical' or 'out of character'). Indeed, singularity of organizational milieux may rely on the progressive entrenchment of certain ideas that all within the organization adhere to and take for granted, and which are not exposed to any bracing challenge from outside. Kenneth Boulding (1956) points to the danger:

As long as the sub-culture is isolated from the rest of the world, with all its lines of communication lying within, its image tends to be self-supporting and self-perpetuating. All the messages which are received by the individuals participating confirm the images which they have, because to a large extent the messages originate in these images. A mutual admiration society is a fine way of persuading us that we are all fine fellows when nobody ever contradicts us.

One critical component of departmental distinctiveness is its educational philosophy, in so far as many departments can be said to have one; some departments and programmes have a more committed and explicit stance than do others. A number of ideas in currency usually relate directly to this stance and represent prominent constituents of the learning milieu. Exposure to these particular ideas in currency – circulating in the background, as it were – may be among the most critically formative of all the forces emanating from the department and acting on the student.

The potency that such ideas may have was evident in an innovative freshman teaching programme investigated by the writer at the Massachusetts Institute of Technology (Parlett, 1971). The programme demonstrated a preoccupation with promoting independent learning. Prominent ideas in currency were that the programme was 'experimental', was a 'home for doers, those who want to shake the system . . . action orientated'; it was 'based on the expectation that students would take charge of their own education'. It was said that the programme forced students 'to see what they are interested in and what they aren't interested in'; and it required them to 'think and figure out what they are doing and why they are doing it, or what they are *not* doing and why they are *not* doing it.'

The students could hardly avoid picking up what amounted to a powerful ideology. They were left in no doubt about how they were expected to work or of what cues they should be conscious for purposes of assessment. Unsurprisingly, many first-year students experienced difficulties with independent study and the terminology used for describing such 'failures' reflected the same ideology: 'he didn't make it here'; 'he never faced up to the problem of how he can do something on his own'; 'he got particularly worried about not being able to find one thing which turned him on more than everything else'. In this milieu, the programme's students were naturally anxious when they met the setbacks, and the programme's staff were naturally delighted when students showed evidence of independent initiatives. The link suggested here, then, is one between 'what the department (or programme) is like' and 'how students are expected to be'.

In this experimental programme the emphasis was on independence; in the environmental sciences department, earlier mentioned, a dominant theme was its informality. One group of students picked up the message that they should learn to manage on their own; the other group that they could approach staff without fear of a 'brush-off'.

Conclusion

Departmental orientations, as reflected in the prevailing ideas in currency, form part of the students' academic surroundings: their formal engagement in departmental activities takes place against this background. This paper has suggested various ways of gaining an understanding of the departmental ethos. The approaches which have been put forward overlap (ideas in currency will emerge during induction week meetings, and certainly in face to face discussions with students); the types of enquiry and observation which have been described are obviously not the only ones available. What is important to emphasize is that departmental milieux all have local special features, marks of individuality, and that these exert influence. Whether they take the form of prominent personalities, old feuds still fizzling, professorial quirks, or accidents of history, any thorough appreciation of the department as a milieu has to acknowledge them and give them due weight. What is proposed, therefore, is necessarily a case-by-case series of studies. General surveys have undoubted uses: but any discussion of milieux must by definition deal with the particular rather than the general.

Two brief points need to be made in conclusion. The first is that the kind of self-study explored here is likely to tap departmental knowledge of an unusual kind: it is partially appreciated but is seldom discussed as serious business. The anthropological observer will be turning the spotlight on those areas of departmental life which are acknowledged to be important but which rarely attract significant notice. He will be deciphering knowledge that is neither altogether 'manifest' nor entirely 'latent' (Polanyi, 1967). Its intermediacy in this respect may account for the emerging discoveries being not only recognizable, but also (discouragingly for the observer) labelled as 'telling us what we know already'. Yet the staff members who engage in such reviews, however they organize or present their conclusions, will be changing the pattern of customary awareness among their colleagues. The extent of change and the practical results forthcoming are hard to tell. What is certain is that such studies — because they are directed at concerns that are central in phenomenological terms — are seldom considered a waste of time by those contributing to them.

The mention of departmental change leads to the final point. Even if improvements to the milieu are identified as being urgently required — say to render it more intellectually stimulating — there is another critical dimension to be considered. A departmental milieu can in most cases be changed only by individuals in positions of influence who 'set a different tone' or 'disestablish the norm'. It is a fact, unfortunate but true, that those in power do not always share an active interest in open-ended organizational self-scrutiny of a kind which might suggest the need for substantial changes affecting themselves. Yet those in such positions cannot fail to respond, in democratic institutions, to grass-roots demands, persuasively argued, for greater attention to be paid to the milieu and its impact – both short and long term – on the students who study within it.

Notes

1. See for instance, Philip Jackson's introduction in Overly, 1970.
2. These quotations from Henry James are taken out of Matthiessen, 1961.
3. The quotations used here are taken from the Students' Experience of Academic Life Project conducted by the Nuffield Group for Research and Innovation in Higher Education, and in related enquiries.
4. The term 'ideas in currency' is used in a slightly different way from that introduced by Schon (1971).
5. This department was studied as part of the Students' Experience of Academic Life Project, Nuffield Group for Research and Innovation in Higher Education.

References

Becher, R. A. *et al.* (1977), *Making the Best of it*, Final Report of the Nuffield Foundation Group for Research and Innovation in Higher Education, The Nuffield Foundation.

Boulding, K. (1956), *The Image*, University of Michigan Press.

Hamilton, D. F. *et al.* (eds) (1977), *Beyond the Numbers Game*, Macmillan.

Matthiessen, F. O. (1961), *The James Family*, Knopf, pp.69-100.

Miller, C. M. L. and Parlett, M. R. (1974), *Up to the Mark*, Monograph 23, London Society for Research into Higher Education.

Overly, N. V. (ed.) (1970), *The Unstudied Curriculum: its impact on children*, Washington DC, Association for Supervision and Curriculum Development.

Parlett, M. R. (1971), *Study of Two Innovative Programs at MIT*, Report to the Committee on Educational Policy, Massachusetts Institute of Technology, part reproduced in Parlett and Dearden, 1977.

– (1977), 'The Wellesley Milieu', in *Educational Studies at Wellesley*, Wellesley College Publication, part reproduced in Parlett and Dearden, 1977.

– and Dearden, G. J. (eds) (1977), *Introduction to Illuminative Evaluation: Studies in Higher Education*, Pacific Soundings Press.

– and Hamilton, D. F. (1977), *Evaluation as Illumination: A New Approach to the Study of Innovatory Programmes*, Occasional Paper 9, Centre for Research in Educational Sciences, University of Edinburgh, reprinted in Hamilton *et al.* (1977).

Polanyi, M. (1967), *The Tacit Dimension*, Routledge & Kegan Paul.

Schon, D. (1971), *Beyond the Stable State: Public and Private Learning in a Changing Society*, Temple Smith.

Simons, H. and Parlett, M. R. (1977), *Up to Expectations*, Group for Research and Innovation in Higher Education, The Nuffield Foundation.

Whitehead, A. N. (1925), *Science and the Modern World*, reprinted by Fontana, 1975.

3.10 Suggestions for a School Self-evaluation Based on Democratic Principles

H. Simons

As a contrast to the previous reading, we include here Helen Simons's prescriptions for what she calls 'the democratic approach to evaluation'. Following Barry MacDonald's argument in this area, (see MacDonald, 1976), Simons stresses the need to recognize democratic principles in school self-evaluation programmes, recognizing the interest of the particular groups of participants involved, and considering what implications these have for the application of research techniques.

In the current climate of the Taylor Committee, the Assessment and Performance Unit and the Great Debate, increasing pressures are being placed on teachers to examine and document their work. Since many of the pressures come from outside the school it would not be surprising if teachers should feel that their autonomy is under threat or that their privacy is likely to be intruded upon. School self-evaluation on democratic principles is one positive way for schools to respond to these demands while protecting and extending their professional autonomy.

School-based evaluation is not a new concept and has been used to refer to quite different practices. Before outlining the democratic principles it may be useful to indicate how the term has been interpreted in the past and why a different approach merits investigation.

Informal evaluations undertaken by heads and/or staff as part of their 'normal practice' or curriculum renewal or policy change are based in and usually remain private to the school or, perhaps, a few within the school. Formal evaluations conducted by outside researchers using the school as a base may become public but are usually conducted and presented in terms defined by the researcher and subject to his or her control. Both kinds of evaluation do not necessarily involve or reflect the views of a large number of staff. In the case of external evaluations, power to control what is made accessible to others lies, with certain exceptions, in the hands of the researcher even though in many

Simons, H. (1979), 'Suggestions for a School Self-evaluation Based on Democratic Principles', in *CRN Bulletin, No. 3.*

cases he or she has consulted over access, aspired to reflect issues relevant to teachers and sought agreement for publication.

The proposal suggested here accepts the need for schools to present accounts of their work to the public but shifts the basis of control for how this should be done to the people within the school. Giving teachers' control over their own evaluation respects their autonomy, protects their 'right to privacy' and, paradoxical though it may seem, provides a process for making the policies and practices of schools more public. School-based evaluation in the context defined here is not a defensive reaction to accountability demands from the centre or outside the school but a positive means for institutional self-development. It will, at the same time, provide a document of self-accountability. The prime aim of the self-evaluation is to assist staff to monitor policies and practices within their school to inform their own decision-making; the secondary aim is to produce accounts of their work which can be made accessible to outside groups such as parents, governors, the LEA and the community.

Principles

The aim of the democratic approach to evaluation is to open up the work of the school to discussion while finding some way of protecting the individual's 'right to privacy'. This is a particularly delicate exercise to carry out within an institution bounded in time and in one building and where the principal researcher/s is/are the head or the teachers themselves. The principles and procedures below may help to create conditions where this might be possible. Each teacher/researcher would be asked to adopt these principles of procedure in conducting research in their schools. These are safeguards to the participants, the teacher/researcher, the school and the objectivity of the evaluation. They should be explicit and all staff and students, whether involved directly or indirectly in the evaluation, should be informed of them. The procedures, summarized at the end, are derived from the following principles.

I. IMPARTIALITY

In a school where the evaluation on a policy issue is initiated and co-ordinated by a member of staff the principle of impartiality is both problematic and essential. It is problematic because the member of staff may have vested interests in the issue and wish to see these represented. It is essential for precisely the same reason. If the evaluation is to be perceived to be objective and the evaluator impartial this principle is crucial to:

(a) safeguard the evaluation against bias and the participants against the evaluator using the evaluation as a platform for the promotion of his/her own views. It is not possible for the teacher/researcher to be entirely free from bias. What is important is that the person be aware of these biases and be prepared to subject them to internal checks and criticism. If the teacher/researcher can find a person outside the school acceptable to the participants and him/herself it might be possible to have an outside check as well.

(b) protect the evaluator and the evaluation against co-option by particular groups within or outside the school. The evaluation should not advocate one group's position, i.e. teachers, pupils, heads of departments at the expense of others, e.g. heads or junior staff; it should treat everyone's point of view as open to justification and attempt to represent different perspectives impartially. To this end the teacher/researcher should forgo putting forward his view. In the event his view may be represented by others but even if it is it should not receive undue emphasis.

(c) establish the credibility of the evaluation outside the school. Self-reports, as is so often said, have low credibility. If the evaluation can demonstrate that through the procedures it has checked for bias and reported impartially it will be more likely to be regarded as non-partisan by those within the school and be more likely to meet those outside critics who dismiss such internal reports as 'too subjective'.

II. CONFIDENTIALITY/CONTROL

The principle of confidentiality is equally problematic in a school where the researcher is also a member of staff. Certain information will already be public knowledge. But there will also be information private to the individuals. So much that is taken for granted in normal day-to-day practice is open in a self-evaluation to critique. What is private may become public, if even to a few, and this may be threatening to some of the staff. Important decisions, it is often claimed, are made during the 'chat in the staff room over a cup of tea' or informally outside of school. Such occasions should not be jeopardized by the evaluation. The line between 'gossip' and informal chat may be perceived to be a narrow one and needs to be checked if informal conversations and observations provide data for the evaluation. Some procedures are necessary to ensure that business carries on as usual and that teachers and pupils are not put at risk by openly and frankly discussing their work or policy issues.

Information that is private to the individual should be governed by the principle of confidentiality. Information that is already public knowledge within the school should be subject to controlled release. The onus is on the researcher to aspire not to gossip and on the participants to take control over his/her own data. If participants have control over what data is given and released they are more likely to offer accurate perceptions and to respond honestly to the issue under discussion.

Giving control also helps to ensure that participants are not made vulnerable by their co-operation and contribution; it reassures them that the person documenting the account and facilitating the information exchange cannot misuse information from any one individual.

Giving control, in summary, protects their 'right to be discreet' and allows them to pace the flow of any information they decide to share. It should not be used, however, to censor relevant information. (Relevant information will be agreed upon by those contributing to the study.) There would be little point in undertaking the evaluation if the aim was not to produce some useful information. Confidentiality, if necessary, and in some cases it might not be, should be seen as a stage in a process of making information that is useful accessible to further discussion. Control should not be used to protect confidentiality. Once accurate and relevant accounts have been negotiated and presented in ways that do not threaten participants (see negotiation principle and procedures) this protection should no longer apply.

III. NEGOTIATION

Negotiation is a central principle in democratic evaluation protecting participants from the evaluator taking total control over the data and using it for his/her own purposes. Confidentiality may be some protection for the individual in some situations but it is no guarantee. Once information has been given the participant has been made vulnerable while the evaluator, now privy to certain information, gains power. Without other principles the evaluator could use his/her position to gain clearance of that information for wider release. After all he/she has the initiative throughout for generating the data. It is the participant who is more at risk. The fact that the evaluator claims to be trustworthy and operating on the principle of impartiality does not necessarily help. It may set up a sense of false security where participants may be quite prepared to give over control of the data to the evaluator. All this serves to do is reverse the situation and put the evaluator at risk. Participants also deny their responsibility to take control over 'their' data.

Negotiation helps to ensure that a balance is maintained between the 'public's right to know' and the individual's 'right to be discreet'. The evaluator should negotiate with participants to set the boundaries of the study in terms of accessibility, relevance of issues and feasibility of procedures and approach. He/she should negotiate clearance of information offered by participants and used as data for the evaluation before distribution to anyone else.

Negotiation does not lead to a 'watered down' account as some people have claimed. On the contrary. It encourages people to participate; gives them room to contribute equally and fairly; improves the impartiality of the account by inviting checks on biases and improves the reliability and validity of the accounts. Aware that other participants are presenting their perspectives participants are encouraged to put their views honestly. Documenting different people's perspectives on the same issue is also a further reliability check.

IV. COLLABORATION

'Who's afraid of evaluation? I am, aren't you?', concluded an article written by an independent evaluator commenting on impending developments in external evaluation of schools (MacDonald, 1976). These sentiments no doubt are not confined to the author. Given the current pressures on schools to 'go public' internal evaluation is just as likely to raise anxieties about the use of information, control of data and appropriateness of techniques of assessment. However harmonious relationships in a school appear to be, however democratic the organization, trust does not automatically exist between professionals. It has to be created. In any institution people will choose their confidants and keep their secrets. School-based evaluation demands a degree of openness which on the face of it might seem to threaten the individual's or small group's right to privacy to keep their classroom practices within the confines of the classroom, department or school and school policies within the confines of the school.

The principles already cited go some way to ensure that participants' 'rights to privacy' are protected while information is gradually shared. But an additional, perhaps prior, principle is collaboration. To engage in the evaluation at all demands a commitment to sharing data relevant to an understanding of the school's practices and policies. The principle of collaboration ensures that teachers begin to share their work with others in the school; the other principles give them control over how and at what pace they do this.

To take account of initial anxieties each participant may wish to choose to collaborate with one or two persons in the school asking them to check self-reports for fairness, accuracy and relevancy. Once a degree of confidence is gained and reliability and validity attributed to the data and procedures these can gradually be extended in the interest of presenting fair accounts to facilitate policy discussions in the whole school. The procedures are designed to promote self-reflection in the school as a whole but can only do so to the extent that participants are willing to co-operate in the study.

V. ACCOUNTABILITY

That schools should be accountable to the public is not at issue in a democratic society. The public have a right to know what is going on in schools which they help to support and to which they send their children. The question is how, in what terms and to whom, in particular, should they be accountable. It is this question which is currently under the microscope of the education profession and lay community alike in terms of who maintains control over the running of our schools.

It should not be assumed in the current debate on opening up the curriculum, the governance of schools and assessment of performance that schools are the most closed of institutions in our society. There are many ways in which schools already provide information about themselves. They keep records of pupil achievement. Parents receive report cards of pupil progress. Examination results are public. Parents and the public may also have access to information on issues such as school rules, staff policy on options, academic and pastoral organization, roles of staff, transfer from primary to secondary, remedial teaching, career guidance, extra-curricular activities. What are less open to view are the decision-making processes for determining policies of teaching practice, curriculum changes, allocation of resources etc., but it should be noted that in these respects schools do not differ from many institutions.

The proposal here suggests that schools take the initiative for further ways of reporting to the public by first accounting to themselves. By opening up their own practices to internal criticism and documenting their perspectives and aspirations on issues central to their development, teachers can facilitate self-reflection within their own school. In so doing they might also produce accounts which meet outside accountability demands. But such reports would be defined in the school's own terms and their distribution to any other group controlled by them.

That the evaluation should also be accountable to individual participants and the school is also not at issue. The procedures help to ensure that the teacher/researcher meets this responsibility.

Procedures

Set out below are a list of the procedures derived from each of the principles just discussed.

I. IMPARTIALITY

1. The teacher/researcher's role is to collect the judgements of others and represent a range of views on policy issues. He/she should withhold his own judgement in description and keep his/her own view out of reports.
2. The role of the researcher is to describe what happens in policy

meetings, staff meetings, the classroom etc. – to report accurately and fairly whatever transpires, not to recommend what should happen: i.e.

he/she should inform decisions without prejudging them;
he/she should present options without prescription;
he/she should come to no final judgement;
he/she should present a range of perspectives on the issue;
he/she should not press particular viewpoints.

3. Self-reports by one person within the school should also be descriptive adhering to the procedures above. 'Critical friends' within the school should check for biases and respond on criteria of fairness, accuracy and relevancy. It is not their role to pass judgement on colleagues.

4. Conditions are the same for all. All participants should have equal access to the data once it has been negotiated. No one has the right to veto what is reported and cleared by participants.

II. CONFIDENTIALITY/CONTROL

1. Conversations are confidential to the individual person; knowledge within the school subject to release by them.

2. The evaluator will not report anything or examine documents relevant to a particular person without his/her consent.

3. Interviews, discussions, staff meetings, committee meetings, written statements are all potential data for the evaluation. But individuals have the right to restrict parts of the exchange or to correct or improve their statements.

4. Contributors to the evaluation have control over to whom it is released.

5. Reports should aspire to be issue- not person-orientated.

6. Pseudonyms or role designation should be used in reporting if attributing quotations to people. While this does not offer anonymity it depersonalizes issues that may be critical to discuss and which, if contentious, might become 'too personal'.

7. Clearance need not be sought for information summarizing findings or reporting general perspectives on issues which involve no specific detail about persons or groups.

8. Where details are included which do identify the person or source, clearance is necessary.

III. NEGOTIATION

1. The teacher/researcher should negotiate the boundaries of the study with participants.

2. The teacher/researcher will seek access only to those data sources

relevant to the issue under discussion. There will be no gratuitous reporting. What is relevant needs to be negotiated with the participants. Potential relevant data sources are people in the school (head, teachers, pupils, ancillary staff) and outside the school (governors, parents, LEA advisers), school records, examples of pupils' work etc.

3. Reports/statements should be negotiated for release to a specific group with the persons whom it concerns (teachers, pupils, head, advisers).
4. Reports should first be checked with the individual or group concerned. Only with their agreement on amendments should reports be made accessible to other people.
5. Reports should be negotiated on criteria of fairness, accuracy and relevancy, not on personal grounds e.g. whether the person looks favourable or unfavourable in the report.
6. On occasions one person may negotiate on behalf of a group (e.g. head of department on behalf of department) providing the group delegate this responsibility to that person.
7. If several people are mentioned in a report, information should be negotiated first with those who would be most disadvantaged if it were negotiated with all at the same time. (The question of who would be most disadvantaged in any one setting needs to be discussed.) This helps to ensure that participants genuinely share control with the teacher/researcher and share control and risk with the other participants.
8. Before taking part in negotiation, participants should be aware for whom the report is intended. If it is subsequently desired for another group its release has to be re-negotiated.
9. The accessibility of any product of the evaluation should be negotiated with all the participants.

IV. COLLABORATION

1. Every person has the right to participate.
2. Every person has the right not to collaborate.
3. The teacher/researcher should choose one or two persons within the school to check reports for fairness, accuracy and relevancy.
4. The teacher/researcher may choose one or two persons outside the school (subject to internal agreement with participants) to help keep biases in check.
5. The teacher/researcher should not expect everyone to participate nor coerce anyone who would prefer not to participate.
6. All collaborators should work to the same procedures.

V. ACCOUNTABILITY

1. The teacher/researcher will be accountable to the participants in the ways outlined in this paper.

2. The evaluation will be accountable to the school by being responsive to their policy concerns.
3. The evaluation will be accountable to internal criticisms and external checks from time to time if the latter is agreed upon.
4. Other ways in which the evaluation needs to be accountable will depend upon local settings and the kind of issues discussed.

CONCLUDING COMMENTS

Within any institution there are likely to be power imbalances in the distribution of roles, tasks and information. Increasing the flow of information increases the possibility that the powerful may gain more influence at the expense, perhaps, of those in the least powerful position (who is the more powerful, of course, may differ on different issues). As the teacher/researcher begins to document the study he or she may come to be perceived as upsetting the balance of power. The procedures are necessary therefore not only to protect all participants but also the teacher/researcher from misusers of information. It is perhaps the case that in a truly open society there would be no need to introduce such explicit procedures. But that does not seem to be the system we work in at present.

Procedures do not, however, provide guarantees. Their effectiveness depends upon the researcher establishing and maintaining an atmosphere of trust. This is best achieved by demonstrating that the evaluation is responsive to the needs of the school and that the teacher/researcher is committed to the rights of participants and the procedures. Onus for upholding the principles clearly lies with the researcher. The ultimate sanction rests with participants. By withholding relevant information, giving the evaluation token support, or refusing to participate, teachers within the school can effectively curtail the school's self-study.

Background to paper
The idea for this type of school self-study stemmed both from evaluation theory and practical experience in studying a school in the SAFARI Project – a Ford Foundation sponsored project looking at medium-term effects of curriculum projects in schools (MacDonald, 1976). In this school six teachers reported how their group discussion of a SAFARI issues report stimulated discussion of 'critical' policy issues within the school of a kind which had not been possible at regular staff meetings or in special sub-committees set up to discuss school policy. Their experience points out the potential of this approach for continuing self-evaluation and professional development. This proposal is an attempt to explore this potential systematically.

The principles and procedures outlined in this paper have drawn on the ethics and practice of SAFARI and the excellent principles and procedures for the COPE evaluation proposed by Stephen Kemmis. For further details of SAFARI see 'Innovation, Evaluation and the Problem of Control: Some Interim Papers',

Centre for Applied Research in Education, University of East Anglia, 1974. COPE, the Committee on Program Evaluation of the University of Illinois at Urbana – Champaigne, is a relatively permanent evaluation of the University's faculty and programs. The evaluation proposal takes an independent stance. Both projects attempt to explore the implications of the democratic model of evaluation in practice. I am indebted to Stephen Kemmis for sharing his proposal with me and for discussing the implications of the model.

Reference
MacDonald, B. (1976), 'Who's Afraid of Evaluation?' *Education 3-13*, Vol.4, No.2. October.

3.11   A Checklist for Planning or Reviewing an Evaluation
W. Harlen and J. Elliott

Harlen and Elliott bring together here all our earlier material in the form of a checklist which can be used both as a basis for planning an in-school evaluation or reviewing a report of such an evaluation. Their ten-point design checklist and sixteen-point review checklist will be found particularly useful for all those contemplating evaluation or attempting to put other evaluations to use in their own educational setting.

When planning an evaluation there are a number of questions to be asked which will help in deciding its feasibility and usefulness. The following is a list of such questions, firstly stated briefly and then discussed with some of the range of alternative responses considered. There are, of course, no answers to these questions which can be specified as acceptable or unacceptable, but posing them raises issues which should be considered before an evaluation is undertaken.

Later the same questions are considered as the basis for reviewing an ongoing or completed evaluation. Suggesting the 'evaluation of evaluations' may seem like setting up a self-perpetuating cycle of events; however, its importance lies not in any purely academic interest in the process but in learning from mistakes and improving the practice of evaluation by reviewing what has been done. All we suggest here are some guidelines for doing this.

Checklist for Planning an Evaluation

1. REASONS, PURPOSES AND MOTIVATIONS

− who wants the evaluation to be carried out?
− what reasons do they have for wanting the evaluation to be done?
− who wants the information it will provide?
− what reasons do they have for wanting the information?
− who else should have the information?

First publication.

2. WORTHWHILENESS

- what possible actions or decisions can be taken as a result of the evaluation?
- what possible actions or decisions have been pre-empted?
- what constraints are there on the planning and execution of the evaluation?

3. INTERPRETATION OF THE EVALUATION TASK

- what views do those involved hold about the nature of the evaluation?
- what is the existing decision-making system and how does the evaluation relate to it?

4. SUBJECTS OF THE EVALUATION

- what will be evaluated?
- what kinds of information are required?

5. THE EVALUATORS

- who will gather the information?
- who will co-ordinate the process?
- who will produce the report(s)?

6. EVALUATION METHODS

- are the methods to be used appropriate to the information required?
- can the methods be devised, if necessary, and applied in the time available?
- what resources, equipment, back-up facilities are required for the methods to be used?
- will the methods for data collection be acceptable to those who will be involved in supplying information?

7. TIME SCHEDULE

- what time is available for the evaluation?
- can the information required be gathered and processed in that time?

8. CONTROL OF INFORMATION

- what procedures, if any, will govern the collection and release of information?
- how will ownership of the information be decided?

9. CRITERIA FOR MAKING JUDGEMENTS OR DECISIONS

- who will decide the criteria to be applied in using the information?
- will there be the need or possibility for applying alternative criteria?

10. REPORTING

- in what form will the evaluation be reported?
- will those involved be shown the report before it is made final?
- who will be the designated audience of the report?
- what steps will be taken to see that the report reaches the designated audience?

The order of the questions in this list follows roughly the sequence of questions which should govern any evaluation or assessment activity:

1. What are the purposes?
2. What information is required to serve those purposes?
3. What methods can be used to gather the information?
4. How should the information be reported?
5. How should the report be used to achieve the original purposes?

Although it is not necessarily important to answer the questions sequentially it is useful to consider the responses in this way. It is pointless to have methods, people and facilities lined up if in fact there is no worthwhile purpose to be served, as when decisions which the evaluation was intended to inform will be pre-empted, or when the purpose is to justify steps that have already been taken. Thus the purposes and worthwhileness of the evaluation should be carefully reviewed before serious planning goes very far on the other matters. The temptation to seize upon attractive research methods and apply them, before considering whether they are best suited to the problem and how the results can be interpreted, should be resisted. Much time and good-will can be lost in that way. Perhaps fewer evaluations would be done if the planning involved a thorough scrutiny of motivations and systems, but those which were done would be worthwhile.

Now we look at the items on the list in more detail and consider some of the possibilities available.

1. REASONS, PURPOSES AND MOTIVATIONS

It is relevant to the success of carrying through an evaluation to ask who is seeking for it to be done. If it is the head of a school or senior staff the consequences for the evaluation will probably be different than if it is ordinary classroom teachers. It may be that those who want the evaluation to be done do not expect to be involved – least of all evaluated – themselves. Expectations of this kind should be examined if possible, for clearly there is the likelihood of lack of co-operation if an evaluation thought to be looking only at 'them' begins to look at 'us'.

It is also advisable to find out if all those to be involved share the same view on who should be the audience for the evaluation. Teachers might readily co-operate in exposing, for example, problems in their teaching in the context of an evaluation which is investigating what changes in class organization may be beneficial, yet would be less willing to be so open if the report were to go to the LEA or prospective employers. Thus the reasons for carrying out the evaluation must be clarified. These may be to inform all those within the school, or only those involved in the evaluation, or it may be outsiders with an interest in what is going on, e.g. parents, governors, LEAs.

2. WORTHWHILENESS

Evaluations arise from a variety of motivations. The most straightforward cases are where a decision has to be taken and the options are clear. Evaluations may reveal information which makes the decision more than 'backing a hunch'. However, the worthwhileness of the evaluation in these cases may not be so obvious; the decision would have been taken one way or the other in any case, and it is not always evident that the evaluation was used. Again, there may be a decision to take but it may be pre-empted before an evaluation takes place. Thus we cannot claim that an evaluation is always worthwhile if a decision has to be made. But the reverse is more certain; that is, if there is no decision to be made or no possibility of action as a consequence of the information, then an evaluation is not worthwhile. Where there is no decision to be taken the motivations for evaluations carried out are often to be found elsewhere: to justify decisions already taken, to show what a good job X or Y is doing, to increase personal status, to gain qualifications for a higher degree, etc.

A further check on worthwhileness is to find out the constraints under which the evaluation will have to be carried out. It may be that an evaluation which could potentially be helpful and informative in decision-making would have to be carried out in such a way that the amount of relevant information would be severely limited. In such cases it may be better not to continue with the planning if the constraints cannot be removed.

3. INTERPRETATION OF THE EVALUATION TASK

Interpretations of evaluation vary widely. Evaluation theoreticians fail to agree on what evaluation means, and an even greater range of interpretations can be inferred from practice. The chief division is between those who hold that the process of evaluation should be regarded only as the collection of information and does not extend to the making of judgements on the information, and those who hold that the process involves making judgements. Comments can be found elsewhere on this matter (see reading 3.2, pp.185-91). A third point of view is that evaluation is concerned with collecting other people's judgements of the value of something. The role of the evaluator will be seen differently by those who hold contrasting views; to some he will be a god-like figure handing down judgements, to others a hand-maiden supplying information for them to judge and to others again a broker who deals in judgements. It is not necessarily better to adopt one view rather than another but it is important for the view which is adopted to be made explicit by all involved and, if necessary, negotiated, so that a common understanding can be reached.

4. SUBJECTS OF THE EVALUATION

The word 'subject' here is used as if in the context of the subject of an enquiry. Thus the subject may not be a person or persons but could be processes, such as interactions between teacher and pupil, between pupil and learning tasks, between head and teachers, between parents and teachers, etc. It could be the organization of a class, department or school as a whole. It could be the school's goals or the extent to which these are achieved, or it could be the unintended outcomes in pupils. The range is very wide and frequently there is a difficult balance to strike between spreading the evaluation over too many subjects, all of which seem relevant, and being able to gather sufficient information about each one. Thus frequently the subjects and the kinds of information about each one have to be considered together. An idea of the wide range of possibilities can be had from the following scheme, where anything from one bracket can be considered with anything from another:

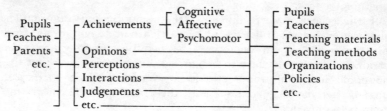

5. THE EVALUATOR(S)

Although we have discussed the evaluator, in the singular, it is not necessary for there to be one person so designated. Far less is it to be seen as a job only for someone who regards himself, by experience or training, to be an 'evaluator'. In the present context anyone who takes part in an evaluation is an evaluator. Thus the role may be assumed by teachers, the head, pupils, representatives of outside bodies such as the LEA, parents, governors, or indeed a consortium representing different groups. These people may be involved in carrying out the evaluation, in data gathering, analysis, interpretation. If duties are spread among several people it will be necessary for there to be some co-ordination, presumably in the hands of one person.

Many of the procedures and methods of evaluation are not complicated or technical; they are not all that different from the skills teachers need as observant, perceptive, systematic operators in the classroom.[. . .] Methods often have to be devised or adapted, thus knowing about a range of conventional methods is some help but only takes one part of the way. Experience of involvement in evaluation is valuable and this can be aided by reading and criticizing evaluations carried out by others. Thus it is important to know about the experience of the evaluator(s), since the scope and pace of the evaluation must be adapted to this, but it is stressed that lack of experience should not bar a potential evaluator – it only means that he or she is in the same position as almost everyone else.

6. EVALUATION METHOD

This includes the overall structure of the enquiry as well as the instruments used to gather information. The special question to ask of any methods being considered is whether they are appropriate for gathering the information required. By 'appropriate' we mean *valid*, that they do actually give evidence of what it is they purport to be about, and *efficient*, that is they use the most direct and least expensive in terms of time and effort. A head who evaluates the teaching methods of his teachers by administering individual diagnostic tests to each pupil has not chosen the most appropriate method for doing this. He is gathering a great deal of information which is not required (about the special difficulties of each child) but not enough of the information he does require (about the opportunities for learning which different teaching methods provide).

The methods used in any particular evaluation can be selected or adapted from the following:

- observation, structured or unstructured
- interview, structured or unstructured
- questionnaire, including rating, ranking, agree/disagree multi-choice, etc., as well as open-ended questions
- audio or video tape recording
- collection of documents, minutes, records, etc., analysed in various ways
- achievement testing

– diary records or self-made reports

Some of these require more resources, equipment and back-up facilities than others. For example, an evaluation depending heavily on audio-tape recording will need facilities and manpower for preparing transcriptions. Questionnaire and achievement testing may need computer analysis or many hours spent in marking, collating and transcribing results. Part of the judgement of 'appropriateness' of a method must therefore be in terms of the whole context of the evaluation, including the acceptability of various methods to those who will be subject to them. What is desirable may not always be possible. Designing an evaluation and choosing methods requires forethought and imagination so that one does not run out of space, time, paper or patience when only part of the information has been used.

7. TIME SCHEDULE

This is perhaps the most difficult part of the planning to judge, particularly if there is little similar work to go on. It will depend to some extent on the priority given to the evaluation as well as the nature of the problem. Rarely can any evaluation be undertaken in less than a year after the planning has taken place. If less time is available the amount and range of information which is gathered must be extremely restricted.

8. CONTROL OF INFORMATION

The plan for an evaluation should include agreements made with those concerned as to who has control over the information which is collected. Who is to decide what is selected for reporting and how the report is to be written? If the report is for a restricted audience, who decides exactly who is included and who excluded from the circulation? The decisions will be different in each case, but what is the same for all is that the position must be clear. Information is given more freely in an atmosphere of trust and it is in the interests of a full and frank evaluation to make agreements which are fair to all concerned and seen to be kept by all involved. This subject is explained fully in the next reading.

9. CRITERIA FOR MAKING JUDGEMENTS OR DECISIONS

Whether or not an evaluator includes recommendations in his report will depend on the stance he adopts in the evaluation (see 5 above). But given that evaluation is an activity directed towards decision-making, the information must, at some point, be judged and used as a basis for action. It is essential for the criteria used in this judgement to be explicit, for in general different criteria applied to the same data leads to different conclusions. Evaluation loses its vigour and becomes little more than a bolster for prejudices if the criteria applied are not known. The planning must therefore include ways of identifying criteria and, if necessary, of collecting alternative conflicting criteria which different audiences may wish to apply to the information collected.

10. REPORTING

The form of the report to be made of the evaluation has to be decided with the intended audience in mind as well as the nature of the information to be conveyed. There is little point in preparing 300 pages of illustrative transcripts if these will not be read and a three-page summary would at least bring the evidence to the attention of the decision-makers. On the other hand it may be essential to provide 300 pages of evidence if there is no other way of showing the validity of patterns drawn from it. Reports do not all have to be in writing – film, video-tape, photographs, even cartoons should be used to help the communication.

Early plans for an evaluation should include the steps to be taken to ensure that those whose activities or views are reported will have a chance to see what is said or shown and to reply to it if they wish to. Some procedure must be adopted for satisfying all the persons mentioned without drawing out the negotiations to unacceptable lengths.

Questions for Reviewing (Evaluating) Evaluations

1. Did the evaluation serve to inform the decisions or judgements for which it was originally intended?
2. What decisions have been taken as a consequence of the evaluation?
3. Was the evaluation task interpreted and carried through consistently as intended?
4. Was the information which was gathered appropriate to the purpose of the evaluation?
5. What steps were taken to allow for bias, unrepresentativeness, and low reliability in the information gathered?
6. Were the actual evaluators in the best position to carry out the evaluation?
7. Were the methods used appropriate to the kind of information which was required?
8. Were the methods systematic and explicit?
9. Did those involved in supplying the information approve of the methods used for collecting it?
10. Was there sufficient time allowed in the evaluation for the necessary data to be collected?

11. Was the evaluation carried out at the best time to serve its purpose?

12. What were the side-effects, positive and negative, of the evaluation process?

13. Were satisfactory procedures used to protect the interests of those who supplied information?

14. Were the criteria by which judgement or decisions were made appropriately drawn and explicitly stated?

15. Was the evaluation reported in a way which communicated effectively with the intended audience?

16. What reactions did the report provoke in the participants and in the decision-makers?

Applying these questions to some examples of completed evaluations can be a useful planning exercise for anyone contemplating an evaluation. In most cases it is necessary to follow up initial answers with the further question 'If not, why not?' Reasons are not always accessible but raising the question brings to light issues which should often be considered *before* and not just after an evaluation is carried out.

PART 4: REPORTING

Editor: Robert McCormick

4.1   School-based Accounting: Communication with Parents

This extract from the research report of the East Sussex Accountability Project reviews their findings on the types of information about what is happening in schools which are, or could be, made available to parents by schools. Much of this evidence is not necessarily limited to specific evaluation studies, but with an increasing concern for communication with parents this wider context is an important starting point for a consideration of reporting evaluation.

The parent interviews reported [earlier] indicated that most parents wanted to know more about what was going on in schools and what standards were being achieved. This section, therefore, reviews the types of evidence which are or could be made available to parents, and which might help to form or modify their judgements of what is being provided for their children. First, however, we wish to present some of the general arguments that have been suggested to us for and against schools spending time and effort on communication with parents, because these arguments provide the criteria by which any school's particular programme of activities must ultimately be judged.

The first argument derives from teachers' professional responsibility for the progress and well-being of their pupils, and was clearly articulated in the Plowden Report. Plowden claimed that good school — parent communication stimulates parental interest and involvement, which in turn improves children's performance; and this assertion is well backed by research evidence, which suggests that at the primary stage parental involvement is as important an influence on pupil performance as the quality of teaching. Many schools take this argument very seriously and, as a consequence, invest considerable time and effort in making contact with individual parents. However, the argument is not fundamentally based on what is good for parents but on what is good for children; and it is the responsibility of professionals for pupils which

East Sussex Accountability Project (1979), *Accountability in the Middle Years of Schooling: An Analysis of Policy Options*, University of Sussex, mimeo, pp.42-54.

provides the motivation and justification for the teachers' efforts to communicate with parents.

Secondly, and of increasing public significance, there is the issue of parents' rights. Not only do parents share the right of the general public to be kept informed about the education service, but they also have specific rights which derive from their status as parents. All parents have a right to information about their children's progress and the schools they are attending. But how much information, and in what form?

Then, thirdly, there is the argument based on enlightened self-interest: that good school—parent communications contribute to the degree of confidence which the public have in the education service as a whole. From this it follows that every member of the service has some responsibility to engage in confidence-promoting activities. Schools recognize the significance of public relations in maintaining their own reputations, but tend to be less aware of the effect on the whole service. Public confidence is reflected in financial support for education as well as in national debates about policy; and it tends to be reduced by undue secrecy at the level of individual schools.

Ranged against these arguments are two major objections. The first is that giving parents too much information allows them too much power and influence. This does not receive much support from our research in East Sussex. The parents we interviewed showed no desire for greater power, though some were a little concerned that other parents might get it. Moreover, our evidence suggests that more information might in fact reduce criticism, in that many of the anxieties and criticisms raised by parents clearly stemmed from lack of information. What the schools were actually doing corresponded much more closely to most parents' wishes than did what the parents thought they were doing. The image was worse than the reality. So if there is a stage of providing too much information, most schools are still a long way from reaching it.

The second major objection is that the school's primary task is to teach children and not parents, and that spending too much time on parent-oriented activities jeopardizes the quality of their children's education. This is clearly true in extreme cases, but the Plowden argument warns against artificially separating teaching from parent communication. Both have an important influence on pupil performance, but the proper balance of emphasis has to be determined by experience.

Each school, therefore, has not only to find the right balance between parent-oriented activities and those directly linked to their teaching programmes, but also to choose the most appropriate procedures within this total allocation, and to find the best ways of implementing those procedures.

Types of Evidence

In this part of the Report, we put forward considerations relevant to the choice of appropriate procedures for the schools' communications with parents, based on the findings of our research. Since many of the procedures in question were tried in different combinations by different schools and implemented in different ways, we are in no position to recommend a 'best buy', even for a particular type of parent. But the evidence of our interviews [. . .] and our considered reflections on the attitudes and climates of opinion we encountered when visiting parents and schools suggest important factors which both schools and the LEA should consider when reviewing their current practice.

We shall need first to introduce the idea of different types of evidence. While a particular procedure, such as a teacher–parent interview, will not necessarily be confined to one category, it is still useful when reviewing a school's programme as a whole to be able to distinguish between types of evidence. The relative merits of the procedures most likely to provide that particular type of evidence can then be discussed with greater clarity. Accordingly, we have identified six types of evidence which a school might seek to provide and have reviewed the possible procedures under these six headings. These categories, which we shall go on to discuss, are as follows: Personnel, Milieu, Curriculum, Teaching Process, Progress of Individual Pupils, and General Performance.

To complete the picture of different types of evidence, we also need to reintroduce the notion of the grapevine which figured so prominently in our interviews. The grapevine carries all the miscellaneous information (or misinformation) which someone may happen to pick up about a school or group of schools. It may include such varied forms of evidence as comments on individual teachers, random observations of children in the playground and the results of asking children to recite their tables to a visiting grandparent. This kind of evidence, though often unreliable, can have a powerful impact. It nearly always lies beyond the control of the school itself, which can only strive to counteract any wrong impressions by developing its own communication procedures. These procedures [. . .] can be either informal or formal.

Informal communication is often, but not always, oral rather than written; and much of it is spontaneous. Formal evidence, on the other hand, will usually be written; and will always be accorded official status by forming part of some official event, record or publication. In general, formal methods of communication are seen as more authoritative but less responsive than informal methods.

Thus there are three main questions which schools need to ask in relation to these different types of evidence:

(1) Is sufficient evidence of each particular type being provided?

(2) What is the relationship between the evidence already being transmitted on the grapevine and that which the school itself attempts to provide? Which evidence has most credibility for which group of parents?

(3) To what extent does the school need to use formal as well as informal procedures?

Personnel

The responsiveness of heads and teachers was of considerable significance in the parents' dealings with the schools, and virtually all parents felt able to discuss problems if the necessity arose. However, this kind of informal access was usually seen as needing a specific excuse to justify it, and did not therefore provide a mechanism for dispelling more generalized anxieties. It might be a relatively simple matter to ask for ten minutes to discuss Johnnie's peculiar handwriting, but less easy to initiate a dialogue about a concern that many of his school friends seem to be noisy and rude.

In this respect, the open door policy practised by most East Sussex primary and middle schools is fulfilling a problem-solving, rather than a routine maintenance, function. Although informal access is appreciated, and made use of, by the parents, opportunities for them to come in with their worries are, on their own, insufficient. Such opportunities may cope with a specific problem, but will not dispel a more generalized disquiet.

A kind and considerate response which shows respect for and understanding of parents' concerns contributes to the trust parents need to have in teachers. Heads themselves acknowledged that some teachers, despite being good with children, fail to impress parents. The head then has the responsibility of ensuring that those parents who bring their anxieties to him are reassured about the calibre of the teacher, and about what will happen to their child. However, some parents could easily slip through this safety net, and teachers might benefit from, and appreciate, some more direct form of help in their dealings with parents. This aspect of their work, which they themselves consider most important, does not appear to be a formally recognized professional duty and is rarely given much attention in initial or in-service training.

Milieu

Opinions about the school milieu are particularly susceptible to the grapevine, and it can be difficult for a school to counteract an unfavourable image, since atypical incidents inevitably arise which are capable of hostile interpretation. Heads were agreed that it was necessary to guard against overdefensiveness, and that nothing was to be gained by pretending that untoward incidents never happened. Nevertheless, it is still easy for a siege mentality to develop in a staff room. For some parents, order and standards of behaviour are the main symbols of a good education, but some of the signs they look for may be inappropriate for an educational, as opposed to a custodial, institution. There is a danger in merely rejecting this viewpoint rather than seeking to explain how the school does, in fact, maintain good order and reasonable behaviour. Order is in the eye of the beholder, and it may take a very honest and practical description of how it is kept, or a prolonged period of observation, before some parents recognize that it is there. Those parents who had, over a period of time, helped in schools testified to this.

Similarly, some parents have opportunities to absorb something of their local school's milieu by attending events such as open assemblies – occasions on which the school is effectively making its philosophy public. Some schools follow an open assembly by a coffee morning, or an opportunity to meet the head for conversation, or by quick visits to the working classroom. On all occasions of this type, incidental observation of the manner in which children behave in corridors or respond when spoken to gives the visiting parents a strong impression of what the school is like. Some schools may take the view that physical or organizational constraints preclude this sort of opportunity for the parents to absorb directly the atmosphere of the institution. It is worth recording that in one school many parents rated such occasions so highly that they took time off work in order to attend.

Both the tales and the notes which children bring home from school are important to parents. 'I question my children very closely about school' one mother told us. While the school can never hope to guarantee the veracity of children's reports, it can ensure that notes home are worded in a manner which will help to convey an accurate picture of school life. A note which informed parents that the school would be closed for a one-day staff conference drew from one parent the caustic comment, 'Why can't they talk to each other at lunch time?' When she discovered – accidentally – that the closure was to enable staff to spend a whole day re-examining and re-organizing their science curriculum, her attitude changed: 'Of course I don't grudge that, it's time well spent'.

Curriculum

For some time, it seems, schools have been so careful to explain new aspects of primary education and elucidate how things have changed since parents' – or even grandparents' – own schooldays, that they have inadvertently given the impression of having abandoned former goals and practices. Our visits have confirmed that this is far from being the case. But the understandable urge to explain the new and unfamiliar leads to a danger that the routine description of the old and familiar will be neglected. Indeed, the omission of the obvious – which parents, unlike teachers, do not take for granted – may even make explanations of new practices difficult to understand. Many teachers are worried that being too specific about the curriculum will limit their flexibility and autonomy. But avoiding specifics can be counter-productive, because it is the specifics that are most easily understood. We encountered considerable suspicion from parents of generalized aspirational descriptions of the curriculum and of philosophic statements of the aims of the school.

Some schools developed written accounts of curriculum policy as an element of their participation in the research project. These consisted of about half-a-dozen pages for each of five curriculum areas – English, mathematics, moral and religious education, expressive arts, and environmental studies (history, geography, science). Several of these accounts were tested with parents, who indicated almost without exception firstly, that they considered the length and language appropriate, and secondly that they would welcome similar accounts of other aspects of the curriculum. Shorter accounts were usually well received but accompanied by requests for more detail. In spite of some forebodings on the part of the teachers, none of these experiments led parents to use the material to make critical comments about the school or its curriculum.

Such accounts are demanding for teachers to produce, especially as they require careful attention to language and detail; but the time taken would diminish if examples from other schools became available as blueprints for consultation. They answer many questions which parents raised at our interviews and also provide a context within which teachers can talk about children's work and the teaching process itself. An additional benefit – which was welcomed by teachers on the project – is the opportunity to read about the practices of colleagues in other schools.

Teaching Process

Our interviews indicated that teachers' status was high with parents, but that it depended more on the teacher's competence and practical classroom skills than on his or her possession of esoteric knowledge. Hence parents who gained access to the classroom world showed increased confidence in teachers, had a greater understanding of their difficulties, and appreciated their expertise.

Although aware of the element of good public relations in having parent help in the classroom, many schools considered it unmanageable to issue open invitations asking *all* parents to help. But several schools make formal arrangements to enable parents to see the children at work on particular occasions – most commonly at open days, or as was noted in 'Milieu' above, at events such as open assemblies. Such direct forms of communication about the teaching process make a more powerful impact on many parents than do indirect accounts. But there is also scope for brief written explanations of classroom life – groupings, topic work, the uses made of textbooks and other teaching materials, even the timetable – which can be linked directly to children's work and activities without necessarily being embedded in technical vocabulary. Informal discussion of these could arise more naturally if curriculum evenings were focused on the work of particular classes rather than on what is common practice for the school as a whole.

Increased familiarity with classroom activity and the teaching process would have the additional benefit – for parents, teachers and children – of assisting parents to a more informed understanding of how best to help their children at home. Many teachers adopt an ambiguous position over parental help. Whilst not slow in decrying the lack of attention paid to their children by the parents of today, they are equally quick to condemn the parent who pushes his child. The margins delineating the correct amount of parental help are seldom clearly defined. Reading stories with your child is applauded; buying your own copy of the school's reading scheme is definitely not. The clear evidence from our research is that, regardless of the teachers' opinions about whether or not, and how, parents should help at home with the three Rs, a very large number of them do it – and several even pay for outside help from private tutors.

Teachers may have sound professional arguments to support the view that parental interference can be disastrous. The arguments are rendered irrelevant, however, by the fact that most parents resolutely continue to act as surrogate teachers – though perhaps with a certain degree of furtiveness – even if the school has indicated its disapproval. There is therefore scope in many schools for greater co-ordination between parent and teacher on this issue, and a case for teachers being prepared to share more details of the educational process. All they would, in fact, be doing would be to exploit and improve a state of affairs which already exists. As there is nothing they can do to prevent it, they may as well settle for a greater degree of influence over what is done.

Progress of Individual Pupils

Reporting on the progress and performance of individual pupils can serve three main functions: (a) informing parents about what their child has learnt, (b) giving some indication to parents of their child's aptitude and motivation, and (c) discussing any matters which either the teacher or the parents regard as problematic. In practice, the second and third receive more attention than the first; and this could well be another example of neglecting the obvious. We referred earlier to the need for specific and concrete reference points in parent–teacher communications, yet nothing is more specific or closer to the interest of both parent and teacher than the child's classwork. Parents usually have access to their child's work on open evenings and at various other times during the school year, but it is often assumed that they can draw their own conclusions from this evidence without professional guidance. However, not only topic work but even work in exercise books can be difficult to interpret out of context and without reference to any sense of an appropriate standard. Explaining and discussing such work, possibly even comparing it with work completed a few months earlier, would seem a strong candidate for fruitful parent–teacher communication. It could counteract some of the less reliable interpretations on the grapevine, illustrate the teacher's comments on the child's report, and provide a natural link with the help that many parents attempt to give at home.

The other two functions – (b) and (c) – are catered for by formal arrangements for parent-teacher consultations, by reports and by informal invitations to 'come and talk if there is anything you want to know or if you think there may be a problem'. The main policy issues would appear to be the nature and frequency of formal consultation arrangements for parent–teacher consultations, by reports and by be placed on informal contact.

The relative merits may need to be considered of open evenings, where parents wait their turn to buttonhole the teacher, and a system of appointments for interviews at specific times. The latter has the advantage of privacy and of showing that parent time is valued as well as teacher time, but the additional formality may be offputting to some, and not all parents want to be tied down to a fixed time. Few schools have the facilities to operate both systems unless they allocate classes to different evenings – and this can inconvenience parents with more than one child. If the classroom is occupied by interviews, there is little opportunity for waiting parents to examine children's work. However, parents could at least inspect their own child's work if it were taken home a day or two before the interview, even though the opportunity to look at other children's work would have to be transferred to another suitable occasion. Some research has been conducted (though not in East Sussex and not with representative samples) which indicated a strong parental preference for the private interview over the open evening as a form of consultation.

It is also a matter for debate how often these formal consultations should take place. All primary and middle schools in East Sussex provide them at least once a year, and many do it twice a year. It remains to be established whether this is sufficiently frequent.

Not all of the schools we worked with issue written reports. Though we did not conduct a referendum specifically on this issue, many of the parents we interviewed indicated that they would like to receive them. Some teachers are wary of committing to paper categorical statements about children which – appearing as they do in an impersonal and decontextualized form – are easily misinterpreted. They feel that the scant information it is possible to convey on a report does not merit the time spent producing it, and worry that, in extreme cases, children might even be physically punished by their parents as a result of a comment on a report.

However, from the parents' point of view, a report acts as a safeguard against the difficulty of remembering oral information accurately. Some children themselves may appreciate the opportunity to read what their teacher thinks of their work: the children, after all, are not present as a rule at parent–teacher consultations. And since teachers fill in record cards anyway, for the school's internal purposes, report writing should not add unduly to the burden that already exists.

It may be that consideration of format and methods is more pertinent than argument about whether or not to issue written reports. If a report is sent home a week or so before the parent–teacher consultation takes place, it can be brought to the interview and serve as a useful opening for the ensuing discussion. The teacher has the opportunity to set his written remarks into their correct context, and the parent has before him a useful checklist of points which he might otherwise forget to raise. For the less articulate parents – those who indicated to us that they often found difficulties in formulating questions – part of their problem might be eased by having the report as a starting point.

Given the difficulty which parents have in making judgements about standards, consultations have a tendency to hinge on either explicit or implicit statements of a child's ability, motivation and potential. Thus, although the discussion may well influence a parent's judgement of a teacher or a school, its primary purpose will be seen as drawing the parents into the school's experience, assessment and expectations of their own child. It is the child rather than the school that is being judged. Moreover, parents often press for more tightly defined judgements than most teachers want to give.

General Standards of Performance

Most of the information which parents receive about pupil performance relates only to their own children, but this has not always been the case. The eleven plus gave opportunities for inter-school comparisons which have now ceased; and there is a natural tendency to look for some 'successor to the 11-plus' to provide a simple indicator of school performance. This kind of data, however, must presuppose that all schools take the same standardized tests and make the results publicly available – a situation which can only arise from decisions at LEA level. Procedures which rely on standardized tests administered on a county-wide basis are discussed [later]. Here we will merely register two main objections to this kind of policy. First, it may encourage schools to coach pupils for specific tests and thus distort the normal educational process. Second, test results must reflect the nature of a school's intake as well as the quality of its teaching. Publicizing these results has the effect of favouring schools with a good intake, giving them a reputation they have not necessarily earned, and allowing them to rest on their laurels. At the same time it discriminates against schools with a poor intake, putting them under pressure to achieve results beyond their capacity, in the vain hope of acquiring the good reputations which some at least richly deserve. These are among the reasons why there is almost total professional opposition to the suggestion that test results should become available in any way that facilitates inter-school comparisons by non-professionals.

It may therefore be necessary to rule out the use of standardized test results in reporting on school performance to parents, but not the use of other kinds of evidence. Apart from what parents glean from their own and other children's exercise books, they have the opportunity to see written work, art work, topic work and sometimes number work on display. Such evidence, if supplemented by copies of classroom tests, comparisons of work over a period of time (e.g. from the beginning and end of the year), or accounts of the current level of work being attempted, could help to allay parental anxieties and dispel the suspicion that the schools had something to hide. Parents might also be informed of the ways in which performance was internally monitored by the school and externally monitored by advisers, as a further challenge both to the claim that the abolition of the 11-plus has led to the abandonment of proper standards and to the belief that in these days schools can get away with anything.

Summary

The procedures discussed above have been listed and classified in a single diagram (Table 1) as an aid to subsequent discussion. Not all types of evidence fit neatly into a single box, but we believe that the grid has the advantage of clarifying the options that are open to a school in deciding how best to communicate with parents, as well as reminding it of the grapevine over which it has little control. We have tried to include all the main procedures mentioned during the course of our research, but make no claim for complete coverage. Perhaps the very existence of the grid will suggest new and useful possibilities.

Table 1 Types of Parent Evidence about Schools

	Grapevine	Informal	Formal
Personnel	Teacher's dress and public behaviour; Teacher's control of children in public; Newspaper reports of teachers' activities; Comments of ancillaries; Comments from children; Comments from other parents.	Responsiveness of head and teachers to queries; 'Meet the teacher' evenings.	
Milieu	Random observations of playground and corridors; Comments from ancillaries; Comments from other parents; Behaviour at bus stops; Child reports of school; Media coverage.	Reports on school trips; Notes to parents; Handling of critical incidents; Newsletters; Parent attendance at assemblies, school concerts and plays.	School prospectus.
Curriculum	Child reports; Comments from other parents; Media coverage of curriculum issues.	Books brought home; Curriculum evenings; Talks with head and teachers; Timetables; Displays of children's work.	School prospectus; Written accounts of curriculum policy; Parent access to schemes of work.
Teaching Process	Child reports of classroom events; Comments from parent-helpers.	Classroom visits by parents; Parent-helpers; *Written explanations of classroom activities (groupings, use of classroom time, role of topic work etc.); *Video recordings of classroom activities.	
Individual Progress of Pupils	Random observations of performance; Home-testing; Inter-pupil comparisons.	Work brought home; Open evenings; Parent–teacher interviews.	Written reports on children's progress; *Parent access to school records.
General Performance	Media coverage on educational 'standards'; Inter-school comparisons.	School concerts and plays; Displays of children's work.	*Reports on test results.

*Not currently in use in East Sussex

Finally, we should like to make some general points that we hope will put some of the foregoing analysis into perspective.

1. Schools have to be realistic about what they can hope to achieve. They cannot please all of the people all of the time, and there is therefore a sense in which they cannot win. Overambition can lead either to the investment of too much time in parent relations or to unjustifiable disillusionment when reasonable effort does not lead to total success.

2. It can be dangerous to evaluate events for parents solely in terms of attendance. A school is not like a football team, with parents as its supporters' club. Supporting one's children does not necessarily mean attending school functions, and attendance figures are not a good indicator of successful communication.

3. Schools are prone to become overdefensive. Questions and initial comments usually reflect anxiety rather than hostility. Criticism often indicates involvement rather than apathy, and parents appreciate it when their views are treated with respect. Parents' respect for a teacher's professional role and judgement is usually strong and need not normally be doubted. But dialogue which does not allow the opportunity for criticism is liable to be dismissed as window dressing.

4. There is a tendency to talk about open days or curriculum evenings as if the only issue is whether or when to have them. Less consideration seems to be given to how best to run them. Yet the setting, the preparation, the quality of interaction are all crucial to their success. Similar considerations apply to written documents.

5. Any and every piece of communication is influenced by local history and tradition. Parents and teachers can become so used to communicating with each other in certain ways that both may be hostile to a change of pattern, even if it is to their mutual benefit in the long run. Some changes may need to be gradual, and if a school tries out a new idea it should not expect an instant success.

4.2 Teacher–Parent Communication
R. Gibson

This is the second extract from the Cambridge Accountability Project research and it focuses on the formal written communications between schools and parents. It thus takes up one dimension (formal) of the grid put forward by Becher et al. in the previous reading, investigating who tells what to whom, how and why, and with what effect?

Introduction

Any school has three major ways of telling parents about its activities and beliefs: by inviting them to *see* what goes on, by *talking* with parents, and by writing to them. Most schools use all three methods and many, particularly at primary level, argue that it is through *involvement* and participation that parent–school relationships are most fruitfully developed. This chapter discusses only those *written* communications a school sends to all its parents. It is not concerned with pupils' reports or with correspondence about individual children[. . .]. Rather, it confines itself to an examination of those booklets, brochures and newsletters which a school produces for all parents. It is therefore a study of how schools engage in (to use an unfortunately ambiguous term) mass-communication.

Communication is one of those important-sounding words much in vogue. Marshall McLuhan wrote once-fashionable books about it from which now only a few clichés remain; contemporary linguists such as Roman Jakobson analyse it in ways impenetrable to laymen; in higher education it forms a distinct field of study; there exists a 'communications industry'. However, in spite of its apparent complexity there is a simple structure that underlies all communication:*who* tells *what* to *whom, how, why,* and *with what effect?* It is this deceptively simple six-point structure that will be used to analyse the written messages schools send to all parents.

1. Who?

'It's from the school' say the parents as the latest Newsletter or forty-

Gibson, R. (1981), 'Teacher–Parent Communication', in the Cambridge Accountability Project, *The Self-Accounting School*, Grant McIntyre.

page sixth-form booklet is brought home by their child. But 'the school' is a convenient corporate fiction: the newsletter or booklet has been written by an individual or several individuals. Who actually writes what parents read? In many small schools the answer is straightforward: the headteacher. In larger schools a variety of practices is to be found: a single individual, a team, a compiler of contributions from other teachers; invariably however the head retains responsibility for oversight, approval and usually signature, of each document.

Behind such an obvious and apparently trivial observation lie three important facts. First, that with the exceptions noted in section (4) below, whatever is communicated to parents is presented as a collective, corporate, school, view, not an individual or sectional one; inter-staff disagreements have no place in such communications. Second, each document presents an *image* of the school to the parents, an image approved by the writer(s) – and by extension, all other members of the school staff. Third, that conscious choice is being exercised by someone over what to include and what to exclude.

To give one small but significant illustration: if you are a teacher and your name is Jane Smith, someone decides how, in a brochure for new parents, those parents may learn of your existence. You may thus be presented as: Jane Smith, or Mrs J. Smith, *or* Mrs Jane Smith, *or* Mrs J. Smith M.A.; Cert.Ed. (the choice of Ms if preferred will probably be your own), but it is possible that no mention be made of you at all! Does it matter? And there is scope for far greater variety of treatment over such matters as school aims, pastoral care, curriculum, discipline and school uniform. An examination of a few school brochures will reveal enormous differences in extent and nature of treatment of every item of school life.

2. What?

What *do* schools tell parents in writing? There is great variety of practice. Some schools tell a great deal, some very little. All six schools in the Cambridge Accountability Project [CAP] provide much information for their parents. To take one example: at one school all parents of third-year pupils could expect to receive, on a conservative estimate, communications totalling around 30,000 words during the course of the year. Indeed, each parent would additionally receive as a matter of course, lengthy reports about their own child's progress.

It is useful to record what might be considered the minimum information that should be provided to all parents. In 1977 Mrs Shirley Williams, the then Secretary of State, set out the nature and extent of the information she considered should normally be available to parents in written form. Her recommendations were:

(i) The name, address and telephone number of the school, the hours it is open and the dates of term times; the address and telephone number of the Local Education Authority and Divisional Education Office.

(ii) Characteristics: e.g. whether county or denominational, mixed or single sex, the age range covered and boarding provision, if any.

(iii) Names of the head, and at least of the senior staff, and also the names and addresses of the Chairman of Governors and of any parent governors.

(iv) How parents should arrange to visit the school and the time at which the head, senior staff members, class or subject teachers, year heads or pastoral tutors are normally available for consultation (bearing in mind the difficulties of working parents and the desirability of contact with the school for both parents).

(v) Other arrangements to enable parents to be kept informed of their child's progress in school.

(vi) The number of pupils and the number normally admitted each year.

(vii) The basis on which places are normally allocated.

(viii) Arrangements for transfer between one stage of education and the next, including, where appropriate, details of the course options available in schools, tertiary or sixth-form colleges, and in further education establishments.

(ix) Any special facilities offered in particular subjects or activities including facilities for careers advice.

(x) Arrangements for religious education and for exemption from it.

(xi) (Secondary and upper schools only) Public examinations for which pupils are prepared, and the range of subjects and options available at the time when the information is issued, together with details of arrangements for consultation with parents on these matters.

(xii) A brief indication of the normal teaching organization (including arrangements for teaching children of different abilities), of any special organization or methods used, and of the school's policy on homework.

(xiii) Clubs, societies, extra-curricular activities, including community service, normally available.

(xiv) Organization for pastoral care and discipline of pupils, including school rules and procedures.

(xv) Whether school uniform is required and if so the approximate cost, otherwise an indication of the type of clothing which is acceptable.

(xvi) Whether any parents' or parent—teacher organization exists, and if so the name and address of its secretary.

(xvii) Local school transport arrangements.

(xviii) The LEA's arrangements for the provision of free school meals.
 (xix) The LEA's arrangements for the provision of free PE kit and the school clothing grants.
 (xx) (Secondary and upper schools) The LEA's arrangements for the provision of educational maintenance allowances and discretionary awards.

(Source: Department of Education and Science circular 15/77)

Such a list is useful and apparently unexceptional. Heads, teachers and parents could usefully compare it with their own schools' practice. Interestingly, there is little available public knowledge of what written information schools actually do produce. Knowledge is often confined to what one's own school does – and this is taken as 'normal'. Only in the pages of *Where?* are actual examples of practice fairly regularly given, and only in *Teacher – Parent Communication* (Gibson, 1980) is it possible to see, in great detail, what actually happens in someone else's school.

CAP evidence points to how parents greatly value written information about such matters as school uniform, bus times and school dinners. Parents wish to know the *detail* that will directly affect them and their children. One mother's remark about an 'Information for New Parents' booklet is typical:

> . . . you feel they want you to know about the place. 'Course you forget – I did read it all at the time and really the only thing I remember is things I wanted to know like school uniform – obviously the things I needed to know . . . Couldn't tell you about it now apart from those things, but I do know that I thought it was really good.

It is such practical, everyday matters that weigh heavily. They are not trivial but of great significance to almost all parents.

Usual practice in secondary schools is that such information as the DES prescribes is presented in booklets or brochures. One Project school provides four brochures:

1. An Introduction for Parents of Middle School Children (7 pages)
2. For New Parents and Students (21 pages)
3. Fourth Year Option Guide (14 pages)
4. The Sixth Form (39 pages)

In addition to such booklets, all the project schools issue newsletters several times per term or on a regular basis: fortnightly or even weekly. Newsletters contain a great miscellany of information about day-to-day school life. Examples of topics included are: Christmas concert, slide evening, careers evening, can you help? dates for your diary, county hockey honours, evening classes, reports, play evenings, old time music hall, meet your governors, PTA AGM, self help, charity efforts, public examination results, road safety . . . the list, over a year, is a very long one.

There is a very wide range of opinion among teachers over what should be included in written information provided for all parents. Three items not mentioned in the DES list are worth remarking upon.

First: aims. It is a difficult exercise to convey to parents, pithily and in a non-banal way, what the aims of the school are. Lists that teachers draw up for themselves might sometimes seem inappropriate when committed to print. It is interesting that some schools which produce extensive brochures for parents do not make a point of specifically stating their aims in a separate section. It would seem sensible to recommend that all schools should give thought as to how desirable and practical it is to include 'school aims' in their documents for parents.

Second: examination results. Project schools vary in the amount of information they provide to all parents about examination results. All give some information; at least one gives a complete breakdown by subjects and grades for both CSE and O level. From 1982, legislation will compel all schools to make results available.

Third: rewards. Most schools make clear their expectations for behaviour in their written documents. Many set out, as Mrs Williams suggests, details of their pastoral care and discipline organization. One of the Project schools lists its nine disciplinary measures (from 'setting of extra work' to 'suspension from school'). However, specific reference to 'rewards' is rare. Certainly, it is invariably easier to compile a list of a school's punishments than of its rewards. It is therefore well worth considering whether this topic merits more attention, and whether parents could not be more fully informed as to the manner in which a school rewards its pupils.

3. To Whom?

It might seem unnecessary to ask to whom are the written documents addressed. The answer is obvious: the parents. However, the question is well worth asking because it serves as a reminder that parents (like teachers) are *not* a homogeneous group. 'The parents' is as much a convenient and necessary fiction as 'the school' or 'the pupils'. Such labels conceal a diversity and richness of human qualities that defy aggregation. The only certain thing 'the parents' do have in common is that they have children who attend *this* school. Given that, each parent is unique; many may share expectations, perceptions, purposes, values; but it is certain that some will not. Awareness of such heterogeneity makes the task of addressing all parents a difficult and demanding one. It also reveals the danger of regarding parental contact simply as mass-communication: the parents are never a 'mass'. Encouragingly, what the following sections show is that it is possible to succeed remarkably well in this potentially fraught enterprise.

4. How?

How does a school communicate with its parents? One obvious answer is that in every case the children themselves take the documents home. But the How? question raises much more subtle and important issues than this (although it should be recorded that some teachers are sceptical about how many children do actually deliver newsletters to their parents – a problem some schools resolve by including a tear-off reply/acknowledgement slip and the collection of these slips by form tutors).

Each of the Project schools gives close attention to the presentation of its booklets and newsletters. Some have their booklets printed, others use offset litho or duplicating machine stencils. For newsletters the offset litho or stencil is employed. There is a very high quality of presentation: layout is attractive, letters and pictures clear cut, impeccable grammar and spelling. Whatever the mode of reproduction, the document received by the parent represents a model of what the school stands for and expects (see the many examples in Gibson, 1980). Many of the resonances of McLuhan's deeply ambiguous 'the medium is the message' can be detected in schools' documents for parents. Thus, certain major assumptions underlying a particular school's approach to education often can be revealed by a consideration of the language, tone and style of its written communications.

The language of parental documents is a matter of concern for many teachers: 'do they really understand what we write?' The answer to that frequently asked question, as will be shown in Section 5 below, is 'generally – yes'. Teachers nevertheless are much concerned whether some of the documents, particularly those relating to curriculum, 'go over the heads' of many parents. This concern is both genuine and realistic: how do you get over to *all* parents the curriculum structure of the school or something of the essence of physics or integrated science? Such topics after all are not usually part of the everyday conversation of most homes, offices or factory floors. How can jargon be avoided and how can (say) curriculum choice be meaningfully presented? An encouraging finding of the Cambridge Accountability Project is that its schools experience much success in teacher–parent communication. This success is due in part to very conscious appreciation of the problem and a policy of keeping documents constantly under review, and a concern to ensure that written documents fit within a wider context of parent–teacher communications: meetings, visits, reports evening and other events. The context of the written documents is all important and no school relies solely on the written word but provides many opportunities for teachers and parents to meet face-to-face.

Style and tone are aspects of language that help to influence how a message is received. Immediately obvious in speech they are no less present in writing, particularly when, as in newsletters, a steady flow proceeds from school to home over the year. Thus the 'ethos' of every school is subtly reflected in the written documents provided for parents.

There is unfortunately not room here to detail with accuracy how, in style and tone, such differences are reflected in each school's booklets and newsletters. Rather, what will be attempted is to sketch some of the common characteristics of the documents of all six CAP schools.

First, there is a friendly, welcoming tone:

> I am writing this letter on behalf of all the staff, to welcome you and your daughter to . . .

> We look forward very much to getting to know you and to working with you in the years ahead.

> Welcome!

Second, a human, personal voice comes through, particularly in newsletters and in heads' letters introducing the various major documents. This is evidenced in a number of ways: for example, by signing first name in addition to surname; by the occasional aside:

> We had another scramble to get ready for opening, but once again we managed to move all the furniture in time. It is rumoured that the idea is to re-train redundant headmasters as removal men!

and by direct acknowledgement of individuality.

> Whatever the need we try to meet it . . . We are attempting to make the school fit the individual rather than force everyone into the same mould.

Although newsletters necessarily begin 'Dear Parents' (they may go to over a thousand homes) it is clear that there is a concern to establish direct, friendly contact to acknowledge the uniqueness of each parent and each pupil, and to show that teachers too, are human. One head signs, 'I look forward to meeting you personally'.

Third, each school attempts to ensure that, as far as possible, everyday, rather than technical, language characterizes its documents. One school rewrote its introduction to curriculum choice for the fourth/fifth years leaving out earlier reference to 'faculty structure' as it felt this hindered, rather than helped, parental understanding. In the same school the head of English periodically carries out readability tests on parental documents.

Fourth, there is an enthusiasm, a vivacity and a feeling of excitement in the documents. The implicit (sometimes explicit) message is that not only is the school an interesting, stimulating and lively place for pupils, but as parents become involved in school activities they too will find it both enriching to themselves and helpful to their children's education. The invitation for parents to participate in extra-curricular activities are legion: Summer Fayres, dances, barbecues, concerts, open evenings, school plays, carol services, curriculum subject evenings, sales, raffles, careers conventions, slide shows, coffee evenings, Caribbean evenings, fetes. . . .

It could be said that the tone is one of sociability, of togetherness. The schools assert, quite directly, that they regard education as a joint enterprise, that success can only come through co-operation of home and school. This concern to build and sustain a community is evidenced in the very style of many of the documents.

Fifth, courtesy underlies and is evidenced in the documents. Such concern for the dignity of others comes through in many ways, particularly in the very full information given on aspects of school life, the professional presentation, and through a stated willingness to listen to individual parents and to meet their children's needs.

Sixth, there is a strong tone of authority in the documents. Not authoritarianism it must be stressed, because the invitation to discuss and the willingness to accommodate is always present. Rather, it is authority in the sense that a very strong feeling comes through that the school *knows what it is about*. Extensive descriptions of curriculum, pastoral care and organization convey an air of confidence and assurance. The full and reasoned documents unequivocally imply that the teachers know their job, and, with the co-operation of parents, can successfully educate their children.

In addition to curriculum expertise, such authority is often reflected in a directness of style that lays clear the school's expectations for pupils' conduct. A single example from a Project school booklet will illustrate:

. . . smoking. While it is a very difficult problem for schools to deal with, most parents are very anxious that we should try to do something about it. We do not allow it for two main reasons.

(a)   If it takes place in the buildings, there is a very real fire danger, as many schools have discovered at their cost.

(b)   Smoking is a serious health hazard.

Having made our rule for sound reasons, to allow people to ignore it threatens the discipline of the school, so this is what we do . . .

(a)   The first time a student is caught smoking on or near the school premises they are fined 25p and the money given to Cancer Research!

(b)   We keep a central register of people found smoking including anyone within a group where smoking is clearly taking place. No one can say 'It wasn't me!' We treat all people within the group in the same way.

(c)   The second time we find a student smoking we increase the Cancer Research funds by another 25p, but we also send a letter to parents saying what has happened and telling them that on health, safety and discipline grounds, if it happens again, the student will be suspended from school until we have had a chance of talking together . . .

(d)   . . . and if it happens again, that is exactly what we do!

This analysis of written documents could be extended much further and with profit by readers of this [chapter]. A comparison of a number of schools' material will quickly suggest many dimensions in addition to the above: is the language plain rather than elegant? crisp rather than curt? formal or informal? cheerful? hectoring? (see Green, 1975), serious, solemn or with humour? succinct or prolix? and a host of others. Although the CAP schools have certain characteristics in common, nonetheless each school has a 'distinctive quality of voice' and on every dimension there are subtle differences of emphasis. But, however they do it, each CAP school 'lays its expectations on the line' in a way that is neither condescending nor authoritarian.

5. Why?

The question is a crucial one: why *do* some schools invest so much time, energy and resources in providing written information for parents? From the wide variety of explanations advanced, three major theories may be detected. They can be called Competition, Control and Common sense.

Competition theories view the parent—teacher communication exercise basically as competition for scarce resources, whether these are materials, cash or children. Thus, booklets are referred to as 'glossies' and communication is seen principally as about 'image building', 'a PR exercise'. The motives attributed are those of personal or institutional self-interest, *viz:* a school gains a good reputation in a community and in the LEA, so that, at times of falling rolls and economic recession, its survival and the security of its staff, is assured. Usually, the unstated inference of these theories is that there is little or no match between 'image' and 'reality'.

Control theories view the whole exercise as one of control by mystification, by overloading or by distraction. Such theories are usually propagated by theorists who have little contact with teachers, children or a wide range of parents. Control by mystification implies that communication is only 'blinding with science': language being used so as to obscure what are held to be fundamental realities of knowledge, social structure or social relations. Control by overloading argues that parents have so much information pumped at them that they are incapable of making rational judgements or seeing the 'true' state of things (advocates of these theories always put inverted commas around the word, true). Control by distraction was identified by Shakespeare's Bolingbroke: 'Busy giddy minds with foreign quarrels'. It argues that leaders with something to hide should focus the attention and resentment of subordinates on trivial, peripheral or external matters or groups. Thus the misled underlings will never protest about, or even recognize, what is really important to them. These theories are even more sharply premised on interest-theory, on false consciousness and the absence of goodwill in human conduct.

Common sense theories to explain teacher–parent communication of the type examined by the project arise from three beliefs: first, that the parents have a right to know what goes on in the schools that their children attend; second, that such knowledge makes for good relationships between parents and teachers; and third, that good communications will result in improvement in pupils' learning and attitudes. Further, such theories are based on the assumption that there is a fairly close match between what is described in the documents and what actually goes on in school. Unlike the two previous theories, there is the assumption that what is obvious is also true.

Why people act as they do is usually a consequence of mixed motives. It is rare indeed that human behaviour has one single simple course or explanation. The Cambridge Accountability Project has found a great deal of evidence to support Common sense theories (see all six case studies: teachers' and parents' views); a certain amount to support Competition theories (see particularly John Elliott's Case Study Part I, Cambridge Accountability Project, 1981) and little or no evidence for Control theories.

6.   With what Effect?

Does it work? Do the written documents do what the schools intend? What needs stressing again is that all schools see their written documents only as one of many channels of communication with parents. They rightly insist that their effectiveness should be judged, in relation to the visits, parents' evenings and other meetings that necessarily complement the documents.

When considering the effectiveness of teacher-parent communication three fundamental questions arise. First, do the documents get across? (i.e. do they result in greater parental understanding?) Second, do they improve relationships between home and school? Third, do they result in improvement in pupils' learning?

On the first question, the evidence from the Cambridge Accountability Project is very encouraging. The newsletters and booklets are not only welcomed, but closely read by parents. Teachers' fears about parents not understanding because of language difficulties seem ill-founded. The conversational, informative style of newsletters appears to work very well: parents genuinely *are* kept in the picture and have few difficulties in understanding what is going on. There is a similarly encouraging finding concerning the first booklet issued by schools, typically called *Information for New Parents*. When schools take the twenty DES recommendations (pp.320-22) as the basis for their introductory booklet and present them in their own individual style, then parents can and do understand the result.

Curriculum documents issued by schools to guide option choices for the last two years of secondary education and for the sixth form present greater problems of understanding for parents. These substantial documents present complex and often unfamiliar information.

In CAP interviews, parents stressed how necessary it was to talk with their children and with teachers in order to grasp the full implications of what they read. Thus, a fairly typical comment was:

> I was clear when we went to the school. We saw the Deputy Head and chatting to him we got it. Reading that (i.e. the Booklet) was difficult but it was sorted out by the time we had to choose.

All the schools see discussion as vital; no school considers its documents sufficient. Curriculum documents in particular are designed to facilitate *individual* choice, and, to this end, each school arranges and encourages meetings as an integral part of that process.

There is encouraging evidence too on the second question: are home—school relationships improved by written documents? Although an occasional parent complained of the sheer amount of information ('you could be reading *War and Peace!*') it was obvious that parents appreciate the schools' efforts to keep them informed and involved. There is little doubt that goodwill towards the schools was increased by the booklet, which informed parents of the schools' expectations and intentions, and by the newsletters, which kept up a running commentary on progress and which sought to involve the parents in the schools' activities. In the great majority of cases a climate of trust was created. Such goodwill was not the result simply of a public relations exercise, but because parents came to recognize that the image presented in the documents matched the realities of school life. Documents are one of the vital means by which teacher—parent contact is established and maintained; the knowledge parents thus acquire undoubtedly makes for good relationships. This finding of the Cambridge Accountability Project receives support from a major accountability investigation of middle schools (East Sussex, 1979). The explanation seems fairly straightforward: people like to know what is expected, what is going on, and how they can be involved in decisions that affect their lives. The written documents help to fulfil just those functions.

The third question: 'Does teacher—parent communication result in improvement in children's education?' is one that professional researchers usually assert to be impossible to answer. There are simply too many variables to take into account. Certainly, the Cambridge Project cannot produce unequivocal evidence. However, it can report that such a *belief* is very widely held by teachers and parents. The six schools do what they do because they believe it will result in better education for each pupil; parents think that the documents help them to help their children.

It seems very likely therefore that as parental support and encouragement *is* a major factor in pupils' achievement, and as parents much value being kept informed and involved by schools, then good parent–teacher communication of the type discussed in this chapter is a vital contributory element in children's learning.

Some Questions for Discussion by Teacher and Parents

1. Who writes your teacher–parent documents? Do all staff make a contribution?
2. Should 'the aims of this school' go in the documents? How would you state them for parents?
3. How appropriate is the *language* of your documents?
4. Do your documents have a characteristic tone and style? What is it?
5. What additions, amendments or deletions would you make to your school's documents?
6. *Why* do you issue written documents to parents?[. . .]

References

East Sussex Accountability Project (1979), *Accountability in the Middle Years of Schooling: An Analysis of Policy Options,* University of Sussex.

Cambridge Accountability Project (1981), *Six Case Studies*, Cambridge Institute of Education.

Gibson, R. (1980), *Teacher–Parent Communication: One School and its Practice,* Cambridge Institute of Education.

Green, L. (1975), *School Reports and Other Information for Parents*, Home and School Council.

4.3 Record-keeping in Primary Schools
P. S. Clift

The Record-keeping Project ran from September 1976 to August 1978. The final report was published in 1981 (Clift et al., 1981). This is an abridged compilation from the newsletters produced by the project team (Clift et al., 1977 and 1978) and one chapter of the final report. It provides a synoptic view of record-keeping policies and practices in primary schools, and makes recommendations for their improvement. It is presented in terms of the questions asked of schools and considers official LEA records, internal formal school records, and records and reports to and from those outside.

Time was allocated to visiting as many schools as possible of those recommended by local education authorities as having developed interesting systems of recording. The data which follows is derived from school visits and postal replies. The information gained from the school visits includes replies to questionnaires and notes from interviews.

What kinds of records are being used in the primary school?

1. *The day to day record* of the teacher — kept for the planning and organization of classroom work, e.g. notes on the levels of reading and mathematical ability, topic work covered etc.
2. *Summary record* for the transfer of information within the school (either teacher to teacher or teacher to head):
(a) half-termly
(b) termly
(c) half-yearly
(d) at the end of each year.
3. *Transition record* sent from school at the end of each educational stage:
(a) from nursery to infant or first school
(b) from infant or first school to junior or middle school
(c) from junior or middle to secondary school.

First publication.

4. *Transfer record* sent from school to school when a pupil changes schools for reasons other than transition.
5. *School report to parents*
6. *Diagnostic records* used either:
(a) at the instigation of the classroom teacher to identify educational weaknesses
(b) at the instigation of the local education authority to identify children 'at risk', e.g. Croydon, Birmingham.

What forms of recording techniques are used?

Progress recorded long-hand – unstructured, e.g. the account of the progress of a pupil written on a blank page.

Progress recorded long-hand – structured; in terms of headings beneath which extensive comments are required.

More detailed headings requiring shorter comments.

Checklist which requires an answer in terms of yes/no or 3-10 point scale (usually 3 or 5).

Records which include several or all of the above techniques.

What kinds of information are usually kept on records?

General background information – address, age, parental occupation, religion, place in the family etc.

Medical information.

Information from outside welfare agencies e.g. educational psychologists, social workers.

Assessment of pupil progress: [pupil skills] comments, observations, marks, grades, rankings, test results.

What has been attempted (as opposed to what has been achieved [pupil experiences]) e.g. topic work covered, interests etc.

In our analysis of the records from the schools we visited and those sending information through the post, we found that pupil skills and experiences were recorded in the following proportions:

*Skill or Curriculum Category	% of schools
Reading development	96
List of mathematical topics covered	81
Social and personal development	55
Writing development	35
Oral language development	34
Physical development	31
Concept attainment in mathematics	29

Skill or Curriculum Category   *% of schools*

Scientific skills and experience	17
Aesthetic development – craft skills	14
Study skills	3

*This data was not taken from a random sample of schools but from those recommended by their LEA for good practice in record keeping.

We have also looked at the purposes which teachers have given for keeping records.

In answer to the question a number of generally agreed typical reasons for school record-keeping were received and also a number of unexpected ones.

The typical reasons given by teachers for keeping records:
1. To chart pupil progress and achievement;
2. To communicate information to other teachers;
3. To ensure continuity of education throughout the school;
4. To ensure continuity of education on transfer to other schools;
5. To guide a replacement or supply teacher;
6. For diagnostic purposes – to spot problems, identify under-achievement and pupils needing extra help;
7. To provide teachers with information on the success (or failure) of teaching methods and materials;
8. As a statement of 'what has happened' – to inform interested parties (parents, educational psychologists, the head);
9. To give headteacher a general picture of achievement within the school.

Some of the less expected replies to the question concerning the purpose of school records included:
10. To be used as a defence against accusations of falling standards;
11. As an insurance policy – the record is an account of what has gone before which may be needed in the face of hostile attacks;
12. For the head to gain control over the classroom curriculum;
13. To keep balance in areas of study;
14. To reassure teachers as to what progress has been made;
15. In a large school, to keep 'tabs' on each pupil.

The great variety of reasons for keeping records has been criticized as being counter-productive to good teaching practice.

One of the strongest impressions gained . . . is that records are expected to fulfil too many purposes simultaneously and that, as yet, insufficient consideration has been given to methods of using the information collected. (Walker, 1955, p.33)

Transfer Records

When children move to other schools the records which accompany or follow them are usually the LEA cards, which were available to us. These were analysed into their content categories.

A questionnaire compiled from this analysis was completed by project teachers. Their responses to this questionnaire were analysed and related to the respondents' length and range of teaching experience. The data revealed that the types of information teachers felt to be important were:

(i) identification: e.g. pupil names, date of birth, address;

(ii) any vital medical or other important personal information;

(iii) names, telephone numbers, or addresses, of persons to be contacted in case of emergency;

(iv) any physical handicaps which may affect learning;

(v) note of particular learning difficulties;

(vi) referrals to psychologists or child guidance, the results of referrals and any recommended remedial treatment;

(vii) information on attainment in basic skills – e.g. stage reached on reading and mathematics schemes;

(viii) any standardized tests taken, their names and the results.

More detailed categories of information on language, mathematics and personal development were ranked lower in importance. Information about physical education and games skills, drama and movement ability, and use of study skills were the kinds of information teachers least wished to know about new pupils. Less experienced teachers require a higher degree of structuring on records, i.e. they wanted many more categories on a record to help them to focus on various facets of pupils' progress and behaviour; conversely more experienced colleagues required fewer categories.

Confidentiality and 'Sensitive Information'

One of our groups of teachers wrestled at length with the issue in an attempt to provide guidelines for teachers. It was decided to focus on 'sensitive information' (i.e. the kinds of information which might be more controversial where a policy of 'open' records exists) rather than the general aspects of confidentiality in record-keeping.

The following is a summary of the guidelines:

(i) 'Sensitive' information is:

● information about an individual which may cause embarrassment or anxiety if disclosed to the child/parents and may include information about home background, personal qualities, and certain medical information;

● any information from supporting agencies, e.g. education psychologists, social workers, medical services, should be treated as 'sensitive' unless stated otherwise.

(ii) Types of records kept in school:

(a) the 'Official Permanent Record' supplied by the local authority;

(b) internal formal school records – records devised by a school staff for use within their school;

(c) records and reports to and from external welfare agencies and parents.

(The guidelines below apply to the three types of record described above but exclude notes jotted down by teachers from day to day which are used as a basis for completing permanent records but are not passed on directly to other colleagues.)

(iii) The purpose of recording sensitive information:

● factual data collected to enable teachers to provide appropriately for and to deal sympathetically with children.

(iv) Teachers' responsibilities when recording and using sensitive information:

● entries on the permanent record should be dated and signed;

● where information is sought by telephone, the credentials of the enquirer and the reason for enquiry should be checked;

● information should be verified before inclusion on records;

● an indication of whether the information is permanent or transitory.

(v) Procedure for updating and protecting 'sensitive' information:

● records should be regularly reviewed (annually at a minimum);

● the current validity of any information should be reviewed prior to communication

● records should not be left open or unattended;

● conversations involving sensitive information should be avoided in places where they might be overheard.

At the present moment parental access to school records depends on the current policy of the local education authority.

Record-keeping in Open-Plan Schools

A study of record-keeping in schools designated 'open-plan' was carried out, principally to find out if practices differed from those used in more traditionally built schools.

From our study it appears that record-keeping practices in 'open-plan' schools differ very little from those in other schools. School architecture, except insofar as it may encourage co-operative teaching, has little impact on methods of recording progress. However there are differences in recording patterns according to methods of organization and teaching style, these being:

Teachers operating in a team-teaching situation favour long-hand written, open-ended profiles and samples of pupils' work other than the more structured checklists. Flexibility of recording technique appears to be the overriding factor in team teaching situations.

Records also seem to reflect the degree to which teachers view children as individual learners rather than the school buildings in which the learning takes place.

Report and Preliminary Recommendations

At a general level there is agreement between teachers as to what good records should be. Factors constituting 'good practice' when designing a record are:

DESIGN

- a clear layout
- clear, stable printing that will not fade
- clear section headings
- prominent position for the pupil's name (official forms generally use the top right hand corner of a sheet)
- sufficient space to be provided when comments are required
- a key placed in a prominent position on the record (or a user's handbook) to explain any abbreviations which may be used.

Acceptable degrees of clarity vary from teacher to teacher when evaluating records. Clarity seems to lie in the eye of the beholder. Records which are printed professionally are consistently favoured for their appearance when compared with those produced on a school duplicator.

It was more difficult to identify 'good practice' factors regarding record content. This depends a good deal on schemes in use and individual practice within schools. Where record content is based on textbook schemes, such records were considered favourably by teachers using the same scheme but *not* by teachers using other schemes.

Record content reflecting a developmental approach to language and mathematics rather than particular schemes, has more general appeal.

CONTENT

Factors of content which are considered important are:
- a clear sequence of development based on available theory or sound educational practice;
- information relevant to the purpose served by the record;
- direct indications for future teaching rather than implications;
- a clear distinction between entries concerned with pupil's school experiences and those which are assessments of attainment;
- clear presentation of assessment information:

(i) the derivation of norms used when grading or rating
(ii) the criteria used when stating pupil's competence
(iii) details of standardized tests used as a basis for grading or rating
(iv) details of other testing techniques used
(v) presentation of teacher-made test marks in a standardized form, possibly as standardized 'z' scores, to indicate the range and distribution of scores. This is particularly necessary where sets of marks supplied by several schools have to be compared.

References
Clift, P. S., Wilson, E. L., Weiner, G. G. (1977 and 1978), *Record Keeping in Primary Schools*, Schools Council/NFER Project newsletters of September 1977 and September 1978, NFER.
—, Wilson, E. L., Weiner, G. G. (1981), *Record Keeping in Primary Schools*, Macmillan Educational for the Schools Council.
Walker, A. S. (1955), *Pupils' School Records*, NFER.

4.4 The School Assessment Programme: Externally Referenced by Public Examination Results
M. Shipman

The results obtained by pupils in public examinations are the most widely-used criteria of the success of secondary schools. The debate over the merits of comprehensive schooling has been largely confined to comparing such results for selective and non-selective schools. They are often the only hard evidence available. Yet the inconclusive nature of this debate indicates the need to use examination results with caution, and in context. Four weaknesses in examination data need to be overcome:

1. Results can be the product of the attainment of pupils at entry to a school rather than of the quality of schooling.
2. Even if the attainment of pupils at entry to school is taken into account, differences in results when comparisons are made with other schools may still not be the result of different quality schooling. For example, as social background is a powerful factor behind attainment, pupils of similar attainment at intake in two schools may still be expected to achieve different examination results if they came from different social backgrounds.
3. The results of examinations in different subjects of different boards at different times, and between GCE and CSE may not be directly comparable.
4. Examinations only cover a part of the school population, sample only a part of the curriculum, and the results depend on the different examination policies of different schools.

Nevertheless, despite these weaknesses, examination results can be used in a school to check the performance year by year of pupils entering five, six, or seven years before with differing attainments and abilities. They are externally referenced and are accorded priority by parents and employers. The teachers consulted asked for extensive cover of ways in

Shipman, M. (1979), 'The School Assessment Programme: Externally Referenced by Public Examination Results', in *In-School Evaluation*, Heinemann Educational Books, pp.65-87.

which examination results could be used. In this chapter methods of collecting and tabulating results for internal consideration are discussed first. Then methods of obtaining comparisons with other schools, nationally or locally, are discussed. Many different tables are presented because the teachers consulted came from schools with very different examination policies. Staff with an open-door examination policy will expect different results from a staff operating a restricted policy of entry to examinations. It is easy to obtain 100 per cent passes by restricting entries. It is easy to ensure that all but a few pupils get some sort of grade at CSE examinations by allowing all to enter. In these cases the information required to monitor the effects of the policies will differ.

Examination results are not the only indicators of the academic quality of a school. They indicate the degree to which some implicit or explicit objectives of the staff of the school are being attained. The sequence of actions should not be to decide on the collection of results and then to analyse these to determine the level of success, but to review the school's examination policies as a reflection of wider academic objectives, and then to organize the collection and analysis of results to assess the extent to which these objectives are being attained. Decisions over objectives still take precedence. The examination results are indicators, means to an end, rather than ends in themselves. Thus the methods of organizing public examination results suggested in this chapter should not be taken as a blueprint. Each school staff will want to organize available information in different ways to meet different objectives. Selection among the methods suggested may help.

The tables are presented without division into boys and girls. Yet this is often an important piece of information and in mixed schools this separation is recommended in case there are wide discrepancies in performance when the figures for the school are laid alongside those produced by the DES or examination boards. For example, while girls obtain a higher proportion of grade A, B, or C on GCE O level than do boys, the latter obtain more 'passes' in mathematics, while girls do very much better in modern languages and English. If evaluation is to produce information for decisions about important educational issues in the school, division into boys' and girls' results is advisable.

The objectives that follow were selected from those stated by teachers consulted before writing this book. These were not volunteered readily. Most teachers had implicit objectives for the examination policy they organized, but few had thought through the purpose of the exercise in any thorough way. The objectives can vary widely. Here are four examples:

1. To maximize GCE and CSE entries.
2. To maximize all passes on public examinations.
3. To maximize the number of passes while minimizing the number of failures.

4. To maximize entries and passes in English, mathematics, and science.

Each of these objectives will lead to different results and will require examination information organized in different ways to provide an adequate indication of the success of the policy.

How not to Present Examination Results

It is rare to find published accounts of the examination results of a school that do not give an incomplete or biased picture. Here are the results of one comprehensive school on O level and CSE 1 grades, described by the headteacher as a 'remarkable academic achievement' (Boyson, 1974).

		GCE O level passes	A and B grades	CSE Grade 1 passes	Total GCE O level and CSE 1
1967	3 contributory schools	372	37	—	372
1968	Highbury Grove	290	33	17	307
1969		204	21	19	323
1970		307	43	20	327
1971		343	36	15	358
1972		345	47	23	368

Now it may be that this is a remarkable achievement if the intake into the school changed between 1962, when the 1967 examination group entered, and 1967 when the 1972 examination group entered. But the reader is only given a part of the total examination picture, has not got the size of the last complete age group from which the examination forms were formed, is not given the national trend across the years 1967 and 1972, or the trend in neighbouring schools. This is not necessarily misleading the reader, but it is denying him or her the opportunity to judge the interpretation given in the text.

The three examples that follow are from schools that asked for advice on how to organize their results. These schools were making results public and were concerned to improve their presentation. They were likely to be among the most thorough in preparing examination statistics.

TYPE 1

This school makes no use of public examination results for internal purposes. For Speech Day it produces the names of pupils with the subjects 'passed' in CSE and GCE although no definition of 'pass' is given. This appears as:

General Certificate of Education O level: A. Adams (Art, English), B. Brown (Maths, Physics, Technical Drawing), etc.

Certificate of Secondary Education: A. Abrahams (English, History, Maths), B. Black (French, English, Geography, History, Music, Religious Education), etc.

TYPE 2

This school produces a simple statistical picture of its results as follows:
Summer Examinations 1978. Number in fifth year = 170.
Number not taking any examination = 40 (23 per cent).
Number obtaining over 5 O level Grade A, B or C or CSE grade 1 = 36 (28 per cent).
Number obtaining CSE grades 2 to 5 = 72 (55 per cent).

There are obscure aspects in this collection of figures. If collected each year they would indicate examination success. The public however needs to be mathematically sophisticated. First, the percentages obtaining grades are expressed in relation to those entering examinations not the whole age group. Secondly, there is no information on the numbers taking examinations but failing. Thirdly, there is no information on successes and failures in subjects or of individual pupils. The separate presentation of each examination conceals the tendency for pupils to accumulate grades in different years or in winter as well as summer examinations. Fourthly, it shows nothing of the pattern of success overall, only indicating selected parts of the examination scene. In the programme for Open Day the results were presented only as total numbers passing GCE and CSE with the figures for the preceding year. The number in the year-group was not given.

TYPE 3

This school prepared its public examination results in a similar form to Table 1. These tables also served to produce the number of entrants and the number of pupils obtaining five or more O level 'passes' or CSE grade 1. The staff used the number obtaining five or more O levels as a way of comparing its success year after year. This school printed a brief summary of examination results annually. This was available for governors and was made available to parents who made enquiries. It consisted of the numbers entering for GCE or CSE summer examinations and the percentage 'passing' each. A pass meant GCE A, B or C and CSE grades 1 to 5. The figures for the year were compared with those from preceding years.

There are many weaknesses in the way the results in these schools were collected together and used for internal purposes. There were no figures on the total, terminal performance of pupils on leaving school. There was no attempt to build up time series showing how examination performance varied year by year. There was information on passes but not on failures. The examination results were not related to the attainment of the pupils at entry to the school five years earlier. There was no attempt to relate the results to national figures or to figures provided by the examination boards. They were not related to the examination policy of the schools. Yet these schools had taken the trouble to seek advice on the use of their results and were probably in a better position than most. The information presented to parents was even less informative. However, the absence of useful examination data sprang from the absence of an articulated examination policy. In none of the schools was there a clear policy agreed among the staff over the object of the examination exercise. The balance between GCE and CSE, the number being entered for each, the number re-taking by staying on into the sixth form, the levels of failure that could be tolerated, the length of courses leading to examinations, even the balance of subjects to be taken seemed to have been decided without explicit decisions having been made. Insufficient evidence was available to help make such decisions. The form in which results were made public was designed to give parents the one piece of information they already had, the performance of their own child. In addition it gave the performance of peers. But it did not give any idea of the examination policy of the school, or its success in achieving the objectives built into that policy. Curiously, where parents were given some idea of this success, the information was incomplete and gave an unnecessarily bad impression.

Methods of Organizing Examination Results

The three schools described earlier all had members of staff who were keen to make greater use of examination results to help in making decisions about public examination entries and about curriculum. In discussion their problem was about priorities. Was priority to be given to maximizing the number of pupils obtaining five or more O levels or CSE 1 in the more marketable subjects or to ensuring that all pupils had a good general education, with examination results being the by-product not the primary aim? Should they press on with integrated studies, social studies, community studies, or place more time and resources into traditional subjects? Should they extend mixed-ability grouping into third and later years or separate a GCE examination group early in their schooling? Should the A-level pattern offered in the sixth form determine the curriculum lower down the school, even though few would stay on into the traditional sixth form? As soon as the results of public examinations were looked at as a useful source for decision-making over the curriculum, questions about the objectives of that curriculum were asked. The wish to assess was forcing these teachers to consider the purpose of the schooling they were offering.

The outcome of discussions over public examinations was usually a policy of maximum success with minimum failure. The discussions were frustrated by the lack of sufficient information on previous examinations. It is hoped that the act of organizing results systematically will enable objectives to be further clarified. But there was another set of priorities to be decided. The staff were rightly worried about the time and trouble involved in the extraction and organization of examination results. Once again the final decision was pragmatic. A few tabulations would be made and if these were useful they would be extended. This could be wasteful, for the statistics only became useful when collected over time. The tables that follow should help in the selection of data of most use in schools with different objectives.

The most satisfactory method of storing information from examinations is to keep a record of the grades, including unclassified, of all the examinations taken in all subjects by each pupil. But to produce tables from record cards is very time-consuming unless the information is punched on to a special card that can be sorted mechanically or processed by a computer. Commercial firms are of course keen to be of service. Once information is stored in this way it can be retrieved for any analyses that are required. Many schools have the facilities to store, retrieve, and analyse in this way, but it would be unrealistic to assume that it will be given a high enough priority in many.

Examination results arrive at the schools from the examination boards on a computer print-out or duplicated list showing the name of pupils followed by the subjects they have taken and the grade achieved.

Table 1 Examination Results of Pupils by Subject

	Art GCE	Art CSE	English GCE	English CSE	Maths GCE	Maths CSE	Geography GCE	Geography CSE	Social Studies GCE	Social Studies CSE	Biology GCE	Biology CSE	Woodwork GCE	Woodwork CSE	French GCE	French CSE	V.R.	Reading
A. Adams		2		3				5						3			98	10 yrs 2 mths
B. Brown	E		B		U		C			1	C				D		119	Absent
C. Cook		4		4										3			92	9 yrs 8 mths
Z. Zavier	B		B		A		C				C				A		126	12 yrs

The easiest way of producing a basic table from which other information can be obtained is shown in Table 1. This merely organizes the information from each examination board in a more convenient form and enables available intake data to be added. Here the reading age and the verbal reasoning score of each pupil obtained five years before have been used to give some idea of the impact of the teaching across these years. Table 1 contains information that can be organized to produce most of the tables that follow. In a large school the table is too long to be useful, but it gives an immediate picture of the successes and failures of pupils and a simple indication of ability and attainment at intake to the school. Read down the columns it gives the level of success in individual subjects.

Another start to the collection of examination statistics can be the DES Form 7d, used for the 10 per cent leavers' survey every autumn term. The back of this form contains space for grades obtained by the leaver on CSE, O and A level GCE on some 60 subjects. This form can be used for 100 per cent of leavers, or as a model for a form for collecting results on summer and winter examinations. It can be filled in for each pupil, or a single, expanded form can be used to give an aggregated picture of all results of all pupils. Here is the layout of this form which provides a useful model for the collection of statistics. Only the first three of 60 subjects listed are shown (Table 2).

The Number of Passes and Failures

It is impossible to present all the many ways in which public examination results might be organized. Different school staffs will have different objectives in entering pupils for examinations and will require different data from the results to check how well their objectives are being achieved. Another complication is that the same results can be used to indicate different levels of success. For example, the A, B and C grades on GCE O level cover the older 'pass' grade. CSE grade 1 corresponds to a GCE pass. But there the clarity ends. The DES presents CSE figures using both grade 4 and grade 5 as a pass. Five passes at grades A, B or C on GCE or CSE grade 1 is frequently used as an indication of a significant level of success among employers and teachers. But GCE grades D and E, while failures, cannot be compared with CSE grades 2 to 5, as each set of grades is the result of different criteria. Particularly where school policy is to enter the same pupils for both GCE and CSE there has to be some arbitrary decision on how results are to be presented. Once the decision is made, it should be continued to give comparable data year after year.

The entry policy of a school staff determines the success and failure rates. This is why public examination results have to be presented not

Table 2 The DES Form 7d

Subject (2)	CSE (4) Please use grades 1, 2, 3, 4 or 5 6 = ungraded		GCE 'O' level papers (4) Please use Grades A, B, C, D, E, or U = ungraded or P = pass, F = fail as appropriate (3)							GCE 'A' level papers (5) In columns J to N please enter A, B, C, D, E, O or F to indicate grades				
	1974/5 or earlier	1975/6	1972/3 or earlier	1973/4		1974/5		1975/6		1973/4 or earlier	1974/5		1975/6	
				Winter	Summer	Winter	Summer	Winter	Summer		Winter	Summer	Winter	Summer
	A	B	C	D	E	F	G	H	I	J	K	L	M	N
Pure Mathematics (6) 501														501
Applied Maths and/or Mechanics (6) 502														502
Pure & Applied Maths (single subj.) 503														503

only within the context of the other work of the school and its environment, but also in relation to the examination policy of the school, or even of subject departments. Maximizing entries may increase both passes and failures. But parents will be pressing for their children to be entered, particularly for GCE. A few CSE grades 4, 5 or unclassified are not a marketable qualification, but may reflect a far more rewarding education than GCE grades D, E and certainly U, the unclassified GCE category. The presentation and internal use of examination results must be educative. They should show parents, employers, and the staff of the school what is being attempted and why, as well as the results of that policy.

To illustrate the possibilities of organizing public examination results, the policies of secondary schools were examined and questions asked about the objectives incorporated in those policies. A selection of those objectives has been made and suggested treatment of public examination results presented.

Objective — To maximize the number of each successive year-group getting five or more O levels or CSE grade 1. However, this success should not be at the cost of excessive numbers failing.

The most widely recognized level of success in public examinations is five GCE grades A, B or C or CSE grade 1, which is the equivalent of a GCE pass. This number of passes is the entry requirement for many courses in further education and for entry to professions. The number of pupils gaining this basic five subjects is a useful single indicator. It can be balanced by the number obtaining U grade on GCE, or grades 5 or U, or U only in CSE. The former is a fail and the latter is the lowest CSE result. There are, however, other considerations in the use of these simple indicators. The subjects included in the 'passes' and 'failures' are important. Five 'passes' including maths, English, a science, and a modern language are more marketable than one including subjects less respected by employers and not accepted for entry to some further education courses. Table 3 shows one way of presenting this information. It is limited in scope but it is easy to accumulate and gives staff an indicator of the extent of success and failure.

Table 3   Success and Failure on GCE and CSE Examinations

		Number of pupils obtaining			
		5 'passes'	*Grade U*		
	5 O level	*inc. maths*	*GCE*	*CSE U*	*Number in*
Year	*or CSE 1*	*+English*	*1, 2, 3, +*	*1, 2, 3, +*	*age group*
1975	29 (18%)	18 (11%)	13 8 4	23 9 2	160
1976	24 (16%)	18 (12%)	11 8 1	22 18 7	150
1977	22 (14%)	16 (10%)	9 6 4	22 14 9	152

Table 3 indicates the tendency for the number obtaining five 'passes' to fall although there is some compensation in the fall in numbers 'failing' GCE. Again, such tables can only be interpreted in the light of events in the school, the characteristics of the intake five plus years before, and against the objectives of the staff.

Objective — to attain an entry to examinations that will keep pass rates (GCE A, B and C, CSE grade 5 or better) high, and failure rates low, for all pupils regardless of how many subjects they take.

This objective is similar to the last objective. But this staff was worried as much by the pupil who took eight or more subjects as the pupil who took only a single CSE. To them, failure could be damaging across the whole range of ability, and success as rewarding. Tables 4 and 5 are not in a form that is suitable for release to the public, although the percentages calculated from them could be. They are in the form used by the DES in their annual statistics on leavers. Read across, these tables give the number of entries of pupils; read down the columns they give the numbers getting a Grade 5 or better CSE or Grade C or better in GCE. The grades specified can be decided by the staff of the school. The DES also provides a table giving CSE grade 4 or better. As the number of entries and number of grades of each pupil is entered into each table it is easy to calculate the total number of subjects attempted and the total number of the specified grades achieved. These have been used to calculate pass, failure, and entry rates. This is probably the most useful information for monitoring the success of the examination policy of a school in detail.

Tables 4 and 5 do not give any information on separate subjects. Neither do they give information on the total examination attainment of individual pupils, for some pupils will take both CSE and GCE. However, any of the five pieces of information extracted from the tables can be used to build up a useful year-by-year picture. Further, the juxtaposition of entries and passes shows up the cases where failures seem excessive. Clearly in this school there were some pupils who were entered for GCE in particular when their chances of obtaining an A, B or C grade were slight.

From Table 4 the following can be extracted:

1. GCE O level (grade A, B, C) pass rate $= \dfrac{165}{236} = 70\%$

2. GCE O level (grade D, E, U) failure rate $= \dfrac{71}{236} = 30\%$

3. GCE O level entry rate $= \dfrac{48}{152} = 32\%$

4. GCE O level average entries (year-group) $= \dfrac{236}{152} = 1.55$

5. GCE O level, average entries (GCE group) $= \dfrac{236}{48} = 4.91$

Table 4   GCE O level – Pupils Gaining Grade C or Better

Number of subjects attempted by pupils	0	1	2	3	4	5	6	7	8+	Pupil total	Total attempts
0	104									104	
1	2	2								4	4
2	1	2	2							5	10
3				2						2	6
4		1	1	1	2					5	20
5	2	1	2	2	2	2				11	55
6			2			4	4			10	60
7			1	3		1		2		7	49
8+								2	2	4	32
Pupil total	109	6	8	8	4	7	4	4	2	152	
Total of grades		6	16	24	16	35	24	28	16	165	236

Table 5   CSE – Pupils Gaining Grade 5 (or Better) Results

Number of subjects attempted by pupils	0	1	2	3	4	5	6	7	8+	Pupil total	Total attempts
0	27									27	
1	9	14								23	23
2	9	5	8							22	44
3	4	1	3	3						11	33
4	2	1		2	5					10	40
5			1		6	8				15	75
6			2		2	8	13			25	150
7	1			4			9	5		19	133
8+											
Pupil total	52	21	14	9	13	16	22	5		152	
Total grades		21	28	27	52	80	132	35		375	498

Some national figures on the results of examinations taken in summer and winter are published annually by the DES. These appear some two years after the dates of the examinations. The national percentages getting A–C grades on GCE for summer 1975 were 58.1 per cent for boys and 60.8 per cent for girls.

From Table 5 the following can be extracted:

1. CSE (grades 1–5) pass rate $\quad = \dfrac{375}{498} = 75\%$

2. CSE unclassified, failure rate $\quad = \dfrac{123}{498} = 25\%$

3. CSE entry rate $\quad = \dfrac{125}{152} = 82\%$

4. CSE average entries (year-group) $\quad = \dfrac{498}{152} = 3.27$

5. CSE average entries (CSE group) $\quad = \dfrac{498}{125} = 3.98$

The DES figures for the 1975 summer CSE examinations show th t 90.8 per cent of boys and 91.7 per cent of girls entering obtained grade 5 or better.

The objectives considered so far have concentrated on the need to ensure that success is not balanced by excessive failure. Statistics produced for each year's examinations might not be sufficient to check on the success of this policy, unless staff can agree on some acceptable levels of success and failure after looking at the rates achieved by all candidates for the relevant examination boards. In any case, staff will want to look at results year by year to see how successful their policy and their teaching is, but also to detect any trends that may need action. Tables 4 and 5, for example, yielded summary information for comparison across years. Table 6 shows the percentage pass and fail rates for a school across three years. Such a table can serve to alert staff to any trends towards excessive failure and can monitor the effects of changes in entry policies to examinations. In this school there had been a gradual increase in the numbers being entered for both GCE and CSE, and this did seem to be raising failure rates. However, not too much should be read into such trends. Changes in the ability of the fifth year could easily account for such fluctuations. The collection of such information across the years would ensure that staff were aware of the consequence of such combinations of changes.

Teachers may prefer a simple indicator of success in GCE and CSE for internal planning purposes. This is straightforward for CSE as the grades run from 1 to 5 and U, which can count as 6. To produce a parallel GCE numerical scale it is convenient to count GCE A grade as a 1, B as 2, down to grade U as 6. Table 7 shows these averages where a low score indicates a high success rate. These could easily be reversed so that the high scores more conventionally indicate the better performance.

Table 6   Pupils Obtaining Pass or Fail Grades in GCE and CSE

			Year			
	1975		1976		1977	
Grades	Subject entries	% obtaining	Subject entries	% obtaining	Subject entries	% obtaining
GCE	186		208		236	
A, B, C		68		73		70
U		6		8		9
CSE	408		414		498	
1		19		21		22
U		22		22		25

Table 7   Average Grade on GCE and CSE on a 1–6 scale for all Subjects Entered

Year	GCE	CSE
1975	2.91	2.60
1976	3.24	2.40
1977	3.08	2.71

Obviously the choice between preparing one table and the next will depend on the audience in view as well as the examination objectives under review. The tables reproduced from Rowe (1971) below, and Tables 3 and 6, are suitable for release to the public. But Tables 4 and 5, while probably the most informative, may be too complicated for release. They, and some of the tables that follow, give details necessary to make decisions among staff, but are not in a form that is suitable for parents as they need too much interpretation.

None of the tables presented so far has been specially designed to give information to the public. Yet this demand is persistent and justified. The difficulty lies in the absence of any detectable agreement among parents or employers about the indications they require. The factors involved – the total numbers in age groups, the numbers entering public examinations, entries to GCE or CSE, the definition of pass or fail, the subject mix required, the level of pass compared with the ability of the pupil – are manifold and no single set of figures is going to satisfy all audiences. A good example of time series used to illustrate changes as a comprehensive school built up its examination entries is

Table 8a Yorkshire Regional Examinations Board Certificate of Secondary Education Examinations

Year	Candidates	Subjects offered	Total subjects taken	Av. no. of subjects taken	Grades						Total no. of passes	Av. no. of subjects passed
					1*	2	3	4	5	U		
1965	7	1	7	1.0	1	2	3	1			7	1.0
1966	45	10	79	1.8	14	23	11	17	9	5	74	1.6
1967	67	19	313	4.7	32	53	72	90	50	16	297	4.4
1968	103	20	471	4.6	70	74	125	141	53	8	463	4.5
1969	177	21	883	5	160	211	198	193	83	38	845	4.8
1970	210	22	998	4.7	180	227	240	222	105	24	974	4.6

*GCE equivalent

Table 8b Joint Matriculation Board, GCE O Level Examinations

Year	Candidates	Subjects offered	Total subjects taken	Av. no. of subjects taken	Grades						Total no. of passes
					1	2	3	4	5	6	
1965	46	13	132	2.9	4	3	8	7	15	15	52
1966	48	16	153	3.2	8	6	13	11	25	25	88
1967	55	18	204	3.7	6	3	17	16	21	24	87
1968	115	21	286	2.5	11	9	43	24	57	35	179
1969	159	25	707	4.4	11	18	94	58	103	94	378
1970	221	26	810	3.2	5	15	98	73	115	101	405

found in Albert Rowe's personal, informative account of the organization of David Lister School, Hull (Rowe, 1971). It has to be remembered that the switch to GCE grades only occurred in 1975 and that the pass grades 1 to 6 presented are now A, B or C. The definition of 'pass' for CSE is a grade 5 or better.

Tables 8a and 8b have many useful features. They give previous years as a basis for comparison. They indicate subject range and level of success. They would not answer questions about the proportion of pupils in an age group taking examinations. Rowe deals with the attainment of the intake to the school over the years elsewhere in his book, and in the early years of a school this is important planning information. The average number of subjects passed column for GCE, which is omitted, rises slowly from 1.1 to 1.8 between 1965 and 1970, with, as in CSE, a peak in 1969. No questions can be answered about the attainment of pupils as the mix of CSE and GCE is unknown. These and other questions that could not be answered are not criticisms of Rowe. To answer all possible questions would require a large number of tables and without a clear expression of the public's interests in advance, they would still not be complete. For example, a favourite question is 'how well does the average pupil do on examinations'. The real answer to this question would come only from a sophisticated exercise to identify this average pupil and his or her results. Even then the definition of 'average pupil' would have to be very carefully spelled out. With the size of each year's age group and a definition of 'passes', these tables for David Lister School would give most teachers and the public of the school sufficient information to judge the success of examination policies.

Here is a selection of results presented by a headteacher of a comprehensive school to his governors. The report on examinations was extensive and each year one examination was analysed in detail. Table 9 dealt with A levels. These were presented as a time series as follows, for summer examinations only. This school kept a record of the pupils' grades on a seven-point scale based on a verbal reasoning score at entry seven years before. There were pupils who joined after entry at 11 years, but a table was included in the report to governors showing the relation between ability at intake and A level results (Table 10). These were designed to show how few pupils would have normally gone to a grammar school and how many of those obtaining A levels were from grades at entry not often considered to have academic potential. Results are for 1976 only.

This school laid its CSE results out in a similar way to that used by Albert Rowe at David Lister. The GCE O level results were, however, designed to show the number of subject passes of those pupils obtaining three or more O level passes or CSE 1 grades. They were tabulated as shown in Table 11.

Table 9 Percentage Entries and Passes

Year	*No. of candidates A*	*4th year 3 years before B*	*A/B %*	*Subject entries*	*Passes*	*Passes per candidate*	*% Passes*	*% Passes national*
1972	36	168	21	81	53	1.5	65	68.3
1973	48	164	29	111	76	1.6	68	68.7
1974	62	169	37	141	93	1.5	66	68.3
1975	59	176	34.5	130	85	1.4	65	67.6
1976	67	167	40	159	105	1.6	66	—
1977	79	181	44	190	122	1.5	64	—

Table 10 A Level Results and Entry Grade Seven Years Before

		Grade at entry 7 years earlier							*Total candidates with known entry grades*
		1	2	3	4	5	6	7	
A level passes	1	—	2	6	4	2	1	—	15
	2	4	4	6	4	2	—	—	20
	3	2	3	2	—	—	—	—	7
	4	2	—	—	—	—	—	—	2
									44

Table 11 Number of Candidates with more than 3 GCE Grades A, B, or C or CSE 1 Grade

	Pupils Passing:								
Year	*8*	*7*	*6*	*5*	*4*	*3*	*Total 3 or more A*	*No. in previous 4th year B*	*A/B %*
1972	2	4	4	5	4	7	26	169	15
1973	2	7	4	10	6	7	36	176	20
1974	3	5	11	9	8	8	44	167	26
1975	3	9	15	12	12	10	61	181	34
1976	2	8	14	13	11	15	63	174	36
1977	4	8	14	7	13	17	63	174	36

These tables have been extracted from a longer report on the examination results of this comprehensive school. There are still important pieces of information missing. While A level results are related to grading at entry, this is only done selectively to show that selection is a dubious procedure at 11 years. There is no evidence on whether the school was receiving a more or less able intake across the years. But these were the most complete set of examination statistics found while preparing this book. At the end of the period the local education authority concerned finally stopped selection for its secondary schools, and the school in question was receiving an intake that was drawn from a representative sample of the population for the first time. The results stored would be a most useful basis for watching the effect of this changed intake and for planning new curricula to take account of these changed conditions.

There is another missing piece of evidence that illustrates the difficulty in covering all the important questions in a few tables. Clearly from the A level Table 9 the proportion of the last complete year (in this case taken as fourth year to avoid the problem of the raising of the school leaving age) taking A levels is high for a comprehensive school. But a look at the supplementary evidence on the numbers for whom grades at entry to the school were known gives a clue to this high proportion. For 1976, only 44 were known out of an A level group of 67. Many of the sixth form had joined from other maintained and independent schools.

Success and Failure within Subjects

The staff of a school will often want to know the pattern of examination policies across departments. They may also want to know how successful such policies are. This is not mere nosey-parkering. It is essential for decision-making. Resources have to be allocated between subject departments on some basis, preferably rational. Examination policies and successes are one possible basis. For example, teachers in one department may decide that they have a claim, based on more entrants to GCE or superior examination performance, for available resources. Staff may want to counter criticism from outside the school, directed at one or more subject departments. Headteachers or inspectors might be concerned about the efficiency of a department, or wish to spread a form of examination policy used by a successful department to other schools, or to have information prior to inspection. The difficulty in collecting together meaningful statistics is that there are often few departments entering enough candidates for comparisons to be made. English and mathematics are usually big enough, but caution has to be exercised when using small numbers from small departments. There are other factors that can confuse results. Girls tend to attain a lower level than boys of equivalent ability in mathematics, but are superior in English. The level of severity of marking tends to differ between subjects. For example, mathematics seems to be marked more severely than English in both GCE and CSE examinations. Only when differences are large and persistent should they be assumed to be a reflection of real differences.

Objective—to ensure that the examination policies of subject departments do not result in excessive failure rates.

Table 12 Average GCE and CSE Grades Obtained by Pupils in Mathematics

Year	GCE A (1)	B (2)	C (3)	D (4)	E (5)	U (6)	Ab.	Total	Average	CSE 1	2	3	4	5	6(U)	Ab.	Total	Average
1975	2	4	1	3	4	2	3	19	3.0	12	4	14	6	5	9	2	52	2.7
1976	5	3	4	2	1	4	4	23	2.6	11	11	9	14	12	7	7	62	2.2
1977	2	2	4	4	7	6	2	27	3.9	3	13	12	5	11	4	6	54	2.6

Table 13 Average GCE and CSE Grades Obtained by Pupils on Selected Subjects (grades translated into numbers as in Table 7)

Year	Maths GCE	Maths CSE	English GCE	English CSE	French GCE	French CSE	Physics GCE	Physics CSE	History GCE	History CSE	Geography GCE	Geography CSE	Art GCE	Art CSE
1975	3.0	2.7	2.2	2.0	3.1	3.2	3.7	2.9	2.4	2.3	2.5	2.5	2.1	2.0
1976	2.6	2.2	2.1	2.2	2.6	2.9	3.5	3.1	2.4	2.5	2.9	2.7	2.6	2.0
1977	3.9	2.6	2.2	2.0	2.4	3.6	3.6	2.8	2.3	2.1	2.9	2.7	2.8	2.2

Subject departments in a school will want their own data on public examinations. Table 12 shows information extracted from an examination board print-out for all pupils in a school taking mathematics. The information on this table can be treated further to give average grades and percentages passing, although with small numbers the layout in Table 12 will probably be safer. Table 13 shows the results from several subject departments gathered together to give a time series which can guide staff in making decisions not only about examinations, but about the curriculum. The numbering of grades is given in Table 13, the higher grades being given smaller numbers. It has to be remembered however that there is not strict comparability between the grades obtained between subjects. It is probably safest to look at the results of each subject across time rather than at the results of different subjects in the same year.

Tables 12 and 13 are suitable for discussion within and between subject departments, but unsuitable for publication. Table 12 would need repeating for all departments and some subjects would be too small to give meaningful figures. Table 13 is convenient for internal discussion but is indicative only, and open to misinterpretation if the basis of the figures is not understood. The public usually wants to know how many enter and pass different subjects. Table 14 is an attempt to give the information required to the public. Again the need to place tables like this in the context of the total examination policy and the attainment of pupils at intake to the school is obvious. Parents often assume that it is usual for pupils to take GCE, and the release of results will inevitably lead to further questions about examination policy.

Table 14   Entries and Passes in GCE and CSE in Selected Subjects

Subject	Pupils in year	GCE entrants	GCE A, B, or C	% pass	CSE entrants	CSE 1–5	% grades 1–5
English	152	31	24	77	75	60	90
Maths	152	22	14	64	67	61	91
Art	152	22	18	82	64	52	81
History	152	24	20	83	40	34	85
Geography	152	26	20	77	64	56	88
Physics	152	18	14	78	50	44	88
French	152	15	12	80	14	13	93

Once again, such a table will not satisfy all parents, employers, and so on. It will give the public a picture of the examination entries and results, but most parents will go on to ask how this compares with other schools. Even if such comparative information were available it would need to be put into the context of the school and the nature of its intake compared with the other schools. This raises the problem of the release of statistics by local education authorities on a school by school basis.

The statistics might reflect very different situations, not the results of teaching similar intakes. When results are prepared within the school they can be placed within context and changes over the years can be included.

Total Pupil Performance

So far only separate GCE and CSE entries and grades have been considered. But each pupil can take a combination of subjects from these two examinations. Staff may find it useful to tabulate these total examination achievements. Read across, Table 15 gives the subject grades above 5 on CSE; read down the columns it gives GCE subjects 'passed' (pre-1975). Only the results from summer examinations have been included. The DES produces results in this form, but for leavers in one school year; these can include achievements accumulated by pupils over one, two, or three years (DES, 1976). Comparisons are unwise unless made for all annual leavers. These problems of comparison with national statistics are expanded at the end of this chapter [not included].

Table 15　CSE and GCE Achievements

		Number of subjects with A, B, or C grade on O level papers									
			1	2	3	4	5	6	7	8+	Total
Number of	0	27	2	3	5	2	4	4	3	2	52
subjects at	1-2	22	2	4	1	2	3		1		35
grade 5 or	3-4	17	2	1	2						22
better on	5-7	38									38
CSE papers	7+	5									5
	Total	109	6	8	8	4	7	4	4	2	152

Table 15 shows a school still running one GCE group which tends not to take CSE subjects, and another that takes subjects from both examinations. Comparison with the DES tables is not possible unless the total achievements of all leavers are used. Those staying on into the sixth form having taken CSE in the fifth are likely to pick up GCE grades, while a few who have taken GCE in the fifth will pick up CSE grades.

The tables presented so far suffer from not showing the achievement of pupils in a simple, single measure. This makes it impossible to tabulate change across the years in a simple way. What is needed is a single scale that will give a picture of the performance of pupils in all their public examinations. This should provide an indicator of performance that will show staff whether their policies in relation to examinations are successful. The indicator need have little meaning by itself, nor is it suitable for public consumption. It can however serve as the examination litmus paper for staff.

There are various ways of combining all public examination results into a single scale. All are arbitrary. Different methods should be used in schools where staff have different examination policies. Fortunately CSE grade 1 is supposed to be the equivalent of GCE grade C, and this helps to produce a single scale from the different examinations. For example, CSE grades 1 to 5 and U can be given scores so that grade 1 counts as 6, grade 2 as 5 and so on. GCE grade A can then be given 8, grade B given 7, and grade C given 6, the same as CSE grade 1. From there on it becomes more arbitrary and the results are not suitable for publication. GCE unclassified grade U could count as 1 or zero, while grades D and E on GCE can count as 5 and 4 or as 3 and 2, or as 2 and 1. Whatever scale is chosen, it should be adhered to year by year, as it is annual results collected across the years that give the indicator meaning and enable staff to assess the success of their work.

This scoring from 8 for GCE grade A down to 1 or zero for unclassified results gives a total positive score for all candidates that can be summed to give an annual indicator of examination success. However, some school staffs may prefer to use a scale that gives less emphasis to higher grades and which indicates successes alongside failures. A method of achieving such an indicator is to give positive and negative scores for grades and keep these separate in the summing of results. For example:

GCE grades A, B, and C, and CSE 1 can count as + 2.

CSE grades 2 to 5 can count as + 1.

GCE grades D and E can count as − 1.

GCE and CSE unclassified can count as − 2.

This scale reveals failures but compared with the previous method over-emphasizes lower CSE grades while under-rating GCE grades D and E. For example, on the first scale, a GCE D or E grade count as 5 and 4 respectively. On the second they both count as − 1. This illustrates the problem with indicators. They will be chosen to illuminate policies agreed among the staffs of schools. But different policies will be illuminated best by different indicators. The first method of producing a single scale would suit a staff interested in maximizing success. The second would suit a staff interested in minimizing failure. It is difficult to design an indicator that combines both. In any case such single indicators, referred to an arbitrary scale, are for internal use only. It is useful to have a single measure of examination results incorporating both GCE and CSE on a single scale. But it has meaning only in relation to that scale and could easily be misinterpreted. The method of keeping positive and negative scores separate is valuable as a check on failure as well as success, and teachers can stretch the scale beyond + 2 to − 2 to suit their own priorities.

In Table 16 the positive and negative scores have been presented as a time series. A ratio of total positive to total negative results has also been calculated for each year.

Table 16 Total Positive and Negative Results on Public Examinations

		1970	1971	1972	1973	1974	1975	1976	1977
Total	+ ve	860	940	940	1060	998	1006	980	961
Total	− ve	210	266	270	266	294	333	324	316
Ratio	$\frac{+ve}{-ve}$	4.09	3.53	3.48	3.98	3.39	3.02	3.02	3.04

Table 16 suggests that the efforts of the staff to raise examination performance succeeded, but at the cost of raising failure rates. Remedial action could be taken by altering the balance between entry to GCE and CSE examinations, and by ensuring that fewer pupils who were unlikely to pass were entered. But these were policies being discussed by the teachers. The actual action taken in any one case would depend on the examination policy, the curriculum of the school, and the ability of the pupils. The figures serve as indicators only, showing that policies are working or failing. If figures are to serve as a basis for action the results will need to be related at least to the attainment of pupils to see if any particular group of pupils is doing unexpectedly well or badly.

References
Boyson, R. (1974), *Oversubscribed*, Ward Lock Educational.
Department of Education and Science (1976), *Statistics of Education*, Vol.2, *School Leavers, CSE and GCE*, HMSO.
Rowe, A. (1971), *The School as a Guidance Community*, Pearson Press.

Index